P9-EDK-259

Approaches to Teaching Early Modern Spanish Drama

Approaches to Teaching
World Literature
Joseph Gibaldi, series editor

For a complete listing of titles,
see the last pages of this book.

Approaches to Teaching Early Modern Spanish Drama

Edited by

Laura R. Bass

and

Margaret R. Greer

The Modern Language Association of America
New York   2006

© 2006 by The Modern Language Association of America
All rights reserved
Printed in the United States of America

For information about obtaining permission to reprint material from MLA book
publications, send your request by mail (see address below), e-mail
(permissions@mla.org), or fax (646-458-0030).

Library of Congress Cataloging-in-Publication Data
Approaches to teaching early modern Spanish drama /
edited by Laura R. Bass and Margaret R. Greer.
p.   cm. — (Approaches to teaching world literature)
Includes bibliographical references and index.
ISBN-13: 978-0-87352-994-5 (hardcover : alk. paper)
ISBN-10: 0-87352-994-4 (alk. paper)
ISBN-13: 978-0-87352-995-2 (pbk. : alk. paper)
ISBN-10: 0-87352-995-2 (alk. paper)
1. Spanish drama—Classical period, 1500–1700—Study and teaching.
2. Spanish drama—Classical peroid, 1500–1700—History and criticism.
I. Bass, Laura R., 1965– II. Greer, Margaret Rich. III. Series.
PQ6105.A67 2005
862'.3071—dc22   2005032966
ISSN 1059-1133

Cover illustration of the paperback edition:
Rebecca Johnson and Katherine Kelly as Doña Leonor and Celia,
in a Royal Shakespeare Company performance of
Sor Juana Inés de la Cruz's *House of Desires*,
London, 2004. Photograph by John Haynes, © RSC.

Published by The Modern Language Association of America
26 Broadway, New York, NY 10004-1789
www.mla.org

CONTENTS

Language, Theory, and (Teaching) Philosophy

Theater History, Practice, and Comparative Contexts

Cross-Cultural Approaches

PREFACE TO THE SERIES

In *The Art of Teaching* Gilbert Highet wrote, "Bad teaching wastes a great deal of effort, and spoils many lives which might have been full of energy and happiness." All too many teachers have failed in their work, Highet argued, simply "because they have not thought about it." We hope that the Approaches to Teaching World Literature series, sponsored by the Modern Language Association's Publications Committee, will not only improve the craft—as well as the art—of teaching but also encourage serious and continuing discussion of the aims and methods of teaching literature.

The principal objective of the series is to collect within each volume different points of view on teaching a specific literary work, a literary tradition, or a writer widely taught at the undergraduate level. The preparation of each volume begins with a wide-ranging survey of instructors, thus enabling us to include in the volume the philosophies and approaches, thoughts and methods of scores of experienced teachers. The result is a sourcebook of material, information, and ideas on teaching the subject of the volume to undergraduates.

The series is intended to serve nonspecialists as well as specialists, inexperienced as well as experienced teachers, graduate students who wish to learn effective ways of teaching as well as senior professors who wish to compare their own approaches with the approaches of colleagues in other schools. Of course, no volume in the series can ever substitute for erudition, intelligence, creativity, and sensitivity in teaching. We hope merely that each book will point readers in useful directions; at most each will offer only a first step in the long journey to successful teaching.

Joseph Gibaldi
Series Editor

PREFACE TO THE VOLUME

Early modern Spain produced one of the great dramatic corpora of world literature. The *comedia*—the term generically applied to comic, tragicomic, and tragic works alike—was the most popular art form from the latter decades of the sixteenth century through the first half of the seventeenth. Its cultural role was akin to that of the movies in the mid-twentieth century and cinema and television today. For the considerable segment of the audience that was illiterate, in particular, the *comedia* supplied a vision of national history, of religious obligation, and of the political order, as well as models of social deportment. Its ideological power was thus formidable.

The paradigmatic *comedia* is a three-act, polymetric drama, freely combining comic and tragic elements and noble and baseborn personae in fast-paced plots, in which character is developed more through action than through introspective monologues. The public demand for new plays was almost insatiable, and three superb dramatists—Lope de Vega, Tirso de Molina, and Pedro Calderón de la Barca—together with many others produced an enormous corpus of works. Along with the dominant three-act comedy, they wrote moving tragedies, history plays, hagiographical plays, elaborate court spectacle dramas, *autos sacramentales* (allegorical dramas performed for the annual Corpus Christi celebrations), and short burlesque pieces to accompany and season the other dramatic pieces. Their works, rapidly translated and adapted, appeared on stages throughout Europe and traveled with Spanish colonizers to the New World.

For the title of our volume, we have chosen the designation "early modern Spanish drama," but in the essays herein and in much of the secondary literature to which they refer, readers will find a variety of other terms applied to the corpus. Most common is the designation "drama of the Spanish Golden Age" or simply "Golden Age drama." A chronologically fluid term that sometimes covers the two centuries from about 1500 to 1700 or shorter periods within that span, "Golden Age" came to be employed in the eighteenth and nineteenth centuries by nationalist literary historians nostalgic for a past retrospectively seen as a conjunction of cultural and political glory (see Pelorson 295–301). Some critics opt for "Spanish classical drama," or simply *teatro clásico* (classic drama); others, particularly in Spain, refer to "baroque drama," since the majority of the works regularly studied and performed come from the seventeenth century. We prefer "early modern" because, avoiding the niceties of a Renaissance-Baroque break, it indicates the transitional nature of the period; moreover, unlike the term "Golden Age," which implies a great-works approach, "early modern" suggests the importance of reading what we now call literature in conjunction with other social discourses and formations.

At the beginning of the twenty-first century, early modern Spanish drama, in Spanish and in translation, is experiencing resurgent popularity among the general public. There are at least two annual theater festivals dedicated to it, one centered in a restored theater in Almagro, Spain, another in the Chamizal park on the Texas-Mexico border; a classical drama school was established in the mid-1990s in Madrid to train actors in performing verse drama; and the Compañía Nacional de Teatro Clásico, based in Madrid, has been a success since its 1986 inception. Another theater, the Teatro Pavón, which reopened after remodeling in 2000, is dedicated primarily to early modern drama performances and is currently the home base of Compañía Nacional de Teatro Clásico while its own Teatro de la Comedia undergoes remodeling. Companies in many other parts of the country are including *comedias* in their repertoire. Performances in Spanish and in translation have been hits on stages across Europe, Latin America, and the United States; for example, a new production of Calderón's *Life Is a Dream* won great acclaim in the Edinburgh Theatre Festival in 2000, and again in London and the Brooklyn Academy of Music, as well as playing to sold-out houses for months in Barcelona and Madrid. Bilingual theaters in New York (the Repertorio Español), Washington (the GALA Hispanic Theater), and Los Angeles (the Bilingual Foundation for the Arts) regularly perform *comedias* in Spanish or in English. In its 2004 season at Stratford-upon-Avon, the Royal Shakespeare Company performed plays by Cervantes, Lope de Vega, Tirso de Molina, and Sor Juana Inés de la Cruz to critical acclaim. Clearly we are at an opportune moment to translate the renewed success of Spanish classical theater on the contemporary stage to new vitality in the classroom.

The *comedia* is regularly taught in a wide variety of academic contexts, in Spanish and in translation. In Spanish, these range from a single drama in survey courses of Spanish literature to specialized undergraduate or graduate courses on early modern Spanish drama or on individual dramatists. Furthermore, professors are teaching the *comedia* to a diversity of students: from those just beyond intermediate Spanish to seminative and fluent speakers, in small private colleges and in large state universities. In translation, it is regularly taught in comparative courses in Renaissance and baroque literature and in history of drama.

Given the steady increase of Spanish as the language of choice in foreign language instruction programs, teaching early modern Spanish drama will surely continue to constitute a regular feature of college curricula. However, because of the prevailing presentism of today's students and the linguistic and cultural difficulties of comprehending the *comedia*, teachers need guidance in helping their students understand and engage with these works. This volume is intended to provide such guidance, both to beginning professors and to more experienced ones seeking renewed pedagogical energy.

ACKNOWLEDGMENTS

From beginning to end, this volume has been produced as a collaborative effort. The enthusiasm generated by the 1998 MLA panel "Teaching the *Comedia* in the Twenty-First Century" was its first motor. Sponsored by the Sixteenth- and Seventeenth-Century Spanish Drama Division of the MLA, the panel showed that a volume dedicated to our subject in the Approaches to Teaching World Literature series would find a warm reception. From the start, Joseph Gibaldi has been the most commited of editors, believing in the value of teaching early modern Spanish drama at the university level and unfailing in his guidance and support. Early on, survey participants, whose names are listed at the end of this volume, took the time to share materials and approaches with generous detail. Also generous in their careful consideration and detailed suggestions were the anonymous readers who reviewed the volume at the prospectus and manuscript stages. Thanks to their input, the final product is much richer and broader in coverage than it would have been otherwise. All the contributors deserve acknowledgment for their labors, patience, and agreeable responses to requests for revision. With unparalleled patience, Ari Zighelboim took care of the mechanics of putting together the manuscript and compiled the indexes. With the utmost professionalism and good humor, Elizabeth Holland carried the volume through final production. Playing for a moment the role of the *graciosos* who take their bow at the end of *comedias*, we extend our thanks and applause to all the participants, named and unnamed, for their part in bringing this production to a wider audience of twenty-first-century teachers of early modern Spanish drama.

Part One

MATERIALS

Editions of *Comedias*

Anthologies in Spanish

The ideal anthology of *comedias* for the undergraduate classroom would include canonical and noncanonical plays, ones by women dramatists as well as men, works that explore issues of immediate interest to students today (such as race and the conquest of the Americas), as well as the standard topics of honor, kingship, and the like. The ideal anthology would provide up-to-date introductions to the *comedia* in its social and historical context, overviews of the dramatists and the plays, metrical tables, and neither too few nor too many annotations of linguistically difficult passages and cultural references. Unfortunately, the ideal anthology does not exist. The standard used in survey courses on Golden Age drama is José Martel and Hymen Alpern's *Diez comedias del Siglo de Oro,* originally published in 1939 and still available in its 1968 revised edition (reissued in 1985 by Waveland Press). Included are *La Numancia, Fuenteovejuna, La estrella de Sevilla, El burlador de Sevilla, Las mocedades del Cid, El esclavo del demonio, La verdad sospechosa, La vida es sueño, Del rey abajo, ninguno,* and *El desdén con el desdén.* All supplementary materials—introductions to authors and works, footnotes, glossary of common terms, discussion topics—are in English. Instructors find the explanatory apparatus inadequate, and the lists of key critical studies need updating.

Also aimed for college students in this country were Bruce Wardropper's *Teatro español del Siglo de Oro: Masterpieces by Lope de Vega, Calderón, and Their Contemporaries,* and Raymond R. MacCurdy's *Spanish Drama of the Golden Age: Twelve Plays*—both of which, while out of print, are still used by some instructors. Wardropper's anthology includes *El perro del hortelano, El caballero de Olmedo, El villano en su rincón, El retablo de las maravillas, El condenado por desconfiado, El médico de su honra, El príncipe constante, El gran teatro del mundo,* and *El lindo don Diego.* MacCurdy's includes *El retablo de la maravillas, El caballero de Olmedo, El burlador de Sevilla, El condenado por desconfiado, Las mocedades del Cid, La adversa fortuna de don Álvaro de Luna, El examen de maridos, Reinar después de morir, El médico de su honra, El gran teatro del mundo, Entre bobos anda el juego,* and *El desdén con el desdén,* as well as a helpful guide to Spanish versification and grammatical notes.

Some instructors mention using Eugenio Suárez-Galbán Guerra's *Antología del teatro del Siglo de Oro,* although they find the annotations inadequate. Included in the volume are the *Paso séptimo (Las aceitunas)* by Lope de Rueda; *El retablo de las maravillas, Fuenteovejuna, El caballero de Olmedo, Las mocedades del Cid, El burlador de Sevilla, La verdad sospechosa, La vida es sueño, El médico de su honra, El gran teatro del mundo, Del rey abajo, ninguno;* and also Lope de Vega's *Arte nuevo de hacer comedias.*

Teresa Scott Soufas's *Women's Acts: Plays by Women Dramatists of Spain's Golden Age,* while not intended specifically for college teaching, is the only anthology of its kind, with editions of eight plays by five peninsular women writers: Ángela Azevedo's *Dicha y desdicha del juego* and *La margarita del Tajo*; Ana Caro Mallén de Soto's *El conde Partinuplés* and *Valor, agravio y mujer*; Leonor de la Cueva y Silva's *La firmeza en la ausencia*; Feliciana Enríquez de Guzmán's *Tragicomedia los jardines y campos sabeos*; and María de Zayas's *La traición en la amistad.* Given the upsurge of interest in teaching the *comedia* in transatlantic courses, one more anthology begs mentioning, though it is expensive: *América en el teatro clásico español: Estudios y textos,* edited by Francisco Ruiz Ramón, with the following plays included: Lope de Vega's *Arauco domado,* Ricardo de Turia's *La bellígera española,* Fernando de Zárate's *La conquista de México,* Miguel de Carvajal and Luis Hurtado de Toledo's *Las cortes de la muerte,* and Lope's *El Nuevo Mundo descubierto por Cristóbal Colón.*

Several anthologies for survey courses on Spanish literature include one or two *comedias.* For classes spanning many centuries, Beverly Mayne Kienzle and Teresa Méndez-Faith's *Panoramas literarios: España* makes Lope's *Fuenteovejuna* accessible to undergraduates with little or no experience reading *comedias;* Barbara Mujica's *Texto y vida: Introducción a la literatura española* provides helpful introductions and notes to Lope's *El caballero de Olmedo* and Cervantes's *entremés El retablo de las maravillas.* Used for the last three decades in introductory classes on medieval to early modern Spanish literature, Antonio Sánchez-Romeraldo and Fernando Ibarra's *Antología de autores españoles,* volume 1, *Antiguos* offers Lope's *Fuenteovejuna* as its example of Golden Age theater.

Individual Editions and Series in Spanish

The number—well into the thousands—of *comedias* in manuscript and printed form from the seventeenth century vastly exceeds the number of those readily available in modern editions. Most instructors teach canonical works available in reliable, generally well-annotated paperback editions published by Cátedra and by Castalia (in the series Clásicos Castalia) or by Espasa (in the Colección Austral): Calderón's *El alcalde de Zalamea* (Castalia and Espasa), *La dama duende* (Cátedra), *El médico de su honra* (Castalia), *El príncipe constante* (Cátedra, Espasa), *La vida es sueño* (Cátedra, Castalia), *El gran teatro del mundo* and *El gran mercado del mundo* (Cátedra); Cervantes's *El retablo de las maravillas,* included in his *Entremeses* (Cátedra, Castalia, Espasa) and *La Numancia* (Cátedra, Castalia); Guillén de Castro's *Las mocedades del Cid* (Cátedra); Lope de Vega's *El caballero de Olmedo* (Cátedra, Castalia, Espasa), *El castigo sin venganza* (Cátedra, Castalia), *La dama boba* (Cátedra, Espasa), *Fuente Ovejuna* (Cátedra, Castalia, Espasa), *El mejor alcalde, el rey* (Cátedra, Espasa), *Peribáñez y el co-*

mendador de Ocaña (Cátedra, Espasa), *El perro del hortelano* (Cátedra, Castalia, Espasa), *El villano en su rincón* (Cátedra); Rojas Zorrilla's *Del rey abajo, ninguno* (Castalia); Ruiz de Alarcón's *La verdad sospechosa* (Castalia, Cátedra); *El burlador de Sevilla* (Cátedra, Espasa) and *El condenado por desconfiado* (Cátedra, Espasa), both traditionally attributed to Tirso de Molina, and two plays definitively his, *El vergonzoso en palacio* (Cátedra, Castalia) and *Don Gil de las calzas verdes* (Castalia); and Vélez de Guevara's *La serrana de la Vera* (Cátedra, Castalia).

Also available from these major publishers, though less frequently taught, are Calderón's *La cisma de Inglaterra* (Castalia), *La devoción de la cruz* (Cátedra), *Entremeses, jácaras y mojigangas* (Castalia), *La fiera, el rayo y la piedra* (Cátedra), *La hija del aire* (Cátedra), *El mágico prodigioso* (Cátedra, Espasa), *El mayor monstruo del mundo* (Espasa); Andrés de Claramonte's *La estrella de Sevilla* (Cátedra); Luis de Góngora's *Las firmezas de Isabel* (Castalia; Cátedra publishes his *Teatro completo*); Lope's *El acero de Madrid* (Castalia); Lope de Rueda's *Pasos completos* (Espasa); Agustín de Moreto's *El desdén con el desdén* (Castalia) and *El lindo don Diego* (Cátedra); Luis Quiñones de Benavente's *Entremeses* (Cátedra); Bartolomé de Torres Naharro's *Comedias* (Castalia); the collection *Ramillete de entremeses y bailes* (ed. Bergman for Castalia); and a compilation of burlesque comedies, *Comedias burlescas del Siglo de Oro* (ed. Arellano et al., Espasa).

Of works by women that are now part of the canon, only Ana Caro's *Valor, agravio y mujer* is available in Castalia's series Biblioteca de Escritoras. A fine paperback edition of Sor Juana Inés de la Cruz's *Los empeños de una casa,* published by PPU of Barcelona, is no longer in print, and teachers may want to use Matthew Stroud's electronic edition (see below). María de Zayas's frequently taught *La traición en la amistad* is available in Soufas's anthology cited above and a recent bilingual edition (see below).

For undergraduate classes, many instructors prefer the series Castalia Didáctica, which aims its editions at high school students in Spain and undergraduates abroad. Each volume provides introductions to literary and historical contexts, illustrations, explanatory annotations, discussion and writing topics, brief bibliographies, and samples of critical appraisals. Available are *El alcalde de Zalamea, La vida es sueño, El caballero de Olmedo, Fuente Ovejuna, Peribáñez y el comendador de Ocaña,* and *El burlador de Sevilla.* Castalia Didáctica has also published *Teatro breve de los Siglos de Oro* (ed. Buezo). Castalia Prima, aimed at younger students in Spain but appropriate for undergraduate classes in the United States, has published *El perro del hortelano* and two collections of theatrical works that span the centuries: Cervantes and García Lorca: *Dos retablos y un retablillo* (ed. Ana Herrero Riopérez) and *Teatro cómico popular* (ed. Beatriz Pérez Sánchez and Angel Muñoz Calvo), which includes works by Lope de Rueda, Cervantes, Quiñones de Benavente, Ramón de la Cruz, and the brothers Joaquín and Serafín Álvarez Quintero and Carlos Arniches y Barrera. Akal's new series Literaturas has recently published *Teatro breve de la Edad Media y del Siglo de Oro* (ed. Jesús Maire Bobes), which offers a sociohistorical and literary introduction, bibliography of critical studies, and discussion and writing activities in a reader-friendly format. Providing similar materials, the series Biblioteca Didáctica Anaya has published *El alcalde de Zalamea, El caballero de Olmedo, Fuente Ovejuna,* and *La vida es sueño.* Put out by McGraw-Hill/Interamericana de España, the series Clásicos Literarios: Colección Didáctica has produced pedagogically oriented editions of *Fuente Ovejuna* and *La vida es sueño.*

Cervantes & Co.: Spanish Classics for Students aims its editions specifically at college students in the United States. *Comedias* available so far are *La verdad sospechosa, Las mocedades del Cid, Fuenteovejuna, El burlador de Sevilla, La vida es sueño, El mágico prodigioso, Peribáñez y el comendador de Ocaña,* and *El caballero de Olmedo.* The following are forthcoming: *El alcalde de Zalamea, Del rey abajo ninguno,* and *El médico de su honra.* All editions include helpful introductions, notes on grammar and versification, and explanations of linguistic and cultural references likely to be unfamiliar to undergraduates. Many instructors prefer these editions over their counterparts produced in Spain, because all the pedagogical materials are in English, saving students the tedious task of looking up words in notes.

For graduate students, paperback editions of *comedias* in the series Biblioteca Clásica, published by Crítica in Barcelona (not to be confused with the series Clásicos y Modernos, also by Crítica), are recommended for their scholarly quality, availability, and price. One of the strengths of the series is that the introductions pay close attention to issues of staging and performance, textual history, and editorial criteria. Each volume has brief footnotes, more detailed endnotes, and an extensive bibliography of critical studies. Golden Age dramas published to date are *El gran teatro del mundo, Las mocedades del Cid, Fuente Ovejuna, Peribáñez y el comendador de Ocaña,* and Francisco de Rojas Zorrilla's *Entre bobos anda el juego.* Forthcoming are *Los baños de Argel, La Numancia,* and *El vergonzoso en palacio,* among others.

Several research centers in Spain are producing excellent scholarly editions of works by the major dramatists of the period. From the Grupo de Investigación Siglo de Oro (GRISO) of the Universidad de Navarra comes the series Autos sacramentales completos de Calderón, which, as of 2005, has published forty-nine of Calderón's *autos* with Reichenberger (Kassel, Germany). (In addition to Calderón's *autos,* Reichenberger has published more than forty scholarly editions of *comedias* and its subgenres in its series Teatro del Siglo de Oro). GRISO is also coordinating editions of Golden Age burlesque comedies, mostly for the collection Biblioteca Áurea Hispánica, of Vervuert-Iberoamericana. Also from the Universidad de Navarra, the Instituto de Estudios Tirsianos has published two volumes of Tirso de Molina's *autos sacramentales,* his *comedia El amor médico* (ed. Blanca Oteiza) and has more editions of Tirso's dramas in preparation. Working out of the Universidad Autónoma de Barcelona, the organization

PROLOPE is publishing the complete theatrical works of Lope de Vega in groups of collected volumes corresponding to the twelve-work *partes* of the seventeenth century. Four *partes* are available to date. From the Universidad de Granada, the Aula-Biblioteca Mira de Amescua is editing the complete works of this dramatist, and a group associated with the Universidad de Burgos, under the direction of María Luisa Lobato, has projected editions of Agustín de Moreto's complete works, with his *Loas, entremeses y bailes* now available through Reichenberger. While the GRISO and PROLOPE editions are beyond the reach of student budgets (and, in the case of undergraduates, their intellectual needs), they are important teaching and research tools at advanced levels of *comedia* studies. In the United States, scholarly editions of several plays by Luis Veléz de Guevara have been prepared by William R. Manson and C. George Peale for Juan de la Cuesta. Also available from that publisher is Eyda M. Merediz's edition of Lope de Vega's *Comedia la famosa de los guanches de Tenerife y conquista de Canaria,* a nice complement to his *El Nuevo Mundo descubierto por Cristóbal Colón,* well edited and with a good brief introduction.

Hundreds of *comedias* are available in electronic version through the Association of Hispanic Classical Theater (AHCT) Web site. Teachers (and students) need to be aware, though, that few of these versions are annotated (Sor Juana Inés de la Cruz's *Los empeños de una casa,* with notes by Matthew Stroud, is an important exception) and that the texts are only as reliable as the printed editions (in most cases, not scholarly) on which they were based. Also useful for teaching graduate students, as well as for doing scholarly research, is the Chadwyck-Healy database of over nine hundred Golden Age plays, Teatro español del Siglo de Oro, available by subscription as an Internet resource. The texts, drawn from early editions, with their vacillations in accidentals, are not reliable enough to ground a scholarly article, but the ability to search for words and phrases over a huge corpus facilitates comprehensive research not otherwise possible. Another invaluable resource is the microfilmed version of the large University of Pennsylvania collection of early *partes* and *sueltas* (singly published *comedias*) available in many research libraries. José Regueiro's catalog of the collection guides the user to authors and texts available in its eighty-six reels.

Bilingual Editions and Translations

While instructors who teach the *comedia* in Spanish tend not to use bilingual editions for fear that their students will rely on the English, such works have an important place, especially in cross-listed and team-taught courses. The best-established series of critical bilingual editions is published by Aris and Phillips. Reliable texts in Spanish are accompanied by accurate translations on facing pages, and each volume includes an introduction situating the play historically and literarily, linguistic and cultural annotations, and a table of textual variants.

Bilingual editions include Tirso de Molina's *The Trickster of Seville and the Stone Guest / El burlador de Sevilla y el convidado de piedra, Damned for Despair / El Condenado por desconfiado, Tamar's Revenge / La venganza de Tamar*; and *Don Gil of the Green Breeches / Don Gil de las calzas verdes*; Lope's *Peribáñez and the comendador of Ocaña / Peribáñez y el comendador de Ocaña* and *Fuente Ovejuna*; Calderón's *The Schism in England / La cisma de Inglaterra, Love Is No Laughing Matter / No hay burlas con el amor; The Painter of His Dishonour / El pintor de su deshonra.* Available through the Bilingual Press and Trinity University Press are critical editions of Calderon's *Celos aun del aire matan* (not bilingual) and *Guárdate de la agua mansa / Beware of Still Waters*; Lope's *The Best Boy in Spain / El mejor mozo de España; El anzuelo de Fenisa / Fenisa's Hook* or *Fenisa the Hooker*; and *Lady Nitwit / La dama boba.* Sor Juana's *Pawns of a House / Los empeños de una casa* is to appear in 2006. Valerie Hegstrom and Catherine Larson have produced a fine paperback edition of María de Zayas's *La traición en la amistad / Friendship Betrayed* in Spanish with a facing prose translation. Also notable is Robert M. Shannon's critical edition of *El Nuevo Mundo descubierto por Christóbal Colón / The New World Discovered by Christopher Columbus* (see Cartagena-Calderón's article in this volume).

The number of fine translations of Golden Age dramas bodes well for the study of the *comedia* in courses in world literature, English, and history. *Three Major Plays:* Fuente Ovejuna, The Knight from Olmedo, Punishment without Revenge, by Lope de Vega, is available in paperback from Oxford. Cervantes's *Eight Interludes* can be found in Everyman Paperback Classics. Edward FitzGerald's nineteenth-century translations—"recastings," as he called them— of *Eight Dramas of Calderón* have recently been reissued in paperback by the University of Illinois Press, with a foreword by Margaret R. Greer. *Comedias* edited for the respected series Carleton Renaissance Plays in Translation (Dovehouse Editions, Ottawa) include Lope's *The Duchess of Amalfi's Steward (El mayordomo de la Duquesa de Malfi)* and *The Dog in the Manger (El perro del hortelano)*; Lope de Rueda's *The Interludes (Los pasos)*; Mira de Amescua's *The Devil's Slave (El esclavo del demonio)*; Tirso de Molina's *The Bashful Man at Court, Don Gil of the Breeches Green, The Doubter Damned (El vergonzoso en palacio, Don Gil de las calzas verdes, El condenado por desconfiado)*; and Calderón's *The Phantom Lady (La dama duende)*. From Peter Lang come *The House of Trials: Translation of* Los empeños de una casa *by Sor Juana Inés de la Cruz* and *Wit's End: An Adaptation of Lope de Vega's* La dama boba. Eric Bentley's *Spanish Plays*, volume 3 of *The Classic Theatre*, was reprinted in part in 1990 as Life Is a Dream *and Other Spanish Classics.* In its series Absolute Classics, the Theatre Communications Group has published translations and adaptations of works by Calderón, Tirso, and Lope; aimed specifically for stage productions, however, these translations can stray rather far from the original. The four translations in this series produced for the Royal Shakespeare Company's 2004 performances of Spanish classics and published by Oberon Books (www.oberonbooks.com) are all excellent, however. They include Tirso's *Tamar's Revenge*, translated by James Fenton and Simon Masterson; Cervantes's *Pedro, The Great Pretender*, translated and adapted by Philip Osment; Lope de Vega's *The Dog in the Manger*, translated by David Johnson; and Sor Juana's *House of Desires*, translated and adapted by Catherine Boyle. A more lengthy (indeed, nearly exhaustive) list of Golden Age dramas translated into English can be found at the *Comedia in Translation* Web site directed by Susan Paun de García (www.denison.edu/collaborations/comedia/translations; also accessible through the AHCT Web site).

The Instructor's Library

Background Studies

The most essential item in the instructor's library is a good history of Spanish Golden Age theater. The best currently available are Melveena McKendrick's *Theatre in Spain* and Ignacio Arellano's *Historia del teatro español del siglo XVII*. Both include concise histories of preceding sixteenth-century theater development, and descriptions of public and court theaters—their structure and their audiences—and dramatic conventions in those venues and in the street performances of the *autos sacramentales*. They also discuss at some length the lives and works of major and minor dramatists and provide substantial bibliographies. Some instructors still rely on older histories of Golden Age theater, particularly those of Margaret Wilson and of Edward M. Wilson and Duncan Moir, no longer in print but available in university libraries. The McKendrick and Wilson and Moir histories have also been published in Spanish. Francisco Ruiz Ramón's two-volume *Historia del teatro español* is useful for an overview; it covers the origins of theater through 1900, in the first volume, and twentieth-century theater, in the second. In-depth treatments of the early development of the theater are provided by Ronald Surtz, *The Birth of a Theater*; Alfredo Hermenegildo, *El teatro del siglo XVI*; and José María Díez Borque, *Los géneros dramáticos en el siglo XVI*. An important recent reference is the massive two-volume, multiauthored *Historia del teatro español*, directed by Javier Huerta Calvo. The first volume, *De la Edad Media a los Siglos de Oro*, contains substantial articles on theater history and theory, theatrical spaces, textual transmission and reception, acting techniques, music in the theater, female dramaturges, and the relation to the commedia dell'arte and French and English theater, as well as articles on individual dramatists, from Juan del Encina to Sor Juana.

Other historical studies help explain the cultural role of early modern Spanish theater. Walter Cohen's *Drama of a Nation* is a superb comparative study of Spanish and English theater from a Marxist perspective. William R. Blue's *Spanish Comedies and Historical Contexts in the 1620s* connects plays to the critical issues of that decade, with a conversational style that makes the work appropriate for undergraduates as well as specialists. Two studies by José Antonio Maravall, *Teatro y literatura en la sociedad barroca* and *La cultura del Barroco* (the latter available in both Spanish and English), contain his influential vision of the repressive ideological function of theater in Counter Reformation Spain. Díez Borque's *Sociología de la comedia española del siglo XVII* takes a historical-sociological perspective in describing the principal human relationships—individual and group, social and political—in the *comedia*. A more profound study of the significance of the commoner in the *comedia*, from a Bakhtinian and Marxist perspective, is Noël Salomon's classic *Recherches sur le thème paysan dans la "comedia" au temps de Lope de Vega*, translated into Spanish as *Lo villano en el teatro del Siglo de Oro*. Jane Albrecht's *The Playgoing Public of Madrid*, which evaluates the nature of the theater audience on the basis of economic statistics and other documents, provides an important reconsideration of the presumed socioeconomic breadth of the audiences.

A growing body of works examines Golden Age drama not just as a literary text but as theater, in performance, in specific spaces and times. Groundbreaking on its publication in the 1960s, N. D. Shergold's *A History of the Spanish Stage from Medieval Times until the End of the Seventeenth Century* is an impressively well documented, detailed study of the stage, from medieval dramatic tropes through elaborate court theater and the Corpus Christi sacramental drama performed on carts in the streets. Although long out of print, it is available in many libraries. John Allen's *The Reconstruction of a Spanish Golden Age Playhouse: El Corral del Príncipe* is a highly accessible source, with drawings of the *corral* and a lively opening narrative of an afternoon at the theater. More technical and thorough—for further study of the history, structure, and staging practices in other public theaters, as well as the Príncipe—is José María Ruano de la Haza and Allen's *Los teatros comerciales del siglo XVII y la escenificación de la comedia*. The multivolume series Fuentes para la Historia del Teatro en España, first compiled by N. D. Shergold and John Varey for the Colección Támesis, offers documents on theaters, theatrical companies, actors, and staging. Varey collected his articles on staging in *comedias* and *autos*, along with interpretative essays, in *Cosmovisión y escenografía. Teatros y comediantes en el Madrid de Felipe II*, by Carmen Sanz Ayán and Bernardo J. García García, documents the early development of theaters and acting companies, while *Teatros del Siglo de Oro: Corrales y coliseos en la Península ibérica* (vol. 6 in the Cuadernos de Teatro Clásico series; see below) contains articles on *corrales* in ten peninsular cities as well as Madrid. Evangelina Rodríguez Cuadros's extensive volume *La técnica del actor español en el Barroco* is a richly considered and illustrated study, broader in scope than Josef Oehrlein's earlier *El actor en el teatro español del Siglo de Oro.*

One would wish to have serious, up-to-date biographies on the major dramatists; at present, scholars must rely on old biographies such as those by Emilio Cotarelo y Mori on Calderón (recently reprinted by Iberoamericana/Vervuert) and Hugo Rennert on Lope de Vega or studies derived from them, or use volumes in the Twayne World Author Series, which are limited in most cases to superficial coverage of the author's life and work. *Spanish Dramatists of the Golden Age: A Bio-Bibliographical Soucebook,* edited by Mary Parker, contains brief articles on nineteen playwrights, from Encina to Bances Candamo, useful for quick reference—although, on Tirso de Molina, Henry Sullivan's article in the *Encyclopedia of the Renaissance* (vol. 6) is more reliable. That six-volume reference work also includes good brief biographies of Encina (by Robert ter Horst, vol. 2), Gil Vicente (C. C. Strathaton, vol. 6), Torres Naharro (Ronald Surtz, vol. 6), Cervantes (Carroll Johnson, vol. 1), Lope de Vega (Emilie Bergmann, vol. 6), Góngora (María Cristina Quintero, vol. 3), Ruiz de Alarcón (Willard King, vol. 5), and Calderón (Margaret Greer, vol. 1).

Certain reference books have proven of particular utility to *comedia* scholars. One is the *Cronología de las comedias de Lope de Vega,* compiled by S. Griswold Morley and Courtney Bruerton, which dates Lope's plays by the proportion of varying types of versification; the study also helps in locating published versions of his less-known *comedias.* Volume 25 of *Biblioteca de Autores Españoles* provides an index to Lope *comedias* published in the series (vols. 24–250). Also useful are *The Characters, Plots, and Settings of Calderón's* Comedias, by Richard W. Tyler and Sergio D. Elizondo, and the *Diccionario de personajes de Calderón,* by Javier Huerta Calvo and Héctor Ursáiz Tortajada. Two valuable recent additions are John Reynolds and Szilvia Szmuk's annotated bibliography of dissertations on the *comedia, Spanish Golden Age Drama,* and *Diccionario de la comedia del Siglo de Oro,* edited by Frank P. Casa, Luciano García Lorenzo, and Germán Vega García-Luengos. Sections of the *Diccionario* cover origin and development, texts and subgenres, sources and themes, poetics, characters, concepts and ideology, representation, reception and study, with bibliography and illustrations.

Along with histories of Golden Age theater, instructors need historical studies on early modern Spain. The most regularly used is J. H. Elliott's classic *Imperial Spain,* followed by Henry Kamen's *Spain 1469–1714: A Society of Conflict;* both are available in Spanish translation. Elliott's volume is a well-narrated political history; it can usefully be supplemented by good social histories such as James Casey, *Early Modern Spain;* Teófilo Ruiz, *Spanish Society, 1400–1600;* and Antonio Domínguez Ortiz, *The Golden Age of Spain, 1516–1659.* All the preceding authors have other, more specialized volumes that are useful for graduate courses. Mary Elizabeth Perry's study *Gender and Disorder in Early*

Modern Seville focuses on the position of women, which is not generally visible in standard histories. Some instructors like to use Marcelin Defourneaux's *Daily Life in Spain in the Golden Age*; it is entertaining for undergraduates, if rather unreliable and negative in its presentation.

On the much debated question of honor in the *comedia,* many instructors cite the classic articles by Peter Dunn, "Honour and the Christian Background in Calderón," and C. A. Jones, "Spanish Honour as Historical Phenomenon." For other important sources, see Renato Barahona's article in this volume. Recent articles by Jesús M. Usunáriz, "Volved ya las riendas" and "El matrimonio," contextualize the question of honor, moral codes, and courtship rituals historically. To help students understand the position of theater in the transition from an oral to a book culture, instructors also cite Sara Nalle's article "Literacy and Culture in Early Modern Castile."

The most influential early modern poetics of the *comedia* is Lope de Vega's *El arte nuevo de hacer comedias en este tiempo,* well edited by Juana de José Paredes. Federico Sánchez Escribano and Alberto Porqueras Mayo provide a brief introduction and an anthology of dramatic theories from the sixteenth and seventeenth centuries, in *Preceptiva dramática española del Renacimiento y el Barroco.* Luis Sánchez Laílla has recently published a carefully edited, thoroughly annotated edition of the *Nueva idea de la tragedia antigua* (1633) of Jusepe Antonio González de Salas. Invaluable for an examination of early modern condemnations and defenses of theater is the *Bibliografía de las controversias sobre la licitud del teatro,* by Emilio Cotarelo y Mori (1904), republished with an introduction and index by José Luis Suárez García in 1997.

Critical and Scholarly Studies

The number and range of critical studies dealing with the *comedia* is so vast that we can cite only the most widely read books and articles. Essays in this volume (e.g., that of Edward H. Friedman) suggest a variety of critical works on the most commonly taught plays; to go beyond these resources, instructors should consult the *MLA Bibliography* and the bibliographies published in the *Bulletin of the Comediantes* (see Journals, below) for research materials on individual authors and plays.

Barbara Simerka's collection of essays *El arte nuevo de estudiar comedias: Literary Theory and Spanish Golden Age Drama* includes a variety of the critical perspectives on *comedia* studies that have largely replaced A. A. Parker's once highly influential formalist-moralist "The Spanish Drama of the Golden Age." Paul Julian Smith's chapter "The Rhetoric of Inscription in the *Comedia*" also offers a wide-ranging analysis of the *comedia* and its place in the history of dramatic theory, informed by Derridean and Lacanian theory. Matthew Stroud's

The Play in the Mirror, which considers the *comedia* as a genre, analyzes several frequently taught plays from a Lacanian perspective. Three chapters of Anthony Cascardi's *Ideologies of History in the Spanish Golden Age* historicize the ideological function of the *comedia* as a cultural institution shaped by, and intervening in, the tensions of its age; most effective is his opening chapter, "The Spanish *Comedia* and the Resistance to Historical Change." Two older, opposing positions on the *comedia* that instructors still find useful points of reference are Arnold Reichenberger's "The Uniqueness of the *Comedia*" and Eric Bentley's countering article "The Universality of the *Comedia.*"

With regard to the subgenres in the field, Parker's work on the *auto sacramental, The Allegorical Drama of Calderón,* has not been superseded; it is complemented by Bruce Wardropper's *Introducción al teatro religioso del Siglo de Oro*; Louise Fothergill-Payne's *La alegoría en los autos y farsas anteriores a Calderón*; and Barbara Kurtz's *The Play of Allegory in the* Autos sacramentales *of Pedro Calderón de la Barca.* For court theater, instructors cite Margaret Greer's *The Play of Power*; for the short burlesque pieces that accompanied *comedias* and *autos,* Eugenio Asensio's *Itinerario del entremés* and Javier Huerta Calvo's anthology and preliminary study, *Teatro breve de los siglos XVI y XVII*; and for music in the theater, Louise Stein's *Songs of Mortals, Dialogue of the Gods.*

In recent years feminist and gender-studies approaches have constituted a major segment of *comedia* criticism. Notable contributions are McKendrick's classic *Woman and Society in the Spanish Drama of the Golden Age,* and her recent *Identities in Crisis: Essays on Honour, Gender and Women in the Comedia*; two collections edited by Anita Stoll and Dawn Smith, *Gender, Identity, and Representation in Spain's Golden Age* and *The Perception of Women in Spanish Theater of the Golden Age*; Teresa Soufas's examination of the small number of dramas by women, *Dramas of Distinction*; Yvonne Yarbro-Bejarano's *Feminism and the Honor Plays of Lope de Vega*; Sidney Donnell's recent *Feminizing the Enemy: Imperial Spain, Transvestite Drama, and the Crisis of Masculinity*; and María José Delgado and Alain Saint-Säens's compilation, *Lesbianism and Homosexuality in Early Modern Spain.*

There are a number of other significant collections that instructors frequently consult. Louise Fothergill-Payne and Peter Fothergill-Payne's *Parallel Lives: Spanish and English National Drama* is one of the few studies comparing the *comedia* with drama elsewhere in Europe at the time; *Echoes and Inscriptions,* edited by Barbara Simerka and Christopher Weimer, also offers several comparative approaches. José A. Madrigal's *New Historicism and the* Comedia: *Poetics, Politics, and Praxis* contains examples of the fruitful use of new-historicist analysis, which McKendrick also uses to explore Lope's treatment of monarchs in her work *Playing the King.* The two-volume collection of landmark articles edited by Manuel Durán and Roberto González Echeverría, *Calderón y la crítica: Historia y antología,* includes a Spanish version of Parker's "The Spanish Drama of the

Golden Age," as well as other classics. Some of the articles also appear in Javier Aparicio Maydeu's two-volume *Estudios sobre Calderón,* along with several essays by more recent Calderonistas.

Worthwhile compilations have been published as *homenajes* to distinguished *comedia* scholars: one dedicated to Vern Williamsen, edited by Charles Ganelin and Howard Mancing, *The Golden Age* Comedia: *Text, Theory, and Performance*; Dian Fox, Harry Sieber, and Robert ter Horst's *Studies in Honor of Bruce W. Wardropper*; R. O. Jones's *Studies in Spanish Literature of the Golden Age: Presented to E. M. Wilson*; *Golden Age Studies in Honour of A. A. Parker* (McKendrick); *Studies in Honor of Gerald E. Wade* (Bowman et al.); and *Calderón 1600–1681: Quartercentenary Studies in Memory of John E. Varey* (Mackenzie).

Journals and Series

The *Bulletin of the Comediantes* is the longest-standing journal devoted exclusively to the study of Spanish Golden Age drama. It began publication in 1949 and now appears twice a year. In most volumes through 2001, one issue includes a useful bibliography of *comedia* studies that appeared during the previous two years. Each year in the series Cuadernos de Teatro Clásico, the Compañía Nacional de Teatro Clásico publishes a volume of articles devoted to a special topic within *comedia* studies; those issued to date include *La comedia de capa y espada, El mito de don Juan, Música y teatro, Traducir a los clásicos, Clásicos después de los clásicos, Cervantes y el teatro, La puesta en escena del teatro clásico, Teatro cortesano en la España de los Austrias, Teatro y carnaval, El vestuario en el teatro español del Siglo de Oro*; the Compañía Nacional also puts out works that describe its productions since its inception in 1986 (see teatroclasico.mcu .es/cuadernos).

Other journals frequently contain articles on the *comedia* and sometimes devote special issues to the subject. The *Bulletin of Hispanic Studies,* or *BHS* (called the *Bulletin of Spanish Studies* from 1923 to 1948), published by the University of Liverpool, has a supplementary monograph series in textual research and criticism (TRAC). Another version of the *BHS*, with different content, appeared between 1996 and 2001 at the University of Glasgow; since 2002, this journal has had the title *Bulletin of Spanish Studies.* Instructors may also consult *Hispanic Review, Hispania, Criticón, Revista canadiense de estudios hispánicos, Gestos,* and a new journal, *Hecho teatral (Revista de teoría y práctica del teatro hispánico),* which puts out annual volumes on particular themes. The Coloquio Anglogermano, dedicated to studies on Calderón, has released the proceedings of a number of its triannual conferences since 1969 under the title *Hacia Calderón,* as has the Asociación Internacional de Teatro Español y Novohispano de los Siglos de Oro of its biannual conferences, issued under varying titles. *Cuadernos de historia moderna,* published by the Universidad Complutense de Madrid, dedicated its 1999 volume to theater: *Ingenio fecundo y juicio profundo (Estudios de historia del teatro en la edad moderna).* Finally, the Association of Hispanic Classical Theater has launched the electronic journal *Comedia Performance.*

To date, eight volumes in the series Critical Guides to Spanish Texts have been devoted to early modern drama: *Gil Vicente:* Casandra *and* Don Duardos (ed. Thomas R. Hart); two Lope plays, *El Caballero de Olmedo* (Jack W. Sage) and *Fuenteovejuna* (J. B. Hall); two plays usually attributed to Tirso de Molina, *El burlador de Sevilla* (Daniel Rogers) and *El condenado por desconfiado* (R. J. Oakley); and three by Calderón, *El alcalde de Zalamea* (Premraj Halkhoree), *La vida es sueño* (Paul Lewis-Smith), and *El médico de su honra* (Don William Cruickshank). These compact treatments by respected scholars provide useful introductions, reviews of major themes, and bibliographies.

Aids to Teaching

Illustrated Books

Bringing illustrated books into the classroom is an effective way to help students visualize early modern Spain and its drama (see Sheppard, on a comparable topic, in *Approaches to Teaching English Renaissance Drama* 43). For descriptions and illustrations of daily life—for example, urban and rural spaces, family life, housing, eating habits, festivals—we recommend *Así vivían en el Siglo de Oro,* by José Calvo, an inexpensive paperback in the series Vida cotidiana, by Anaya Biblioteca Básica. Exhibition catalogs are an excellent, if more expensive, resource. Two recent ones particularly rich in illustrations are *Teatro y fiesta del Siglo de Oro en tierras europeas de los Austrias,* which sets the culture of Spanish spectacles and theater in a wider European context, and *Calderón de la Barca y la España del Barroco,* which includes maps, objects from religious and secular life, portraits, landscapes, urban streets and plazas, and mythological figures, presented alongside selected passages from Calderón's oeuvre (many of the images from the latter work are available at the Centro Virtual Cervantes [cvc .cervantes.es/actcult/calderon], although downloading is slow). For illustrations of period dress and accessories, see—in addition to the articles mentioned in Laura Bass's essay in this volume—Brian Reade's classic *The Dominance of Spain;* the magnificent *El traje y los tipos sociales en* El Quijote, by Carmen Bernis; and Maribel Bandrés Oto's recently published *La moda en la pintura: Velázquez. Usos y costumbres del siglo XVII,* which draws heavily from the *comedia* corpus as well as from Velázquez's paintings. Detailed illustrations of playhouses are found in John J. Allen's *Los teatros comerciales del siglo XVII* (published in the same volume as Ruano de la Haza's *La escenificación de la comedia*). Although not widely available in libraries in the United States, *El corral de comedias: Escenarios, sociedad, actores* (ed. David Castillejo) has color illustrations of public theaters and costumes.

The illustrations in Jonathan Brown and J. H. Elliott's *A Palace for a King: The Buen Retiro and the Court of Philip IV*—many reproduced in color in the revised and expanded edition—can be incorporated into discussions of historical events, the monarchy, and propaganda, as well as court theater and the theatricality of courtly life. So close was the link between art and theater in palace life that two canvases painted for the ceremonial hall of the Buen Retiro—Maino's *Recapture of Bahía* and Velázquez's *Surrender of Breda*—had direct counterparts in plays performed at court: Lope de Vega's *El Brasil restituido* inspired Maino (Brown and Elliott 186), and Calderón's depiction of chivalrous sentiment in *El sitio de Bredá* finds a visual counterpart in the Velázquez (182). Rosa López Torrijos's *Mythology and History in the Great Paintings of the Prado*, with its beautiful color plates, is useful for illustrating allusions to classical mythology. Painting can help students visualize, as well, key concepts and preoccupations; for example, Pereda's sumptuous *The Knight's Dream* is effective in discussions of *desengaño* (disenchantment); Murillo's self-portrait offers a visual analogue to the metatheatrical play common in the *comedia;* Ribera's famous bearded *Magdalena Ventura with Her Husband and Son* stimulates conversation about gender and, more generally, the contemporary fascination with oddities of nature. A well-illustrated source on painting of all genres in the period is Jonathan Brown's *Painting in Spain: 1500–1700* (an expansion of his *The Golden Age of Painting in Spain*). A survey with reproductions, the majority in color, is Janis Tomlinson's *From El Greco to Goya: Painting in Spain 1561–1828*. Another recommended survey is Nina A. Mallory's *El Greco to Murillo: Spanish Painting in the Golden Age*.

Films

Films for the Humanities and Sciences (www.films.com) has made available for purchase RTVE (Radio y Televisión Española) productions of such classical works as Calderón's *La vida es sueño* (1968, Spain, black and white, 74 min.) and *Fuenteovejuna* (1980, Spain, color, 2 hr., 22 min.), as well as others. These productions tend to be relatively uninteresting on an artistic and dramatic front, but inasmuch as they re-create period dress and spaces (*Fuenteovejuna* was filmed in the town where it takes place), they give students a flavor of the world of Golden Age drama and allow them to hear the poetry of the plays. Several instructors have found Pilar Miró's acclaimed 1996 version of Lope de Vega's *El perro del hortelano* (Spain, color, 104 min.) a stimulus for lively discussion, especially on the way the director's identity as a woman inflects Lope's original play (unfortunately the film is not widely available in the United States, though it can be purchased online through www.fnac.es). The Assocation for Hispanic Classical Theater (AHCT) rents to members, from its extensive collection, videotapes of plays performed at the annual Siglo de Oro Drama Festival, at El Chamizal National Monument (to become a member, consult the Web site www.comedias .org). Since the taping is done by a stationary, single camera, the quality of AHCT videos is not ideal, but, as one survey respondent put it, "they at least serve to give students an idea of how these plays look in performance, and clips of performances can illustrate very different interpretations of a single play." The AHCT also has an archive of videotaped plays from around the world. In addition, the organization lends videotapes of lectures and discussions by well-known *comedia* scholars.

While not based on an actual *comedia,* the 1991 film *El rey pasmado* (Spain, dir. Imanol Uribe), which won several Goya awards, was recommended by one survey respondent as "a fantastic visual reproduction of the Spanish baroque" that, like numerous *comedias* themselves, explores "how political, religious, and aesthetic discourses converge on individual subjectivities." (*El rey pasmado,* though not available in the United States, can be purchased online through www.fnac.es). Some teachers recommend another acclaimed Spanish film, *Abre los ojos* (Spain, France, Italy, 1997, dir. Alejandro Amenábar), available in the United States through Facets Multimedia (www.facets.org.) as *Open Your Eyes,* in Spanish with English subtitles. Amenábar's film (see Carmen García de la Rasilla's article in this volume) and its Hollywood remake *Vanilla Sky* (2001, dir. Cameron Crowe) can be discussed as late-twentieth-century takes on *La vida es sueño.* Also recommended is *Don Juan de Marco* (United States, 1995, dir. Jeremy Leven), a twentieth-century take on *El burlador de Sevilla,* with Johnny Depp convinced he is the arch-seducer and Marlon Brando playing his psychiatrist.

Several instructors find it useful to draw analogies between the plays they are reading in class and American films: the Hollywood western and movies like *Braveheart* (1995, dir. Mel Gibson) exemplify the participation of cultural production in the creation of myths of national identity; *West Side Story* (1961, dir. Robert Wise and Jerome Rogers) can be referred to in discussions of tragedy, and *The Matrix* (1999, dir. Andy Wachowski and Larry Wachowski) and *The Truman Show* (1998, dir. Peter Weir) in those of *engaño* and *desengaño.* (See also the conclusion of McKendrick's article in this volume.)

Internet Resources

While many respondents are hesitant to incorporate the Internet widely in teaching the *comedia* at the undergraduate level when, as one instructor put it, "we are struggling just to get them to read," most recognize its increasing importance in class preparation and research. A major *comedia* Web site is that of the AHCT, managed by Matthew Stroud at www.comedias.org. Particularly valuable is its electronic library, which contains searchable and downloadable texts of more than 220 *comedias, autos sacramentales,* and *entremeses* in Spanish and several *comedias* in English translation. There is also a Teaching and Research Tools library, which includes such pedagogical materials as a guide to grammar in the *comedia,* a list of poetic terms, and rules of scansion, as well as several bibliographies. In addition to a long list of plays available in English translation, the site's Translation Project, directed by Susan Paun de García, offers a bibliography of some forty-five reference books and secondary studies on the *comedia;* in many cases, contents of the books are listed. The AHCT Web site also provides links to several academic sites related to the *comedia,* theater studies in general, and Spanish and Spanish American literature; among the focused links is a database on Tirso's plots and characters, a searchable Web adaptation of Jean S. Chittenden's 1964 doctoral dissertation. Finally, this site contains information on AHCT activities, including conferences, and its journal *Comedia Performance.*

The Asociación Internacional de Teatro Español y Novohispano de los Siglos de Oro (AITENSO) also has an excellent Web site, created and meticulously maintained by A. Robert Lauer at faculty-staff.ou.edu/L/A-Robert.R.Lauer-1/AITENSO.html. The AITENSO site provides a thorough, regularly updated international bibliography on individual playwrights and plays; New World as well as peninsular dramatists are included. Other valuable offerings include several of Lauer's course syllabi; guides to rhetorical terms, Spanish verse form, and grammar; links to professional organizations, academic Web sites, publishing houses, journals, and conferences devoted to Hispanic studies in general and the Golden Age in particular, as well as to theater festivals and companies; and a directory of AITENSO members from around the world. As scholarly communities, both AITENSO and AHCT maintain a Listserv (go to their respective Web sites to sign up). They are not intended for students but can help teachers keep abreast of publications, conferences, and performances.

Another treasure trove for scholars, teachers, and students is the Ars Theatrica section of the Parnaseo site run by the Universidad de Valencia (parnaseo .uv.es/ars). José Luis Canet, Evangelina Rodríguez, and Josep Lluís Serra have assembled a superb corpus of visual documentation—including diagrams, drawings, and reproductions of paintings and engravings—related to theatrical spaces in ancient Rome and early modern Spain; actors and acting in ancient Greece and Rome and medieval and early modern Europe; stage sets and scenery; and theatrical festivities and spectacles. Ars Theatrica also has an electronic library of critical editions of some twenty rare theatrical texts, mostly from the sixteenth century. In addition, Ars Theatrica publishes scholarly essays under the heading "Sobre las Tablas: Estudios e investigación." The GRISO (Grupo Investigación Siglo de Oro) Web site of the Universidad de Navarra, while not devoted exclusively to drama, is an important resource for specialists, offering up-to-date information on the conferences and publications sponsored by this prolific center of Spanish Golden Age studies; it also maintains an international directory of Hispanists. Another valuable site is the Biblioteca Virtual Miguel de Cervantes (www.cervantesvirtual.com/index), which includes digital editions of all his plays, as well as a variety of resources on Cervantes and other canonical writers.

The Université du Québec à Trois-Rivières hosts a Web site called Teatro de los Siglos de Oro (www.UQTR.Uquebec.ca/dlmo/TEATRO), organized by Ricardo Serra, Alfredo Hermenegildo, and Marc Vitse. Like other sites mentioned here, it provides a bank of play texts (albeit not as extensive as the AHCT electronic library), information on conferences and theater festivals, and links to related sites. Unique to this site is a complete list of articles and accompanying abstracts of articles on Golden Age theater (141) published in the journal *Criticón* (Université de Toulouse–Le Mirail) from 1978 to 1995. Also from Canada comes José María Ruano de la Haza's magnificent virtual reconstruction and description of Madrid's theater the Corral del Príncipe (1583–1744) (http://aix1.uottawa.ca/%7Ejmruano/Corral.html). Seven views of the theater (façade, women's staircase, lateral buildings, stage, etc.) are shown and meticulously described in both their architectural and their social dimensions.

Through the Web sites of the annual Festival Internacional de Teatro Clásico, at Almagro (www.festivaldealmagro.com), and the Compañía Nacional de Teatro Clásico (teatroclasico.mcu.es), teachers can follow comedia productions in Spain. The latter Web site also has information about the CNTC's monographic series Cuadernos de Teatro Clásico (see Instructor's Library, above) and its editions of *comedias* performed. Going beyond the *comedia*, Infoescena (www.infoescena.es) is a gateway to the performing arts throughout Spain and Latin America.

Part Two

APPROACHES

Introduction

Whether the *comedia* is taught in courses devoted mainly to this genre or in broader surveys of early modern Spanish history, literature, and culture, fundamental aspects of context need to be outlined from the start. Students should know that there were three main types of theatrical spaces: commercial *corrales de comedias* (public playhouses), court theaters, and the streets on which *autos sacramentales* were performed. In Madrid and other cities, the *corrales* were the principal venue of *comedia* performance from about 1580 onward. The designation derives from the fact that earlier, temporary theaters were erected in the patio or courtyard (*corral*) of multifamily houses, inns, or hospitals, and the arrangement they afforded was carried over to buildings specifically adapted for theatrical performances. The rectangular patio was surrounded on three sides by viewing windows or boxes opened or constructed in the neighboring houses and the building's facade; the stage and multistory acting and dressing-room structure stood on the fourth side, opposite the façade. Paying the relatively low entry cost (about one-fifth of a laborer's daily wage) entitled men to stand in the patio, which could be covered by an awning to protect them from the sun or rain; if they paid an extra fee, they could sit on benches in the raked seating that lined the lateral walls. Women paid about one-fifth more, entered by a different doorway, and were seated in the *cazuela* (literally, "stewpot"), a gallery that occupied the second level of the façade. There was an upper level *tertulia* (gallery) for clerics. Nobility (men and women) and other wealthy viewers or dignitaries occupied the windows and boxes, at much higher prices. Seating arrangements for viewing thus reflected the hierarchical structure of the society. Despite the pressures of moralist opposition to theater in general and to public theaters in particular as places of moral corruption and social disorder similar to those that would close theaters in Puritan England, the Spanish *corrales* were protected, from the outset, by the fact that performances were sponsored by charitable brotherhoods (*cofradías*), who used the proceeds for the care of the sick and indigent in public hospitals.

The basic *comedia* was performed with iconic stage props and minimal scenery; each scene was described by the text itself, although curtained spaces in the dressing-room and acting structure could be opened to reveal painted scenery. Performance was continuous within the three acts, with the exit of all characters indicating a scene change. Performances of the *loa* (prologue), the three acts, and the burlesque pieces—an *entremés* (interlude), *baile* (dance), *jácara* (ruffian ballad), *mojiganga* (farce), and *fin de fiesta* (finale)—lasted about two and one-half to three hours and took place in the afternoon, without artificial lighting. The sequence of the accessory pieces and the subgeneric boundaries between them were variable; as the seventeenth century progressed, the *loa* was sometimes omitted, except at the opening of the theatrical season, when each company presented its actors and actresses in a new *loa,* and before *auto sacramental* or elaborate court performances. Typically, an *entremés* was performed between the first and second acts of a *comedia,* and a *baile* or *jácara* between the second and third acts; a *mojiganga* or *fin de fiesta* would conclude the festivities (see Asensio; Buezo, *Teatro breve*; Greer, "Embodying the Faith," Caballero Fernández-Rufete; Madroñal Durán).

The court was another important venue for plays, whether in improvised theaters in various palaces or in the Coliseo (Coliseum), which opened in 1640 in the Buen Retiro palace to accommodate elaborate court spectacle productions. Court performances became increasingly frequent and elaborate during the reigns of Philip III (1598–1621) and especially Philip IV (1621–65), and *corral* lessee-managers complained of the drain on their revenues resulting from royal command performances by the best companies and performers.

The third, but certainly not least significant, type of theatrical activity took place during the annual Corpus Christi festivals, in which *autos sacramentales* (one-act allegorical religious dramas) were performed in the streets of all Spanish cities. In some ways, the *autos* were the theatrical highlight of the year, free of charge and open to all, the only drama that all residents of Spanish cities and towns could see.

Students should be cautioned not to assume an easy identity between the texts they read, the works as originally written, and the *comedias* performed in those spaces. Dramatists sold their play scripts to an *autor de comedias* (theater company owner-director), and the works were thereafter the property of the *autor,* to use and dispose of as he or she pleased. The terminology of early modern Spanish drama, therefore, recognizes that "authorship" of *comedia* performance is as much that of the player-director as of the dramatist. Scripts were jealously guarded for a number of years, since new plays drew larger audiences. After a decade or so, texts were sold for publication either in *partes* (collected volumes of a dozen plays, by one author or a variety of dramatists) or as single-play editions (*sueltas*). Between composition and publication, scripts suffered many changes, as *autores* adapted them to suit the tastes of their audiences and the talents of their company, and as copyists, editors, and printers did their work faithfully or, more often, carelessly.

After preparing students by presenting the technical aspects of *comedia* production, teachers face the vexing issue of making this drama come alive to today's students, while developing their understanding of its cultural and historical specificity and significance. The Approaches section of the volume thus begins under the rubric "The Past in the Present: Historical Frameworks and Visual Contexts." Melveena McKendrick, in the lead essay, sets out key issues of *comedia* studies—the degree to which the drama served or challenged the interests of a monarchical state, the ambiguous treatment it gave to women, the use (or abuse) of the honor code—and asserts the pedagogical necessity, as well as the dangers, of making connections between the plays and the present-day world. As

McKendrick discusses, the obsession with honor in the *comedia* was very much a preoccupation of the nobility; in the next essay, Renato Barahona turns to the on-the-ground workings of honor, showing that even women of modest means had high stakes in defending their reputations. Although mere suspicions of dishonor lead to wife murder in classic dramas like *El médico de su honra*, the historical record analyzed by Barahona reveals a more flexible application of the honor code in real life. Of course, the real-life versus literary representation dichotomy is never clear-cut, and a major task in teaching complex works of literature is to guide students toward an appreciation of the power of art to shape a culture's understanding of its past and of its present vis-à-vis the past.

As Frederick de Armas shows in his discussion of *Fuenteovejuna*, in the third essay in this volume, drama could paint foundational moments in Spain's national history in mythic terms, creating a picture of the past against which to comment on an imperfect present. It is through painting and also Renaissance emblems that de Armas illuminates the interpenetrating layers of myth and history in the play while instructing us, more broadly, on the visual culture of early modern Spain.

Laura R. Bass and Enrique García Santo-Tomás likewise advocate the use of visual aids in the classroom. Bass is interested in communicating the key role that costume played in both the meaning-making and the viewing pleasure of the theater. *El vergonzoso en palacio* is the paradigmatic example here. Bringing in a range of images, from clothing catalogs to period portraits, she encourages her students to appreciate Tirso's baroque exploration of dress and cross-dress as it anticipates our culture's fascination with clothing and identity and—at the same time—as the play is grounded in the material culture of seventeenth-century Spain. Another one of Tirso's plays, *Don Gil de las calzas verdes,* invites García Santo-Tomás's analysis of urban geography and the *comedia.* Illustrating the play's references to Madrid's promenades, plazas, and gates with maps and paintings, García Santo-Tomás argues that the theater not only grew up with the capital city but also helped shape its landscape. Turning to another visual medium, Carmen García de la Rasilla discusses the transfer of plays and themes from the early modern Spanish stage to the late twentieth-century silver screen, in her essay on Pilar Miró's enormously successful *El perro del hortelano* and Alejandro Amenábar's postmodern take on *La vida es sueño, Abre los ojos.* With its use of period costumes and faithfulness to Lope de Vega's seventeenth-century verse, Miró's film allows students to watch—and hear—this early modern comedy of manners come alive, while it invites reflection on the cultural reception of the past in the present. Translating the baroque obsession with illusion and disillusionment into the contemporary idiom of virtual realities, *Abre los ojos* reminds us that, although technologies change across time, fundamental philosophical preoccupations remain.

Although the teaching of the *comedia,* like that of literature in general, is increasingly taking a cultural studies orientation, our survey respondents were concerned that the nuts and bolts of textual analysis not be left behind. Of course, the two go hand in hand: as Mary Malcolm Gaylord demonstrates in the first of the next group of essays, out of poetic language are constructed the very issues of power, identity, and gender and class relations on which cultural studies focus. Specifically, Gaylord proposes paying greater attention to verse form. Using *Peribáñez y el comendador de Ocaña* and *La vida es sueño*, she demonstrates that teaching students to recognize traditional Castilian *redondillas* (quatrains) and *romances* (ballads) as distinct from Italianate sonnets, for example, is no mere formality but rather a vehicle for appreciating the dramatic conflict encoded in the juxtaposition of verse forms. In his essay, Edward H. Friedman outlines a graduate seminar on the *comedia* in which individual works are explored through close reading of and attention to the critical and theoretical complexes that have been constructed around them. As they become versed in the key issues of *comedia* criticism, students adopt their own points of emphasis.

Teresa S. Soufas provides guidance for teaching a combined graduate–undergraduate seminar focused on women writers. As she explains her presentation of the five early modern women writers whose plays we know, she considers the issues, such as essentialist versus constructivist explanations of gender (or as she prefers, relational and individualist philosophies), that are central to feminist approaches to the *comedia* in general, whether written by men or women. Manuel Delgado is interested in the complex philosophical and theological underpinnings of the Calderonian plays *La vida es sueño* and *El mágico prodigioso*, two of the richest dramas of the Spanish baroque. Using the saintly prince Fernando of *El príncipe constante* as a foil for the struggle toward moral good undergone by Segismundo and Cipriano, he describes how he teaches undergraduates to appreciate such concepts as synderesis and baroque *desengaño* (disenchantment with false goods) as these heroes achieve a sense of social responsibility akin to that advocated by Emmanuel Lévinas.

The next group of essays examines early modern drama in terms of the history and social practice of the theater and in broader comparative contexts. Bruce R. Burningham presents two narratives of the development of the theater in the West: an "official" one that focuses on playwrights, written texts, and architectural settings, and an alternative history that stresses improvised performance practices, such as those of street mimes and jongleurs. The *comedia,* he argues, emerged at the meeting of high literary tradition and popular performance. Such a perspective can best be examined by comparing, for example, Guillén de Castro, Sor Juana Inés de la Cruz, and Alarcón with dramatists of the other national theaters in early modern Europe and the degree to which they embraced or rejected their jongleuresque ancestors. Committed, like Burningham, to the study of theater in social practice, Vincent Martin shares his course on the festive drama of early modern Spain, specifically the burlesque *entremeses* and *mojigangas* and one-act *autos sacramentales* that were performed during the Catholic feasts of carnival and Corpus Christi. While teachers of Spain's classical theater tend to focus on the three-act *comedia,* Martin reminds us that the subgenres played a key role in the cultural life of both small towns and cities; he outlines his techniques for overcoming the linguistic and conceptual barriers they present.

Susan L. Fischer also pays close attention to performance, in her comparative undergraduate seminar on the *comedia* and Shakespeare, which pairs *Henry VIII* and *The Schism in England, Measure for Measure* and *The Painter of His Dishonour, The Tempest* and *Life Is a Dream*. In addition to discussing these works in their sociohistorical contexts, Fischer addresses the question "Why these plays now?" exploring them in the light of modern-day theory and performance possibilities. Leah Middlebrook's comparative course juxtaposes the *comedia* and the French *comédie*. As she demonstrates, the ways in which writers like Corneille and Molière adapted the plots of Guillén de Castro, Lope de Vega, and Ruiz de Alarcón, streamlining them and trimming away low characters, shed light on the contours of theater and absolutism in the writers' respective societies. Both the French and Spanish plays analyzed by Middlebrook portray the emergence of early modern model subjects. In contrast, the figure of Don Juan examined in James Mandrell's essay is the archetypal seducer who refuses subjection to the social order. It is the unruliness of his desire that accounts for his appeal across time, space, and artistic medium. Mandrell traces Don Juan's incarnation from the seventeenth-century *comedia* through Mozart's opera to the philosophy of Kierkegaard and later Ortega y Gasset and, finally, to two plays set on this side of the Atlantic: Derek Walcott's *The Joker of Seville* and Carlos Morton's *Johnny Tenorio*. In the end, this navigation across the ocean and three centuries allows Mandrell to go back to Tirso's original play, foregrounding its itinerary on the imperial map of early modern Spain.

Mandrell's essay forms a logical bridge to those by José R. Cartagena-Calderón, Frederick Luciani, María Antonia Garcés, John Beusterien, and Cory A. Reed. Cartagena-Calderón shares his approach to teaching the *comedia* from a transatlantic perspective. The example here is Lope de Vega's *El Nuevo Mundo descubierto por Cristóbal Colón,* whose engagement with Spain's American enterprise is illuminated through the writings of Bartolomé de Las Casas and López de Gómora and visual representations of the New World. While Cartagena-Calderón focuses on the Americas on the stages of Spain, Luciani looks at works produced in the New World itself—specifically, plays from Mexico (the *Coloquio de los cuatro reyes de Tlaxcala,* of uncertain authorship, and the *loa* to *El divino Narciso,* by Sor Juana Inés de la Cruz) and Peru (the anonymous *Tragedia del fin de Atahualpa*) that take as their subject the conquest and conversion of the Amerindians. Garcés turns to Spain's borders with the Islamic world, exploring the relation between literary testimony and history in Cervantes's captivity plays *El trato de Argel* and *Los baños de Argel.* Beusterien draws from new historical, postcolonial, and race studies in his teaching of Andrés de Claramonte's *El valiente negro en Flandes.* Reed discusses the challenges of making the *comedia* meaningful to students who have had little exposure to literature and languages and who, coming to Hispanism from a Latin American perspective, have little interest in the Spanish Golden Age. As he shows, however, Lope's *Fuenteovejuna,* and Cervantes's *Numancia* and *El retablo de las maravillas* resonate in the classroom when taught through issues of imperialism, *convivencia,* and ethnicity and conceptions of self and other.

The next two essays describe concrete ways of making early modern Spanish drama come alive for students through embodied practices. A. Robert Lauer shares his method of putting characters on trial, as he playfully and critically enriches the teaching of *La vida es sueño*; even the historical complexities of Polish succession start to make sense to students when they must decide on Basilio's guilt and Segismundo's right to the throne. Dale J. Pratt and Valerie Hegstrom recount their experiences mentoring undergraduates as they prepared a production of *La dama duende.* While few literature professors have the resources and institutional support to stage a full-length drama the way their group did, the interactive methods can be implemented on a smaller scale.

The last two essays address the use of technology in teaching Spain's classical theater. Diane E. Sieber provides guidelines for creating and implementing multimedia instructional tools and offers examples of the successful use by students of interactive Web sites, 3-D digital modeling, and hypertext editions. Finally, Matthew D. Stroud describes a course in which students created electronic editions of six *comedias,* three by women (*Valor, agravio y mujer*; *La traición en la amistad*; and *Los empeños de una casa*) and three by men (*El burlador de Sevilla, El castigo sin venganza,* and *La vida es sueño*). Having students annotate the assigned texts allowed for much closer readings than the usual one-act-per-fifty-minute session. Creating editions, in other words, is an excellent tool for working through the challenges of early modern Spanish drama—its language and its cultural and literary references.

Communicating the Past

Melveena McKendrick

I was fortunate to receive my training as a *comedia* specialist from two great British Hispanists, Alexander A. Parker and Edward M. Wilson. Although both were influenced by New Criticism, their attitudes to teaching the *comedia* were very different. For Wilson the text was paramount, and he strayed from it only to make references to other texts. Parker, too, paid close attention to textual detail but always in the elaboration of a larger moral and philosophical canvas— the Catholic world picture of sixteenth- and seventeenth-century Spain. His approach offered both an intelligible way into individual texts and a template for making sense of an entire period. His concern was, at once, to present the text as an integral part of the historical moment and to explain its enduring significance, in educational terms probably the most effective strategy. The young need help to see why the past is interesting and relevant, to discover what it has to say to them.

Our perception of what constitutes the early modern period has changed since Parker's generation, profoundly influenced as it was by E. M. W. Tillyard's *The Elizabethan World Picture*. We now know that this work offered a very partial picture indeed of a world that was in reality ideologically fractured and socially and politically complicated. Historians no longer think of Spain then as a monolithic, wholly conformist society, and scholars have become more sensitized to evidence of dissent, tension, and anxiety in the texts we teach. The expansion of research on the period into all areas of human activity—socioeconomics, culture, class, race, gender, demography, crime, the law, the city—has opened doors into plays that simply did not exist before. Context is no longer understood as the backdrop against which to read dramatic texts but as a crucial shaping force that determines meaning. A play, particularly one that belongs to a national, commercial theater, is not an accidental recorder of the social process but a product and agent of it.

In some ways this approach has made our task easier. Extending the cultural and sociohistorical reach of the *comedia*—talking about money, clothes, transgressive sexuality, crime, racism—renders it more accessible, makes it seem more modern. But the approach also creates problems, the least of which being that we do not yet have at our disposal the rich variety of historical research in these new fields that is available to Shakespearean critics. A more taxing problem is the ineluctable fact that while the present inherits the past, it does not reproduce it. Students respond more readily to aspects of a text that are familiar to them and that fit comfortably within a twenty-first century mind-set: discussing issues of gender and race are infinitely more appetizing to them than trying to get their minds round Neoplatonism or the debate about justification by faith or good works. Yet when faced with what is strange to them, at least they know where they are. They identify the material as arcane and exotic, and learn what they need to in order to make sense of the text. It is when they fail to identify, or when they misidentify, the familiar that they flounder, and it is in the delicate balance between cultural invisibility (failing to see the present in the past because the social circumstances and moral vocabulary are different) and anachronism (treating the past as if it were no different from the present) that the hermeneutical challenge of teaching the *comedia* lies. Meaning then and relevance now must be allowed to illuminate each other without being fuzzily confused or conflated. Reading a seventeenth-century work solely in the light of our own preoccupations is an intellectual and aesthetic cul-de-sac—what comes out of it is what goes in; little new is learned; horizons are not expanded. Even so, willfully denying a seventeenth-century text its enduring resonances and insisting on reading it as if it were necessarily confined to its historical moment is an arid form of literary archaeology at best, a rejection of the leading condition for literary survival. Students need encouragement in identifying modern transformations of archaic practices and beliefs, but they need restraining in their tendency to apply present-day measures and evaluations to familiar but nonetheless contingent issues.

The overarching preoccupations of the seventeenth-century Spanish theater as a whole—honor with its related issues of class and power, kingship, and what one might call proto-feminism—all present problems of reception and interpretation. Honor is a problem for students because they consider it an outdated concept with no application in the modern world. By the time they have read a handful of plays, they perceive honor as the overworked resort of murderous husbands, vengeful fathers and brothers, and sword-happy aristocrats and judge it to be an unconvincing psychological motivation. Distracted by terminology, they have not made the right connections. They have not looked beyond the label "honor" and recognized that as a dramatic motif it encompasses a complex set of interrelated concerns and values. Change the signifiers, however, and things begin to fall into place. Talk about self-worth, self-respect, self-image and public image, good name and reputation, and they begin to feel more at home. Refer to the laws of slander, libel, and blackmail, and the light begins to dawn. Explain that honor is a social concept with strong gender implications, and they begin to be interested. Invoke Italy, Greece, Germany, and Japan, to name but a few societies in which a ritualized concept of honor has flourished, and they identify patterns and stop thinking of honor as a bizarre obsession unique to seventeenth-century Spain. Inform them that even now in some countries hundreds of women are killed every year in order to preserve men's honor, and they begin to see things in perspective.

It is useful to get out of the way the distinction between *honra* (social esteem) and *honor* (moral integrity). I explain the elusive and unstable difference between them, but I tell students that they need not worry about terminology, since in the seventeenth century the idea of honor was so closely equated with social reputation that the two terms were used interchangeably, as both the plays and the *Diccionario de autoridades* show. What they do need to know is that the conflation of honor with reputation provoked an ongoing debate in Spain about the nature and meaning of honor, with moralists like Mateo Alemán and Francisco de Quevedo insisting that there could be no honor without moral integrity—that honor was not constituted solely by birth and social recognition. The playwrights of the day weighed into the debate by using the stage to explore the ideological tension in the workings of honor between personal worth and public perception, individual will and social prescription. That honor was generally understood as being in the eye of the beholder, something bestowed or withheld by a man's peers, is a difficult concept for students to grapple with, even when they read the Veinticuatro's speech in act 2 of Lope de Vega's *Los comendadores de Córdoba,* where the notion is clearly set out, but again familiar equivalences can help—undeserved campus reputations, harmful gossip, tabloid papers, Internet rumor sites, and popular assumptions like "there's no smoke without fire." A full and nuanced understanding of the inflections of honor as reputation, however, requires wider input. Why reputation mattered so much and why honor was a question of such vital concern to seventeenth-century Spanish society can be thoroughly probed only by summoning the aid of sociopolitical history, political theory, and anthropology.

The bottom line in trying to convey the significance of honor is that since it was perceived as emanating not from worth but from recognition, without any necessary relation between the two, honor was lost not through one's misdeeds but when one's fellow men withdrew their respect, with or without good cause. Since without that respect one could not function in the hierarchical society of seventeenth-century Spain, honor was equated with life and dishonor with death. The world of the *comedia,* for its own dramatic and theatrical reasons, takes the metaphorical equation between honor and life literally, but it was not an analogy peculiar to Spain—in Renaissance France, too, reputation was so vital that the unjust loss of it through calumny was called "civil murder." This obsession with reputation had much to do with the nobility's loss of function and identity in a world in which power was now centralized in the monarchy and where upward mobility seemed to be threatening the nobles' preeminent position. By stressing honor as part of their birthright, as something distinct from virtue and integrity as well as from wealth, the nobility were seeking to establish a hurdle the nouveaux riches could not jump, and therefore to increase the distance between themselves and the new social-climbing middle classes. Because this middle class in Spain was largely of *converso* origin (of Jewish descent), *limpieza de sangre* (purity of blood) operated as another class barrier. Honor and *limpieza,* in theory, went hand in hand: both obsessions had their origins in insecurity, were preoccupied with the idea of immaculacy (pure wife, pure blood), and were fueled by the fear of loss of control over one's life, since whether one was *honrado* or *limpio* depended on the witness of others.

The concept of honor implicated the entire social structure, including the nation-state itself. A key factor of seventeenth-century political thought was the idea that a country's image was important not just to an appearance of strength but to the nation's actual strength and health. As the political philosopher Diego de Saavedra Fajardo put it in his *Idea de un príncipe político-cristiano* (1640): "los imperios se conservan con su misma autoridad y reputación. En empezando a perderla, empiezan a caer. . . . [E]n no estando la corona fija sobre esta coluna derecha de la reputación, dará en tierra" (*Empresa* 31)("[E]mpires survive by dint of their very authority and reputation. As they begin to lose it, they start to fall. . . . If the crown be not firmly secured upon the upright column of reputation, it will fall"). And again: "Es el honor uno de los principales instrumentos de reinar" (*Empresa* 7) ("Honor is one of the principal instruments of royal government" [my trans.]). With his careful use of *honor* rather than *honra,* Saavedra is referring here not only to the public perception of the ruler who embodies the state but to the integrity on which that perception should be based. Lope de Vega's *El castigo sin venganza* is a stunning problematization of the state dimension of honor in which reason of state (another contentious issue) and personal motivation become infamously and tragically confused. What we explore here with our students is Lope's own exploration, with his audience, of the role of ethics in politics.

Below the level of the state, honor continues to collide with morality. The newcomer to the *comedia* needs to understand that at the heart of the idea of honor as reputation lies a logic enshrined in the legal concepts of slander and libel. Honor was a form of social control, a restraining and inhibiting influence on behavior. What the *comedia* reveals, however, is the danger of this essentially constructive principle degenerating into a social and mental tyranny that separates man from his feelings and from the workings of his moral conscience.

In seventeenth-century Spain the greatest insult a gentleman could suffer was to be called a liar. His honor was most vulnerable, however, in relation to his family. In patriarchal societies like those of early modern Europe, the traditional model for the family was the monarchical model. Marriage was connected with political and economic systems, sexual economy with the economy of property. In family and state a single person symbolized the group whose collective identity, welfare, and honor were vested in his person, and a threat to the authority of the family was, by implication, a threat to the state. Adultery challenged more directly than any other form of dishonor the three principles—authority, order, and unity—on which society and the state were understood to be based. It was incumbent upon the head of the family to maintain control over his little kingdom, particularly his womenfolk. If he neglected or failed in the task, he was effectively unmanned and society withdrew its respect, leading to a sense of social and psychological isolation. While this was true at every social level, it was the gentleman who had most to lose, since so much depended on his standing— posts, preferment, titles, marriages. In Calderón's *El médico de su honra* (act 1) and *El pintor de su deshonra* (act 2), husbands are explicitly linked with the notion of power, and the perceived challenge to the husband's authority is associated with an invasion of patriarchal territory. The anthropology of honor shows that in such plays, where murder becomes the ultimate form of control and of preservation of the social self, the rhetoric of honor is not simply a coded rationalization of jealousy but the articulation of a nexus of issues ranging from atavistic notions of defilement to interconnected economies of sexual, social, and political organization whose imperatives run counter to Christian morality.

The problem for men living within such a system was that the authority granted them was vested in the behavior of a creature—woman—that they had long condemned as willful, unpredictable and untrustworthy, and governed by uncontrollable sexual urges. Such assumptions about women's nature bred insecurity and suspicion precisely because they conceded to wife or daughter the power to threaten not only the husband or father's peace of mind but his social role and thus his identity. The motif, in serious or comic form, is a constant of the *comedia,* and it is developed in ways that introduce other variations in the crises that honor creates.

The *comedia* takes us down the social scale into the world of peasant honor, and across gender boundaries into a world in which women, too, have a highly developed sense of personal and social worth. Students are particularly attracted to the plays of peasant honor, not least because they are surprised to come across such democratic takes on a preoccupation they have assumed to be the province of aristocratic males in a bygone elitist age. They are both wrong and right to be so. Anthropologists have established that in all cultures, honor works horizontally, not vertically, operating within and not between peer groups. A noble could not be dishonored by a peasant, nor a peasant by a nobleman—the respect a man cared about was the respect of his own kind, of those he had to live among. At the same time, since a seventeenth-century gentleman derived his honor from his birth, in his own eyes his honor rendered him not only socially and economically superior to the lower orders but morally superior as well. The entrenched idea that the poor were morally inferior to the rich—an idea encapsulated linguistically in the double meanings of words like *noble* (in Spanish and English) and *gentleman*—was challenged in plays like *Peribáñez y el comendador de Ocaña* and *Fuenteovejuna,* both by Lope, and *El alcalde de Zalamea,* by Calderón, which expose the wrongs done to the people in the name of a spurious concept of honor and nobility. The abuse of social and sexual power perpetrated by nobles in such plays requires no explanation, but the ideology that produces both it and its condemnation does. Yet the idea that nobility should be understood as both cause and effect—that the nobleman's origins and upbringing imbue standards and sensibilities that require that he behave nobly (noblesse oblige)—is not as alien as it might now seem. The moral connotations of the word *gentleman* may have overtaken its social significance, but they derive from the same assumptions, and we are still less forgiving of disreputable behavior from the prosperous and educated than from the poor and deprived.

Laura Bass has observed to me that issues of class in the *comedia* are some of the hardest for American students to grasp. European students have less of a problem, because many superficial traces of class structure still survive in their societies, but they, too, find many of the traditional assumptions about class hard to relate to. However, exposure to class subtleties and anxieties in the novels (and their film and television versions) of Jane Austen, Henry James, and Edith Wharton should familiarize students with the ideas of social embarrassment and shame, socially unacceptable marriages, and so on. And reference to the social standing and power that come with wealth and education in new as well as old societies can also be illuminating. Success everywhere buys status, and continuing success perpetuates it. All countries have their elites, who see themselves as special and entitled, and statistics show that people generally mix with and marry others from the same socioeconomic milieu. Social divisions are still there, although they are less fossilized and less visible because attitudes to authority have changed and social patterns are more fluid.

Where social divisions in the *comedia* are concerned, it is helpful to explain the functional principle behind the medieval concept of the three estates (clergy, nobility-military, and peasantry) and the related Renaissance representation of the state as a human body of essential parts that serve different purposes; the idea that the order and unity of family, society, and state reflected the order and unity of the divinely ordered cosmos; and the entrenched conviction (Aristotelian in origin) that the individual served society, not society the individual. The *Autor's* explanations to *Mundo* and *Pobre* in Calderón's *El gran teatro del mundo* ([ed. Frutos Cortés] 39–66 and 409–28) are an excellent metatheatrical introduction to the social ordering of Christian life. This pressing desire for order, of course, was in reality the response to a world in flux. The anxieties generated by social tensions and social mobility, changing values and behavior, civil strife, generational conflict, and female assertiveness are what the plays explore, and students need to recognize that the containment provided by apparently conformist endings can be deceptive, even transgressive—that negotiated resolutions dictated by generic convention, commercial demand, or the specter of censorship do not cancel out what has transpired in the body of the play and can contrive to resist closure. The *comedia*'s vision of the workings of class and power is a very troubled one indeed.

The part played in it by *limpieza de sangre* is implicit rather than explicit. For theatrical purposes, honor and *limpieza* constitute a seamless garment worn by every stage hero. The *comedia* is full of puns on *raza* (race) and *tribu* (tribe) and jokes about Judaizers and pork, but the issue of racial purity was both too sensitive and theatrically unrewarding (because unresolvable) to become a central dramatic motif. Nevertheless, students need to know about the inflections of race, religion, and class to come to grips with the social hierarchy of the *comedia*'s world. Since most nobles owed their titles, lands, and wealth to the services they had rendered their race and religion during the Reconquest, noble legitimacy had become identified with pure Christian blood and the Christian faith. The decline in the military function of the nobility, extensive intermarriage between noble and wealthy *converso* families in the fifteenth century, the emergence in the sixteenth century of an aspirational, largely *converso* middle class, and in the seventeenth century the sale of titles to fill the crown's coffers all conspired to undermine noble exclusiveness and produce a deep-seated sense of insecurity—particularly among the more vulnerable minor nobility—which we see reflected in the reputation-obsessed husbands and gallants in the *comedia*. The fact that the peasant laid claim to what he considered a superior form of honor and nobility—*limpieza de sangre* combined with personal merit (Peribáñez, Pedro Crespo)—merely compounded the threat.

The apex of the social pyramid was of course the king, and early modern ideologies of kingship contain some tricky concepts and terms—the prince is head of the republic, the king has two bodies, the monarch embodies the law but is not above the law, the king is a mirror for his people, the king is divine, the will of the prince is or is not absolute. While most Spanish political philosophers, unlike those of England and France, did not subscribe to the principles of absolutism and divine right, and while Spanish kings have never been anointed or crowned and never wear crowns and other regalia, monarchy was the only available, viable model of social and political organization. It was nonetheless seen as problematical, and the theater became the largest forum for public debate of the issues. For all their antiquated shaping, the plays talk about governance, leadership, and the proper exercise of power. The qualities necessary in the leader, the exercise and mediation of authority, the role of advisers, and, above all, the tension between the role and the individual—these are political concerns still with us today, constantly aired in newspapers and on television.

Students are fascinated when I point out that the trail that leads to the Bill

Clinton and Monica Lewinsky scandal starts with Machiavelli. In his treatise *The Prince* he argued that there were qualities more important to effective leadership than personal virtue, and a large section of the American public ultimately agreed with him. Yet there is no doubt that people find it easier to admire and trust their leaders if they are personally irreproachable. Kings in the *comedia* are almost without exception dysfunctional, and, interestingly, sexual excess is one of the commonest ways in which political dysfunction is signaled, largely, of course, because it makes for compelling drama. The message, however, then and now, is clear: when you are at the top, the personal is always political. Lope, in particular, reveals the flawed individual behind the public icon; he also reveals the consequences of royal inadequacy, consequences susceptible in the political framework of the seventeenth century of no solution other than death. Ask a student to see the deeply unsatisfactory reign of an early modern monarch who has no limit of tenure as a modern dictatorship, and she or he will quickly understand both the dilemma itself and the seventeenth century's preoccupation with the ethical problem of tyrannicide. Lope's *El duque de Viseo* is a superb dissection of the weaknesses of a political system in which there is no recourse against a prince who believes that his own will is law.

The concerns I have looked at so far reveal the dangers of expecting too little of the *comedia,* of assuming that it portrays a hermetic world with little to say to us now. The theater's representation of the condition of women, conversely—so clearly in touch in many ways with modern perspectives and sensibilities—reveals the danger of expecting too much. Students must realize that it is historically illiterate to judge the *comedia*'s women by the standards of modern feminism. They can be assessed only against the perceptions and prescriptions of the day. Woman was understood to be by physical constitution unruly and unstable, morally weaker, less intelligent, and more foolish than man. Simultaneously vulnerable and dangerous, she needed to be kept silent, submissive, and enclosed. While the reality of women's existence through the different levels of society was inevitably more complex, this was the model that determined expectations of women, and it is consequently the model against which their representation in the plays must be judged.

Students identify with Casandra's protests in Lope's *El castigo sin venganza* about being treated as an object, a possession, a piece of furniture by her husband the Duke; with Campaspe's fury in Calderón's *Darlo todo y no dar nada* at being gifted by one man to another; and with Julia's defiant defense of her free will when faced by forced enclosure in a convent by her father, in *La devoción de la cruz* (also by Calderón). They applaud the wisdom and nobility of Tirso de Molina's queen, María de Molina, in *La prudencia en la mujer*; the exemplary spirit and guts of Laurencia as she humiliates the village men into action in *Fuenteovejuna*; and Rosaura's triumphant proclamation of female selfhood, signaled by her physical appearance (feminine skirts, masculine weapons), at the end of Calderón's *La vida es sueño*. They recognize Calderón's wife-murder plays as powerful statements about the way men have sacrificed women to the egocentric values of an androcentric world; they see that the *comedia* is full of women who contrive to triumph over the destinies to which men try to relegate them; and they appreciate the ease and imagination with which women are allowed to run rings around men in the comedies. What they find difficult is to reconcile the display of female intelligence, resourcefulness, and self-awareness in the body of these plays with what happens to most, if not all, of the heroines at the end. They get married, for goodness sake, they knuckle down, they give in. So the playwrights cannot really be sympathetic to the cause of women after all. The slack they allow their female characters is ultimately a dramatic and theatrical convenience, and they ensure that the status quo is eventually reestablished, illustrating not only the conservatism of their audiences but their own.

This notion that marriage in the plays is at best a copout, at worst an admonitory lesson learned, is innocent and literal-minded. That generic conventions required the comforting restoration of order and stability, after all the disruption that has gone before, is also an inadequate explanation that merely reinforces the impression of ingrained conformism. The crucial response, it seems to me, is the question, What other sort of life do you think was open to women in the early modern period? Life was lived and plays were written not just within a given horizon of expectations but within the limits of what was socially and culturally available. Getting married and having children was the norm for both women and men. The only respectable sexually active life was lived in marriage, and the woman who did not marry went into service, retired to a convent, or lived on suf ferance on the margins of her own or a relative's family. For young women of good family, service was not an option. For daughters with dowries, convents could be a comfortable solution offering security, female company, reading and contemplation, escape from an unwanted match and the perils of childbirth. For most women, however, being mistress of their own homes, however modest, was infinitely preferable, offering status, influence, and control within a limited spectrum, the pleasure of children, and, if they were lucky, close companionship. In Spain women retained their own property within marriage and, as widows, often ran their deceased husbands' businesses, theater companies and printing firms included.

Marriage is what most heroines in Golden Age plays, like those in nineteenth-century novels, want. They want it on their own terms, however; they want to choose their life partners; they want restitution when they are ill served by lovers. They stand up for what they see as their rights, and by intelligence, imagination, and guile they achieve them. Victories have been won, and they should not be underestimated. The status quo has been restored, but it has not been restored unchanged. It is not easy now, when the range of life choices is so very much wider, to get students, even women students, to see this. In a strange way they dissociate themselves from the women in the plays. Ask them whether they themselves do not envisage family life as being part of their future, and they invariably answer, "Yes, but . . ." in a bemused way, as if they have never made that simple connection before. They concede that the *comedia* was extraordinarily willing to see things from the female perspective and to give women a voice with which to express thoughts and feelings that could easily be those of a modern feminist. And they are impressed to learn that the *comedia,* particularly comedy, was in its own day regarded by churchmen and moralists as dangerous and subversive. Yet until they become much more familiar with the period, they still have residual doubts, related, I think, to their expectations of endings in general as well as of proto-feminism. *Comedia* endings are sly, elusive things, and even marriage endings, which restore the cycle of human life and its social organization, are rarely unproblematic. By and large, the young expect endings to be a denial or an affirmation of closure, and are uneasy with resolutions that contrive to evade both.

The problems of cultural invisibility and anachronism in approaching texts produced outside our own present are acute in the case of the *comedia:* in its vastness and detail, it seems so convincingly rooted in an identifiable past that it is difficult to get the balance right between faction and fiction, and between diachronic and synchronic readings. The solution is not to ignore the diachronic perspective but to embrace it, mapping connections and differences between then and now in order to create a more sophisticated degree of historical understanding. Even at the simplest and most obvious level, demonstrating what links us to and separates us from the past can contribute to the processes of historicization and humanization that bring a text alive. The links can include those that operate below the surface of formally documented history. Since the *comedia* was a commercial venture with wide popular appeal, fictional as well as real-life continuities may productively and entirely legitimately be plucked out of the *comedia's* modern-day equivalents—cinema and television. What are *Thelma and Louise* and *Crouching Tiger, Hidden Dragon* but contemporary versions of the *bandolera* (woman bandit) and female warrior plays? What was Wonder Woman in the 1980s "in her satin tights, fighting for her rights" but an archetypal *mujer varonil* (masculine woman), simultaneously unruly and seductive? As for the *comedia's* depiction of an ideal of aggressive heroism that in real life would have been both unfeasible and extremely undesirable, one has merely to invoke the spaghetti western, the *Mad Max, Lethal Weapon,* and *Die Hard* films to illustrate the poetic truth of the way in which fiction allows male spectators a space in which to fantasize about themselves where the constraints of real life do not operate. Such analogies are not facile stratagems but cultural evidence, like the genres of comedy and tragedy themselves, of the enduring patterns traced by the human imagination and human psychology, and tapped into by drama then as now. They manifest themselves in contingent ways that need exploration and explanation; the conventions in which they are clothed change, but the deeper structures of representation remain the same.

Between Ideals and Pragmatism: Honor in Early Modern Spain

Renato Barahona

> Mi honor conservo en pajas
> Como fruta sabrosa,
> Vidrio guardado en ellas
> Para que no se rompa.
> —Tisbea, *El burlador de Sevilla,* act 1

> I preserve my honor in straws
> Like delicious fruit,
> A glass protected by them
> So that it will not break.

The compelling image of honor as glass is a recurrent one in Golden Age drama. It is an exaggerated conceit to be sure, but one that vividly conveys the purported fragility of honor and the difficulty, indeed the impossibility, of putting it back together once it has been broken. Presented as such, honor—perhaps especially that of females—is a priceless possession and quality, one that when damaged is beyond repair (see Honig; D. Larson; Stroud, *Fatal Union*; Mandrell; Yarbro-Bejarano; Dopico Black, *Perfect Wives*). At the other end of the spectrum, however, honor is a tangible commodity that can be quantified, repaired, and partially restored. Honor and related issues, such as shame, in Spanish and Mediterranean societies have been generally examined with an eye toward the first position—honor as a kind of zero-sum game, and in effect something that is nearly always lost (see Peristiany; Gilmore; Caro Baroja, "Honor y verguenza"; Maravall, "Función del honor"; Bennassar, "Honor"). Historical studies, in contrast, present a far more benign and accommodating view of the way in which individuals faced with predicaments of honor dealt with questions of honor. The totality of the evidence reveals a broad range of ideas and attitudes toward the concept and the way it was understood by contemporaries. In other words, the concept—or concepts—of honor reflected in the historical record appear far more flexible and less delicate than has been commonly believed (see Bazán Díaz; Bennassar, *Valladolid*; A. Dyer; A. Castro). In the lives of historical protagonists—socially, economically, and legally—honor takes on vastly different meanings than in the highly idealized works of literature and political and religious commentaries (see Chauchadis). The following observations are based on extensive historical research centered in the Spanish Basque country during the early modern period (see Barahona).

It has become almost commonplace to assert that from antiquity through the

early modern period, male honor for the most part was based on social considerations while female honor revolved primarily around sexual virtue. This gendered view of honor finds echo in the *Diccionario de autoridades* (1734, 172–73),
which defines *honra* as, among other things, "virginity in women" ("*la integridad
virginal en las mugeres*") and *honor* as "honesty and modesty in women" ("*la
honestidad y recato en las mugeres*"). Of course, the terms are not similarly applied to men. But what about the women who were deceived, deflowered, and
abandoned by their seducers? Such women clearly experienced a loss of honor,
not only because their virginity had been taken but also because—and perhaps
more important—they now found their marriage prospects impaired and their
social standing diminished. However, in the cases I have studied, the women's
modest rank and absence of strong family supports made difficult a reparation of
lost honor that entailed physical violence. Unlike dishonored women in the
comedia who sought revenge against their victimizers (see Honig; McKendrick,
Woman and Society 261–75; Welles 210–11 n18), women in early modern Vizcaya (Basque provinces) who lost honor would appear to be best redeemed by
way of practical, nonviolent courses. To understand this, consider women's main
choices following their seduction: first, they could do nothing and consequently
bear their disgrace grudgingly; second, they could seek out-of-court monetary
settlements, such as those found in other parts of the Peninsula, from their seducers (see Barahona, ch. 1, n71); third, they could stand their ground and take
their case to court, obtaining concrete remedies to their damaged reputations.
In effect, the legal system became a surrogate family and community support
for victims of misconduct. The course chosen by female litigants and their families raises the important question of whether women effectively regained their
lost honor. It would appear that although honor was not completely recovered—how could it be, after seduction, loss of virginity, abandonment, and disgrace?—a monetary award obtained through the courts would enable a woman
to marry and thereby regain a measure of respectability and honor (see Bazán
Díaz 603–20; A. Dyer 251; Córdoba de la Llave 47; Narbona Vizcaíno 126–27).
Successful litigation, therefore, probably redressed lost reputation to a considerable extent, allowing women to resume their places in society on reasonably
good terms.

It is worth emphasizing that the legal process for the reparation of female
honor was, from all appearances, a highly individual one, affecting primarily, perhaps even exclusively, the woman in question. Little, if anything, is ever said, either in the complaints or in the judgments, about sullied honor that extended to
family or that shamed others; female dishonor does not appear to have affected
lineage and household (A. Dyer 98–99, 101). Consistent with this, the monetary
remedy sought in litigation was for the woman's marriage, redress, and use. If
there was damage to women's reputations, then, the harm generally did not extend, in any immediate or ostensible way, to their parents or families. In fact,
claims of dishonor to parents and family as a result of sexual misconduct by sons

or daughters are exceedingly rare, even when family members themselves (or other parents) initiate the complaints on the women's behalf.

Given the purported centrality of honor in ancien régime Spain, one would expect to find, in this study's lawsuits, a substantial spillover to kin and house in matters of honor, and yet, except for isolated instances, this is not the case. Is it possible that Spain's alleged obsession with parental and family honor has been grossly overstated by the reliance on literary texts and those of elite commentators? Or could it be that Basque families, unlike Castilian ones and those of other Iberian and Mediterranean peoples, were not concerned about having their honor adversely affected by their daughters' soiled reputations? This seems unlikely. Or were Basque parents perhaps more practical and realistic when it came to women's honor? Another possibility, of course, is that questions of female honor were primarily an issue of social class, and that since many—indeed most—of the plaintiffs came from society's lower orders, concerns of sexual honor were not as significant as they might have been to those of the upper echelons. In other words, when a poor family's daughter was deflowered and abandoned, what was most important to the victim and family was seeking a material solution, not invoking some less tangible and difficult-to-satisfy ideological affront to house and lineage. If defendants failed to make good on their promise of marriage, as some victims' accusations demanded they do, seducers would be held financially accountable to the women through the legal process.

After a woman was courted, seduced, and abandoned, how did she, her family, and her advocates litigate her honor and obtain reparation for damages? First, it was essential for plaintiffs to establish the victims' virtue and reputation from the outset. Honest and virtuous (*honesta y recogida*) was the most commonly used formula to characterize the moral condition of women before their seduction. Distressed and angry parents, in particular, offered persuasive—and, of course, partisan and charged—testimonials of their daughters' admirable qualities. There were excellent reasons, from a legal standpoint, for stressing the plaintiffs' prior honesty and other qualities: generous assertions of virtue stood in stark contrast to how profoundly these good women had been victimized. In sum, underscoring female honesty magnified male culpability.

Second, and probably even more important, was for victims to establish their respectable social condition. The accusations reveal three fundamental paths to this objective: assertions of good family background and wealth, claims of dowry amounts commanded by victims' families, and allegations of the monetary damage to plaintiffs and kin. These considerations were at the heart of litigation for defloration and lost honor; from the outset, victims attempted to prove their creditable status to recover honor and respectability through reparations equivalent in some fashion to their rank and condition. If claims of women's moral reputation highlighted masculine sexual misconduct, assertions of social standing underlined the specific harm victims had suffered—damage that defendants would be obligated to repair through the legal process. And if victims and their families pressed their claims vigorously in the courts, defendants, for their part, subjected plaintiffs to a second victimization through relentless double-barrel attacks against the women's good name and social standing.

Litigation was usually a rough-and-tumble legal process, in which defendants hammered away at plaintiffs, tainting their sexual reputations and lowering their socioeconomic status. Ultimately, both were profoundly interrelated: a disreputable woman commanded less respect and money and was not as marriageable as an honorable one. While many defendants' assertions seem mean-spirited, rarely were they gratuitous insults; each allegation, even if exaggerated, was entered into the record to rebut plaintiffs' claims. Victims' ages, sexual histories, occupations, and socioeconomic conditions were all fair game for the defense.

Women's second victimization was a natural continuation of the first, during which they had been dishonored in the public arena. Now, before the court of law, defendants attacked the plaintiffs' and families' reputations to gain every ounce of legal advantage, to minimize offenders' liabilities and deny accusers their due. Already defeated in the court of public opinion, plaintiffs were assailed by defendants whose generally superior socioeconomic status and age had facilitated the seductions and the victims' ensuing social disgrace. Despite the uphill battles they faced before the courts, plaintiffs had nowhere else to turn.

Consider, too, the significant obstacles plaintiffs confronted. Numerous victims lived in precarious situations: marginally employed in menial work and odd jobs (domestic service in particular), with limited income, often saddled with children, without husbands or family support, and at times downright poor. Every circumstance appears to have given defendants the upper hand in litigation: monetary resources, status and rank, literacy and knowledge of the law, and age and experience. That plaintiffs and victims were able to succeed against such odds as often as they did is as much eloquent testimony to their tenacity and skills as litigants, as it is to the helpful role played by local authorities and royal courts.

The justice system, for example, showed a remarkable flexibility in allowing some accusations to be brought forth after the time specified by the statute of limitations. Nor was the burden of proving defloration, and its concomitant loss of honor, particularly difficult for plaintiffs and victims. In fact, the bar appears to have been set quite low, with the courts in general agreement with plaintiffs' claims that "indications and conjectures" were sufficient to prove that a woman had lost her virginity (Barahona, ch. 5, n85). In the light of the difficulties in establishing the culpability of certain defendants, the courts appear to have sided consistently with the plaintiffs and given them the benefit of the doubt on key matters of proof.

As we might expect, plaintiffs and defendants had divergent objectives in litigation: accusers primarily sought to redress lost honor and reputations through marriage or monetary compensation for damages; offenders struggled to prove their innocence or, if they should be found guilty, to keep the awards for the victims as low as possible. How well the parties succeeded in their aims is borne out by a detailed examination of the verdicts. The evidence clearly shows that while both sides benefited from litigation to some extent and in different ways, the plaintiffs, on balance, fared considerably better. Plaintiffs were able to hold offenders responsible for damages nearly ninety-three percent of the time (Barahona, ch. 5, n86). The lawsuits indicate that there were tangible rewards for plaintiffs determined to obtain the compensation they considered was owed them for dishonor and damages.

A case in point: in 1613, Catalina Ruiz de Muncharaz, a nineteen-year-old orphan, who was apparently in the care of an aunt, brought charges against Miguel de Arteaga, a lawyer. Catalina recounted how, four years earlier, Miguel had violently taken her virginity; after she had complained about it, the incident had become public throughout the region, from which, according to her words, she was now with "irreparable harm" (*"daño irreparable"*) (Barahona, ch. 5, n106). Were her words an exaggerated rhetorical device to elicit sympathy from the authorities? Unquestionably. But were they accurate? To a considerable extent, yes. Her predicament was at once dire and completely understandable: having been deprived of her sexual honor, she could do little immediately to amend the wrong. Barring physical revenge or direct action against her assailant, avenues unlikely to be pursued by women of her condition, her disgrace appeared beyond reparation. But Catalina had a fundamental legal course at her disposal: by pressing criminal charges against her victimizer, she could use the justice system to reacquire part of her respectability through a monetary award from the court; the money would enable her to marry, to remedy her situation in some other fashion, or to provide for her children.

Like other plaintiff-victims of her modest condition, Catalina went on to litigate successfully against her assailant, eventually obtaining a hard-earned compensatory award: an appellate court in Valladolid—where lawsuits from Vizcaya went for review—awarded her 100,000 *maravedís* (266.66 ducats) in 1616. It was not an enormous sum, nor would it return Catalina her lost honor, but if she eventually collected it, the award would doubtless alleviate some of the "irreparable harm" she had eloquently bemoaned three years earlier. The lessons of this case are instructive: though honor could be easily and swiftly forfeited and though its litigation was prolonged and arduous, women such as Catalina could at least regain part of their reputation by acquiring honorable conditions for themselves and their families through monetary reparations.

The totality of the evidence strongly indicates that litigation was the most viable and effective course for women to hold wrongdoers accountable. Women of humble social condition proved determined and resourceful in their quest to overcome the consequences of misconduct. That they eventually prevailed in a patriarchal society speaks volumes about the significance of the early modern Spanish courts for these women, but equally so about the unquestionable agency and initiative of these resolute women.

Even though much has been written about questions of honor in ancien régime Spain, little has been known of the specific ways in which lost honor was assessed and repaired. Was it an invaluable, irreplaceable quality—indeed, a

fragile glass—or was it a commodity that could be recovered, albeit perhaps partially, pragmatically and without violence? The evidence that emerges from early
modern lawsuits involving sexual misconduct against women strongly indicates
that the loss of female honor and reputation could be—and often was—settled
in orderly, legal processes. While this approach to the reparation of female honor
may have had regional characteristics based on Basque tradition and culture, I
am inclined to believe that class considerations were much more influential in
the course chosen by victims. It is safe to conclude that they and their families
opted for a practical legal remedy because, as suggested earlier, their modest socioeconomic status prevented other paths, including physical vengeance, for obtaining satisfaction to their loss of honor. If victims could not completely repair
the broken glass, they could mend it patiently, restoring it as carefully as possible
to a semblance of its original condition.

NOTE

Original parts of this essay appear in my *Sex Crimes, Honour and the Law in Early
Modern Spain: Vizcaya, 1528–1735* (U of Toronto P, 2003). Reprinted with the permission of the University of Toronto Press. Most of the passages in question appear in
chapter 5.

A Woman Hunted, a City Besieged:
Spanish Emblems and Italian Art in *Fuenteovejuna*

Frederick A. de Armas

First-time readers of Spanish drama of the Golden Age assume that, like most modern theater, spectacle and the visual have an important role to play. They fail to recognize that the plays of the late sixteenth and early seventeenth centuries were performed with little scenery. In general, the visual was limited to the gestures and movements of the actors on stage, their costumes, a small space covered by a curtain to reveal violent acts or spectacular displays, rudimentary machines that brought down or elevated characters from the stage (used mostly in hagiographic plays), and the division of the stage into three levels (two balconies above, a main stage, and a trapdoor for falls or demonic apparitions) (Varey, *Cosmovisión* 23–36). With the rise of Philip IV to the throne in 1621, a new form emerged, the court spectacle play, but earlier, spectators had to imagine most of the setting. As spectacle became increasingly prevalent, playwrights insisted that scenery was the mere body of the play, while their poetry provided the soul.

And yet Spain was very much a visual culture during the sixteenth and seventeenth centuries, and playwrights were clearly aware that they must satisfy both the sense of hearing and the sense of sight. Thus in many of my courses on Golden Age theater I emphasize the hidden visual nature of many of the images and actions in these dramas. I begin by addressing the development and importance of the relation between the visual and the verbal, to set the stage for studying the *comedia* as a poetic yet visual genre. The sisterhood and competition between painting and poetry has an ancient heritage, one that writers of the Golden Age often evoked and emulated. When Cervantes writes, in chapter 71 of part 2 of *Don Quixote*, that "el pintor o escritor, que todo es uno" (*El ingenioso hidalgo* 2: 574; "the painter and the writer are one and the same" [my trans.]), he is voicing a notion prevalent in classical literature and the Italian Renaissance and continuously echoed during the Spanish Golden Age. Lodovico Dolce, in his *Dialogue on Painting* (1557), asserts that "good poets are painters themselves" and that "the painters often draw on the poets for their inventions, and the poets on the painters" (Roskill 131, 169). In Spain, López Pinciano and Vicente Carducho reiterate these views. Both arts, after all, were said to be based on the emulation of nature and on the imitation of authoritative works (be they verbal or visual). In Lía Schwartz's words: "Poetry and painting share in many features, one reads in several seventeenth-century treatises. They are both based upon the aesthetics of imitation; they both use fiction to create artistic texts; both are the products of imagination and craftsmanship" (137). Each of the arts would thus render homage to the other (while competing for supremacy). Raphael, for example, painted a *Parnassus* exalting the image of blind Homer; both Homer and Vergil competed with the visual arts by including ekphrases (descriptions of works of art) in their epics, such as the famous murals of the Trojan War in Carthage. An overview of the sisterhood and rivalry between the arts is necessary, then, before instructors enter on a discussion of the visual nature of theater in the Spanish Golden Age.

But even this context is not enough. I also tell my students that the notion of writing for the eyes was inspired by three other currents: the Neoplatonist view of hieroglyphics, emblematic literature, and the art of memory (see de Armas, *Writing for the Eyes*). To explain the importance of these three currents, I bring to class copies of Horapollo's *Hieroglyphica*, Sebastián de Covarrubias Orozco's *Emblemas morales* (*Moral Emblems*), and Giovanni Battista Della Porta's *Ars Reminscendi* (*The Art of Memory*). Although the *Hieroglyphica*, published in 1505, was filled with mistakes concerning Egyptian lore, it promoted the visual symbol. Taken up by the Neoplatonists, these images were regarded as a way to contemplate the Platonic ideas in visual form. Images, then, were ways to represent ineffable ideas or complex concepts. Thus, when Andrea Alciato prepared a collection of epigrams in 1531, his editor decided that each one of the poems should be illustrated, to clarify and render them memorable. Thus was born the tradition of the emblem books—collections that combine the visual and the verbal to create the ideal didactic tool for the humanist. Because the emblems have a tripartite structure, composed of the lemma (*inscriptio*), image (*pictura*), and poetic explication (*subscriptio*), the visual, at the center of the emblem, teaches through the grasp of objects that form an emblematic code. The ensuing explication employs verbal discourse on some of the complexities revealed by the image. The brief lemma and the image also stimulate the memory, while the image and the explication appeal to the understanding. In class, students begin to comprehend the sibling rivalry between the visual and the verbal by looking at the emblems. In fact, examining emblems helps them discover the visual elements that are at play in the *comedia.*

Visual writing was also used as a mnemonic tool. To demonstrate how pictures aided memorization, I show the class a copy of Della Porta's treatise (1556), with his many strange, interesting ways to develop memory. Other Renaissance and Golden Age treatises would be equally effective, because most of them explain how to enhance memory through visualization. Indeed, Giovanni Della Porta contends that one of the best ways to memorize is to use images by famous artists: "pictures by Michelangelo, Raphael, and Titian stay in the memory" (Yates 206). Thus the Spanish dramatists would write for the eyes, since pictorial writing allowed them to compete with the artist and create a "capacious" language (Krieger 10), permitted them to develop difficult concepts, and helped stimulate the memory and imagination of the reader or viewer; and, they did so, finally, because the eyes were the highest of the senses according to the Neoplatonists.

Della Porta adds that amazing or erotic images are particularly easy to remember. If we conjoin this statement with his foregrounding of famous paintings as mnemonic images, we realize why much of the visual writing in the secular *comedia* derives either from the strange images in the emblem books or from Italian Renaissance art, which stressed the erotic in its mythological representations. When I turn to texts of the Golden Age, then, I bring to class Spanish emblem books (such as Covarrubias's *Emblemas morales* or the 1999 emblem anthology of Bernat Vistarini and Cull) and slides, generally of Italian Renaissance paintings. *PowerPoint* images may be easier for faculty members with better technical skills than mine. I also try to have a Web page where sudents can view the paintings before and after class.

I use Italian Renaissance art rather than Spanish Golden Age paintings for several reasons. First, the choice allows students to realize that most of Italy was in Spanish hands during the Golden Age, with a viceroy governing Naples (most of southern Italy) and Sicily. Philip II's establishment of "Spanish hegemony in Rome" deeply influenced the cardinals and the papacy (Dandelet 53). In the north, Milan had a Spanish governor, while Mantua was under the rule of the Gonzagas, who favored Spain. Even the Medicis in Florence tilted toward Spain. The rest of northern Italy was a space of contestation, as France and Spain fought to gain control. Thus what was not Spanish was always being talked about in Spain.

Second, the use of Italian art reveals an important element of Spanish culture at the time. Although most art created in Spain was religious, Italian art imported to Spain was secular. Jonathan Brown has shown that mythological subjects were "nearly absent" from Spanish art of the period, since the "home market was confined mainly to an ecclesiastical clientele" (*Golden Age* 4). The secular and even "immoral" character of classical mythology, together with the propensity of the ancients and their imitators to sculpt or paint these figures as nudes, caused the ecclesiastical clients to shun this art. Indeed, as Rosa López Torrijos notes, those characteristics made the works subject to censorship, following the dictates of the Council of Trent (*Mitología* 9). It has been argued that many Italian Renaissance paintings use the "cloak of mythology" to revel in sensuality and sexuality (Talvacchia 46). Kings and nobles of the Spanish court were well aware of the beauty, eroticism, and value of Italian Renaissance paintings and exhibited them in palaces and in private collections. It is fair to say that the Spanish court had the best collection of Titian's paintings in all of Europe. The concern with exhibiting wealth through collections of Italian art is clearly documented in the *comedia*. For example, in Lope's *La prueba de los amigos* (*The Proof of Friendship*), Feliciano, to display his riches, shows his art collection to Ricardo and Fulgencio. Here they discover a Lucretia drawn by Raphael and an Adonis that is most likely Titian's *Venus and Adonis* (1553–54), now in the Prado.[1] To demonstrate his magnanimity, he gives the two works to his supposed friends. Of course, once he spends all his money in the pursuit of a courtesan, none of these "friends" will help him. The paintings suggest both the urge to exhibit Italian art and the erotic images of women that were forbidden in Spanish theater.

References to Italian painting, in other words, allowed the dramatists to impress on their audience's imaginations taboo images of sensuality. Whether exhibiting on stage Titian's portrait *Rossa Sultana,* of the Russian redhead who came to control the sultan's heart, the harem, and the politics of Constantinople in *La santa liga (The Holy League)*(de Armas, "Allure"), or pointing to nymphs pursued by satyrs in *El castigo sin venganza,* Lope de Vega often turned to Italian art. In fact, he was aware that the art served as counterpart to Christian piety. In *Virtud, pobreza y mujer (Virtue, Poverty, Woman)*, the chaste but poor Isabel, who is deceived by don Carlos with a promise of marriage, is surrounded by pious images and not (as the text explicitly states) by the paintings of Titian or Jacopo dal Ponte (called Bassano), artists of the Venetian school, whose sensuous colors are more suited to pagan desires.

To address the question of how members of the audience would be able to visualize the works of Italian artists—which sometimes were openly exhibited in the plays, sometimes carefully hidden in allusive passages—I explain the migration of images throughout Europe. Italian artworks, particularly those by the painters canonized by Giorgio Vasari, were the most prized of all. Thus it was common for lesser-known painters to go to Italy or to Spanish palaces and copy these works. In many cases, the difference between the original and the copy was glossed over. More important, a huge traffic in images or engravings began when Marcantonio Raimondi was given permission by Raphael to make prints of some of his major works. These illustrations traveled throughout Europe and were in the possession not only of the nobility but also of the middle classes. As a result, a Golden Age audience would be well aware of the image being evoked. For example, in Lope de Vega's *La viuda valenciana (The Valencian Widow)*, one of the suitors of Leonarda enters her home in the guise of a "mercader con estampas" (165; "merchant with prints" [my trans.]). He shows the lady, among the prints, Titian's *Venus and Adonis* and works by Raphael and Federico Zuccaro. The previous suitor had come disguised as a book merchant with works by the likes of Cervantes and Gálvez de Montalvo. Clearly, Italian Renaissance art was as prized by lovers as Spanish amatory prose. The erotic images referred to in the theater would have been known, through prints or copies, by members of the audience who would use their imagination to place them on the stage and view Leonarda as a Venus who allows Adonis (Valerio) to depart her company without regret. Playing on the ominous denouement suggested by the painting, Valerio concludes, "Pues muero desesperado / y él murió favorecido" (167; "But I die in despair, while he [Adonis] died while being favored [by Venus] [my trans.]).

Italian painting can be equally useful in teaching works that do not explicitly turn to art, as I will demonstrate through discussion of the peasant honor play *Fuenteovejuna,* which combines history, questions of honor, and amorous concerns. Its use of history may create difficulties for students with little interest in the past. How, then, does one present historical events in a way that will both capture students' attention and make history into something worth studying? Bringing in a combination of Spanish emblem books and Italian art can help engage today's visually oriented students and bring to the fore many of the important conflicts and concepts of the work.

From Javier Herrero to William R. Blue, a number of critics have underlined the importance of *Fuenteovejuna* as a vision of past glory. Blue asserts, "Lope, rather than accurately representing the weak, indolent king who ruled Spain, draws from nostalgic popular beliefs and invents strong, practical monarchs. It is the myth of the Reyes Católicos, the myth of the utopian state" ("Politics" 313). The play thus establishes a contrast between the present ruler, Philip III, "a bland, indolent king dependent upon and accompanied by his 'favorite'" ("Politics" 299) and the Catholic monarchs. To help students understand what Lope is subtly creating in his play, I turn to Covarrubias's emblem 3.97 of *Emblemas morales*. The picture recalls actions on stage: a judge, seated on a throne, listens to two suppliants, while in the background we see instruments of torture and a scaffold. The image is followed by a poetic explanation that shows little compassion for the rebellious inhabitants of Fuenteovejuna. As Duncan Moir has shown, Covarrubias's message "may well have shocked the dramatist" whose "sympathies are clearly on the side of the villagers" (541). The brief, severely moralistic, authoritarian emblem serves as contrast to the nuanced play, which presents the king and queen as ultimate arbiters, as both just and magnanimous. The emblem, then, can trigger discussion of how to turn a concept into a carefully crafted play.

To develop the myth of the ideal monarchs, Lope must include an antagonist within the play, a figure with many flaws who opposes the Reyes Católicos. Fuenteovejuna's Comendador, who persuades the Maestre to attack Ciudad Real and wrest it from the control of Ferdinand and Isabella, is an ideal antagonist. When the Maestre, aided by the Comendador, takes the city, the stage is set for the eventual reversal and triumph of the Catholic kings. But what interests us here is how the victory at Ciudad Real relates to the tradition of triumph that often accompanies the capture of a city. During the Renaissance, European cultures became obsessed with the recuperation of the past, and particularly of the classical civilizations of Greece and Rome. Among the myriad topics for archaeological study and emulation was the Roman triumph—"the procession of a Roman general who had won a major victory to the temple of Jupiter on the Capitol" (Hornblower and Spawforth 747). As the republic gave way to the empire, the celebrations were reserved for the emperor and his family, while the victorious general was considered secondary. Renaissance and baroque art reveled in the depiction of ancient victories, from Andrea Mantegna's *Triumphs of Caesar*, to Giovanni Battista Tiepolo's *Triumph of Aurelius*. And generals, kings, and emperors during the Italian Renaissance and the Spanish Golden Age sought to be represented as ancient heroes who were worthy of triumphs. Elaborate arches and complex allegorical entries served, in European politics, to glorify the authority of rulers.

To bring out the importance of this motif, I show woodcuts from Petrarch's *Triumphs* as well as slides of the many Italian paintings on the same theme. The works contrast with the events in the play, which is nothing more than a rustic mock triumph that debases the Comendador (and, in the process, further exalts the Catholic kings). As he approaches the town, Flores declares, "recebidle alegremente, / que al triunfo, las voluntades / son los mejores laureles" (act 1, lines 526–28) ("Receive them joyfully, for no victor's laurel is so welcome to the returning hero as the good will of those he left at home"; *Five Plays* 68). While Roman soldiers exhibit the booty taken from the conquered, the villagers of Fuenteovejuna offer the Comendador their riches, to celebrate his triumph. The notion of a world turned upside down is thus foregrounded as the four-horse chariots of the Roman victor are transformed into villagers' carts carrying all manner of rustic treasures: geese, hogs, skins of wine, cheeses, and so on (1.549–78 [*Five Plays* 68–69]). The peasants admit that they are lacking "armas ni caballos, no jaeces bordados de oro puro" (1.566–67) ("arms or horses or trappings adorned with gold" [*Five Plays* 69]). These displays would be typical as seen, for example, in the nine paintings by Mantegna known as *The Triumphs of Caesar* (c. 1484–1505), in Hampton Court, Surrey. The golden jars in the painting also contrast with the earthenware crocks offered by the villagers. But the Comendador does not miss these elements from the Roman celebration. He asks, instead, that two of the peasant women, Laurencia and Pascuala, be brought to him. Such a request further ties the moment to a Roman triumph while distancing itself from it. Renaissance representations of these events, from Mantegna to Tiepolo, often featured women prisoners. In Tiepolo's *Triumph of Aurelius* (1760–61, Palazzo Dolfin, Venice), for instance, Queen Zenobia is chained to the back of Emperor Aurelius's triumphal chariot. But in *Fuenteovejuna* the Comendador is asking women from his village to assume the role of the conquered. Once again, he has turned the Roman tradition upside down. As the peasant women are ushered towards the Comendador's house, Laurencia complains, "¿No basta a vuesso señor / tanta carne presentada?" (1.623–24) ("Has not your master received enough flesh for one day?" [*Five Plays* 70]). She is referring here to all the animals given to the Comendador for his victory—and to her own flesh. In ancient triumphs, numerous animals were brought for sacrifice. In the play, the two women figure as such creatures to be sacrificed at the altar of the Comendador's lust. He is indeed a mock Jupiter who revels in the pursuit of women. Of course, Laurencia's very name precludes such a conclusion. As the laurel tree, she is a Daphne who repulses, through metamorphosis, the pursuit of another lustful pagan god, Apollo. While Flores seeks to grant the laurel of triumph to the Comendador, it is Laurencia who personifies the triumph. The Comendador seeks to appropriate only that which does not belong to him: the riches of the town and the honor of its peasant women.

The play, in equating the siege of a city with the pursuit of a woman, shows that both endeavors are flawed. The Comendador seeks to gain a city that belongs to the Catholic kings, and he desires a woman who wishes to marry another. This second pursuit is associated with the motif of the hunt of love (see E. R. Rogers;

Gerli; Chaffee-Sorace). It is clear that the Comendador views himself as the hunter who wants to kill (dishonor) his prey. When the villagers ask him about the greyhound they sent him, he expresses interest in a hare (Laurencia): "que le hiziérades pariente / a una liebre que por pies / por momento se me va" (lines 958–60) ("I am more interested in a certain young rabbit which I have pursued many times in vain. That would be an even more welcome gift" [*Five Plays* 77]). The greyhound that pursues a hare—a creature of Venus and symbol of female genitalia (Barbera)—is a common image, and students can be encouraged to look for it in Renaissance art, emblem books, and medieval bestiaries. The Comendador again employs animal imagery in his erotic hunt when he encounters Laurencia in the woods and states: "No es malo venir siguiendo / un corzillo temeroso / y topar tan bella gama" (lines 779–81) ("A happy stroke of fortune! I was hunting a deer, but did not think to find such dear game as this!" [*Five Plays* 72]). To bring out the many implications of the hunt of love, I show a slide of Botticelli's first canvas (1483, Prado) on the story of Nastagio degli Onesti, as told in Boccaccio's *Decameron*. In this haunting painting, a woman is indeed hunted; we see a dog biting her and bringing her down while a knight on a white horse holds up his sword, ready to strike. Botticelli's painting and the story told by Boccaccio trigger discussions of woman's supposed "cruelty" to men (and vice versa), of women pursued, and of the relation between erotic desire and violence. Indeed, *Fuenteovejuna* clearly links war and erotic desire, the forbidden siege of a city and the forbidden pursuit of a woman. In both cases, the Comendador will fail.

Returning to the mock triumph staged after the conquest of Ciudad Real, we observe many other parallels with Roman and Renaissance triumphs, which often included paintings, music, and song. The Comendador's rustic victory also partakes of these elements, as musicians sing his praises and laud the victory at Ciudad Real. However, once again, the Comendador's triumph is ridiculed when he is offered a flock of geese—as Teresa Kirschner has pointed out, geese were often symbols of the bad poet—who sing of his martial valor (1.557–59; *Five Plays* 69). But perhaps the high point is Flores's lengthy narrative of the battle at Ciudad Real, to which he was an eyewitness. Flores's speech takes on the function of the paintings of battle scenes in the Roman triumphs. As if to underscore the painterly aspects of his words, he constantly turns to colors. Two-thirds of his narrative is spent in describing the colorful dress of the Maestre and the Comendador, along with the adornments on their horses. The visual impact of the images is dazzling: green surcoat, silver bracelets, white ribbons, white plumes, red and white garter, red cross versus blue crescent. Just a few lines are devoted to the beheading and flogging of the captured. The horrors of war are painted over with beautiful colors. This technique takes to an extreme Paolo Ucello's glorifying vision of war in his three-part *Battle of San Romano* (1450s), now separately located in Florence (Uffizi), London (National Gallery), and Paris (Louvre). The three paintings, which I show in slides, narrate "an episode from the unpopular and eventually unsuccessful Florentine war with Lucca" (Hale 155). Here, battle becomes pageant—or even processional entry. The savagery of war is further minimized through the "coloristic background" of brightly painted flowers and fruit trees (Hartt 254), reflected in the colors of Flores's narrative, even down to certain details. The color orange is evoked twice, becoming an image of the Comendador's helmet, its white plumes compared with orange blossoms (1.493–96; *Five Plays* 67). In Ucello's painting in the National Gallery, London: "Any notion of serious killing is downplayed by background groves of oranges and roses that produce the effect of a garden more than a battlefield" (Maiorino 128). In painting over the horrors of war, Flores, whose very name recalls the actual and rhetorical flowers of his narrative, fashions an ambience of springtime renewal surrounding the Maestre and the Comendador. But an audience alert to his negative role in the play is invited to look through his attempts to replace the violence of Mars with the beauties of Venus. In exposing Flores's ability to transform and mythologize a historical event, the play opens itself up to a scrutiny of its own mythologizing acts. The myth of the Catholic kings becomes just that, another myth that paints history anew and colors the way we perceive it.

NOTE

[1] Most of the artworks discussed in this essay are readily available in art books and on Web sites, such as the *Web Gallery of Art* (www.wga.hu).

Early Modern Geographies: Teaching Space in Tirso de Molina's Urban Plays

Enrique García Santo-Tomás

A Sense of Space, a Space of the Senses

In the past three decades the discipline of geography as a "positive" science has been questioned in favor of a humanistic approach in which the landscape has become a privileged area of study. Modern human geography has been influenced by the geographical imagination of the past, in which the idea of space becomes anchored in the experience of human life. Since the early 1970s, a materialist geography has emerged, inspired by Henri Lefebvre, who asserted that the dominance of capitalism assumed the creation of spatial practice, a production and reproduction of an unequal landscape with homogeneous tendencies, fragmentations, and hierarchies. Especially since the 1980s, these sociological approaches have been broadened, entering into the realm of the postmodern. Beginning with a recent reelaboration of what has been coined the "geographic imagination," geographers such as David Harvey, Edward Soja, Derek Gregory, and Yi-Fu Tuan have established a powerful connection between the concept of urban space and the notions of capital, perception, and sensibility. These are the three fundamental concepts that organize my introduction to urban theater. Moreover, focusing on these four thinkers in particular has been extremely useful as I work with graduate students in my seminars on the *comedia urbana*. Exploring the writings of Soja and Gregory has enabled me to introduce an overview of other pivotal notions such as space, perspective, and human geography, whereas Harvey and Tuan have been of great interest as the seminars examine questions of urban capital (Harvey) and the sense of place and escapism (Tuan). Their discussions have helped students appreciate how the experience of space is connected to ideas of religion, economy, and sexuality.

Early modern Spanish literature and visual arts offer many views of Spain's cities from varying social and physical perspectives. The vision of Toledo in Renaissance poetry; the depiction of the River Tagus by Garcilaso; the Manzanares by Góngora, Lope, and Quevedo; the Barcelona of *Don Quixote*; and the Sevillian portrayal of the exemplary novel *Rinconete y Cortadillo* all serve as loci for a coherent study of this urban stage of characters. Many of these spatial discourses have a long literary tradition, like the River Manzanares, which serves as a basis for an array of fictions, from the burlesque to the idyllic, from parody to exaggeration. From different perspectives—the physical, the symbolic, the allegorical—the notion of space is a difficult one to grasp, communicate, and enjoy in the classroom. The more we delve into this topic, the more kaleidoscopic it becomes.

Teaching cloak-and-dagger plays (*comedias de capa y espada*) frequently entails traveling to urban spaces (street corners, churches, gardens) that no longer exist. Among the Spanish cities, Madrid is often the favorite setting because of its position as the new bureaucratic and cultural center. Yet traditional research on early modern Spain has usually considered space as a category in which things *happen*, and the notion of the theatrical city has simply perpetuated this idea. Baroque Madrid has been perceived as a fixed site, a rhetorical artifact much like the monumental city we are introduced to in tourist guides or visual portraits—the mute, reliable witness of history, the cultural cradle of the imperial Golden Age. Recent studies on other European cities of the period (mainly Paris and London, but also Naples, Venice, and even Spanish Rome), however, have illuminated a more sophisticated view of the symbiosis between the landscape and the aesthetic, whereby space becomes not only an active category but also an entity *in process.* The idea of space as being created (and not as the final product) presents, in the case of Madrid during the early seventeenth century, three prominent features: renovation, centralization, and accumulation. These processes are not only physical; they are related to the symbolic organization of Madrid's demography, as indicated by the location of palaces, government offices, theaters, art schools, convents, brothels, and gaming houses, which constitute the fabric of what we conceive, in modern terms, as the cityscape.

The "urbanization of consciousness" (a term coined by Harvey) not only assumes the logical accumulative processes of capital and its consequences but also suggests a political understanding that values this process as a social, cultural, and aesthetic phenomenon. The dynamic of the accumulation of wealth creates conflict, confusion, and struggle, which are treated, in some way or another, by the great artists of this generation. Consider, for instance, Tirso de Molina's satires on the Duke of Lerma's pompous palace, Calderón's concerns about the proliferation of gaming houses, and Salas Barbadillo's critique of greedy women as some of the literary topoi of the new urban territories. The Spanish historian Alfredo Alvar Ezquerra has insisted on the "malleable" character of this young city, one that is organized "to the liking of the king" under the orchestration of its architect Juan Bautista de Toledo (who, along with his disciple Juan de Herrera, was Philip II's main architect from 1563 to 1584) (191). Suddenly, cartography, economy, and anthropology become suitable subjects to frame the teaching of early modern Spanish theater.

Tirso de Molina's dramatic production is no doubt influenced by the social conditions of Hapsburg Madrid, where power relations established the dynamics of a highly volatile cultural field. During his years as a playwright, some of the most notorious episodes in the social chronicle of the court are defined by permanent rivalries among consecrated poets: Francisco de Quevedo's dislike for Luis de Góngora, Tirso's antipathy for Antonio Hurtado de Mendoza, and Lope de Vega's constant puns about Ruiz de Alarcón's deformed appearance are part of the canonical testimonies of the literary field of the 1620s and 1630s. This cartography of violence and displacement was also the Madrid of Tirso's upbringing, and would become the grid of his life: a crucible of literary ambitions, economic forces, and social interests. The settings of his urban plays inform the reader of a fascinating time during the formation and maturation of Madrid, as the works become cultural artifacts of the city itself. Thus the need to posit this theoretical balance in the classroom, appropriately placing more emphasis on space and less on time, overcomes a traditional historicism that has tended to hide, according to Edward Soja, "the social production of space and the restless formation and reformation of geographical landscapes" (11). A city that so powerfully lives through the texts is worthy of attention in the classroom.

Reading the Country, Reading the City

Numerous plays subscribe to this new perception of the city (Blue, *Spanish* 85–135). Born in Madrid in about 1584, Tirso lived from 1621 on in the Mercedarian monastery, near the Rastro and the palace of the duke of Alba (one of the wealthiest patrons of the time), not far from some of the most ingenious minds of the Golden Age. Lope de Vega, Vélez de Guevara, Ruiz de Alarcón, Suárez de Figueroa, and Salas Barbadillo were among the first to establish themselves in Madrid, followed later by Mira de Amescua (1616), Góngora and Villamediana (1617), Quevedo (1618), Guillén de Castro (1619), and Esquilache (1621). Tirso enjoyed many distinguished neighbors, including Lope de Vega, who immortalized the garden of his house in the Calle Francos (today, Calle Cervantes); Calderón, who grew up on the Calle de las Fuentes, close to the Plaza de Guadalajara, and later moved to the Calle de Platerías; an elderly Cervantes, who lived on Cantarranas (today, Calle Lope de Vega); Salas Barbadillo, on Calle Toledo; Ruiz de Alarcón, on Calle de las Urosas; Paravicino, in the Trinitarian Monastery; Góngora as well, who had lived on Calle del Niño until 1619, before Quevedo arrived (and where today this street preserves Quevedo's name).

Most of these streets were near the artistic and bohemian quarters surrounding the two major playhouses (Príncipe and Cruz), where, according to the testimonies, these artists spent their afternoons drinking, chatting, and watching *comedias*. Students can profit from examining fascinating early modern maps like those of Pedro Texeira (Madrid, Archivo de la Villa), Julius Milheuser (Madrid, Museo Municipal), Frederick de Wit (Museo Municipal), and Antonio Marcelli (Museo Municipal), to learn about the cartography of seventeenth-century Madrid. These visual aids have been reproduced countless times in books and catalogs on Madrid and on Golden Age theater, and most of them are easily accessible through the Web. My method, however, has been to make them into transparencies or colored copies and to use them as the background for introductory lectures at both the graduate and the undergraduate level. They have been particularly useful when the class discusses some of the frequent places visited in the texts—the Manzanares, the Paseo del Prado—or simply to locate the playhouses and the cultural activity surrounding them. The experience, especially at the undergraduate level, has been twofold: if Tirso's plays, along with Lope's, Calderón's, and Alarcón's, help students learn about the city, the contextual aids guide them in the spatial design of its representations.

We see, then, a city converted into a cultural center, one that in the following years would attract artists like Diego Velázquez, Cosme Lotti, and a long list of European actors, musicians, scientists, diplomats, and architects. Often the influx generated dynamic tensions between political and cultural forces, evoking a struggle between the individual and certain institutions. The result of these clashes produced literary testimonies of all kinds, even by well-established artists like Quevedo, who spent some time in jail; Lope de Vega, who suffered banishment in his early years; Salas Barbadillo, who was prosecuted for some of his works; and Tirso himself, who was expelled from Madrid in 1625 because of political hostilities. Danger and fascination are thus triggered by the appeal of the court, which functioned as the center of forces in constant motion. We see, then, how the concentric structures of power undergo conflicts and alliances that point toward a symbolic center where material and social capital is located, as Norbert Elias, in *Court Society,* and Clifford Geertz have observed in their classic studies. Fundamental in the lives of these early modern *ingenios* is a problematic relation with the court that accentuates the concepts of center and periphery and the privilege of belonging to the right social circles. Social capital often becomes a symbolic capital that must be acquired, preserved, and reproduced. Madrid is presented as a representation of the cosmos and of the labyrinth, as a site of hidden experiences, through the portrayal of flirtatious lads and damsels (*escondidos* and *tapadas*) in some of Tirso's best plays: *La huerta de Juan Fernández, En Madrid y en una casa, Los balcones de Madrid, Marta la piadosa, Por el sótano y el torno, La celosa de sí misma,* and *La villana de Vallecas.* By the time of Tirso's death, this cultural axis had acquired a structural anatomy that would be preserved for centuries afterward. Its layout symbolically relevant, the city was sometimes considered a "mother figure" (based on a mistaken etymology of the name *Madrid*), as, for example, in one of Tirso's most rewarding plays to teach: *Don Gil de las calzas verdes (Don Gil of the Green Breeches).*

The representation of the ever-shifting urban landscape is one of the challenges that confront Tirso in *Don Gil de las calzas verdes,* a play that reflects important political changes. Philip III (1598–1621) had moved the court from Madrid—the capital of a still peripatetic court in 1561–to Valladolid from 1601 to 1606. However, it soon became evident that Madrid was a much better option because of its proximity to El Escorial and its position in the geographical center of Spain. From the end of the sixteenth century, the arteries of Madrid, its various districts, and commercial nuclei were already structuring a "professional distribution" of the village, at a time when it was establishing professions in response to the rapid growth of the population (Ringrose). Agriculture, construction, supply of services, and operations linked to the court were part of primary, secondary, and tertiary sectors that were developing rapidly in Madrid before 1606. It was only natural, then, that the circulation and accumulation of capital would become important in the best-known contemporary testimonies, whether literary or not. Allusions to popular places in Madrid are numerous in *Don Gil,* where metonym becomes a major tool of urban depiction: doors of exit from and entry to the city, the River Manzanares, the Puente de Segovia, the churches of Carmen Calzado and the fashionable Victoria, and the Puerta de Guadalajara appear as settings for duels and seduction. Moreover, references are made to important trade centers like Vallecas (famous for supplying bread and construction materials) and Alcorcón (provider of the ceramic used in Madrid's elegant kitchens). Like the hustle and bustle of carriages and pedestrians navigating the city's geography, an accelerated rhythm of change in the landscape was brought about through urbanization and demolition, renovation or reorganization, and readjustment in social hierarchies. Paintings like Juan Gómez de Mora's *El alcázar* (Museo Municipal), Louis Meunier's *Puerta del Sol* (Museo Municipal), Juan Bautista Martínez del Mazo's *Un estanque del Buen Retiro* (Museo del Prado), Félix Castelló's *Vista del Alcázar* (Museo Municipal), and Juan de la Corte's *Fiesta en la Plaza Mayor* (Museo Municipal) are excellent visual aids that can be incorporated into the classroom as slides in *PowerPoint* presentations, photocopies, or transparencies.

From *Don Gil*'s very beginning, Tirso traces a move from the periphery to the center that parallels many of these changes. Doña Juana is on her way from Valladolid to Madrid. She has had an affair with Don Martín, who promised to marry her but whose father has now arranged for him to marry Doña Inés, a lady from Madrid who is richer than Juana. Because Martín is already promised to Juana, he presents himself in Madrid to Inés using the name Don Gil. Through bribery, Juana has learned of Martín's scheme and plans to thwart it, dressed as a man in green breeches; she is now "Don Gil de las calzas verdes." The subsequent mistaken identities open the door to humorous situations, confusion, and chaos. It should be pointed out to students, however, that there is a pivotal connection between space and identity, for only cities like Madrid, Lisbon, and Seville offered the anonymity for these plots to succeed. Such is the experience of *Don Gil*'s characters, as they compare provincial Valladolid with the pleasures and perils of the new metropolis. Doña Juana speaks of Madrid as "esta corte, toda engaños" (Aris ed.; act 1, scene 1, line 170) ("this Court, where all's deceit"); and Caramanchel, the play's *gracioso,* is defined by the numerous urban archetypes he has worked for (1.2.273–487). Madrid's magnitude and cosmopolitanism is depicted, as well, in marine metaphors. For example, when Don Pedro tells his daughter Inés that he has a suitor from Valladolid for her (Don Martín), she responds: "¿Faltan hombres en Madrid / con cuya hacienda y apoyo / me cases sin ese ardid? / ¿No es mar Madrid? ¿No es arroyo / desde mar Valladolid? / Pues por un arroyo ¿olvidas / del mar los ricos despojos?" (1.5.684–90) ("Are there no rich men in Madrid / with whose estates and whose support / you'll wed me off without this trick? / Madrid's an ocean, is it not? Is not its stream Valladolid? / Then for a stream do you ignore / the bounteous riches of the sea?"). Later on, Inés remarks that Gil is a distinctive bumpkin name: "¿Don Gil? / ¿Marido de villancico? / ¡Gil! ¡Jesús!, no me lo nombres: / ponle un cayado y pellico" (1.5.698–701) ("Don Gil? / A husband from the pantomime? / Gil! Glory be! Don't speak his name: / Give Giles his farmer's crook and coat."). At other times, the urban condition is depicted through cultural (mis)conceptions of the period—for instance, the belief that the Basques were unsophisticated simpletons: "En lo corto / tengo algo de Vizcaíno" (3.5.2379–380) ("in my shy / approach I've something of the Basque") says a manipulative Doña Juana to Doña Clara—who comfortably lives in one of the most popular neighborhoods, La Red de San Luis (3.5.2390). Thus Madrid's "urbanization of consciousness," like that of other European metropolises such as Paris and London (as Greer, in "Tale of Three Cities," and Egginton, in *How the World*, have indicated), is frequently expressed through topoi that stress the unique conditions of a place in constant renewal.

Urban Symptoms, Material Pleasures

Once the value system of the *madrileños'* geographical imagination is identified, teaching about space requires paying attention to the way it shapes identities. Despite its negative aspects, Madrid offers a brilliant spectacle through the possibilities that are celebrated in leisure and in the city's visual pleasures. What is staged in the playhouses becomes not only a reflection of what goes on outside them but also an updated guide to the official and forbidden pleasures of the shifting urban landscape, an invitation to explore and discover new realities. Gender, money, and domesticity are discourses negotiated in Tirso's cloak-and-dagger plays. When Juana announces that she has just rented a nice house, her servant Quintana mentions how expensive rents are in Madrid: "Aunque no saldrá barato / No es nuevo agora el haber / en Madrid quien una casa / de, con todo su apatusco / el por qué la alquilas busco." (2.1.1098–101) ("Although it won't be cheap to lease, / it's nothing new for there to be / a person in Madrid who lets / a house with its accoutrements"). Despite all the transformations Madrid has undergone since 1625, the feeling of the city in Tirso's plays, the "urban condition" of his characters, can be related to postmodern experiences of the urban. The city is composed of a conglomeration of productive forces that resemble those of present-day cities. In *The Condition of Postmodernity,* Harvey develops the notions of "crucible," "palimpsest," and "alienation," which I find useful in connecting space to urban feeling. The "crucible" becomes an urban cohabitation under permanent pressure, where short-term qualities are fused in precarious equilibrium; "palimpsest" alludes to blueprints in which established elements combine with additions superimposed over existent layouts; "alienation" refers to the anxiety caused by the frenetic environment.

These are symptoms to be explored in the classroom. The most emblematic scenes in Tirso are exterior settings in public spaces, frequently in three or four distinctive sites. Promenades like the beautiful Paseo del Prado and the Prado de San Jerónimo, with its horse-drawn coaches, were well known by the *madrileños* of the time. In Tirso's theater they become the ideal settings for young *flâneurs* to observe and be observed, as well as familiar references that can be visually and thematically incorporated into the plot as the background of love affairs and random encounters. Consider, for example, the central scene at the fashionable duke of Lerma's *huerta,* one of the best private gardens in the city: Juana (as Gil) arrives, in her green breeches, before Martín does and presents himself to Inés, Clara (Inés's cousin), and Juan. Both Inés and Clara are attracted to Don Gil, who promises Inés an amorous visit that night. It certainly is a comical scene, but students should understand that this pleasant, springtime setting takes on a negative character, where lust can be confused with love, and promises can turn into deceit. The River Manzanares is, likewise, symbolic of false grandiosity: Quintana jokes about "la humilde corriente / del enano Manzanares, / que por arenales rojos / corre, y se debe correr" (1.1.15–18) ("watch the gentle stream roll down / the Manzanares' shrunken cheeks, / which flows through sands as red as rust, / and runs on past, as well it might"). Thus the overwhelming presence of an ever-changing world translates into a pessimistic reading of the urban milieu, one in which the dangers of Madrid are frequently mentioned. *Don Gil* offers an example: when a confused Don Martín sings to the trees and fountains in the Prado de San Jerónimo, he complains about Madrid as "confuso Babel" (3.18.3064) ("Babel's wild confusion"). If Doña Juana was quick to get herself a nice house, Martín can only regret the high number of "casas a la malicia, a todas horas / de malicias y vicios habitadas" (3.18.3067–68) ("bawdy-houses, which with vice and malice / are permanently peopled at all hours") that reflect the demographic saturation of the court.

The city offers a real and metaphorical cartography that allows us to consider these cultural and social transformations, the theater of Tirso being one of the best illustrations of urban restlessness. At a time when churches had become sanctuaries of seduction, the prohibition of the *tapadas* by the Royal Decree of Philip IV in 1638 reflects the situations that some of these plays had already portrayed. Thus *Don Gil de las calzas verdes* can be read as an aesthetic negotiation with radically new lifestyles and ideas. Space becomes fundamental not only as an act of physical occupation but as the stage of new possibilities: seduction, robbery, duels (there is a failed one between Don Juan and Don Martín), and even voyeurism in plays like *Los balcones de Madrid* and *La celosa de sí misma.* Therefore, we should ask our students how these cloak-and-dagger plays act as inspirations for aesthetic creation and, also, and perhaps more interesting, how these representations are produced with such intensity during the period. A materialist interpretation of the history and geography of Madrid provides a useful optic through which to read the urbanite Tirso, allowing us to analyze the relationship between the playwright and his milieu. Even though my choice here is not an exclusive one—after all, contemporaries such as Lope de Vega, Rojas Zorrilla, and Calderón de la Barca are equally informative—I believe Tirso is one of the few playwrights who provide a multifaceted vision of Madrid in a time (the 1620s and 1630s) of demographic expansion and economic growth. As a result, through Tirso's urban theater, we can better teach early modern Madrid and understand a city not too distant from our own.

Costume and the *Comedia*: Dressing Up
El vergonzoso en palacio in the Classroom

Laura R. Bass

At the center of *El vergonzoso en palacio,* the play's heroine, Serafina, voices one of the most famous defenses of the *comedia* made in the Spanish Golden Age. She does so cross-dressed, about to rehearse the part of a man in a play-within-the-play. That Tirso de Molina's woman character extols the pleasures and benefits of the theater while wearing the clothes of a man is no accident. As Marjorie Garber has argued, theater is by its nature transvestite; for a character (already in costume) to cross-dress within the action of the play is to bring to the forefront that already transvestite ground. And that is precisely what Tirso does when he has Serafina rehearse in drag. The rehearsal makes *El vergonzoso en palacio* a play not only about acting, as others have observed, but also about the role of costume in constituting the fabric of theatrical illusion.

In my teaching, I emphasize that costume was especially important in the Spanish *comedia*. With set decoration in the *corrales* relatively sparse and performances taking place in the light of day, costume provided an essential visual index of dramatic space, time, and character. Brightly colored capes located the action on the street at night; shepherds' dress situated it in the mountains; brocaded fabrics communicated a character's prominence (Ruano de la Haza, *Puesta* 90–91). Costume also held a sensuous appeal key to the *comedia*'s popularity. In a society in which frequently reinstated sumptuary laws aimed to limit the use of costly silks, velvets, taffetas, lace, brocades, and gold and silver trims, the stage was one place where sartorial luxury was permitted, allowing actors to dress up and inviting audience members to partake in the visual pleasure of watching them (Díez Borque, *Sociedad* 198–203; Ruano de la Haza, *Puesta* 76). Stage costumes were the most valuable, abundant items in the estate inventories of *autores de comedias* (see Pérez Pastor; Esquerdo; García García), who could spend as much as three times on costumes as on plays themselves (Ruano de la Haza, *Puesta* 75); wardrobes represented the fixed capital of theater companies (García García 171; also see Argente). Antitheatricalists and defenders of the *comedia* equally recognized the appeal of rich fabrics and adornment. The former decried sartorial richness for contributing to the theater's corrupting effects, while the latter allowed actors luxurious costume to attract theatergoers whose purchase of tickets helped fund city hospitals (see arguments made by the town council of Madrid in 1598 for the reopening of the theaters, in Cotarelo y Mori, *Bibliografía,* 421).

As a growing body of scholarly work makes clear (Oriel; Juárez; Sánchez Jiménez), the dramatic centrality of costume was not lost on the playwrights. For Tirso de Molina especially, costume was essential to his conception of the

theater. In his defense of the *comedia nueva* in *Los cigarrales de Toledo,* Tirso an-
swered the classicist objection to this art form as an unnatural hybrid by employing horticultural and sartorial analogies: just as human industry invented
fruits by crossing those God created and as tailors designed clothing since the
first "tailor" (i.e., God) dressed our "original parents" in animal skins, it is only
natural that the *comedia nueva,* in imitation of both the horticulturist's "nature"
and the tailor's "art," should create dramatic forms out of those inherited from
the ancients (in Sánchez Escribano and Porqueras Mayo 211).

Unfortunately, though, the importance of costume in the drama of seventeenth-
century Spain is all too easily lost on students. The difficulty is largely one of
medium: costume works on the register of the visual, and our students read *comedias,* rarely having the opportunity to see them, and tend to skip over unfamiliar sartorial references despite notes provided by editors. But the problem
isn't just one of vocabulary and medium; it is also one of culture and context. Inhabitants of a world where mass-produced clothing is sold at ubiquitous chain
stores, even the most fashion-conscious students have only vague awareness of
the specific meanings that clothing had in the past and of its powerful role in the
social construction of identity.

When I teach a work like *El vergonzoso en palacio,* which makes self-
conscious use of stage costume, I begin the discussion by accessing the students'
often implicit understanding of dress and cross-dress in their own world. I show
a page from a catalog of clothing for newborns in blue, pink, and yellow. What
color would you choose if you were buying baby clothes? Invariably someone answers that the choice depends on the baby's sex, and from there we talk about
when, how, and why blue came to be for boys, pink for girls. I bring in other catalogs to encourage discussion about how clothing communicates socioeconomic
status, profession, age, lifestyle, and gender. I ask my students how their posture
and gait change when they dress up for a formal dance or a job interview. Finally,
I show an image that challenges the categories of identity that clothing is meant
to reflect. Man Ray's photograph of *Rrose Sélavy, alias Marcel Duchamp* in the
Philadelphia Museum of Art (www.philamuseum.org/search), is a good example.
The image, which teases us with the question of who is more real, Rrose Sélavy
or Marcel Duchamp, her alias, thereby interrogates the foundations of the gendered self. Moreover, it invites us to reflect on the pleasures and power of transvestite performance: in dressing up, we become our fantasy selves (Blessing 15).

I teach *El vergonzoso en palacio* precisely because of the brilliant ways in
which it explores the possibilities and the limits of transvestism. The main plot
centers on Mireno, the son of Lauro, really the exiled brother of King Pedro of
Portugal. Raised as a shepherd but convinced he is destined for higher things,
Mireno leaves the countryside, in the hope of winning glory as a soldier. Instead,
he enters the court of the duke of Avero, whose daughter Magdalena falls in love
with him and arranges to have him employed as secretary. Painfully bashful in

this new role, Mireno does not take up Magdalena's amorous hints until the end of the play, when he discovers his real identity and marries her. In the secondary plot, Don Antonio falls in love with the duke's other daughter, Serafina. He commissions a painter to sketch her portrait secretly during her rehearsal of the play-within-the-play. When, later, Serafina rejects his declaration of love, he throws the portrait of the cross-dressed woman to the floor, and she falls in love with her likeness, albeit believing it is of a man. Taking advantage of her deception, Don Antonio pretends to be that man and seduces her. At the end, she has no choice but to marry him. Cross-dressing—in the former case, of class; in the latter, of gender—weaves these plot strands together.

The proverb "El hábito no hace al monje" ("The cowl doesn't make the monk" [Covarrubias Orozco, in *Tesoro* 1018]) frames our discussion of *El vergonzoso en palacio*. Tirso's *comedia* plays on that proverbial wisdom, calling attention to the materials of identity and tantalizing us with the question, To what extent do clothes make—or not make—the man and the woman, the aristocrat and the peasant? To answer that question in the classroom is to explore the very fabric of seventeenth-century Spanish society: the role that clothing had in shaping, sometimes fraying relationships of class and gender; the *comedia* as a platform on which fantasies were given form and expression; the potential for the visual to free and entrap us. We focus on the scenes of transvestism—when Mireno and his companion Tarso exchange their shepherd's clothes for the courtiers' dress and Serafina rehearses a man's role. Hoping to shed light on theater and material culture in seventeenth-century Spain, I illuminate our reading of the play with passages from contemporary treatises on dress (Civil and Vigil provide good examples; Sempere y Guarinos remains the classic source); debates on the *comedia* taken from Cotarelo y Mori and Sánchez Escribano and Porqueras Mayo; and visual images such as portraits and costume illustrations (see esp. Bernis's article "Los trajes" and the plates in *El vestuario en el teatro español del Siglo de Oro*, ed. Reyes Peña; also see Bernis, *El traje*, for its ample illustrations, and Reade).

Even before Mireno himself arrives on stage, the lackey Tarso describes him through a reference to cloth: "que debajo del sayal / que le sirve de corteza / se encubre alguna nobleza" (act 1, lines 283–85) ("beneath that smock / which serves him as a shell, a nobleman / of highest rank from Portugal lies hid").[1] A gloss is needed here: the *sayal* was a roughhewn sackcloth worn commonly by *villanos* (peasants) and considered perfectly suitable to their supposedly "vil"— in the sense of "base" and "rustic"—nature (Bernis, *El traje* 413). In this case, though, the fit isn't right—a hint, from the start, that Mireno does not naturally belong in a shepherd's clothing. Far more suitable is the courtly dress that Ruy Lorenzo, fleeing from the authorities, gives him in exchange for his shepherd's garb. The twenty-seven-line speech (596–623) in which Ruy describes how well Mireno looks in "las galas del traje noble" (605) ("a nobleman's finery"

[trans. mine]) begs close attention. To illustrate, I bring in any number of reproductions of portraits and engravings (e.g., the Spanish Gentleman shown at
www.costumes.org/stibbert/199.jpg) that feature the outfit of the typical Spanish
courtier: doublet (*jubón*), trunks (*calzas*), cape (*capa*), lettuce-like ruff (*gorguera*
or *cuello de lechuguilla*), and gloves (*guantes*) (Bernis, *El traje* 138). The overall
appearance was one of controlled elegance. According to Ruy, the average peasant looks lifeless in the nobleman's attire; no matter how much he dresses up, his
rusticity still comes through, just as a mere adobe wall is apparent even under a
tapestry of silk (604–10). Mireno, in contrast, moves with such "donaire" and
"desenfado" (613–14) ("grace" and "ease") that the court dress is clearly a perfect—indeed, a most natural ("hallo en ti más natural" [616])—fit. Mireno's
transformed appearance points to the nobility of his essence: "Alguna nobleza,
infiero que hay en ti" (620–21) ("I see nobility in you"). To answer our question
about the transformative power of clothing, then, these lines suggest that clothes
cannot make just anyone into an aristocrat, for they constitute the fabric of class
identity in a fundamental way, having the power to affirm the aristocrat's superiority or divest him or her of social privilege. Mireno's new costume carries with
it not only a different look but also a transformative feel. Comparing himself to a
humble horse suddenly invigorated by a saddle of gold, he describes how the
courtly attire has elevated his ambition. In the classroom instructors can suggest
the meaning of *feel* here by discussing the adage "dress for success" and asking
students to stand as if they were wearing tight stockings, jerkin, and a stiff collar.

The change of costume should also be linked to the period when Tirso wrote
the play, in 1611. While *El vergonzoso* takes place in fifteenth-century Portugal,
its preoccupations, as well as the costumes used, belong to Tirso's world. The idea
of a natural aristocratic suit tapped into anxieties about social mobility and rising
consumerism in seventeenth-century Spain. Merchants, artisans, and other non-
nobles were imitating aristocratic fashion and hence usurping the upper classes'
presumably inborn, exclusive right to sartorial refinement. To appreciate the socially transgressive power of clothing, students can consider the fact that treatises were written urging the reinstatement of regulations (the well-known
sumptuary laws) that promulgated a kind of dress code according to profession,
class, and status. Seen in such a light, Mireno's change of costume is a matter not
so much of cross-dress as of social redress, a step toward discovering—and recovering—his noble patrimony.

The court lackey's *calzas* given to Tarso in exchange for his shepherd's *sayo*
(smock) give a more complicated view of costume and identity. Tarso angrily describes his new trunks as a maze of streets and crossings ("confusión de calles y
encrucijadas" [678–79]); sliced melons ("rebanadas [de] melon" [680–81]); an
unintelligible sphere ("esfera . . . menos intelligible" [682–83]); an impossibly
constructed building ("enmarañado edificio" [689]). The accumulation of metaphors mirrors the excessive layers of cloth. I explain that it was a literary commonplace for *villanos* who suddenly found themselves employed at court and

wearing the requisite *calzas* to make fun of their slashes, linings, inner pockets, and stuffings (Bernis, *El traje* 156). The joke was not just on the *villanos,* presumably too simple for these convoluted trunks, but also on a court culture whose obsession with appearance and penchant for intrigue were seen to be materialized in the labyrinthine folds of their garments.

The jest applies here too: the description of the *calzas* subtly warns of what is to come. Particularly significant is Tarso's exasperated reference to the difficulty of locating the *faltriquera* (money pouch) under the maze-like layers of fabric (685). Could that all-important money pouch function as a symbol for the phallus—lost, it seemed to many, in the lax world of the court, whose fashion contributed to the emasculation of a nobility no longer involved in the military occupations that had been its raison d'être? According to moralists like Tomás de Trujillo, the tanned leathers, flimsy shoes, delicate fabrics, burdensome collars, and impractical trunks that dressed up courtly life only added to its supposedly softening, effeminizing effects (see esp. fols. 18–19 and 58). Rather than don a uniform and win glory on the battlefield, as he had planned, Mireno, *el vergonzoso* (the bashful man) of the play's title, will be unmanned when he finds himself at Magdalena's mercy and in the role of palace secretary (see González García; Cartagena-Calderón 247–82).

More masculine than Mireno in his role as court secretary is Magdalena's sister Serafina, in her rehearsal in drag. When I teach the rehearsal scene, I want students to read it in as visual a way as possible, to appreciate how Serafina's use of costume, voice, and body movements worked together on stage to tantalize audience members by teasing the boundaries of sexuality and pushing the limits of gender. For, indeed, this was a transgressive scene, as Juana—echoing the countless moralists in the period who considered female-to-male cross-dressing to be one of the *comedia*'s most reprehensible practices—makes clear when she admonishingly asks, "¿Qué aquesto de veras haces? / ¿Qué en verte así no te ofendes?" (2.731–32) ("But why dress thus? / Are you not troubled by your image in the glass?").

Students need to understand that the appearance of women on stage was of much concern at the time. While women were not allowed on the Shakespearean stage and boy actors were employed in their place, the authorities in Spain decided, from as early as 1587, that female roles should be performed by women themselves. For the Spaniards, the threat to masculinity posed by cross-dressed boys was more serious than the threat to feminine propriety posed by women on stage (see Heise). Still, actresses were forbidden to wear male attire, a prohibition whose reinstatement at various times alerts us to its regular violation. As Lope de Vega well knew ("suele / el disfraz varonil agradar mucho" [*Arte nuevo,* in Sánchez Escribano and Porqueras Mayo 162]), cross-dressed women in the *comedia* were a major selling point.

Why, more exactly, were actresses in men's clothing such an attraction to theatergoers and a danger in the eyes of moralists? The answer might seem obvious to Golden Age scholars, but it is not to students. Again, period likenesses of male and female costumes prove particularly instructive; one example available on the Web is Bartolomé González y Serrano's portrait of Margarita, Duchess of Parma, who dresses in the Spanish style. Students should quickly realize that while female attire would conceal the actress's body from neck to feet, that of a man would reveal much more, the tights clearly outlining the shape of her legs, the close-fitting doublet showing the contours of her waist and breasts. The class should also understand that cross-dressing gave actresses a freedom of movement impossible in their own clothing; no matter how rigid male attire was, it was not nearly as confining as female garments. A woman's clothes were meant to enclose her: the obligatory corset (*corpiño*) flattened her breasts and stiffened her torso; the ruff (*gorguera*) kept her neck and throat not only absent from view but upright and rigid; her skirt, held in shape by the farthingale underneath (*verdugado*), turned the lower half of her body into a stiff cone; her high-platform shoes (*chapines*) rendered her steps small and slow (Bernis, "La moda" 87; also see Stallybrass). Wearing men's clothing, though, offered her literal, physical liberation. Hence, the allure and threat of female-to-male cross-dressing in the *comedia:* it indulged the scopophilia (pleasure in looking) of male (and female) audience members; in an era before shorts and tank tops, much more of women's bodies were displayed than theatergoers would ever see in daily life. Lascivious thoughts and licentious behaviors, the moralists never tired of decrying, were incited: men were overcome by sexual excitement, and women, not satisfied with the vicarious fulfillment of fantasy that the theater offered, imitated their cross-dressed sisters (for an example of this argument, see Ferrer in Cotarelo y Mori, *Bibliografía,* 253).

No playwright in the Spanish Golden Age better understood the dramatic power of transvestism than Tirso de Molina. Recall his *Don Gil de las calzas verdes,* surely the most virtuoso exploitation of this device in the *comedia.* So intrinsic was transvestism to that comedy of errors that, in the last line, the gracioso, playing on the feminine gender of the word *comedia,* referred to the play itself as a "comedia con calzas" (3.3272) ("a comedy clad in breeches"). In the rehearsal scene in *El vergonzoso en palacio,* however, Tirso offers his most self-conscious reflections on the fascination and dangers of transvestism on the stage.

He does so by flaunting the materiality of the transvestite persona. Before beginning to rehearse, Serafina appears dressed as a man, wearing black, but her feminine hair hanging loose. Black, I explain to students, was the preferred color of members of the royalty and of the upper classes who imitated them (think of the row of noblemen clad in black who attend the burial of the Count of Orgaz in El Greco's famous painting). Black conveyed an austere, distant elegance that would forever be associated with Habsburg Spain (on Spanish black, see J. Harvey 71–81; I am also grateful to McKim-Smith's conference paper on the subject). Against the dark clothing, Serafina's long hair, a traditional marker of the passionate woman, must have enthralled audience members. Tantalizing them further with a kind of reverse strip tease, Serafina finishes getting into costume before their very eyes, putting on a collar, wrapping herself in a cape, pinning up her hair, and tucking it under a hat. She is now ready to rehearse: "Ensayemos el papel, / pues ya estoy vestida de hombre" (2.843–44) ("Come, let's rehearse. / I have my costume on"). As the causal *pues* makes clear, the change in costume is a necessary condition for acting.

And the cross-dressed Serafina is a consummate actor, rehearsing the role of the rejected prince now with jealous passion, now with sadness, now with rage; in one moment dancing, in another hiding behind her cape, in another drawing her sword. At times she gets so carried away with her persona that Doña Juana puts a stop to the rehearsal, most humorously when Serafina goes to hug her, threatening the limits of normative (hetero)sexuality. The powers and dangers of transvestite performance are great, indeed.

Scholars, including Dawn Smith, have argued that the rehearsal scene celebrates the art of acting. In the classroom, I emphasize that costume is inseparable from the art. To Juana's objection to her penchant for cross-dressing, Serafina had responded, "Me apetece el traje de hombre, / ya que no lo puedo ser" (2.738–39) ("I like to dress like a man, since I cannot be one" [my trans.]). How better to show off the actor's talent than to have her virtually become what she cannot actually be? Transvestism is cast here as the trope of theatricality, its maximum expression and metaphor. Indeed, this is probably the only instance in the *comedia* in which a woman dons the clothes of a man not for instrumental reasons, such as to avenge a dishonor, but for the pure pleasure of acting. And costume makes that pleasure possible. Could Serafina act like a man so compellingly if she didn't dress like one? Would her onstage audience members marvel at her movements were she wearing her own clothes? Would she even be able to make those movements, including her dangerously amorous gestures toward Juana, if she weren't wearing pants? Absolutely not, as my discussion of female and male attire in the period prepares students to appreciate.

Few of my undergraduates have heard of Judith Butler, but this scene invites me to introduce her work. At the end of the rehearsal, Serafina tells Juana that she will put on her own dress over her male costume until her actual performance later that evening. If costume constituted Serafina's theatrical, male persona, then, by extension, putting on her dress suggests that her female self is likewise the stuff of fabric, something performed, as Butler theorizes. But my students have already intuited that: when they see Serafina play the role of a man so convincingly that she virtually becomes one, they almost always say that she "really" is a man trapped in a woman's body and that playacting is important to her because it frees her from that body. In cross-dressing, she becomes her true self.

Is Tirso making a parallel here with Mireno, who also becomes more truly himself when he puts on the clothes of another? Yes, but there is a difference. Mireno's fantasy becomes reality when his noble birthright is at last revealed.

Serafina's fantasy lasted only momentarily during her rehearsal; deceived by a portrait of her transvestite self and fooled by a man, she has no choice in the end but to marry as a woman. Perhaps theater is safe after all, capable of sewing up the social fabric even after it has tugged at its seams. But that is for debate in the classroom.

NOTE

[1] Throughout, I quote from Francisco Ayala's edition of the play. Unless otherwise indicated, translations are from John Browning and Fiorigio Minelli, *The Bashful Man at Court.*

Teaching Golden Age Theater
through Filmic Adaptations

Carmen García de la Rasilla

Film is an important though complex tool in teaching Spanish Golden Age the-ater. At the most basic level, film versions of *comedias* can help make up for the fact that students rarely have the opportunity to see live performances of works originally composed more for the stage than the page. But film has its own ad-vantages in getting students interested in something as seemingly alien to their concerns as four-hundred-year-old plays written in difficult Spanish. Unlike theater, which many students are unaccustomed to seeing, film is a familiar, ac-cessible medium, conveying nonverbal meanings often overlooked or ignored in academic interpretations of plays (see Jorgens's study of Shakespearean cinema). While casual conversations among students are probably not normally about plays or dramatic texts, young people do discuss movies, which seem to them more vibrant and realistic. Translating into a contemporary format what often strikes students as archaic drama, film effects an invaluable historical and cul-tural transference between the past and the present. Of course, the transforma-tion is not without its perils and pitfalls: in the search for relevance and audience, film versions often intentionally or unintentionally distort crucial textual mean-ings, messages, and historical contexts. Still, even the misrepresentations can open the way for fruitful discussion. Given the proper analytical and factual tools, students come to appreciate the modifications of filmed dramas. In the process, they become more sophisticated viewers of films and sharper readers of classical dramas.

In the following pages I examine two recent instances of Golden Age theater in film: first, the Spanish director Pilar Miró's 1996 adaptation of Lope de Vega's *El perro del hortelano* (*The Dog in the Manger*) (1618); second, Alejandro Ame-nábar's *Abre los ojos* (*Open Your Eyes*) (1997), a highly transformative, free ver-sion of Pedro Calderón de la Barca's *La vida es sueño* (*Life Is a Dream*) (1636) (see part 1 for other film versions of *comedias*). Both adaptations have the ad-vantage of posing questions at once modern and transcendental. In Lope and Miró's comedy, the key concerns are the role of gender in society and the tension between private and public value systems and hierarchies. At issue in both Calderón's drama and Amenábar's film are the pursuit of happiness through the management and interpretation of perception and the flimsy boundaries be-tween dreams and reality, virtual and otherwise.

Miró achieved substantial box office success with her version of Lope's com-edy, and the film received several Goyas, the Spanish equivalent of the Oscars, and other important prizes. Its positive public and critical reception suggests that under the right circumstances Golden Age theater retains its capacity to engage a wide audience. Undoubtedly, the film's high production values and cinematography, as well as effective acting, contributed to its success. But that is not all: the appeal of a four-hundred-year-old comedy of manners suggests the modernity of its message. Lope's play questions—however subtly or blatantly can be a topic for classroom discussion—the ethical and social mores of the Golden Age; it celebrates the triumph of private emotional experience (love) over public hierarchies (class); and, through its protagonist Diana, it presents what might be considered a proto-feminist image of women. Much to their surprise, students discover that they can identify with the play's characters and their dilemmas and that topics such as social and gender inequality could be treated openly—almost subversively—in a work written in a society associated with conservative Catholic and patriarchal values.

With its varied scenery and fluid pace, *El perro del hortelano* is one of Lope's best comedies and easily lends itself to visual narration and screen adaptation. The play deals with the troubled love of two individuals separated by estate or class: Diana, countess of Belflor, and Teodoro, her secretary of commoner origin. The social code prevalent throughout early modern Europe that prevented socially mixed, or "unequal," marriages (that is, marriages across class lines) generates an ingenious game of pull and tug between the protagonists, torn by their attraction to each other, on the one hand, and the categorical need to conform to existing norms, on the other. In the midst of this dilemma, Diana emits ambivalent signals that drive Teodoro to despair and give meaning to the title of the work. The countess is "el perro del hortelano que ni come ni deja comer," the proverbial "dog in the manger" who cannot or will not eat and yet will not let others eat either. The central theme of this excellent comedy is the clash of two of the major forces in Golden Age theater, love and honor or duty. Although in the end there is a compromise solution when the invention of a fictitious pedigree endows Teodoro with the nobility necessary to marry Diana, in reality the social code suffers from being implicitly compared to an invented game of appearance and pretense, a kind of social theater. In the midst of obliquity and deception, love and desire appear as the most authentic and also subversive forces in the play, capable of overwhelming the obstacles of class hierarchy.

Pilar Miró chose to produce a relatively faithful, historically accurate version of Lope's play and to respect his rhymed script. At the same time, she managed to provide the text with considerable cinematic impact by varying the scenery and background, compressing the dialogue, introducing dance, music, and even new scenes, and employing colors to symbolic effect. In other words, Miró reformulated Lope's comedy by accentuating genuinely cinematographic elements in what amounts to a filmic rewriting of the play. And this is what I want students to appreciate: how the film amplifies and diversifies the rhetorical possibilities of the text and how it transmits its implicit psychological, social, and historical content in a visual format.

Providing a list of technical terms, I ask students to consider how the *didascalias* (the playwright's original stage directions) have been translated or transformed on the screen through cinematic techniques, such as camera work, visual scale and perspective, as well as the use of colors, close-ups, montage, and sound track. Miró skillfully deploys these devices to elide some passages and emphasize others. We might note, for example, that the director adds dramatic significance to certain scenes by transferring them from Lope's generic settings to symbolically charged spaces. A case in point occurs when the director places the protagonists in an aquatic garden, where they rhyme their coded love verses while rowing in the still waters of a pond, which might well be a metaphor for the stagnant social circumstances they will have to stir up to achieve their objectives. Miró also locates scenes of quarrels, misunderstandings, and breakups between the two lovers against a background of gushing garden fountains, as if to indicate that, despite their words, their passion continues to flow and overflow.

The film constantly provides ancillary information and subtle hints that underscore the nuances of the text. In this regard, clothing often functions as a kind of visual shorthand to complement or even replace Lope's verses. For instance, Miró deletes a long passage of purple poetry in the overblown speech of one of the Countess's suitors, the Marquis Ricardo (act 1, lines 721–36), but dresses him in a ridiculous costume. In a comparative analysis of the play and the film, one of my students, Jack A. Griffin, paid special attention to the director's use of color, observing how Diana's many dresses, each in a distinct color, reflect, in various scenes, her whimsical personality and emphasize her internal, often unexpressed mood. Miró may have been directly inspired by the words of Diana herself when she points out, "que lo que niega la lengua, / confiesas con las colores" (1.1002–03) ("What your tongue denies, your [facial] colors reveal" [my trans.]). In addition, in most scenes the physical position of the characters denotes the prevailing class hierarchy and suggests the tension between love and status. Diana always stands or sits above her servants, and she descends to Teodoro's level only when love, the equalizer, is under discussion. In one important scene she stumbles while climbing a set of steps in the palace garden and chides Teodoro, who stays below, to come up and lend a hand. The incident is in Lope's text, although there it occurs on a flatter, less suggestive setting: the floor of Diana's palace.

These examples could easily be multiplied, and students generally enjoy identifying them. Instructors as well as students with an interest in the transmission of social values through visual and theatrical conventions may consult John E. Varey's *Cosmovisión y escenografía* (esp. the sections "Cosmovisión y niveles de acción" and "Valores visuales de la comedia española en la época de Calderón"). For a comparative analysis of film and theater, I find useful William K. Ferrell's subchapters "The Written Narrative" (31–36) and "How Film Communicates" (36–47), as well as Trevor Whittock's chapters on the expression of metaphor on screen. Also helpful have been Ramón Carmona's *Cómo se comenta un texto fílmico*; José Luis Sánchez Noriega's *De la literatura al cine,* especially the chapters "Convergencias y divergencias entre cine y literatura," "Teatro, el falso amigo," and "Tipología de las adaptaciones teatrales"; and María Asunción Gómez's comparative study of films and twentieth-century dramas in *Del escenario a la pantalla.* A number of major scholarly works on the concepts of honor and estate and their expression in the Spanish Golden Age, such as Walter Cohen's *Drama of a Nation,* Donald Larson's *The Honor Plays of Lope de Vega,* Melveena McKendrick's *Theater in Spain, 1490–1700,* and José Antonio Maravall's *Poder, honor y élites en el siglo XVII,* may contextualize Lope's play and explain its surprising modernity. Another way to illustrate and update the unfamiliar structures of seventeenth-century Western society is to discuss the formal and informal racial and ethnic barriers that persist in various parts of the world and, as in the past, thwart marriage between individuals of different origin.

Given its presentation of an independent woman in control of her destiny and the lives of her servants, *El perro del hortelano* is a natural starting point for discussions of gender and its social implications. Two questions I raise are these: To what extent does Diana, like her namesake the Roman goddess, represent the forces of the untamed female in her drive to satisfy her desire? To what extent is she a woman very much in control? Indeed, Diana manipulates the other characters and moves the plot forward. At the same time, she is the source of a potential erosion of the social order, even as the deterioration is contained within the text and the social coordinates of its time. Breaking the stereotype of the submissive or passive woman, Diana questions the class barriers that stand in her way, and ultimately rearranges the social order for her private benefit. Much to the surprise of students with stereotypical views of gender roles in the Hispanic world, defiant women like Diana were not unique to literature; as scholars are increasingly aware (see, e.g., Stoll and Smith, *Perception of Women;* Vollendorf), women such as Saint Teresa of Avila, Sor María de Agreda, Mariana Carvajal y Saavedra, and María de Zayas played important roles in shaping the religious, cultural, literary, and even political history of early modern Spain.

Diana herself may have been modeled on Catalina de Mendoza (1542–1602), who administered her father's vast landed estates (see McKendrick's *Woman and Society*). Following Yvonne Yarbro-Bejarano's arguments in *Feminism and the Honor Plays of Lope de Vega,* teachers might point out that the proliferation of *comedias* examining honor resulted from anxieties about women who eluded male control. As executive director of Televisión Española (1986–89) and the first woman to occupy the post of directora general de cine (1982–85) in the Socialist government of Prime Minister Felipe González, Miró would have been well attuned to the gender dynamics in Lope's play and in his day. But again, it is important to relate her film version to the political and social circumstances of Spain in the 1990s. Teachers might assign John Hooper's *The New Spaniards,* especially chapters 11 and 12, which deal with the role of women in democratic Spain and with shifts in gender status. Also valuable, although perhaps more useful as background material for instructors than reading for students, is Amando de Miguel's *Los españoles*.

In contrast to Miró's work, Amenábar's *Abre los ojos* diverges significantly from its Golden Age antecedent, Calderón's *La vida es sueño*; it employs a new script and new characters and brings its thematic preoccupations squarely into the postmodern world. Still, while there is no explicit reference to Calderón's play in the film's credits, critics such as Sandra Robertson and Antonio Sempere have recognized its presence in Amenábar's script. As Robertson argues, the film reinterprets and updates the metaphysical and ethical dilemmas of Calderón's play: "I had just watched a masterpiece of the Golden Age dressed up in contemporary costume, as has been done many times with Hamlet" (115). Students who have been exposed to similar themes, in films like *The Matrix* and *The Truman Show*, have the opportunity to reflect again on the nature and construction of reality, this time on the basis of a Golden Age drama. Although he also lives in a tower, Amenábar's Segismundo, called César, is a modern-day, pleasure-seeking prince of Madrid's nightlife. He has trouble waking up after a night of carousing and, ordered by a voice to "open your eyes," finds himself unable to distinguish dream from reality. The problem becomes more critical after a terrible car accident that deforms his handsome features. From that moment on, the plot fluctuates between dreams and a virtual reality that casts the spectators into a situation that mirrors that of César: like him, we are captivated and disturbed by a succession of incidents whose significance remains obscure until the end of the movie—perhaps even beyond.

Like Calderón, Amenábar underlines the precarious plight of his protagonist by switching him between drastically different locales and situations; Segismundo goes from the dungeon to a palace and back again, and César from a life of luxurious, superficial sensuality to a cell in a psychiatric facility, where, after a series of traumatic events, he attempts, with the aid of his therapist, to organize his memories. They finally discover that following his accident, César had tried to commit suicide after signing a contract with a company named Life Extension; the contract had guaranteed him a future existence through cryonics. But until his revival is scientifically possible, his life would be made up of dreams controlled by his desires. However, the procedure is not perfect, and the return of disturbing memories interferes with his private paradise. Eager to put an end to his nightmares, César goes back to the headquarters of Life Extension, where he realizes that his life, up to that very moment, is exclusively virtual and that nothing exists outside his mind, not even himself. To start a new life César jumps from the top of Life Extension's skyscraper, but before his body hits the pavement, the voice command to "open your eyes," heard in the initial scene, returns to destroy any remaining shred of certainty.

Clearly, then, the film avoids resolution, which is an added attraction for creative students. Viewers are unsure whether its plot has been one of César's dreams, from which his alarm clock is about to awaken him (and us), or if there is a new life, dreamed or real, ahead for the protagonist. Amenábar takes great pains to involve the spectator in the experience, and this is one of his film's great pedagogical assets. The command to "open your eyes" seems directed at us and hints, like several of Calderón's plays, at the imagined and imaginary texture of our lives and also at the constructive, dream-making act of watching a film. However, as I ask my students to ponder, the film's command is more open-ended: lacking a Calderonian or Christian concept of ultimate reality, Amenábar's work does not offer any clear moral message. In the world of Life Extension, the nature and reality of the only possible moral agents, human beings, are themselves uncertain, and thus César does not get to pronounce a didactic monologue. Still, this difference between the play and the film did not prevent one of my students from writing a "César's monologue" along the lines of the famous passage in Calderón (1.2148–187).

For an advanced or upper-level audience, the film is a treasure trove of discussion and research topics. Amenábar describes his work as "the story of a man who wants to live in heaven and ends up in hell" (Sempere 85), and it offers an examination of the ancient Greek theme of hubris, the self-destructive arrogance of reaching for the impossible. While Segismundo renounces his violent, grasping nature, restrains his will, and accepts the parameters of Christian ethics, César goes on experiencing life in the Nietzschean sense, as a field for the unrestrained exercise of the will. Caesar of his own dreamed-up empire, Amenábar's protagonist ultimately fails to construct a perfect life. Paradoxically, through a character who, unlike Segismundo, refuses to acknowledge that life is a dream and can be nothing else, Amenábar succeeds in communicating Calderón's pessimism regarding the capacity of the unfettered will to achieve happiness. The director explores the dilemmas of the major early modern and modern paradigms of human thought and action, from the Cartesian doubt of all but the thinking self, to the psychoanalytic model of human beings as fulcrums of hidden drives and desires in search of an illusive mastery over circumstances. Untethered by a valid transcendental standard, modern-day individuals can make life a dream through virtual reality but cannot avoid the price of their illusions or come to firm conclusions about them.

Comparative assignments using both Calderón and Amenábar can explore these questions in greater detail, and, depending on the preparation of the class, may provide a starting point for fascinating expeditions into intellectual history and cultural criticism. For example, I ask students to reflect on the film's commentary on modern values, to trace the origins of Amenábar's perspective to the literature and thought of the Spanish Golden Age and beyond, and to analyze the strategies he uses in updating the conflict between reality and dreams. That this latter-day Segismundo is a young man, living in a modern city, who looks, dresses, speaks, and acts in ways immediately understandable to a young audience may help students identify with his complex dilemma. Most discussions eventually come around to tackling the major question posed by Calderón and Amenábar:

What is the price of dreams and of living in them? Many who are familiar with the problem of drugs and alcohol in American life are ready to evaluate the physical and ethical consequences of constructing artificial paradises through destructive means, at the expense of personal freedom. For today's audiences, Amenábar's film is much more accessible than Calderón's play, because it updates the baroque concept of illusion and *desengaño* (disillusionment), grounding it in the contemporary concept of virtual reality. However, instructors should remind students that these basic questions have a long pedigree in the culture of the Spanish Golden Age and that even today, their dramatic expression enjoys a "life extension" on the silver screen.

How to Do Things with *Polimetría*

Mary Malcolm Gaylord

It was Lope de Vega himself who inaugurated the long-standing critical tradition of extolling the polymetric verse language of the *comedia*. Dismissing prose comedies as "common" ("vulgares"), Lope celebrated the recent restoration to Spanish drama of the "Attic elegance" ("Atica elegancia" [*Arte*, ed. José Prades, line 119]) of verse.[1] In the expansive rhetoric of his *Arte nuevo de hacer comedias en este tiempo* ("New Art of Writing Comedies in This Time") (1609), drama without verse is seen as not fully developed ("que eran entonces niñas las comedias" (218; "for back then comedies were children"): coming to verse language is a rite of passage, the coming of age of an art form. Most Hispanists follow Lope's lead, citing polymetry as the Spanish theater's mark of distinction and a feature central to its understanding. Since the 1930s and 1940s, when scholars used evolving metric preferences, in plays whose date has been identified, as a guide for placing other works of major dramatists, versification has been considered an important tool for literary historians and editors, as Victor Dixon reminds us. But the exhaustive metric analyses by Harry Warren Hilborn, S. Griswold Morley, Courtney Bruerton, and others do not yet have interpretive analogues. With some notable exceptions (Bakker; Marín), critics have focused on uses of individual forms—the sonnet (Delano; Dunn, "Some Uses"; Greer, "[Self]Representation"), the silva (V. Williamsen, "Rhyme," "Structural Function"), traditional song and music (Alín and Barrio Alonso; Díez de Revenga; García de Enterría; Querol; Sage; Umpierre; Wilson and Sage), and the ballad (*romance*) (Carreño; Fox; Silveira y Montes de Oca; Swislocki)—rather than on the interaction of many forms in a single dramatic structure.

In recent decades, the study of versification has been largely eclipsed by approaches to the language of the *comedia* through poetic imagery and rhetorical figures. Thanks to the work of Dámaso Alonso, Joaquín Casalduero; Wardropper, "Dramatization" and "Implicit Craft"; and others, figuration serves today as a standard point of critical entry into the structural, archetypal, philosophical, theological, psychological, sociological, and ideological heart of Spain's national theater. Because meters and compositional forms have strong ties to rhetorical codes, the approach to polymetry through figurative language can illuminate some of the ways poetic forms are made to confront one another in the theater. Yet paying attention to the *semantic content* of rhetorical figures risks overlooking the important signifying work done by prosody and sonority.

Reasons for general neglect of the metric architecture of this dramatic poetry are not hard to find. Despite heightened interest in performance practice and in the material conditions of representation, we still rarely get to see Golden Age plays staged. With even seasoned scholars of Renaissance and baroque poetry less accustomed to hearing verse recited than to reading it in silence, our ears cannot be as attuned to subtle modulations of rhythm as those of Golden Age playwrights and theatergoers must have been. It is hardly surprising that our students have little sense of the varied poetic traditions that flow into the *comedia*. Heightened interest in historical and cultural understanding of literature, moreover, draws our collective attention more forcefully to context, ideology, and identity politics than to the materiality of form.

In the introduction to his edition of *La vida es sueño* (*Life Is a Dream*), Ciriaco Morón calls for a rewriting of the history of Spanish theater that would take into account the role played in the *comedia*'s development by its defining polymetric form. Critical focus on political, theological, and aesthetic issues, he argues, does nothing to explain the genre's success with a diverse public, which would have understood little of such subtleties. Two features of Golden Age plays had the power to keep an audience of restless Spaniards in their seats: enactment of ritual rewards and punishments and the familiar rhythmic sound of octosyllabic verse (*Vida* 49–52). Although he does not explore links between those two forces, Morón challenges us to look more closely at the contributions of sound to a venerable partnership. In the present context, we may wonder how a feature of dramatic poetry that has been given short shrift by specialists can find a place in twenty-first-century classrooms. One thing is clear: if *polimetría* is to claim the attention of today's students, it must be shown to be more than a relic of a distant era. It must be recognized as an active participant in the signifying operations of the *comedia*.

My title's allusion to the work of J. L. Austin is more than a playful nod to speech act theory. Finding the emphasis of earlier philosophers on the truth or falsity of utterances inadequate to the task of accounting for the complex workings of ordinary spoken language, the author of *How to Do Things with Words* proposed the distinction between two groups of utterances, which he called constatives and performatives. Whereas constatives state—that is, they make statements, affirmations, descriptions—performatives do not aim merely to say. To pronounce a performative utterance is to do something, or to attempt to do something, in the act of saying it. Austin's analyses of common linguistic acts or locutions, such as greeting, naming, judging, promising, threatening, ordering, or telling, bring to light both the active force that speakers regularly assume their words possess and the underlying conditions that determine the success or failure of particular utterances in carrying out their aims. The "felicity" or "infelicity" of these speech acts depends not only on the behavior and intentions, sincere or insincere, of the speaker but on the conventional value assigned to particular words, uttered in particular circumstances, by a given group of speakers.

This double focus—on individual behavior, on the one hand, and on the expectations shared by a community, on the other—has made speech act theory a valuable instrument, as Inés Azar proposes (e.g., 1–3), for examining the verbal encounters of speakers and the significance ascribed to their speech in the classical Spanish dramatic tradition. In recent decades, Austin's seminal lectures have underwritten a number of powerful readings of early modern dramatic texts in English and Spanish (e.g., Fish, "How to Do Things"; Rivers; Azar; Felman). At the same time, Austin's early thinking on speech acts paved the way toward a much expanded understanding of the concept of the performative. No longer restricted to fixed classes and conditions of utterance, the desire to do things with words has been detected in myriad spheres of communicative discourse. The following pages propose that, in Golden Age plays, not only words and grammatical structures but the particular metric forms in which they are uttered are called on to add to dramatic speech acts the persuasive energy that Austin calls illocutionary force (force intentionally invested in an act of speech). Meter thereby claims partial responsibility for illocutionary effects, in John Searle's sense (consciousness of one speaker's forceful intentions registered by other speakers), and even for perlocutionary effects (verifiable, intended consequences of the speech act) detailed in the play's action. In the particular speech context that obtains in theater (Elam), illocutionary force operates on at least two levels: on stage, characters address one another; through and beyond their exchanges, the poet communicates with the audience. The resources of metric variety are available to speakers and listeners in both communicative situations: in the first instance, to playwrights and the speakers they create; in the second instance, to playgoers and readers. Just as *comedia* poets and their characters do things with meter, we too, as members of their audience in the broadest sense, can do things with the same prosodic means, in order to gauge the sense and weigh the significance of their words.

Lope may be thinking of Aristotle, who credited the enhanced role given to spoken lines for the historical rise of tragedy, when he makes speech the sine qua non of drama and the key to its verisimilitude ("que se tome del uso de la gente" [*Arte* 260; "let it be taken from popular usage"]; "ha de imitar a los que hablan"

[*Arte* 264; "it should imitate those who speak"]). The *Arte nuevo* offers aspiring playwrights a set of tools that are both rhetorical (plain speech; sententious sayings, or *sentencias;* and conceits, or *conceptos*) and prosodic (*décimas, sonetos, romances, redondillas,* defined below). Its famous formulas—

> Las décimas son buenas para quexas;
> El soneto está bien en los que aguardan;
> Las relaciones piden los romances,
> Aunque en otauas lucen por estremo;
> Son los tercetos para cosas graues;
> Y para las de amor, las redondillas.   (307–12)

> *Décimas* are good for plaints;
> The sonnet works well for those who wait;
> Narratives demand ballad form,
> Though in octaves they are especially splendid;
> Use tercets for serious subjects;
> And for talk of love, *redondillas.*

—appear to make choice of meter a simple matter of matching poetic form to situations and subjects. By giving priority to plot construction, Lope seems to accept Aristotle's subordination of both speech and character to action. But the seventeenth century dramatist also takes from the *Poetics* the insight that spoken words serve to reveal characters in the throes of moral choice, poised on the brink of the actions that will define them (ch. 19; see Halliwell's commentary, 154–57). Lope's recipe for the soliloquy reads like an emblem of the power of poetic speech, first to transform the actor into a character, then to sway the passions of the spectator (*Arte* 274–77).

As a practicing playwright, Lope knew that meters and compositonal forms were not neutral options. When he promotes his version of tragicomedy—monstrous by virtue of hybridity ("como otro Minotauro de Pasife" ["like another Minotaur for Pasiphae"]) but by the same token a mirror of the variety of nature (174–80)—Lope recalls by implication the role of versification in ancient theater, where polymetry belongs to comedy and farce, as well as to the tragic chorus of Greek drama (Cohn 304–05). There, as in the *comedia,* metric variety is charged with representing social variety—that is to say, social hierarchy. When Lope remarks that octaves and tercets outshine *romances* and *redondillas* or outrank them in seriousness, he speaks from a sociopolitical understanding of meters. As inherited vehicles for poetic expression, these metric forms and compositional types came to their seventeenth-century users wearing the traces of human dramas they had previously been charged with portraying. Because the history of those uses shows poetic form thoroughly immersed in the representation of differences—class, race, ethnic, sexual, political, national—verse form itself could serve as an effective, economical means of evoking social tensions and foreshadowing conflicts.

This remarkable capacity of poetic form, what might be called its political unconscious, was well known to accomplished verse dramatists like Lope and familiar in a less reflective way to the seventeenth-century theatergoing public. It can prove much more elusive today. Students whose primary experience of Golden Age poetry—based on the widely used anthology of Elias Rivers, for example—is that of Italianate verse may be only dimly aware that Garcilaso and his followers shared literary territory with poets who cultivated verse forms inherited from Spanish medieval practice. Yet it is these traditions, still the bedrock of poetic expression in Spanish, rather than forms then recently imported from Italy, that ground the *comedia*. In most plays, traditional Castilian forms account for well over ninety percent of the lines. And, whereas most sixteenth-century poets opted to cultivate one or the other of these traditions, virtually all seventeenth-century poets were fluent in a number of poetic languages and agile in moving among them. For prosodic and rhetorical polyglots who wrote plays, *polimetría* held many advantages. Not only do particular meters have the capacity to shape characters and inflect their words: when a play is structured by changing forms, polymetry becomes an essential force in the drama. As different rhythms and sonorities are juxtaposed, they are made to dialogue and often to compete with one another. In order to decode this dramatic play of verse languages, students need an introduction to the range of poetic forms available to playwrights, and a sense of the ethical, political, and cultural baggage each form had accumulated by the time it was pressed into dramatic service.

For a Golden Age poet, the choice between foreign and native metric types was neither arbitrary nor insignificant. Italian seven- and eleven-syllable lines (heptasyllables and hendecasyllables) and strophic forms (Dante's terza rima, or tercets; Petrarch's sonnet and canzone, or song; Ariosto's octaves) had become the new standard for high style, displacing medieval Castilian high style (*arte mayor*) and playing host to serious themes from history, philosophy, theology, ancient mythology, and the pastoral. The imported types enabled Spanish poets to participate in Renaissance humanism and offered them membership in a new elite of secular culture. But to some, the "new poetry," made less familiar still by the Latinate syntax, lexical borrowings, and dense figures of Góngora's *culterano* (excessively cultivated) style, seemed to threaten not only traditional aesthetics but social mores and even religious orthodoxy (Collard). Of greatest concern to cultural conservatives was the expanded role Italianate poetry gave to metaphor. They fretted not simply over concrete sets of figures but also over the rhetorical operation of substitution itself, which had the capacity to transform human beings, their actions, and their contexts into something other than what they properly were. Because Italian meters stand out as conspicuous exceptions in the overwhelmingly octosyllabic universe of the *comedia,* poets can be expected to use them pointedly as prosodic markers of inner conflict or risky projects.

The native poetic territory of the period had political arrangements of its own. Castilian low style, or *arte menor,* reserved its elite status for troubadouresque love lyrics, or *poesía de cancionero* (songbook poetry), that circulated in musical anthologies (available in the edition compiled by Álvaro Robayo Alonso). This poetic kind offered the cultivated poet peacetime exercise on the field of language, with Wit as its armament of choice. Much of its *conceptista* (conceit-centered) wordplay (ingenious comparisons, paradoxes, puns) serves the cult of courtly love. Heavy with stilted declarations of fealty and a scripted set of metaphors, its diction rearranges the structure of medieval society, transforming icons of power and belief (cathedrals, castles, prisons, battlefields) into a sentimental reality of willed male erotic bondage and idolatrous devotion. There is almost nothing of nature in this world: at its lightest, it mimics indoor court gallantry; at its darkest, it shuns images of vitality in favor of morbid passion. The courtly code is given expression increasingly in the *quintillas* (five-line octosyllabic stanzas) and *décimas* (ten-line octosyllabic stanzas) of Golden Age plays. Linked with metaphoric substitution, verbal trickery, and illicit love, these forms, too, can prove suspect when set against the backdrop of prosodies coded as natural.

In the polymetric drama, the most frequently used Castilian verse forms are the *redondilla* ("little round," or stanza composed of four octosyllables, with assonant rhyme [rhyme of final vowels] usually patterned *abba*) and the ballad, or *romance* (eight-syllable lines, loosely structured, with assonant rhyme on even verses). Although in practice both forms welcome many different rhetorical codes, literary tradition gives them a set of thematic and rhetorical affiliations. With their nearest antecedents in carols (*villancicos*), couplets (*coplas*), and songs (*canciones*) of the late Middle Ages and early Renaissance—short and variable forms often organized around a repeated refrain (*estribillo*)—the *redondillas* of the *comedia* readily take on the dramatic role of love talk and love songs (Navarro Tomás 90, 126, 216). Its ties to the troubadour tradition notwithstanding, the *redondilla* inherits a number of its strongest strains from the *poesía de tipo tradicional* (poetry in the traditional style; available in the anthology edited by Margit Frenk), born in early Romance orality and inscribed into the fifteenth-century *cancioneros* alongside *conceptista* verses, as it had been incorporated still earlier into Hispano-Arabic court poetry (Cummins; Frenk). In the polymetric context of the theater, traditional forms and a variety of dance songs (Navarro Tomás 286–95) play opposite courtly love poems. Songs from the popular tradition work their effects with minimal means: colloquial diction shaped into simple repeated formulas; in place of metaphor and allegory, metonymic evocations of the world of nature (Frenk; Gaylord Randel; Reckert). Traditional songs codify mountains, rivers, flora, fauna, and the routines of rural life (washing, harvesting, milling) into a language of natural love that celebrates sexual passion as part of nature's cycles of fertility and renewal. Their speakers (*niñas en cabello,* or young girls who still wear their hair down; virgins; novices; village girls undone by itinerant knights, or *caballeros;* and unhappily married women, or *malmaridadas*) offer dramatists a model for the speech of young women. In the comparative context of plays, traditional poetry's direct expressions of female desire are called on to connote emotional authenticity and healthy sexuality. From the standpoint of the dramatic poet, who may for ideological reasons use archetypal voices to keep peasants and women in their "natural" places, the choice of this idiom is anything but artless.

Among originally oral forms, the *romance* brings with it the richest thematic tradition. As improvisational offshoot of epic *cantares de gesta* (songs of epic deeds), early ballads (see *El romancero viejo* ["The Old Balladry"]) become vehicles for variations on the received narratives of Reconquest history and legend. But the form soon gathers up and passes along stories from ancient and biblical history, Carolingian chivalric legend, and fictional narratives of solitary knights, political prisoners, sexual predators and their victims, faithful or faithless wives. The *romance*'s steady rise to prosodic dominance in Golden Age theater suggests that the form supplied far more than a repertory of shared stories. In rhetorical and poetic terms, ballads work with simple diction, word repetition, easily recognized assonant rhyme, and narrative formulas that, taken together, as Stephen Gilman, in "On *Romancero*," has proposed, create a unique poetic language. No one would have assigned, even to *romances* based on real events, the status of historical truth. But as favorite stories—received, repeated, reworked, passed on, ingrained into the national imaginary—ballads had the ring of poetic truth. They bestowed rewards and meted out punishments in accordance with a culturally endorsed poetic justice; their heroes and villains carried a force of exemplarity the dramatist could choose either to exploit or to subvert, by marrying familiar sounds to new kinds of sense. The *romance* offers a privileged window onto the competition among *polimetría*'s diverse codes for the most coveted dramatic roles: vehicle of poetic truth and voice of poetic justice.

For the moment, the prosodic structure of two frequently taught plays, Lope de Vega's *Peribáñez y el comendador de Ocaña* ("Peribáñez and the commander of Ocaña") and Calderón's *La vida es sueño*, can serve to indicate some of the many shapes that metric rivalry could take. In *Peribáñez* (c. 1610), Lope makes the "mother's milk" of traditional Castilian poetics a sustaining presence in the idealized agrarian world of his play. He sprinkles each act with carefully tailored snatches of folk song, sung by a chorus of anonymous musicians: a rustic epithalamium, or bridal song, "Dente parabienes / el mayo garrido" (act 1, lines 26–65; "May bright May heap blessings on you"); a *trébole* (clover or trefoil), or fertility song, sung as tension mounts (2.411–28); and a song, "Cogióme a tu puerta el toro, / linda casada" (2.633–42; "The bull gouged me at your door, pretty wife"), that mimics the comendador's voice to prove Casilda's indifference to his suit. The opening *quintillas* of the wedding scene in act 1, where trouble is already hinted at, give way to the reassuring *redondillas* in which the newlyweds proclaim their mutual devotion. For their homespun ABCs, Lope borrows the traditional lyric's "song of the earth." But he bends the code of folk song, often used to voice socially unacceptable desires, to celebrate instead the joyous, fertile continuity of marriage and to make conjugal love the solid ground on which the social order rests. When she spurns the comendador's advances in the *romance* "Labrador de lexas tierras" (2.505; "Laborer from far-off lands") Casilda calls on the form and the inaugural formula of a well-known ballad, "Caballero de lexas tierras" ("Knight from far-off lands") (*Romancero viejo* 270; see Swislocki, "El romance"). Against this homey backdrop, the sparse Italianate *liras* (five-line stanzas combining seven- and eleven-syllable lines), sonnets, and unrhymed hendecasyllables stand out as alien. Not only do they connote a higher class than octosyllables; their formal links to a Petrarchan poetics of idolatry cast an immediate shadow over the comendador and his lackey Luján, who produces a perverse sonnet allegory about lustful conniving. While lacing the verses of these villains with transgressive metaphors, Lope takes extraordinary care with the language of the devoted couple, who use, not destabilizing figures that might transform them into what they are not, but simple similes. Change of meter emphasizes Peribáñez's brief flirtations with jealousy and political ambition, in the *quintillas* (2.808–67, 880–94) that vent the doubts stirred when he discovers Casilda's portrait in an artist's workshop in Toledo. Between these two monologues the dramatist places a traditional ballad (2.868–79), sung by reapers who lend a hand with both material and poetic harvests and vouch for the bride's innocence by quoting her earlier rejection of the would-be seducer. The four central verses of Casilda's speech—"Más quiero yo a Peribáñez, / con su capa la pardilla, / que al comendador de Ocaña, / con la suya guarnecida" ("Much more do I love Peribáñez, / with his little brown cloak, / than the commander of Ocaña, / in his cape with its fancy trim")—repeated nearly verbatim in the space of one act (2.545–48, 876–79), moreover, echo the bold love declarations of the young woman of traditional lyric. Finally, although in this play meter follows rank (the King gestures toward his imperial majesty and ponders Peribáñez's crime in the octaves of 3.823–94), the royal verdict, in the end, like the Queen's plea for clemency and the accused peasant's final self-justifying monologue, is delivered in the language of the folk and of poetic justice, the steadfast *romance*.

Because the world of *La vida es sueño* (1631–32) is aristocratic, predominance of traditional forms encodes a different set of meanings. Where kings, princes, nobles, and their servants all speak in octosyllables, Italianate meters signal moments of heightened tension, as characters struggle with desires and sense of self. Calderón uses only two Italian verse types in this play: eleven-syllable octaves (*octavas reales*) for the brief exchange in act 3 (2428–91), where Basilio, Astolfo, and Estrella plot their ill-fated alliance, and *silvas*. Favored increasingly by Calderón, *silvas pareadas* (paired alternating seven- and eleven-syllable lines rhymed *aabbcc*, etc.) here open the play as vehicle for Rosaura's desperately seeking monologue (1–102). As the least structured of Italian types and prosodic figure for the forest (Latin, *silva;* Spanish, *selva*), *silvas* lend their rambling form, which has no stanzaic divisions, to two others of the play's most confused moments: Segismundo's second meeting with a disguised Rosaura in his father's palace (2.1548–723) and the reckoning of the monarch-elect with his coward servant Clarín (3.2656–89). The most courtly of Castilian forms flag three other pivotal scenes: Segismundo's existential distress, both philosophical and erotic, is rendered in *décimas,* while Astolfo and Estrella enact their formally choreographed courtship in *quintillas* (1.475–599). Behind and beneath these metric excursions, the *romance* grounds the play's vision of political and theological rightness. Seven ballad sequences—for the most part extended monologues, with help from assonant rhyme tailored to underscore themes from the developing action (see V. Williamsen, "Rhyme")—reveal the stories of Clotaldo's past transgressions, Basilio's misguided motives, Rosaura's devotion to her honor, and the commitment to self-control that finally proves Segismundo worthy of kingship. If Italian meters show Calderón's characters consumed in inner turmoil, ballad form enjoys the privilege of restoring order to the represented world.

That the *romance* came to be the preferred means of closing acts and plays suggests that *comedia* authors understood ballad form to carry special illocutionary force, particularly as a way of opening theatrical space to its audience (see Swislocki, "Discurso"). Two well-known examples suggest that the form's connotations of proverbial truth could be exploited in very different ways. Whoever he was, the author of *El burlador de Sevilla y convidado de piedra* (*The Trickster of Seville and the Stone Guest*), attributed to Tirso de Molina, lets a socially mixed range of characters like Don Pedro Tenorio and Tisbea deceive others and themselves with ballad speeches and dialogue, but the author does not allow his archtrickster to speak in *romance* until the play's third act, when the web of deception unravels and Don Juan faces the stone guest and the wages of sin. In the socially homogeneous world of *La verdad sospechosa* (*The Suspect Truth*), by contrast, where a few *romances* stand out against Ruiz de Alarcón's favored *redondillas,* ballad form is used counter to type. Here, the *romance* is kidnapped by Don García as a vehicle for three very fat lies before it is called on, in the play's final scenes, to clear up mysteries and pronounce society's judgment. Yet with his protagonist's prosodic deviance, and with his interlocutors' quickness to be taken in, Alarcón vouches, however ironically, for the persuasive powers of form. Such variations in strategic use of meters suggest that a focus on dramatic prosody can contribute much to an understanding of how seventeenth-century speech was understood and of how its speaking subjects were allowed to voice, or to threaten, the values of their historical community.

NOTE

[1] All translations from the Spanish are mine.

The *Comedia* and the Theoretical Imperative

Edward H. Friedman

It now seems as anachronistic as Don Quixote's chivalric undertaking to separate the study of literature from the broad, interdisciplinary realm of theory, which informs and guides the scholar. These days, one engaged in literary analysis is far more likely to find challenges to traditional principles than reverence for established poetics. Theory often is, in the best sense of the term, confrontational; it defies complacency, plenitude, and accepted bases of authority. How can one usefully incorporate theoretical issues into a graduate seminar on early modern Spanish drama? It is obvious, yet important to remember, that going against the grain presupposes a sense of direction, or directness, in approaching a text, something on the order of a standard, mainstream, or canonical reading. Instructors need to convey this set of conventions as part of the process of contextualizing and justifying counterconventional, and potentially subversive, readings. If the traditional center becomes the margin and vice versa, the student has to perceive the bases of the shift. There are, of course, multiple ways of introducing the plays and their contexts. The approach that I am proposing, while by no means revolutionary, looks at the study of the *comedia* as a progression that reflects literary history, the theoretical present, and a faith in the critical (and metacritical) skills of graduate students.

A checklist of topics to be covered in the seminar would contain the following: the Spanish *comedia* in its literary and historical contexts; the concept of the Golden Age; distinctions between Renaissance and baroque drama; cinquecento Italian theory and modes of drama in England, France, and Spain; dramatic experiments in sixteenth-century Spain; Lope de Vega's formula for dramatic practice; drama from Lope to the school of Calderón; the *dramaturgas* of the Golden Age; the *comedia* as poetic discourse; the major themes of the *comedia* and their variations; types of drama; the dramatic spectacle and dramatic space; the idea of early modern Spanish tragedy; gender issues in the *comedia;* critical approaches to the *comedia;* and theory (including performance theory) and its relation to *comedia* studies.

Because *comedias* are examples of dramatic poetry, the reader can examine the poetic language and its links to the thematic core of a play. Language involves artistic creation, emotion, rhetoric, speech acts, and matters of gender, authority, and censorship; that is, language is intimately related to dramatic conflict, broadly interpreted. An exploration of the construction of a play can start with its poetic structure: verse forms and variations, rhetorical figures, patterns of imagery, elements of decorum, the relation between speech and characterization, the linguistic space allotted to individual characters, the uniqueness of dramatic voices, the text as a uniform poetic vision. The instructor may use Lope de Vega's *El arte nuevo de hacer comedias en este tiempo* as a guide, for, as Lope calls attention to the protocols of writing, he brings to the fore the juncture of poetry and drama. He refuses to separate literary invention from dramatic action and audience reaction, and one may consider this combination as a key to textual analysis. Similarly, Lope's emphasis on pleasing the theatergoing public, coupled with his interest in the unity of action, suggests that he sought a fit among the formal and conceptual aspects of the play. The idea of unity, then, would seem to be a reasonable starting point—if not the end point—of an analytical reading. For example, the motif (and metaphor) of dying for love orients both the poetry and the action of *El caballero de Olmedo*. Similarly, Finea's journey from foolishness to discretion in *La dama boba* involves linguistic as well as behavioral modification, in a blending of Neoplatonic discourse with the Neoplatonic motif of love as teacher, in which both the language and the lesson are grounded in irony. Although students come to the seminar with a background in literary studies and in Hispanic culture, the instructor should set the stage for the discussion of the individual plays. This is a phase that I call "directed spontaneity," for it gives students the information that allows them to recognize the semiotics of the *comedia* on their own.

The initial focus is on the Golden Age of Spain, in its historical and literary dimensions. In the first class, I discuss, in brief, the legacy of the Catholic monarchs and the Habsburg dynasty in Spain, accentuating the role of the Inquisition and censorship, the notion of blood purity, the social hierarchy, honor, the situation of women, and the question of subjectivity. For supplementary reading, I look for about one hundred pages of straightforward historical narrative, such as chapters 12 through 17 ("The Institutions of the Catholic Kings" through "The End of the Golden Century") in Rhea Marsh Smith's *Spain: A Modern History*. Another option would be Felipe Fernández-Armesto's "The Improbable Empire" and Henry Kamen's "Vicissitudes of a World Power, 1500–1700" from Raymond Carr's *Spain: A History*. I then move to literature from 1550 to 1700, starting with several key dichotomies: Renaissance-baroque, idealism-realism, high culture–popular culture, mimetic forms–antimimetic forms, the verbal arts–the plastic arts. Using passages from José Antonio Maravall's *Teatro y literatura en la sociedad barroca* and *The Culture of the Baroque* to help explain these points, I recommend his essay "From the Renaissance to the Baroque: The Diphasic Schema of a Social Crisis" (Godzich and Spadaccini 3–40). I address picaresque narrative as a break from idealistic fiction, as a form of "Renaissance self-fashioning" (a phrase borrowed from Stephen Greenblatt), and as a predecessor of the perspectivism of *Don Quijote*. In class, I use carpe diem sonnets by Garcilaso de la Vega ("En tanto que de rosa y azucena") and Luis de Góngora ("Mientras por competir con tu cabello"), the prologue to *Lazarillo de Tormes*, selected passages from *Don Quijote* and Francisco de Quevedo's *El Buscón*, and a slide of Velázquez's *Las meninas* to elucidate specific points. The next topic is the review of a series of terms associated with the study of literature, including the canon, intertextuality, metafiction (and metatheater), semiotics (and theater semiotics), psychoanalytical theory, performance theory, structuralism, poststructuralism-deconstruction, and cultural studies. Before proceeding to the *comedia nueva,* I review fifteen of the most common rhetorical figures (metaphor, simile, metonymy, synecdoche, antithesis, oxymoron, anaphora, chiasmus, periphrasis, epithet, hyperbaton, apostrophe, personification, hyperbole, and alliteration), together with verse forms, rhyme, and syllable count. There are excellent materials on tropes, versification, and the grammar of Golden Age literature, as well as the text of the *Arte nuevo,* a large number of plays, and other reference materials available on the Web site of the Association for Hispanic Classical Theater (www.comedias.org).

In introducing the *comedia* and outlining the *Arte nuevo,* I demonstrate what is new and not so new about Lope's new art of writing plays. My goal is for students to understand the influence of Renaissance theory and the state of drama in Spain before 1580. At the same time, I want to convey the formulaic aspect of the plays as a foundation for the study of variations. Lope wrote the *Arte nuevo* when he had nothing to prove; he was king of the *comedia,* and he was reveling in his triumphs. The treatise is a playful poetics, but it is a poetics nonetheless, replete with rules concerning composition and representation. Lope believes that art can be entertaining and even egalitarian, and in this he seems to have ties to the Cinquecento moderns (see Weinberg). In Lope's model, as in Shakespeare's, there is room for artistic creativity and crowd pleasing, as well as a challenge to neo-Aristotelian precepts. For a sense of the poetics, the politics, and the performance of the *comedia,* I ask students to read three chapters of Melveena McKendrick's *Theatre in Spain, 1490–1700:* chapter 3, "The *Comedia:* Some Definitions and Problems"; chapter 7, "The *Corrales* and Their Audience"; and chapter 8, "Theatre at Court." (I also recommend chapter 2, "From Drama to Theatre," and Margaret Wilson's *Spanish Drama of the Golden Age* for the historical backdrop.) The discussion of Lope's dramatic theory and practice leads to a general consideration of the school of Lope, Tirso de Molina, Calderón and his school, and the women dramatists of early modern Spain; the major themes of the *comedia,* including the often-cited triad of love, honor, and religion; types of *comedias* (urban comedies, *comedias de capa y espada,* honor plays, wife-murder plays, historical plays, theological-philosophical plays, *comedias de santos,* mythological plays, etc.); and short dramatic forms (the *entremés,* the *auto sacramental*). The introductory assignments (the *Arte nuevo* and selections from Smith and McKendrick) are not large, but, with the opening class materials, they mark a path for reading, reflection, and reinforcement.

I put other resources on library reserve, including works by Frank Casa, Luciano García Lorenzo, and Germán Vega García-Luengos; Enrique García Santo-Tomás; Mary Parker; and Barbara Simerka. I also point out that a perusal of *Bulletin of the Comediantes* enables readers to note trends in *comedia* scholarship over the past half century. Similarly, students can discern changes in focus and approach by examining the lists of completed dissertations and dissertations in progress in the May numbers of *Hispania*.

For the seminar, I choose ten plays and from two to five critical essays per play. Each student picks an additional play for the seminar paper and class presentation. In a typical class session, we begin by concentrating on the critical essays on the play discussed in the previous session. We explore the validity of the thesis, the strength of the argument, and the particular approach employed by the critic. At times I ask the students if, as members of an editorial board, they would have accepted or rejected the essays and what revisions they might have suggested. Such discussions allow the essays to serve multiple functions: to aid in the analysis of the play, to foster dialogue on the theory that informs the criticism, to show the range and linear progression of scholarship, and to inspire students to think about constructing a solid critical essay. As we leave the play, I give the students a copy of a virtual test—the examination I would have given on the play were I to have chosen that option. We then move on to another play. A week before the discussion, I give students a list of topics to consider as they read the play. Before the class, students write a two- to three-page essay on one of three topics (as well as one-page abstracts of the critical essays). In a seminar of fewer than ten students, I divide the class into groups of two and give them a specific topic to consider for ten to fifteen minutes. The topics cover language, questions of genre, characterization, gender issues, honor, endings, and other aspects. We initiate the general discussion with comments from the members of each group and from the class at large. Given the prominence of unity of action in Lope's scheme, I ask students to identify the events around which the play is constructed and to indicate how language and ideology merge in the dramatic structure. As we talk about what elements blend in the play and focus on selected passages, we are likely to find ambiguities, tensions, unresolved conflicts, or what Alan Sinfield has termed faultlines, in the representation of authority, gender, and social class.

Although the selection of criticism changes for every seminar, a representative (and recent) sample, limited to thirty essays, chosen for their insights and approach, includes Willard F. King, Paul Lewis-Smith, and Jesús González Maestro on *La Numancia*; Ronald E. Surtz ("Daughter"), Robert ter Horst ("True Mind"), and Emilie L. Bergmann on *La dama boba*; Geoffrey W. Ribbans, William R. Blue ("Politics"), and Paul E. Larson on *Fuenteovejuna*; David H. Darst, Charles Oriel, and Dian Fox on *El caballero de Olmedo*; Daniel Rogers, Peter W. Evans, Joan Ramon Resina, María M. Carrión, and Elizabeth Rhodes on *El burlador de Sevilla*; William Whitby, Everett W. Hesse, Francisco Ruiz Ramón ("Segismundo"), Ruth Anthony (El Saffar), and William Egginton ("Psychoanalysis") on *La vida es sueño*; Amy R. Williamsen, Georgina Dopico Black, and Henry W. Sullivan on *El médico de su honra*; Margaret Rich Greer ("[Self] Representation"), Bradley J. Nelson, and J. M. Ruano de la Haza ("Staging") on *La dama duende*; and Teresa S. Soufas ("Traición") and Mercedes Maroto Camino on *La traición en la amistad*. The tenth play for the seminar in question was Guillén de Castro's *Las mocedades del Cid,* read after *El caballero de Olmedo.* Instead of assigning essays on the play, I asked students to use their critical time during the following week to seek plays for their seminar papers and to develop a bibliography. I encourage students to pick plays related to their research interests. In this seminar, for example, a student working in colonial Latin American literature wrote on Lope's *El Nuevo Mundo descubierto por Cristóbal Colón,* and a student with a background in classical literature wrote on Calderón's *El monstruo de los jardines.*

The collection of essays traces patterns in *comedia* criticism that mirror the theoretical models of the past fifty years. It is possible to observe the influence of formalist approaches, genre criticism, archetypal criticism, Lionel Abel's *Metatheatre,* structuralism, semiotics, speech-act theory, reader-response theory, poststructuralism, and cultural studies, among other models. History is present in numerous, and changing, ways, as are psychology, gender, and the canon. Emulating theoretical currents, critical commentary becomes increasingly self-conscious, self-referential, and complex, and less text centered; the theorist and the critic can have strong personalities, and they can become as stellar as those whose works they are surveying. The term *movement* comes to have a variety of applications. One can note in an article such as Ribbans's 1954 commentary on *Fuenteovejuna* an interest in the big picture and in the ties between form and content, an interest that evokes the "vida y obra" and "sentido y forma" models. To read Ribbans is to grasp the play more fully and also to recognize a type of critical center that would be decentered, problematized, in the wake of poststructuralism. Surtz's 1981 essay on *La dama boba* uses verbal imagery—the movement from darkness to light—as an analogue to the protagonist's progressive enlightenment. Here Surtz implicitly acknowledges the work of the North American New Critics, who sought to elaborate the structural unity in a self-contained poetic object. Their analysis stands in contrast, for example, to readings such as those on *Fuenteovejuna* by Blue, who does not separate the dramatic events from Lope's personal and professional life or from the politics of seventeenth-century Spain, and by Larson, whose focal point is the reception history of the play. The essays on *La vida es sueño,* manifesting trends in scholarship on the play, deal with the relation of plot and subplot (Whitby), of drama and theology (Hesse), of father and son (Ruiz Ramón), and of dramatic text and psyche (Egginton; Anthony). Following a deconstructionist inversion of the norm, Egginton deploys the discourse of psychoanalysis to address issues raised in the seventeenth-century text, and Anthony foregrounds the absent mother Violante as a symbol of Poland's unconscious, the place of its deepest secrets. In the essays that fall under the rubric of cultural studies, history, gender issues, psychoanalysis, power politics, and linguistics merge in fascinating ways.

If asked to define the principal connecting threads between the dramatic texts of the Golden Age and their criticism, I would cite an interest in *dispositio,* or the putting together, structurally and poetically, of the plays and the ways in which they can be classified; the relation between theater and life, through the metaphor of the world as a stage, on one end of the spectrum, and through textual analysis as historical re-creation, on the other; and social and sexual mores, including the institutions and the rhetoric of authority. In other words, one could say that the studies of the *comedias* tend to place them *against* something, be it history, philosophy, theology, psychology, political ideologies, performance theory, or the literary intertext. The process involves a double struggle, a confrontation with a text and with its criticism (and with the theoretical premises that inform the criticism). Students have remarked, though rarely begrudgingly, that it is often as difficult to decipher a critical essay as to comprehend a play. A fundamental point for students is that the two analytical enterprises are inseparable and that this particular dialectic gives meaning, momentum, and continuity to academic dialogue. Contextualization takes many forms, and one way of approaching the *comedia* is analogous to diverse stagings of a play; the critic becomes an auteur of sorts, determining a frame from which to read and contemplate a work of art. (See Oriel on *El caballero de Olmedo* as an example of an effective framing—or, in this case, weaving—of elements and as an instance of criticism as a creative act unto itself.)

I would like to mention three additional cases that indicate how the critical essays can complement and supplement the study of the texts. Analyzing the representation of control in *La dama duende,* Greer begins in the textual margins by evoking an exchange of sonnets between the supporting characters Don Juan and Doña Beatriz as a means of access to the thematic center of the play. By interrogating the economic and legal subtexts of the sonnets, and of the play in general, the critic ponders the ideological presuppositions of the period and, from another angle, Calderón's stance on questions of authority and power. In "Mencía Perfected," Dopico Black, arguing that *El médico de su honra* exposes the effort by men to contain and reify the female body, observes that ultimately Mencía's corpse resists strategies of containment. I find the essay especially valuable because Dopico Black relies heavily on the language of the play, while relating the symbolic events to broader ideological issues. She notes a debt to Valerie Traub's reading of *Hamlet, Othello,* and *The Winter's Tale* in *Desire and Anxiety: Circulations of Sexuality in Shakespearean Drama.* Calderón hardly gets lost in this picture, and neither does Mencía, but one has the opportunity to evaluate *El médico de su honra* as placed alongside Elizabethan theater, psychoanalysis, and cultural studies. The same is true for Carrión's study of *El burlador de Sevilla,* "The Queen's Too Bawdies." Carrión discovers in Don Juan Tenorio's macho deceptions "the pleasure of rereading the history of staging different masculinities, such as the king, the hero, or the lover" (49). The play effects a disorganization of the concept of "the king's too bodies," the public and the private, in the form of "'the queen's too bawdies,' a queer rendition of the displacement of the power of the royal persona onto a subject of control, Don Juan, who evades punishment with his fantastic tricks, and finds a way out in a nonorthodox management of sexuality and death" (48). This "teasing of historicity" (62) compels one to read the play in an unconventional light, to focus away from traditional approaches to the structure, moral lessons, and theological admonitions by reframing not only the character of the protagonist and the historical backdrop but the inscription of death itself. This shaking of critical foundations should promote an understanding of the play and an evaluation of theory in, or through, practice.

While guarding against the appearance of self-absorption, I share aspects of my critical itinerary with students and suggest that my approach to criticism was clearly affected by structuralism's insistence on process, on reflection on the critical act. Starting with an essay published in 1974, I explain that new directions in genre criticism, discourse analysis, feminist theory, theater semiotics, deconstruction, postmodernism, and cultural studies have had a bearing on my reading and writing about the *comedia.* I ask the students to read one of my essays, on theater semiotics, and I encourage them to look for "open spaces" in my work and in the ongoing commentary, and metacommentary, on early modern Spanish drama. I talk a bit about the theory wars (definitely on a minor scale) among *comedia* scholars and about the revolution (also minor, though less so) in research areas and models. Theory has gone hand in hand with a rise in interdisciplinary studies, and this paradigm shift has had a major impact on academic discourse. Students should become familiar with the underlying history, and drama, of the changes that have helped determine the parameters of their graduate education.

In many ways, academic life was simpler when a search for authorial intention and individual reader-response were deemed fallacies, when reading by way of history was considered unfashionable, and when comprehensive, definitive interpretations were feasible and disciplinary and national boundaries were respected. That world no longer exists, and in its place has come a more sophisticated, more chaotic, and ultimately more exciting critical domain, with labels and frames marked for deconstruction at their inception. The Spanish *comedia* is intriguingly vague, and its playwrights intriguingly ambivalent. Lope and his followers looked to the past with an eye on change, and they dealt with a dangerous and at times oppressive present. They render conflict from many perspectives, and in verse. Comedy and tragedy interact in various manners, and classification can be problematic. The dramatic microcosm may parallel or diverge from social and political macrocosms, and thus gender relations, codes of behavior, and message systems may be rendered contradictorily. When one adds the theoretical template, the critical task can seem daunting. The ongoing dialogue of the seminar setting helps keep the process moving, not so much by lightening the burden as by sharing the load and sharing ideas, and by "teasing historicity," literary and otherwise, in all the right ways.

Unanswering the Question: A Course on Spanish Golden Age Plays by Women

Teresa S. Soufas

Entering a classroom full of undergraduate and graduate students who have registered for my course Women Dramatists of the Spanish Golden Age, I look around at an academic audience of different backgrounds and levels of preparation for the undertaking we are about to tackle together. Some are there to satisfy requirements for a major or for graduation. Others have been attracted to a course about women, either because they are specializing in our women's studies program or because they have never had much exposure to women writers in courses across the disciplines. Still others are there because, unlike their classmates, they have studied the Spanish theater and want to expand their investigation to authors not read in other classes. This mixture is the perfect grounding for sharing information about the five women dramatists who have been the focus of my research (Soufas, *Dramas*) and who continue to be the basis for this course: Ángela Azevedo, Ana Caro Mallén de Soto, Leonor de la Cueva y Silva, Feliciana Enríquez de Guzmán, and María de Zayas y Sotomayor.

During the first two meetings of the seminar, I present the questions that will inform our discussions throughout the semester. As I explain, women dramatists of the Golden Age, writing from an intersection of proto-essentialist and proto-constructionist perspectives, depict what various scholars (e.g., Constance Jordan and Karen Offen) have demonstrated as two models in early modern epistemology for describing and accounting for human behavior with regard to the sexes. The relational model focuses on the differences in experiences of men and women and ponders the essential, or natural, definition of women vis-à-vis that of men; in other words, it is interested in what women are and do in contrast to what men are and do. The individualist model, by contrast, understands men and women as autonomous in relation to politics and law; refusing to take essence as the basis for women's (or men's) behavior, it is akin to current constructionist views of gender and counters what essentialists consider self-evident categories rather than multifaceted discursive practices. Constance Jordan's cogent examination of the way Renaissance feminism embraces both the individualist and the relational models is an important point for students to recognize as we take up the dramatic pieces produced during the early modern period in Spain.

My class is not, therefore, one in which we will find a fixed way to read all the plays. That is, the writers are woman centered insofar as their dramas evince an appreciation of the social, political, and cultural conventions that assign activities and opportunities to men and women differently. Their positions as women authors are frequently raised in their works. Likewise, through their struggles to right wrongs or meet goals, their female characters often engage in activities conventionally associated with men. Yet at the same time, the playwrights' questioning of the individualist stance endures as long as an episode of depicted social mayhem lasts, whereupon the dramatized world resolves itself into one in which women move closer to the relational model and resume behaviors usually attributed to the "perfecta casada" ("perfect wife"; see Dopico Black) and the men continue their public roles and hegemony over decision making. As a result, students who want to experience the literature of a subset of authors who differ from the canonical male writers will not be entirely satisfied. No revolutionary overthrow of the cultural norms is depicted in any of these plays. Nor will there be satisfaction for students who are certain that female-authored plays are indistinguishable from the male-authored counterparts they are familiar with. Taking cues from Diana Fuss, we evaluate the works throughout the semester by questioning the fixity of the essentialist versus the constructionist divide, recognizing that one stance is often embedded in the other.

Where to begin the formal study of the primary texts? The start for me is to make certain that the students understand the theater in Spain's sixteenth and seventeenth centuries. Margaret Wilson's *Spanish Drama of the Golden Age* is a helpful literary-historical resource. Other works I reserve in the library for consultation include Melveena McKendrick's *Theatre in Spain*, J. H. Elliott's *Spain and Its World*, Henry Kamen's *Spain, 1469–1714*, John Lynch's *Hispanic World* and his *Spain, 1516–1598*; I assign chapters or sections from these writers to the class or to individuals, according to students' background knowledge and preparation.

Having digested the preliminary readings and discussions, the students and I are ready to investigate the woman-authored plays. What I offer is a context for considering each play; in addition, I encourage students to ask questions that they can ponder with me, and I remind the class that I am not looking for any single right answers. I invite them to recognize the early modern double focus that, on the one hand, accepted the relational, essentializing models of the humanistic discourse, which insisted on the natural place for women in society and, on the other, acknowledged the individualist paradigm, which recognized the construction of social and cultural identity and admitted more fluidity to role assumption (Soufas, *Dramas* 20). Within this double perspective we find an identifiable thread in the woman-authored plays: the male characters fail to fulfill their socially assigned role; they leave it to the women to behave in ways that the men around them can emulate. In some of the plays, the authors portray cross-dressed characters or cross-gendered roles or affects, while others depict women refusing to accept the limitations imposed on them by normative traditions. Yet in neither case do the characters and situations suggest that it is appropriate to end the represented social structure. The traditional social roles are resumed at the end of each play. Nevertheless, the idea of a counterdiscourse has been raised, with its implications for permeable boundaries of roles and identities.

The playwrights we explore are no longer authors to be discovered. There are many wonderful investigations dedicated to each of them; the largest body of critical analysis and research is dedicated to Ana Caro and María de Zayas. One of the students' weekly assignments is to find at least one such study–usually an article in a journal or an essay in a collection. Each student must bring to class an annotated entry on the work consulted, use its contents in contributions to the class discussion, and submit the written bibliographical information for inclusion in a bibliography that the class and I formulate. Many of the studies come from the excellent collections, edited by Golden Age scholars since the 1990s, such as Charles Ganelin and Howard Mancing; Valerie Hegstrom and Amy R. Williamsen; Barbara Mujica, *Women Writers*; Anita K. Stoll and Dawn Smith, *Gender*; and Lisa Vollendorf.

In outlining class readings, I make Ana Caro's *Valor, agravio y mujer* the first play studied; my anthology *Women's Acts* is the primary text in the course. This play is a premier work and evinces the components of the conventional *comedia* with elements such as an abandoned and thus socially disgraced woman, Leonor, once loved by the central male character, Juan; Leonor's cross-dressed role-playing as Leonardo in her attempt to follow Juan and force, if not rekindle, his earlier stated intention to marry her; and gracioso figures whose liminal quality allows them flexibility in speech and reactions. Caro, I emphasize, was a professional playwright who earned good money for some of her dramatic pieces (students have found useful, at this point, sections of Dolan's *Whores of Babylon*). In *Valor* Caro lets the audience know that she understood the theater conventions of love intrigues and honor dilemmas, but in representing the by-then-typical story of romance lost and regained, she allows some unconventional vehicles for communicating the complications of her narrative and its solutions. Her recourse is to a carnivalesque role reversal of the *mujer varonil* (manly woman) that questions the validity of gender identity when Leonor pretends to be her own beau and challenges the unfaithful Juan in his pursuit of the princess Estella as well as in his supposedly abandoned wooing of Leonor herself. How her performance as a *galán* interrogates the stability of social status and its dependence on symbols of identity leads to discussions of Caro's reliance on a preference for the relational harmony in which men and women function as halves of a successful partnership. We look at the way dramatic moments are arranged to heighten the message. For instance, in act 3, lines 2605–630, it is Leonor, dressed and accepted as Leonardo by the other characters on stage, who delivers a speech to Juan about the abominable treatment "his" beloved, Leonor, has received and how "his" affection and dedication to her are firm and unaffected by the duplicitous treatment shown to her by Juan.

In Azevedo's play *El muerto disimulado,* by contrast, the cross-dressed male figure Clarindo, as Clarinda, speaks the words of a once-loved, abandoned woman to an audience of young female aristocrats who believe "she" has come in search of the offending male. In many other honor or love intrigues in Golden

Age plays, the numerous monologues typically spoken by the offended woman receive multilayered valence through the cross-gendering of the speaker. Azevedo's comedy includes a cross-dressed woman whose role-playing problematizes a version of the patriarchal attempts to enclose and silence women. This character is joined by the rare figure of the cross-dressed male, a subject that inspires discussion of the opinions of the Spanish moralists and critics of the theater about women's place on stage and the alternative, but even more derided, use of men or boys to play female parts, as was the practice in England. But as Azevedo demonstrates in this play—just as Caro does in hers—to be proactive in redressing a grievance, the female character must abandon language and affects labeled as feminine and adopt, for a time, gestures and behavior accepted as masculine, becoming invisible, as it were, as a female. Whereas the cultural expectations carry serious implications for the woman undertaking such a masquerade, the male figure in *El muerto disimulado* enacts his subterfuge out of curiosity and even playfulness. Here it may be interesting to read early chapters of Thomas Laqueur's study (*Making Sex*) on the evidence that in the sixteenth and seventeenth centuries, sexed identity was not an ontological phenomenon but rather a social and political one; also useful is Ania Loomba's cogent arguments, in *Gender, Race,* on the importance of dress as a signifier of both sexual and social identity. In the Spanish plays studied in the seminar, the closed quality of the social system is reinforced, since the women can gain access to the male-dominated realm of communication and action only by temporarily renouncing female identity, thus the disguised female character simultaneously negates and promotes the system, serving as the icon of its destabilization.

María de Zayas's play *La traición en la amistad* provides discursive room for questioning the relational-essentialist vision of woman's place as a chaste, submissive partner for males, through a female protagonist who causes confusion and discord among the other characters because she behaves like the philandering *galanes* in Golden Age plays in general. And she does so without changing costume or cross-dressing. What students find interesting is that the appropriation by Fenisa of male behavioral attributes sets in motion a misrule that is no more chaotic than the order that it overlays. Questions about space—the space of the female body, social space and its flexibility or lack thereof, and the theatrical space that is left open at the end of the play—are all aspects of the work that students ponder with enthusiasm.

In another investigation, my students and I contemplate the second part of Feliciana Enríquez de Guzmán's *Tragicomedia los jardines y campos sabeos* and its witty subversion of theatrical expectations. A reading of Lope's *Arte nuevo* is a must at this point. Whereas Lope addresses his manifesto to the theatrical establishment of which he was a principal participant, Enríquez de Guzmán revels in her play's departure from the norm and her sense of being different as a woman writer, as expressed in her "Carta ejecutoria" (attached letter of response), which immediately follows the play. I allow students more time to read her play than I do for other works because it is not an easy one to take in at first: it is a complex melange of ingredients from Golden Age theatrical conventions.

During the reading of this work (normally in the latter part of the semester), the students consider the primary play (*segunda parte*) with its *entreacto* (between act) choruses, and two theoretical proclamations, a rarity in the Golden Age theatrical corpus. What tends initially to be most problematical and then a source of admiration and lively fascination are the subversive qualities identifiable in this complex work. Whereas in her theoretical addresses to a reading audience she asserts her sympathies and alignment with the classical dramaturgical principles, Enríquez de Guzmán composes a play that contradicts these tenets in numerous ways. The second part of her *Tragicomedia* actually disorganizes the order with which the *Primera Parte* ends. The pairings of royal protagonists are dissolved by the time the action begins in the succeeding play.

Although she adheres to a classical five-act structure, she does not link action to action or follow much of a cohesive plot or spatial unity. Playing on the multileveled definitions of *novedad* (*newness* or *novelty*), she eschews the novelty of the Lopean *comedia nueva* and its appeal to the *vulgo* (*masses*) while insisting that her drama, with its purported connections to the classical theater, is new and that she herself embodies novelty. The students and I investigate the political, social, and artistic resonances of the term *novedad* and the myriad ways in which the author focuses on precisely the place of a woman dramatist in the theater of early seventeenth-century Spain. Looking at the unconventional mixture of mythological and mortal characters and the dependence on the verbal dimension that all but excludes action, we consider how Enríquez de Guzmán plays with multiple theatrical customs–love intrigues, royal succession, mythological stories and characters, comic servants–and many ridiculed versions of these ingredients. Throughout, despite her claim of adherence to the authority of the classical theater, Enríquez de Guzmán mocks authority and proclaims her practice of taking poetic license with the dramatic tenets she professes to uphold. By the play's end, she has entered it, conflating herself with Spain itself, asserting as her basis the Christian symbols of the Cross and the Immaculate Conception. My students are often puzzled by Enríquez de Guzmán's departure from tradition and her recourse, finally, to the invocation of national and religious symbols to justify to her audience (proclaimed not to be the *vulgo* of the *corrales*) her recognition of the importance of church and state that the nation holds dear and that dominates literary debates and poetics in seventeenth-century Spain. Our discussions are often informed by such studies as Ann Jones's "Writing the Body" and her investigation of women authors' development of writing as a "conscious response to socioliterary realities" (374).

Other issues raised during the semester include the place of a female monarch on the throne without a spouse (Caro's *El conde Partinuplés*). In addition, theoretical commentaries on the difference between power and authority are cogent points when the class studies Leonor de la Cueva's *La firmeza an la ausencia.* This play, like Azevedo's *Dicha y desdicha del juego* and *La margarita del Tajo,* presents the female characters with social and familial dilemmas they cannot avoid, even though each is steadfast in her adherence to cultural norms of morality and culturally acceptable behavior.

In seminars such as this one, in which I have a mix of advanced undergraduates and graduate students, I assign different sorts of writing exercises. For the undergraduates, I include two short assignments (five pages each) turned in during the first month and immediately after midterm, respectively. The first focuses on a problem that a play or a critical commentary presents; the student must find alternative ways to explain or argue for or against it. Each of these papers—written in Spanish—is handed in first in draft form, which I critique for grammar, expression, and content. A second draft is optional, but neither one is graded. Only the final paper receives a grade. By the end of the semester, undergraduates submit a fifteen-page term paper, again with an ungraded first draft. This paper differs from semester to semester with regard to topic assigned. Often I allow the students to pick the subject, after meeting with me to discuss the topic and the resources to be used. When I assign a topic, I usually choose something that challenges easy explanation: for example, the lack of closure implied at the end of all the plays studied. With a nod to Barbara Mujica's helpful work on staging of Golden Age plays, *Women Writers,* I have permitted students interested in this dimension, for instance, to write about the physical, performative aspects of one or more of the plays. In particular, Azevedo's use of stage machinery is relevant to such a study. Other students may be interested in the editing process of early modern works; I have encouraged them to consider problematical sections in the original texts and compare the editorial decisions that have resulted in the version in my anthology with the editorial solutions in another edition, such as Valerie Hegstrom's fine treatment of Zayas's play *La traición en la amistad.*

The graduate students write a review essay (five pages) on three related critical articles or two such essays (three pages), each one a review of an article of particular interest to them. For the final writing assignment I ask students to write a *ponencia* (conference paper) that is then submitted to an appropriate panel at an upcoming conference. Again I ask for a draft before the final version is submitted to me for grading. My aim is to give the graduate students experience in professional writing that will help prepare them for positions at research universities.

By the end of the semester, the students and I have grappled with issues and problematical elements of the plays and the situation of women authors in sixteenth- and seventeenth-century Spain. What I hope to impart through our readings and discussions is an appreciation of the historical, social, political, artistic, and cultural complexity embedded in each text and in the context of its composition. I want students to be able to transpose some of the notions of gender construction and gender norms to other topics and readings in the future, just as I want to give them the experience of learning about Spanish Golden Age theater through authors and works on our reading list. And every student should be able to tell me why he or she thinks that such a reading list should or should not be gender-specific.

Toward an Understanding of Moral Philosophy and the Theme of *Desengaño* in Calderón

Manuel Delgado

Studies on ethics or moral philosophy have assumed multiple, often contradictory perspectives during the past century. Three main schools flourished in the first half of the twentieth century: the positivist-analytical, the phenomenological-existentialist, and the Marxist-Frankfurtian (Ferrater Mora), schools that tended to undermine reason as the foundation of practical philosophy (Bonete 12–15). The second half of the century, however, witnessed a reevaluation of practical philosophy, thanks to the works of such thinkers as John Rawls, Emmanuel Lévinas, and Jürgen Habermas, all from these three respective traditions (Bonete 15).

A positive result of such reevaluation can be seen in the commitment by a number of colleges and universities to provide students with a grounding in ethics, in preparation for the difficult choices they will encounter in their personal and professional lives. Faculty members who share this goal may find that discussions of Pedro Calderón de la Barca's works lead to productive examinations of broader topics related to ethics and values. Calderón's careful formulation of moral problems and the portrayal of his characters' solution to those problems can help students explore a key period in the development of moral philosophy in Western culture.

Although, strictly speaking, Calderón cannot be considered a philosopher, his education at the University of Salamanca emphasized moral philosophy according to Patristic and Scholastic teachings, which in turn were shaped by Aristotelian, Platonic, Stoic, and Boethian principles. As Alexander Parker, one of the foremost critics of Calderón, observed, his work is imbued with a "deep sense of ethics" (*Imaginación* 435). Indeed, I would argue that to appreciate in full such works as *La vida es sueño, El mágico prodigioso,* and *El príncipe constante,* we must come to some sort of understanding of his moral philosophy or ethics. In keeping with Patristic and Scholastic philosophy before him and anticipating the *Practical Reason* of Immanuel Kant, Calderón's moral philosophy is based on three fundamental principles: the immortality of man, free will, and the existence of a God who must be considered as the only source of human happiness.

In the light of most undergraduates' unfamiliarity with free will, I assign readings that I find helpful in introducing the subject. In "Free Will and Free Choice," for example, J. B. Korolec traces the Aristotelian and Christian background for the medieval discussion on free will, or *liberum arbitrium,* and offers an insightful explanation of the meaning of the concept and its most relevant applications. Concisely but effectively, Korolec summarizes the ideas of William of Auxerre, Albert the Great, Thomas Aquinas, John Duns Scotus, and William of

Ockham, among others, on the relation between *liberum arbitrium* and divine will. Considering that Calderón studied at Salamanca at a time of great controversy on free will, I also ask students to read Luis Martínez Gómez's "Síntesis de historia de la filosofía española," with special attention to the theories of Domingo Báñez and Luis de Molina, two prominent theologians who maintained opposing polemical views on the subject of human freedom and divine grace. Among the many documents devoted to free will on the Internet, I recommend David Pérez Chico and Martín López Corredoira's "Sobre el libre albedrío: Dos únicas opciones, dualismo o materialismo," an analysis I find enlightening for undergraduate and graduate students. Pérez Chico and López Corredoira present an excellent review of Greek and medieval philosophers' interpretations of freedom; the authors explore, as well, the way Protestant Reformers, rationalists, empiricists, and materialists viewed the subject. The Internet site helps students understand Catholic and Calderonian perspectives on free will, while providing a broad perspective on other writers who deny the freedom of choice in matters of sexual desire.

With regard to moral philosophy or ethics, I give students the definition provided by V. Catherein in *The Catholic Encyclopedia,* not because I consider this definition to be the best among the many in existence but because of its proximity to Scholastic and Calderonian thought:

> Moral philosophy is a division of practical philosophy. . . . Practical philosophy, on the other hand, concerns itself with what ought to be, or with the order of acts which are human and which therefore depend upon our reason. It is also divided into logic and ethics. The former rightly orders the intellectual activities and teaches the proper method in the acquirement of truth, while the latter directs the activities of the will; the object of the former is the true; that of the latter is the good. Hence ethics may be defined as the science of the moral rectitude of human acts in accordance with the first principles of natural reason.

The protagonists of *La vida es sueño, El mágico prodigioso,* and *El príncipe constante* represent, each in his own way, the wise man or philosopher dedicated to practical philosophy, both as the logician in search of truth and the moral philosopher who strives to obtain ultimate perfection or the highest good. Segismundo's itinerary can be summarized as a theatrical demonstration of how man's rational nature can lead him to moral good. Cipriano's life can be divided into three stages: his original search for a god who may possess the supreme good; his deviation from this good as he seeks personal pleasure; and his final discovery that this good resides in the God who has protected Justina's honor against Cipriano's and the Devil's machinations: "Luego ése es suma bondad" (*Mágico* act 3, line 2672) ("Therefore that one is the supreme good"). Prince Fernando of Portugal, however, is linked from the beginning of the play with the highest perfection, symbolized by the city of Ceuta. Identifying Ceuta with the perfect beauty and the highest good, Fernando sacrifices his life rather than see the city surrendered to the Moors, its churches, degraded and profaned, converted into mosques, stables, and mangers.

When Segismundo and Cipriano act like beasts or brutes, they contribute to the degradation of themselves and their world and become the prisoner of Basilio and the slave of the Devil, respectively. By fighting their own sexual desire and anger and exercising their free will in carrying out good actions, they are able to reach the moral level already possessed by Fernando. But first, Segismundo and Cipriano must undergo a long journey during which they argue and strive for the freedom that, according to Thomist philosophy, makes human actions moral. Under the premises of the same Thomist philosophy on human action and moral end, or telos, this freedom lies deeper than that which they attain physically in shedding the chains and leg irons that have made Segismundo a prisoner of the king of Poland and Cipriano the Devil's slave.

When Segismundo states in his introductory monologue, "Nace el ave . . . Nace el arroyo" (*Vida* 1.123–53) ("A bird is born . . . A stream is born"), he is referring to the fact that all creatures have a natural tendency to seek their own good. According to Thomist philosophy, however, this tendency, or natural instinct, as well as man's emotional or instinctive knowledge of the good, is not sufficient to provide a foundation for moral action. Thus Segismundo insists that he has "más alma" (1.131) ("more soul"), "mejor instinto" (1.141) ("better instinct"), más albedrío" (1.151) ("more free will"), and "más vida" (1.161) ("more life") than animals, endowments that make him a rational and spiritual being. Behind Segismundo's long speech lies Calderón's argument that as a rational and spiritual being, superior and distinct from the animals that surround him, Segismundo cannot act morally or put into practice the knowledge of the good presented to him by his reason as long as he is unable to perform good acts freely and voluntarily. As Mikel Gotzon Santamaría Gari has said in his analysis of Thomas Aquinas's philosophy, "moral good is the characteristic perfection of human beings, of people who possess intelligence and freedom. Moral good is man's good, and consequently the end (*telos*) of his actions" (168).

The faculty that enables human beings to perceive and pursue the good, synderesis, has been known since the time of the Roman jurisconsult Domitius Ulpianus (d. AD 228) as the "natural instinct" (*instinctus naturae*) of the soul, and was associated by Patristic and Scholastic philosophy with natural reason. According to Robert Green, "synderesis refers to both the power of the intellect to recognize the primary principles of practical moral action and the habitual inclination in the will towards the good" (189). Traditionally associated with the Greek *syneidesis* (= Latin *conscientia*), the term was introduced to the West by Saint Jerome (d. AD 420) in his interpretation of the four living creatures of Ezekiel's vision (Ezek. 1.1–20): the human, the lion, the bull, and the eagle. Following the Platonic interpretations of Ezekiel's vision, Saint Jerome identifies the human, the lion, and the bull with, respectively, the rational, the irascible, and the concupiscent (appetitive) parts of the soul, while the eagle, the superior part, is above and outside these three: "This the Greeks call synderesis, which spark of conscience was not extinguished from the breast of Adam when he was driven from Paradise" (Lottin 103–04).

As I have argued elsewhere, understanding Patristic and Scholastic explanations of synderesis and, above all, Saint Jerome's interpretation of Ezekiel's vision can help students grasp the moral meaning of a number of images in *La vida es sueño:* Rosaura's description of the hippogriff, her reference to its lack of natural instinct, the tenuous light that accompanies Segismundo in the tower, and the eagle—all interconnected images contributing to the unity of the play.

Segismundo's insistence on the superiority of his instinct and freedom over those of the animals that surround him, as well as his identification with the eagle, has prompted some critics to describe him as a proud, arrogant prince; they forget that Calderón's purpose in emphasizing man's superiority to animals was to establish the natural potential of human beings to seek the supreme good through the exercise of virtue. Rather than encourage Segismundo's self-satisfaction and arrogance, his superior instinct and his assimilation to the eagle lead him to master the basic instincts, such as the urge to possess Rosaura sexually and the anger that prompted him to try to kill his father and Clotaldo. By asserting Segismundo's superiority to lower animals, Calderón falls in line with Renaissance authors such as Pico della Mirandola and Fernán Pérez de Oliva, who defended the dignity of homo sapiens against those who "described man as a stepchild of nature" and as a "worthless and miserable creature" (Kraye 308).

While *La vida es sueño* portrays Segismundo as a human being caught in a struggle between his evil impulses and his virtue and aiming at the supreme good with the help of his free will and natural reason, *El mágico prodigioso* explores the possibility that the human being, in this case Cipriano, may depart from the highest good and from virtue and reason in pursuit of a self-gratifying good. The philosopher Cipriano has been deeply affected by ignorance, which the Devil describes as having knowledge in sight without knowing how to take advantage of it: "Esa es la ignorancia, a la vista de las ciencias, no saber aprovecharlas" (1.119–21) ("That is ignorance, within sight of the sciences, not knowing how to make use of them").

As I have also argued elsewhere ("La melancolía"), Calderón shows Cipriano's departure from truth, virtue, and reason by portraying him as affected by erotic melancholy, or love sickness, an illness that was considered, since the Middle Ages, as affecting both mind and body. Deeply moved by his desire for Justina, Cipriano not only abandons the study of philosophy but sells his soul to the Devil in exchange for the possession of her body. Rather than attribute Cipriano's illness to the humors of the body, Calderón establishes as its main cause the Devil's magic. In this way Calderón preserves the principle of free will, which would have been undermined if he had adhered to the determinism of the theory of humors. As with Segismundo in *La vida es sueño,* there is always a "medrosa luz" (1.52) ("tenuous light") of natural reason, a *scintilla conscientiae,* or synderesis, that no matter how low human beings fall leads them to appreciate the good and carry out virtuous acts.

The movement toward the good and its final embrace by Segismundo and Cipriano is a complex process that includes the realization that the particular, or terrestrial, good they are pursuing has no value in relation to the ultimate end or supreme good. At this stage of their lives, Segismundo and Cipriano come to understand, with the help of the *scintilla conscientiae,* that they have embraced evil voluntarily, that this evil contradicts the dictates of right reason, and that to become good again they must do good deeds: "obrar bien es lo que importa" (3.2424) ("What matters is to do good works").

Although the process of arriving at this moral conclusion differs among the three plays, it is based on the same intellectual and spiritual sensation, *desengaño*—literally, "undeceit." The word refers to our experiences after discovering that the belief or value we had until that moment is false and without consistency. In my opinion, Calderonian *desengaño* is closely related to the Stoic notion of pathos and detachment, a concept that has been explained by John M. Rist: "A pathos is a special kind of 'disturbance' (Cic., *de Fin,* 3.35), or better 'disease' which affects basic human impulses. . . . All such diseased impulses should be extirpated and replaced by others that are totally subordinate and obedient to reason" (259). While for Fernando this *desengaño* exists as an a priori with which he is identified since he first appears on stage, in the case of Cipriano it is created by the experience he has when he assaults Justina. What he considered until that moment as the object of his desire or pleasure reveals itself to be a corpse—death and illusion. As a consequence of this revelation, which implies the conviction that pleasure is not a moral good, Cipriano's strong sexual attraction to Justina is extinguished.

Segismundo's *desengaño* and his adherence to moral good come as a result of the filtering of the experiences created for him by his father and Clotaldo through his natural reason, whether with the help of the eagle, the *scintilla conscientiae,* or synderesis. Now we can see why, when Clotaldo reminds Segismundo of his experience with the eagle and the corresponding principle that one must do good deeds even in dreams, the latter responds: "Es verdad; pues reprimamos / esta fiera condición, / esta furia, esta ambición, / por si alguna vez soñamos" (2.2148–51) ("It is true; so let us repress this beastly condition, this fury, this ambition, in case some time we are dreaming").

In the lives of Segismundo and Cipriano, *desengaño* is the turning point that enables them to seek the good and the truth, which have always been with Fernando. It is the moment in which the "tenuous light" of the "fiera" (1.212) ("beast") Segismundo and of the cave dweller Cipriano shines fully in their consciousness, transforming their illusions and dreams into light and truth. It is the theatrical moment in which Calderón brings up and synthesizes past and contemporary philosophical, literary, and pictorial influences from, among others, the Stoics, Boetius, Jorge Manrique, Francisco de Quevedo, Valdés Leal, Antonio de Pereda, and Jusepe de Ribera. Fernando, Segismundo, and Cipriano share with the Stoics the conviction that wealth, beauty, health, pleasure, and life do not constitute the highest good, and that poverty, pain, and death may lead the human being to that good. This explains, for example, why Fernando, emulating Job and the Stoics, wishes to experience further pain: "siquiera / un instante más viviera / padeciendo" (*Príncipe* 3.2257–259) ("If only I could live another moment suffering"). On reaching the conclusion that human beauty—Fénix, Rosaura, Justina—is vain in comparison with the divine good, they need no external reasoning to convince themselves to abandon the former to pursue the latter. As Segismundo states when he decides not to take advantage of Rosaura:

> Mas con mis razones propias
> vuelvo a convencerme a mí.
> Si es sueño, si es vanagloria,
> ¿quién por vanagloria humana
> pierde una divina gloria?   (3.2967–971)

> With my own reasoning
> I convince myself again.
> If it is a dream, if it is vainglory,
> who for the sake of human vainglory
> would lose a divine glory?

To help undergraduates and graduate students visualize the idea of *desengaño* not only in Calderón's drama but also in seventeenth-century Spain, I strongly suggest the fourth part of *Saturn and Melancholy*, by Raymond Klibansky, Erwin Panofsky, and Fritz Saxl, as well as Fernando Rodríguez de la Flor's *Barroco: Representación e ideología en el mundo hispánico*. Teachers can also prepare a collection of paintings featuring melancholy or *desengaño*, by such artists as Valdés Leal, Ribera, and Pereda, to be shown as slides or with *PowerPoint*. By reading and analyzing the texts and paintings, students should realize that, like many characters in works by Valdés Leal, Ribera, and Pereda, Fernando, Segismundo, and Cipriano are touched by what Klibansky, Panofsky, and Saxl have called the positive side of melancholy, whose portrait, according to them, appears fused, in seventeenth-century Italian vanity paintings, with the most representative image of Vanitas, death (386–90). The consciousness and presence of death—be it the phantasmal skeleton in *Mágico*, its moral remembrance in *Vida*, or its embrace by Fernando in *Príncipe*—elicit Fernando's moral philosophy in the famous sonnet to flowers "Éstas que fueron pompa y alegría" (2.1652) ("These that were once pomp and joy") and explain his willingness to die for the sake of Ceuta and his faith. It also explains Cipriano's and Segismundo's conversion and, above all, the former's search for martyrdom after his experience with Justina's skeleton and the accompanying words, "Así, Cipriano son / todas la glorias del mundo" (3.2547–548) ("So, Cipriano, are all the glories of this world").

Much as Klibansky, Panofsky, and Saxl have observed with regard to seventeenth-century Italian paintings on Vanitas, the consciousness of death and the rejection of worldly realities enable Fernando, Cipriano, and Segismundo to make "great creative achievements" (390) and to seek the moral good and religious fulfillment. While Segismundo's moral attainments—justice, prudence, and self-renunciation in a chaotic, self-centered court that does not recognize the difference between good and evil—fall within the realm of Aristotelian political ethics, Fernando's and Cipriano's martyrdom can be described as the final stage of a harsh asceticism. This "unbalanced asceticism," as the *Internet Encyclopedia of Philosophy* calls it, is definitely more Stoic and Platonic than Aristotelian, since there is no middle term between their passions and their virtues.

The good pursued and achieved by Calderón's characters has not been recognized as such by all critics and scholars. Otto Rank, for example, who based his conclusion on principles quite different from those that guided Calderón's characters, diagnosed their renunciation of sexual assault and self-gratification as an "inability to enact" their desires and as "traits found also in neurotic sexual abstinence" (*Incest Theme* 407). In the same manner, these characters' persistent recourse to reasoning and, above all, Fernando's and Cipriano's extreme asceticism may lead some critics to believe that Calderonian ethics favors personal solipsism and spiritual narcisism. On the contrary, and based on Emmanuel Lévinas's studies on ethics (*Alterity and Trascendence* and *Totality and Infinity*, among others), we can say that Calderón's moral philosophy has a strong foundation in the consciousness and presence of the other. On carefully analyzing the three protagonists' attitudes toward the female other—Fénix, Rosaura, and Justina—and after examining Segismundo's treatment of Basilio and Clotaldo, as well as Fernando's concern for his fellow captives ("¡Quién pudiera socorrelos!" [2.1109–110] ["If only I could help them!"]), we must conclude that alterity is not only the foundation for their conversion to the moral good but one of the best ways to find the other or God. The hidden "superior causa" (3.146) ("superior cause") that makes Cipriano stop sexually harassing Justina is made more explicit when Eusebio, the protagonist of *La devoción de la cruz*, acts in a similar way with his sister, Julia, after seeing a strange divinity in her arms: "voy huyendo / de tus brazos, porque he visto / no sé qué deidad en ellos" (2.1597–599) ("I leave fleeing from your arms, because I have seen I know not what deity in them").

It is not surprising, then, that when these and other Calderonian characters discover, recognize, accept, and respect the other, they embrace the moral good that implies self-renunciation instead of the exploitation and abuse of their fellow human beings. While Calderón places this process in the Christian moral tradition, we may find a similar attitude in the thought of the modern Jewish philosopher Lévinas. Using Lévinas's words, we could conclude that by embracing moral good, these characters develop an "unlimited sense of responsibility. . . . A responsibility that harbors the tenet of sociability, the total gratuitousness of which, though it be ultimately in vain, is called the love of one's neighbour, love without concupiscence, but as irrefrangible as death" (*Alterity* 30). As Cipriano and Fernando declare when they face death, never before has the wise man or the philosopher been closer to truth and the supreme good.

NOTE

All translations from Spanish are mine.

Placing the *Comedia* in Performative Context

Bruce R. Burningham

Given the overwhelming dominance in contemporary culture of dramatic mass-media texts such as television shows and films, most students enrolled in university-level literature courses—whether taught in Spanish, Italian, English, Japanese, or another tongue—have had little contact with live theater in any language, either as spectators or as performers. Because early modern culture, especially that of Spain, seems far removed from the experiences of an increasingly multicultural student body, the *comedia*'s imperial themes, baroque aesthetics, and often archaic poetic language can be doubly alienating. Many students come to the classroom predisposed to view the *comedia* as an ancient (and inherently inaccessible) literary form whose exacting canonical authority demands nothing less—though, curiously, nothing more—than reverential awe. One of the most effective ways of surmounting these ingrained literary prejudices is to help students locate the *comedia* within a series of performative continua: first, diachronically, within a trajectory of theater history in which the *comedia* occupies a kind of midpoint between Greek tragedy and the American sitcom; second, synchronically, within a spectrum of other sixteenth- and seventeenth-century European dramatic traditions, especially those of England, France, and Italy; and third, as performance texts in the here and now that form part of an infinite chain of all conceivable iterations. By highlighting the intrinsic theatricality of the *comedia*, we can encourage students to see these literary texts for what they essentially are: residual scripts initially composed as blueprints for an open-ended series of potential performances—the Spanish term *guión*, of course, ultimately means "guide"—that are infused from the outset with traces of the intersecting performance traditions that gave rise to them.

The Comedia *and Theater History*

Unless they have previously taken a theater history course, most literature students have only the most limited knowledge of the long performance tradition that encompasses not just the ancient Greek tragedians and the seventeenth-century Spanish *comediantes* but their favorite Hollywood movie stars as well. They may have read one or two plays by Sophocles, Euripides, or Aristophanes at some point during their academic career; they may be familiar with the juxtaposed tragic and comic masks that symbolize the theater itself; and they may even include the term *thespian* in their functional lexicon. But beyond these meager details, students probably know less about the origins and development of the theater they see on television than they do about the physics of *Star Trek*. For this reason, I find it useful to spend the first two or three class sessions of any theater course giving students a basic overview of theater history. This is as true for undergraduate surveys of Spanish and Latin American drama as it is for graduate seminars on performance theory. And I usually divide the discussion into two narrative threads: one traditional, one alternative.

The traditional narrative is the official version of Western theater history found in such textbooks as Oscar G. Brockett and Franklin J. Hildy's *History of the Theatre* (a book I highly recommend for those wishing to prepare the kind of overview I outline here). It is a narrative I generally subdivide into two chapters that describe the ritual origins of Western drama. The first chapter deals with the ancient world. As legend has it, sometime during the sixth century BCE, a Greek dithyrambic choral leader named Thespis separated himself from his ritual chorus to engage its members in a dialogue. With this constitutive separation Thespis is said to have invented Western drama by making himself the world's first actor. His crucial contribution to the Western performance tradition coincided with the Athenian creation of the City Dionysia in 534 BCE, an annual theater festival that served as a competitive showcase for the great playwrights of the day. Combining a discussion of Aristotle's *Poetics* (ed. Hutton) with images of architectural structures like the theater at Epidaurus—as well as with any knowledge (however vague) students may already have of such plays as *Oedipus* and *Antigone*—my narrative helps students gain an appreciation of the increasingly complex ancient Greek stage and its scenery; of the spatial relations that developed first between the actor and chorus who encircled the dithyrambic altar and later between the actors who performed in front of the *skene*, or stage; and finally of the social context of classical Greek theater as both religious and civic event. From this starting point, I outline the ways in which the Romans both adopted and adapted the Greek paradigms, creating free-standing amphitheaters and coliseums in place of the hillside theaters, and staging the literary dramas of playwrights like Plautus, Terence, and Seneca alongside mock naval battles, chariot races, and gladiatorial competitions.

The second chapter of this traditional narrative recounts the so-called rebirth of Western drama in the medieval Catholic liturgy, specifically in the tenth-century *Quem quaeritis* trope, in which two choruses of singers (assuming the roles of the Three Marys and the Angels in front of Christ's empty tomb) exchange an antiphonal dialogue. Again, as with Thespis and the dithyramb, a religious ritual is said to serve as the monologic urtext that explodes into a burgeoning dialogic drama that evolves into the mystery and morality plays of France and England, and still later into the secular dramas of the sixteenth- and seventeenth-century European stages from Italy to Germany to Spain. O. B. Hardison's *Christian Rite and Christian Drama in the Middle Ages,* which represents the most extended, articulate reinscription of the Thespis myth into the narrative of Western theater history, is worth consulting on this point. And, as with the earlier discussion of the Greek and Roman traditions, the use of architectural images to illustrate the mansion stages in the church and the later processional stages outside the church can give students a sense of the spatial relations particular to medieval liturgical drama and its audiences. (While discussing the processional stages, I usually comment briefly on the Spanish *auto sacramental,* although I stress that the *auto* is decidedly not a product of the Middle Ages. I also point out, to students who may feel that this medieval ambulant theater is nothing but ancient history, that the annual Tournament of Roses Parade in Pasadena and Macy's Thanksgiving Day Parade in New York are both enduring vestiges of the medieval processional tradition.) I conclude the second chapter of the traditional narrative with a discussion of the increasing secularization of medieval liturgical drama and of the ways in which the European national theaters of the sixteenth and seventeenth centuries developed into the high-tech spectacles we see today on stages from Tokyo to Berlin to Los Angeles.

What characterizes this traditional approach to theater history, of course, is its emphasis on literary playwrights, written dramatic texts, and architectural edifices. Thus, after concluding this narrative, I move to an alternative history that revolves precisely around the poetics of street performance, to challenge students to think about theater in ways that do not depend on the traditional elements. I return to ancient Greece and, following Albert Lord and Walter Ong, discuss the Homeric bards as genuine actors whose mimetic performance anticipated Thespis's invention of drama by several hundred years. I comment on the anthropologically informed writings of Victor Turner and of Richard Schechner (*Performance Theory*) on shamanism and non-Western performance, and I engage Peter Brook's and Hollis Huston's ideas on simple staging. Taking these various theorists into account, I highlight the importance of mimes, satyrs, and rhapsodes on the streets of Athens and Rome; I remind students that these performers did not need a physical stage, an a priori playwright, or even a stable linguistic text to entertain their audiences. Moreover, since these itinerant street performers did not abandon their craft simply because the Roman Empire collapsed in the fifth century CE, I discuss the Teutonic scops and the Latinate jongleurs of the Middle Ages, pointing out that the Iberian *mester de juglaría* represents as much a theatrical tradition as a poetic one, despite the so-called lack of medieval Spanish drama. I emphasize the commedia dell'arte as one of the high points of the jongleuresque tradition, and I comment on Mikhail Bakhtin's concept of the carnivalesque. At the end of the alternative history, I ask students to consider all the ways in which street performance remains an active force in locations like the subway platforms of Chicago and the sidewalks of the Champs-Elysées.

The Comedia *among Other Early Modern Theaters*

Having provided students with a sense of the long performance trajectory that connects Homer and Thespis with Blue Man Group and Tony Kushner, I spend most of the semester examining the place of the *comedia* in theater history, and specifically in the context of the pan-European tradition of early modern performance—although I include an analysis of other important literary issues as well. To contextualize the *comedia* texts on my reading list, I note that—despite the intellectual tendencies of the past century to pigeonhole the theatrical traditions of Western Europe based on the categories of nationalism and national literatures (in which the *comedia* is often extolled as a manifestation of the zeitgeist of Spain's Golden Age)—the legacy that encompasses the *comedia* was a transnational phenomenon whose geographic permutations frequently arose along architectural, spatial, and performative lines that had nothing to do with national temperaments or linguistically determined interpretive communities (to borrow Stanley Fish's terminology). In fact, the theatrically substantive division among early modern national theaters (even within the countries themselves) occurs more often between traditions linked to popular entertainment (jugglers, acrobats, mountebanks, and so on) and those linked to cultural developments in theology, philosophy, archaeology, and mathematics (church, court, and university dramas). In this regard, one useful—though by no means only—way to classify the theatrical world is to distinguish between traditions tied to the indeterminate performance spaces of theaters like the Globe and Swan in England and the Corral de la Cruz and Corral del Príncipe in Spain, and those tied to the overdetermined performance spaces of theaters like the Teatro Olimpico and Teatro Farnese in Italy and the Hôtel de Bourgogne and Palais Royal in France.

    For the latter, what clearly matters most is the re-creation of Greek and Roman architecture and the exploration of the newly discovered mathematical rules of visual perspective in scenic design (see Serlio). Ironically, the plays written for these intellectually committed spaces tend to delimit the performative possibilities of the actors, given that their work necessarily takes place within the visual and theoretical discourses of Renaissance humanism. The significance of the (often allegorical) characters depends precisely on the relationship of individual audience members to the (often aristocratic) singular point of view privileged by the mathematically and philosophically constructed spectacle itself. Aristotle's unities of time, place, and action predominate in these plays not only because neoclassical literary theory insists that they do but also because stages so mathematically constructed and constricted do not allow for a great deal of spatial and temporal movement. Jean Racine's *Phèdre* is a perfect example of the kind of static performance engendered by the neoclassical stage. Although its rhetoric is undeniably eloquent (and one could argue that *Phèdre*'s linguistic performance, like that of *My Dinner with Andre,* is what matters most), Racine's play presupposes an allegorical and declamatory mode of acting. Its characters, who inhabit a world regulated by Aristotelian theory, function less as people than as embodied concepts: they speak but do not talk; they move but do not walk. Their purpose on stage is to complement a cultural nostalgia for a long-lost world whose visual parameters disappear into a vanishing point located somewhere at the back of the painted scenery. (Similar performative stasis can be found—to varying degrees—in many of Ben Jonson's courtly masques, Gil Vicente's *autos,* and Juan del Encina's *églogas.*)

By contrast, for the indeterminate spaces of Spain and England, what matters most is the enclosure of the medieval jongleuresque tradition within a theater structure designed to maximize the performative potential of the actors. To demonstrate this, I often display architectural diagrams of the Teatro Cervantes, in Alcalá de Henares, and indicate an ancient town well at the inner core of a performance space that once functioned as a gathering place for jongleurs and their spectators (see Coso Marín, Higuera Sánchez-Pardo, and Sanz Ballesteros). I also point out, as I have argued elsewhere, that Lope de Vega's *Arte nuevo de hacer comedias* is a dramatic manifesto that grapples with the theatrical impact of the jongleuresque tradition on the Spanish stage at a time when Aristotelian theory dominated European intellectual debate ("Barbarians"). Thus the plays written for these sites—in which a thrust stage often diminishes the separation between actors and spectators—tend to ignore Aristotle's unities in favor of an unconstrained performance that can take audiences on fantastic journeys through time and space precisely because the mostly bare stage can be every place and no place at all.

When we compare the works of Lope de Vega, Tirso de Molina, Guillén de Castro, Juan Ruiz de Alarcón, Sor Juana Inés de la Cruz, and Calderón de la Barca with the works of other early modern playwrights, we can trace the influence of the jongleuresque tradition on the development of the Spanish and English stages, particularly in the enduring performative dialogue between actor and spectator. For example, Lope's *Fuenteovejuna* (in act 1, lines 455–528),

Shakespeare's *Henry V* (in the prologue, spoken by a singular Chorus), and Calderón's *La vida es sueño* (act 1, lines 49–72) depend heavily on the stage presence of de facto jongleurs who—whether speaking directly to the audience or indirectly, through onstage listeners—performatively create the imaginative settings necessary for the presentation of scenes that were unstageable without the kind of scenic technology we routinely take for granted today. In fact, in Alarcón's *La verdad sospechosa,* Don Juan's response to Don García's elaborate description of a party that never occurred can be read as nothing less than a homage to the power of jongleuresque performance: "Por Dios que la aueys pintado / de colores tan perfetas, / que no trocara el oyrla, / por auerme hallado en ella" (1.749–52) ("You've painted such a picture of last night, / My friend, with such detail and in such bright / Colors that I could not be sure, I swear, / If I was hearing it—or actually there"). Likewise, plays like *A Midsummer Night's Dream,* whose final act consists of a burlesque play-within-a-play presented by a group of rustic mechanicals, and Sor Juana's *Festejo de los empeños de una casa,* particularly in the second *sainete,* where rambunctious members of a seventeenth-century audience threaten to destroy a performance of a *comedia* by whistling at it, facetiously stage the jongleuresque tradition that lies at the heart of their theatrical worlds. Nick Bottom, who expresses a desire to insert an impromptu ballad into "Piramus and Thisby" to please his audience, and Castaño, who speaks directly to the spectators as they watch his performance unfold, are embodiments of the enduring presence of the medieval jongleur on the early modern stage. (The same jongleuresque energy can be discerned—again, to varying degrees—in the works of Lope de Rueda, Flaminio Scala, Molière, and other performers connected to the commedia dell'arte tradition.)

Perhaps the dichotomy between the indeterminate and the overdetermined theaters—between dynamic and static modes of performance—is no better represented than in two versions of essentially the same play: Guillén de Castro's *Las mocedades del Cid* and Pierre Corneille's *Le Cid* (based on Castro's work). Castro's text, coming out of the Lopean school, is full of jongleuresque energy. Closely following the ballad tradition from which it takes most of its material, it encompasses several years, numerous plots, and a number of locations. More important, the play relies on jongleuresque narrators who—like many Lopean characters from *El último godo, El caballero de Olmedo,* and *Peribáñez y el comendador de Ocaña*—recite the very ballads that inspired the play (ballads perhaps sung at one time or another by the spectators who now sit watching the spectacle). Corneille's version, in contrast, eliminates most of the jongleuresque elements in an attempt to accommodate itself to the neoclassicism then in vogue in the French capital. It is not surprising, of course, that *Le Cid* has more in common with the classically inspired *Phèdre* than with the seventeenth-century *comedia* on which it is based. And the divergence stems from Corneille's conscious decision to move his play toward a performance model based more on rhetorical declamation than on mimetic representation. Performance—even if merely latent—makes all the difference.

The Comedia *in Performance*

And this point brings us to our final performative context. Although we often talk about the importance of close reading in literature courses, there can be no closer reading of a dramatic text than that undertaken by actors in rehearsal. A reader, sitting alone with a book, can fixate on certain elements of the text, to the exclusion of other important aspects, especially if the poetic language seems to constitute a psychological barrier to understanding. But when actors rehearse the text aloud—particularly if they are serious about their work—no unfamiliar word, no difficult line, no complicated subtext can be easily glossed over. Moreover, as actors synergistically interact, new impulses are discovered and explored, even if most of these (often contradictory) motivations are eventually discarded. Thus I require students to engage in a process of scene work (similar to exercises at acting workshops). These exercises challenge them to test the possibilities—as well as probe the limits—of the *comedia* by fleshing out its characters and conflicts in an exploration that evolves, over time, as they play off each other in a series of performative permutations.

I usually begin this segment of the class (even in courses devoted to the *comedia*) with a brief discussion of a scene from *Bodas de sangre*, summarizing Federico García Lorca's tragedy, if necessary, for those students who may not know it. Toward the end of the play, the Novio, who has been pursuing the Novia and Leonardo during the third act, finally catches up with the two lovers. Shortly thereafter, the two men kill each other in an offstage climax described as follows. "La escena adquiere una fuerte luz azul. Se oyen los dos violines. Bruscamente se oyen dos largos gritos desgarrados, y se corta la música de los violines" (155) ("The stage takes on a strong blue light. The two violins are heard. Suddenly two long, piercing screams are heard and the music of the violins stops"). After reading this passage aloud, I remind students that we do not find out until the following scene what exactly has happened offstage, and I ask them to consider how the written text maintains our suspense. What I hope they discover—although, in truth, I usually end up having to explain—is that the passive voice in the stage directions ("*se oyen . . . dos gritos*") enables the reader to turn the page not yet knowing who has died. But I also point out that in performance there is no such thing as a *passive* voice: all voices—being always already embodied—are necessarily *active*. Hence, the director and the performers do not have the luxury (as does the reader) of deferring the meaning of those passive screams into the final scene. Choices have to be made at the moment of performance as to which of the actors will scream, how the screams will be articulated, and what semiotic information will be conveyed by the recognizable human voices that produce the screams.

At this point, I divide the students into groups of two or three and ask them to rehearse a scene (outside class) from one of the *comedias* on our reading list, and to present it (in class) to their colleagues for discussion and feedback. Although students in Spanish and Latin American literature courses cannot be expected to perform the scenes like theater majors, much less like professional actors, the corporeal engagement with the text in performance can be illuminating. The process works best—and I emphasize the importance of process over product—when students are given ample time to rehearse, especially during a second phase, after the initial performance, so that they can incorporate and explore ideas generated through the postperformance feedback. Ideally, the semester culminates in a series of final performances that involve a class discussion about the process of bringing a *comedia* to life. The discussion includes commentary on the obstacles faced, the strategies employed in overcoming the obstacles, and discoveries that resulted from choices specifically made in performance. Under the best of circumstances, students' final research papers should examine issues they have explored in rehearsal, so that their written work can incorporate discoveries they have made while bringing the text to life. Having located their *comedia* first in the context of Western theater history, then in the context of other early modern European traditions, and finally in the context of an embodied performance in the here and now, students may well leave class knowing at least one play extremely well. And their detailed knowledge can provide a strong foundation for any number of encounters with the theater, whether as readers, spectators, or even (perhaps) performers.

On Teaching Non-*Comedia* Festive Drama of Early Modern Spain

Vincent Martin

Despite the tremendous impetus in Spain since the 1960s to analyze the theories and practices of non-*comedia* festive drama (Arellano; Arellano et al.; Asensio; Bergman; Buezo, *Carnaval, Mojiganga, Prácticas,* and *Teatro*; Díez Borque, *Fiesta,* "Relaciones," and *Teatro*; García Lorenzo; García Valdés; Huerta Calvo, *Teatro breve en la Edad de Oro*; Rodríguez and Tordera, and others), the subgenres that constitute this vast corpus of works continue to be undertaught in the American core curriculum. A recent analysis of graduate reading lists in the United States reveals serious shortcomings in the inclusion of drama that we could call "festive"; specifically, from among the many available specimens of such non-*comedia* drama, only Cervantes's *Entremeses* and Calderón's *El gran teatro del mundo* appeared on more than fifty percent of the lists examined (Brown and Johnson 14). While the canonical *comedia* enjoys scrutiny from innovative as well as more traditional perspectives, the *teatro breve* (particularly the *jácaras, mojigangas,* and even, to a large extent, *entremeses*) and *autos sacramentales* are, with few exceptions, absent from United States classrooms. Since the exploration of festive drama lies at the crossroads of many disciplines—anthropology, sociology, philology, and religious and cultural studies—classroom suppression of these dramatic subgenres undermines current trends in pedagogy and deprives our students of a more contextualized approach to early modern Spanish theater.

Poststructuralism has successfully insisted on the text beyond the text, a notion that is fundamental to all dramatic theory, but especially to popular forms of comic drama in which the script "achieves its maximum degree of effectiveness" in conjunction with extratextual elements such as gesture, movement, costume, makeup, acrobatics, music, and dance (Rodríguez and Tordera 43). The teaching of literature as culture, clearly one of the goals of our profession, is well served by an encounter with the interplay of festival and theater: "If we wish to penetrate the daily life of the people of Velázquez's era, it is particularly important to understand what their favorite amusements and diversions were and in what contexts they were developed" (Sanz Ayán 195). To this multidisciplinary end, I regularly teach a course titled Fiesta y Teatro, which studies the relations between fiesta and theater in early modern Spain, with a focus on the shorter plays written for the Catholic feasts of carnival and Corpus Christi. I prefer to teach this course, which I have offered on an undergraduate level as well as to a mixed group of graduate (MA) students and undergraduates, in the spring semester, to follow the rhythm of the liturgical calendar that grounds the material. Because the beginning of our spring semester tends to coincide with carnival, I initiate the course by giving students a general overview of this Catholic feast of inversion, and I ask them to imagine ways in which Spaniards might celebrate the eve of Ash Wednesday; they submit a list to me before leaving class. Students read and prepare the chapter on carnival in María Ángeles Sánchez's *Fiestas populares* as well as Max Harris's "Carnival in Galicia" and Mariana Regalado's "*Entroido* in Laza, Spain" for group discussion in the next class, after which I show selections of Jesús Lozano's film *Entroido en Laza*. The "shock value" of the Laza carnival offers American students a radical experience with another culture and introduces them to thinking about the liturgical year and the festivals that mark its cycles.

My next step is to take students from carnival as celebrated today in a village in rural Galicia to the practices in Madrid during this holiday under the reign of Philip IV; the project is carried out by reading a few key selections (from Buezo, *Carnaval*; Deleito y Piñuela; Sanz Ayán). While José Deleito y Piñuela provides a wealth of information and writes in a quaint style, many undergraduates have commented that they find his book not only difficult to read but also boring. I have since altered my dependence on this book and now have students learn about carnivalesque practices from the initial chapters of Buezo's *Carnaval*, which is then complemented by selections from Deleito y Piñuela to cover remaining materials. The first dramatic text that I assign is Calderón's *Las carnestolendas*, a brief interlude that encapsulates perfectly the customs and practices described in the secondary readings.

If language is a barrier to American students of the *comedia*, the obstruction is heightened in these works that are teeming with seventeenth-century street slang, which is typically bawdy or scatological. Curiously, Mikhail Bakhtin, the sine qua non of carnival studies in the United States, underscores carnivalesque language as a "stumbling block" for readers of Rabelais, who considered such elements a "filthy depravation" (La Bruyère) or sheer "impertinence" (Voltaire) (145). After going over the high jinks described by the secondary readings, students receive a detailed vocabulary sheet with English equivalents (see app., at the end of the essay), which I compile for all plays to be read during the semester. I also distribute a scene breakdown as an aid in comprehending the different moments, or "scenes," of these plays; the scene divisions are of course my own. Finally, students are given study questions for each play, to test reading comprehension as well as theoretical or cultural aspects.

Such aids facilitate students' preparation of the reading for the next class meeting and reduce the severe frustration caused by the linguistic impediments inherent in the *teatro breve* in general. While instructor preparation of study sheets (vocabulary, scene division, study questions) for each of the works requires a considerable investment of time, the payoff is evident. Students have remarked that they have to know a great deal about carnival practices before the jokes are funny; customs we examine include the throwing of eggs, the foods eaten during the festival, and the mocking of the other (in Calderón's interlude, a black African and a German); students have told me that the handouts are crucial to their success in this course. Subsequent sessions can therefore concentrate on interpreting jokes and cultural references that are beyond the students' grasp—such as the *vejete* (old geezer) as a stock character, the fact that Prado was a popular stage manager of the time, and the folkloric characters personified on stage—without having to summarize the plot; explanation of vocabulary is also reduced. Consequently, the class can focus on elements that are, ironically, given short shrift in Spanish drama courses in the American academy: ideas about scene blocking, staging techniques, casting, and the like.

Once the customs of carnival and the first example of this dramatic literature have been discussed, the next step in our journey is a theoretical introduction that I present to students through selected readings (Buezo, *Teatro breve*; Huerta Calvo, *Teatro breve en la Edad de Oro*; Rodríguez and Tordera). This approach allows us to explore the concepts and development of the three subgenres of the *teatro breve* taken up in our course—the *jácara*, the *mojiganga*, and the *entremés*. Graduate students are given additional readings of a more theoretical nature (Bakhtin; Caro Baroja, *Carnaval*; Cox; Heers). I find Buezo's *Teatro breve* extremely useful, since her introduction describes succinctly the parameters and nuances of the subgenres, followed by carefully selected dramatic examples: interludes by Francisco de Quevedo, Cervantes, and Luis Quiñones de Benavente; a *jácara* by Calderón; and a *mojiganga* by Vicente Suárez de Deza. While Buezo's selections are exemplary in their ability to define the subgenres, and her didactic apparatus aimed at students is helpful, these dramatic pieces do not, in my opinion, provide much entertainment—a key ingredient to both theater and festival. Thus, for reasons having more to do with the spirit of the *fiesta* than with a strictly intellectual endeavor, and after several years of trial by fire, the following burlesque short pieces make up my repertoire: Quiñones de Benavente's *Los coches, El doctor Juan Rana*; Cervantes's *El juez de los divorcios, El vizcaíno fingido, El retablo de las maravillas, El viejo celoso*; Calderón's *Las carnestolendas, La garapiña, Las visiones de la muerte, Los instrumentos, El desafío de Juan Rana, Guardadme las espaldas, El toreador*. In preparation for *Las visiones de la muerte*, students are naturally required to read, in advance, part 2, chapter 11, of *Don Quixote*. Colleagues may be interested to note that I have attempted to teach Calderón's burlesque comedy *Céfalo y Pocris*, but I found the manifold difficulties insurmountable for undergraduates, despite the excellent annotated edition produced by GRISO (see Arellano et al., *Comedias*) and a videotape I own of Teatro Estudio Alcalá's stellar performance of this play in 1995.

Since the spectator (*theoros*) as participant lies at the center of any theoretical dialogue on (and hermeneutic approach to) festive drama—"To be present means to participate. . . . watching something is a genuine mode of participating" (Gadamer 124)—class discussion on the particulars of these subgenres points toward a visualization of the material; I never let students forget that they are not just reading a funny story. Since these carnivalesque plays can be performed with a minimalist set design, our visually oriented students "in the era of television and cinema" (Bloom 491) tend to undertake with great eagerness practical aspects such as scene blocking. For this exercise, students are divided into small groups and asked to stage one of the scenes (each group is given a different scene to en-act during the next class session); rather than memorize their lines, students read while they act out the situations. Those without lines participate as scene direc-tor, costume and set designers, and so on. Without any cue from me, students inevitably make imaginative use of classroom space and incorporate the chalk-board for the drawing of elaborate backdrops. While each group represents its scene, the other groups watch (participate) and take notes. Peer discussion with critical analysis follows.

This hands-on approach to theater grounds my work with students, particu-larly in my course on festive drama, since these texts are nothing short of an in-vitation to play (see Martin, "Play")—the crux not only of the relation between festival and theater but of the study of culture itself: "culture arises in the form of play" (Huizinga 46). In this regard, the Spanish stage director Luis Dorrego's work with American university students in Madrid is exemplary and worthy of our attention (and applause). In spring 2004, for example, his New York Univer-sity students adapted and performed Calderón's interlude *La casa de los linajes,* which they fittingly retitled *¿Jugamos?*; they even designed and created the pro-motional flyer for their production. That summer, under Dorrego's direction, students from the University of Delaware staged—to a packed house—their ingenious adaptation of Cervantes's interlude *El retablo de las maravillas* in Madrid's intimate Karpas Teatro. The pedagogical merits of using festive drama as a playful learning medium go beyond the mere linguistic application and ac-tually lead students to make self-discoveries, as many in the Delaware program confessed to me in their final reports.

This "play element of culture" (Huizinga i) is the thread that runs through my course, from the *teatro breve* to the *autos sacramentales.* Some aspects of the feast of Corpus Christi, which the *autos* were written to celebrate, have already been discussed in the first half of the course when students read Sanz Ayán's chapter as well as Calderón's burlesque pieces *Los instrumentos* and *Las visiones de la muerte,* two plays that I never omit from my curriculum. In the second half of the semester, after discussing briefly how Holy Week fits into the liturgical cycle that we are studying, I add selections from Deleito y Piñuela's book as well as certain passages of my monograph on the *autos,* to show the surprising con-nectedness between the carnivalesque pieces and the *autos,* the "marriage of the sacred and the profane" (Martin, *Concepto* 20). This transition, made easier by a reexamination, in these two interludes, of the ludic elements having to do with the *autos* or with Corpus Christi, allows students to see the festive flow that runs through the liturgical year and manifests itself in diverse ways but always toward the purge of emotions. In this regard, it is useful to point out the almost Pavlov-ian response by Rechonchón (the "old Christian" mayor in *Los instrumentos*) to the promise of a theatrical performance on this feast of Corpus Christi (which the audience is also celebrating with a play), as well as his anti-Semitic pun with the word *auto*, which again underscores the sense of community and alterity that is crucial to ritualistic drama. Similarly, Calderón's *Las visiones de la muerte*, a masterful rewriting of Cervantes's chapter on "the wagon or cart of 'The Parliament of Death'" (in *Don Quixote* 478), opens with the last moment of a performance of an *auto* that the players must hurry off to enact in another town, which is why they cannot change out of their costumes. The entire space of the interlude occurs in the profane "in-betweenness" marked by the officially sanctioned public performance of allegorical religious characters and actions, and the work highlights once more the close relation between the burlesque pieces and the *autos*.

Calderón's *No hay instante sin milagro* is an excellent *auto* to include in this course: not only is it one of the playwright's finest works, it also highlights the bond between ritual and drama and makes for an exemplary play for graduate students doing theoretical readings in performance studies (Turner; Schechner, *Essays, Performance Studies*; Rappaport, "Aspects," *Ritual*). Calderón seems to anticipate the ritual-theater-ritual continuum that Richard Schechner would study in his well-known essay "From Ritual to Theatre and Back" (63–98); the playwright opens his *auto* with the citizens of Madrid celebrating the feast of Corpus Christi, just as the citizens of Madrid who are watching the play offstage are doing. As in *Las visiones de la muerte*—as well as in many other works—Calderón holds up for scrutiny the notion of onstage and offstage, a key concept in the study of festival and theater. Into this ritualistic celebration steps Apostasy (allegorical personification of King James I of England), the other who comes to rain on their Catholic parade through her inability to grasp the reason for joy on this holiday that she believes is better suited for tears. This allows Faith (allegorical personification of the Spanish Jesuit theologian Francisco Suárez) to become a stage director and represent scenes that will help Apostasy comprehend the theological mysteries of the Eucharist, as well as the fact that miracles are not simply a thing of the past but are happening all the time. This "intellectual duel" (*No hay instante* 122) is the agon that sets in motion the stunningly modern series of visual proofs that allow Faith to defeat her opponent. Once the conversion of Apostasy takes place, the characters onstage return to their celebration of the feast of Corpus Christi, thus marking the end of the play and the return of the audience to their celebration of the feast: "from ritual to theatre and back." In addition to giving students a vocabulary sheet, I assign the chapter of my book on the *autos* that analyzes this play in detail (Martin, *Concepto* 152–83). Although perhaps a bit expensive for students to purchase (28 euros), the critical edition prepared by Arellano et al. is doubtless the best edition available and certainly worth putting on reserve in the library.

Another *auto* that follows the ritual-drama-ritual continuum is Calderón's *A Dios por razón de estado*. Calderón opens the play with pre-Christian Greeks celebrating holy festivities, a situation that clearly mirrors the audience of *madrileños* who are celebrating their holy day. As in *Instante*, the festivities are interrupted so that a theological dilemma—in this case, the search for the Unknown God (*Ignoto Deo*) of the New Testament (Acts 17.23)—may be resolved through a debate that will become the play within the play and finish with the return to the festivities. Curiously, the debate takes place between the figure of Ingenuity (allegorical personification of Dionysius the Pseudo-Areopagite) and his Thought, culminating in his famous conversion to Christianity. Significantly, this confrontation between paganism and Christianity belongs not only to the realm of religious history but also to that of carnival: "Carnival is virtually the representation of paganism itself face-to-face with Christianity" (Caro Baroja, *Carnaval* 153). In the light of this remark by the authoritative voice of Spanish carnival studies, it is useful to incorporate this *auto* into the curriculum, in order to compare the syncretism of this piece with the clash of symbols seen in carnival (e.g., the *peliqueiros* [carnivalesque figure in an animal mask] appearing in Lozano's film and described in the essays by Harris and Regalado).

While these two *autos* are exemplary in their manifestation of the interconnectedness of *fiesta* and theater, students are extremely fond of what may be Calderón's best-known *autos*, at least in the United States: *El gran teatro del mundo* and *El gran mercado del mundo*. Also, that these two pieces have been published together by Cátedra, edited and with helpful notes by Eugenio Frutos Cortés, makes them easily accessible, more economical, and possibly more teacher-friendly for the American classroom. The play within the play of *El gran teatro del mundo* begins with the Autor (God as stage director and, by extension, creator of the *auto*) invoking a celebration of his power through the performance of a play, precisely the combination of theater and *fiesta* that grounds this course:

> I mean to celebrate
> My power infinitely great.
> . . . .
> Now as we know
> That the most pleasing entertainment is a show
> . . . .
> I choose that Heaven shall today
> Upon your stage witness a play.   (*Great Stage* 2)

The rest of the festive play within the festive play is an acid test of each character's charity, the theological virtue that will determine the destination of his or her soul. In *El gran mercado del mundo*, the paterfamilias (God) gives each of his two sons a "talent," to see who will make the best use of the coin at the "vanity fair" of the world. The well-disposed son (Buen Genio) naturally wins the girl of his dreams (Grace) while the ill-disposed son (Mal Genio) is sent off with

Sin. In my experience, undergraduates prefer the allegories of these two *autos* over the dogmatic density of the previously discussed pieces, which are better suited for graduate students.

Statistics show that non-*comedia* festive drama of early modern Spain is not adequately represented in the American college curriculum, and students are consequently coming away with a fragmented view of the theater and culture of this period. In a recent review article, Ingrid Rowland writes: "Despite prevailing gossip in the groves of academe, people still like their Renaissance" (21). If Rowland's assessment of postmodern taste for early modern European culture is correct—and I believe it is—we owe it to our students to open the door onto this multidisciplinary field of dramatic art that challenges students to think outside the box of *comedia* studies. By leaving that door closed, by limiting—and, on many campuses, even reducing—our offerings in early modern dramatic literature, we shall never satisfy our rumored desires to create approaches and to rethink the canon, nor shall we satisfy our audience's desire for their renaissance.

NOTE

Translations of secondary sources in Spanish are mine.

APPENDIX: Calderón's *Las carnestolendas*

Glossary

Alborotar to agitate

Aljófar small pearl or dew drop (here, drop of wine)

Alzar to lift

Antiguallas relics

Aporreadas beaten up

Arre *harre* expresses someone having left without saying goodbye

Arrebozada covered by a cloak

Avariento greedy

Ayunar to go without

Azareños filled with orange flower water

Besallos *besarlos*

Bonete *fez* (hat worn by North Africans)

Buchorno *bochorno* stifling heat

Calamerdos perhaps a combination of *calamento* (flowering mint) and *mierda*

De capirote without consideration

Capón castrated chicken

Casadillas *quesadillas* cheesecakes

Casamueza *camuesa* pippin apple

Chamuscadas singed

Chanza fun, joke, mockery

Chasco trick

Chata flattened

Cizaña discord

Cochelate chocolate

Col cabbage

Colacione *colaciones* light meals, snacks

Cómante *que te coman*

Concomer to consume

Convaleciente convalescing

Convidar to invite
Cosquilloso ticklish
Criar callos *lit.* to get corns (on feet); also, to get used to something (usually bad habits)
Decillo *decirlo*
Demo *demos*
Derretidos in love
Desconcierto confusion
Destos *de estos*
Dinerillo pittance, small amount of money
Diluvio universal the Flood
Disparate foolish remark
Enaguas petticoat
Engullir to gobble down
Enjuta dry
Enmoñarse to get drunk
Ensartar to string together
Entonarse to put on airs
Escabeche marinade, pickle
Escollos obstacles
Esportillero a mover, hauler
Estopas burlap
Estregadera scrub brush
Exenta shameless
Fregonicar perhaps a combination of *fregar* (to wash) and *fornicar* (to fornicate)
Fregona scrubwoman
Grana maroon
Gualdada *guardada*
Habas beans
Herraduras horseshoes
Hojaldre puff pastry
Jarro pitcher
Jeringa syringe
Judiguelo *judihuelo* little Jew
Mamola trick
Mancebos young men
El mantenga y el sepades the laws
Maza tail
Mentar to name or mention

Merdelada combination of *mierda* and *mermelada*
Meterse de gorra to stick one's nose in
Morcilla blood sausage
Mozalbete small boy
Navidades many years
Noramala *en hora mala* dammit
Palillos spindles
Palos de tambor drumsticks
Pandorga variety of instruments making lots of noise
Papanduja soft from old age
Parda used to express deep reflection
Pasapán throat
Pedrada exclamation indicating someone deserves punishment for an action
Picarona crafty devil
Pimpollos shoots, buds
Ponzoña venom
Pringar to dirty, soil, scorch with boiling oil
Pullas gibes
Quelemole *querémosle*
Raída shameless
Rancia old, rancid
Randas lace trimming
Relamida wearing too much makeup
Remedar to imitate
Requebrar to flatter
Rociar to spray or sprinkle
Rollonas plump, chubby
Roscón ring-shaped pastry
Retozar to frisk, romp about
De sainete dressed up
Sotanilla short cassock
Sueñecillo drowsiness
Supitaña sudden
Tapete rug
Tarabilla jabber, chatter
Tararira festive saying
Testa head
Tetuán city in Africa
Tizne soot

Tizona sword (the name of El Cid's sword)

Torcer to twist

Tudesco German

Uchoó a shout used to provoke falcons or bulls

Usasted *usted*

Usté *usted*

Vejigas bladders

Volaverunt *Lat.* they have flown

Vuesancé *vuestra merced*

Vuesarced *vuestra merced*

Zampar to gobble down

Zancadilla trick

Zangamanga trick

Zarabanda lascivious dance

Scene Breakdown

SCENE 1 (lines 1–70)

The daughters want to celebrate the feast of carnival with a play, but their father is old and miserly and he adopts an antifestive position. To help Rufina pull off her trick, Luisa pins a tail on Rufina's boyfriend. Meanwhile, the old man launches his complaint about carnival.

SCENE 2 (lines 71–121)

Rufina's boyfriend comes onto stage in the role of the gracioso (comic actor), with a tail pinned to his backside, which turns him into the object of derision. He gets mad and tells a few jokes with double meanings. The old man apologizes for his daughter and attempts to send the gracioso off, but then decides to satisfy the "addiction" of his daughters to see plays. Coincidently, the gracioso is a stage director and he promises an amusing, professional production. The old man wants to feed the director before the show begins, but the gracioso decides that he will eat and drink at the same time as he puts on the performance. All are amazed by his ability to eat and drink so much, and so quickly.

SCENE 3 (lines 122–87)

The gracioso comes out to stage a series of imitations or representations of various characters or types. First he imitates Prado, a famous director. The humor lies in the fact that Prado was actually the director of *Las carnestolendas* and that the characters of Rufina and María were actually actresses named Rufina and María. Then, the gracioso, who is actually Prado, comes out imitating himself (i.e., imitating the well-known director Prado). He drinks wine while he imitates himself. The next character that he imitates or represents is an old man (whose similarities to the father of the girls is no coincidence). Then he imitates or represents a black African, and finally a German. Since Germans were known to be heavy drinkers, Prado/gracioso falls down drunk and passes out (was he really drinking wine?).

SCENE 4 (lines 188–215)

The old man goes to look for a laborer to take away the drunken gracioso, and when he leaves the house, the gracioso (Prado) gets up and puts his plan into action: to steal the old man's money and jewels and to run off with Rufina. Rufina's sisters are accomplices to her escape. When the old man returns, he finds that they have stolen his jewels and he considers that these are atrocities from another era (*son del tiempo del rey que rabió*).

SCENE 5 (lines 216–75)

Now a whole series of characters from Spanish folklore parade onto stage and say ridiculous things, but they all underscore the fact that the old man is not in the playful spirit of carnival: the raging king; Marta with her chicks; Perico el de los Palotes; Maricastaña. We also see the personification of the baroque topos of the world turned upside down and the lady Quintañona (a character from *Don Quixote*).

SCENE 6 (lines 276–87)

Happy ending for everyone except the old man. Music, song, and dance bring the *fiesta* to a close.

Sample Study Questions

1. What are the names of the *vejete*'s daughters?
2. Who is the gracioso?
3. Why won't the *vejete* let his daughters go out and have fun? (Hint: see footnote 9.)
4. What link between festival and theater do we see in the daughters' desires?
5. What do the daughters and the gracioso steal from the *vejete* at the end of the *entremés*?
6. Who comes back to torment the *vejete*?

Reinventing Texts in a New (Historical) Context: Spanish *Comedia* and Shakespeare

Susan L. Fischer

My course Reinventing Texts in a New (Historical) Context: Spanish *Comedia* and Shakespeare is designed to provide a comparative view of the drama of two nations—England and Spain—in a past and present context. It is offered as an undergraduate seminar (a handful of graduate students in English also enroll from time to time) and cross-listed in the departments of English and Spanish and the Program in Comparative Humanities. A number of Shakespeare plays are examined alongside Calderonian counterparts (e.g., *Henry VIII* and *The Schism in England*; *Measure for Measure* and *The Painter of Dishonor*; *The Tempest* and *Life Is a Dream*), which exist in good bilingual editions or English translations and, in many cases, have been performed on the British and Spanish stages. The plays raise equivalent sorts of social, political, and moral questions, which are studied intertextually, both against the historical time of production and the contemporary moment of reconstruction. (Other combinations might include *Measure for Measure* and Lope de Vega's *Punishment without Revenge*; Calderón's *The Physician of Honor* and *Othello*; *Hamlet* and *Life Is a Dream*.) The initial pairing of *The Schism in England* and *Henry VIII* affords an overview of the way the Reformation and the Counter Reformation changed the course of history in early modern England and Spain. The Spanish *comedia* is more profitably apprehended, not in terms of its formal dissimilarity to other national European theaters but as a forum for dialectical engagement with "an emerging secular ideology that gains an irreversible momentum by the seventeenth century" and with historical phenomena and their contemporary understanding in relation to postmodern sensibilities (Soufas and Soufas 294).

Students read articles on Calderón and Shakespeare that employ distinctive critical approaches (e.g., reader response, new historicist, cultural materialist, feminist). We evaluate the strengths and weaknesses of the articles according to what they enable the reader (or spectator) to discover or interpret about the texts and what they obfuscate or ignore. Alternatively, we examine directorial choices in the light of (post)modern performance practices through actors' explorations of the way they created their roles with the Royal Shakespeare Company (RSC), recounted in the four-volume series *Players of Shakespeare* (Smallwood); and through information on stagings by the Compañía Nacional de Teatro Clásico in Madrid, drawn from my research on the *comedia* in performance. Besides the usual format of readings, lectures, discussions, oral presentations of critical articles, and essays written on prescribed topics, the seminar includes viewings of plays in production, subject to availability (e.g., the BBC Shakespeare series; and clips from Pilar Miró's film version of Lope de Vega's *El perro de hortelano* [*The*

Dog in the Manger], which makes *comedia* construction and latter-day staging visually, if not verbally, accessible to Hispanophones and Anglophones alike).

From a performance perspective, the motivating question of the course is the one that virtually every director asks before mounting a classical text: Why *this* play now? Before the first class meeting, students peruse François Laroque's *The Age of Shakespeare*, a delightful little book with almost as many pictures as words, as well as some basic material on early modern acting traditions in England and Spain, from *Actors on Acting* (Cole and Chinoy). The background reading prepares them for the course focus on the theatrical and historical context of a play in relation to its initial performance, followed by subsequent interpretations on stage, under the impact of changing sociopolitical and cultural contexts in the (post)modern period. Video excerpts from *Playing Shakespeare* are most effective for establishing the idea of performing *comedia* and Shakespeare. John Barton, former artistic director of the RSC, along with a group of well-known Shakespearean actors, investigates before the cameras how Shakespeare's text actually works, examining the use of verse and prose, set speeches and soliloquies, language and character, and other topics. However different *comedia* is from Shakespeare, the third tape in the series, "The Two Traditions: Elizabethan and Modern Acting," bridges the gap between the "heightened"— poetic—language of the earlier texts and the more "naturalistic" acting style of the modern age, while it shows a need for a "marriage" between the two. This glimpse into contrastive acting styles and the handling of verse on stage becomes all the more meaningful if it is accompanied by video clips of opening scenes from two wholly dissimilar film versions of *Henry V*. The earlier, and presumably more authentic, starring a youthful Lawrence Olivier, allows students to see how public theater functioned in Shakespeare's day (and, by implication, Calderón's). Contrastively, in Kenneth Branagh's (post)modern screening of *Henry V*, the audience is urged by Derek Jacobi, the player interpreting the Prologue, to let their "imaginary forces work" on the bare backstage set transformed into a latter-day "wooden O" before their very eyes. At the outset, then, students come to realize that the dramatic text of any period is a script for performance and, moreover, that staging is a matter of interpretation.

In the next phase of constructing a so-called companion to Shakespeare and the *comedia*, students are assigned background material on the sociopolitical and religious weltanschauung of the early modern period—Elizabethan (and Stuart) England and Habsburg Spain. They commence the leap backward with E. M.W. Tillyard's polemical book *The Elizabethan World Picture* as a way of demonstrating that, however much the age was obsessed with the idea of hierarchy, order, and degree (captured in the overruling notion of the Great Chain of Being), the very idea of such a world picture is fundamentally reductive. Clearly, not everybody during the period thought in the same way, nor could Shakespeare (and, by association, Calderón) be reduced to an all too simple political or metaphysical scheme. (The same issue arises with respect to A. A. Parker's conception of "*the* approach to the Spanish drama of the Golden Age" ["Approach"], but by then students should be sensitive to the reductiveness of such a totalizing viewpoint.) Tillyard is explored against certain pivotal essays in Shakespeare studies that, in critiquing and deconstructing his essentialist argument, underscore the radical contingency of reader, writer, and historian, historicized as they are by their material conditions and social contexts. For example, the class reads chapters from Michael Mangan's *A Preface to Shakespeare's Tragedies* (religious and philosophical developments, in particular Protestantism and scientific thought; issues of government and authority in the reigns of Elizabeth I and James I; and notions of hierarchy and degree in Elizabethan and Jacobean society); Jonathan Dollimore's "Shakespeare, Cultural Materialism, and the New Historicism"; and Jean E. Howard's "The New Historicism in Renaissance Studies." This material is intended to enable students to play off Tillyard's mind-set with reference to the pervasiveness of the orthodox scheme of salvation in the Elizabethan Age: "You could revolt against it but you could not ignore it" (18). The idea is for them, too, to revolt, to discern that Tillyard's error (from a materialist perspective) is not so much to identify a metaphysic of order in the period but falsely to combine history and social process in the name of "the collective mind of the people" (Dollimore 5). The point is made early on, then, that just as students probably would not want to be homogenized as "contemporary Americans," they should be wary of constructing the people of early modern England and Spain as "Elizabethans" or as "people of the Golden Age" rather than as individual men and women from various social, economic, political, and educational backgrounds. A good clincher to the debate is that, as Mangan observes, the world picture painted by the myriad writers Tillyard cites is, in large measure, a representation of the world as certain people thought it *should* be, rather than as it was, born of a need to defend the status quo (30).

Given the plethora of alternative approaches to, and deconstructive interrogations of, historical process, we can easily lose sight of the delicate balance that perforce must be maintained between abstract theoretical discourse and concrete dramatic representation. A useful antidote can be found in the Royal Shakespeare Company's *Great Performances* video screening of scenes from the 1994–95 production of *King Lear*. Lear's raging against the terrors of the storm on the heath in 3.2.1 ("Blow, winds, and crack your cheeks! rage, blow!") are a graphic depiction of the disintegration and chaos implicit in the images of hierarchy, order, and degree that Tillyard has scrupulously tried to defend as the norm of the Elizabethan universe. On the Spanish side, passing reference can be made to Edward M. Wilson's classic essay "The Four Elements in the Imagery of Calderón," which examines how Calderón lets the confusion of the elements tell their story by allowing the creature or attribute of one element to be that of another.

Poststructural critical theory is complemented by historical material taken primarily from T. A. Morris's uncluttered, innovative course book for British A-level students, *Europe and England in the Sixteenth Century,* which offers an intertextual approach to the histories of British and continental countries in the era of the Renaissance, the Protestant Reformation, and the Catholic Counter Reformation. Through selected readings in Morris's integrated historical survey, students are introduced to the cast of characters they will meet, dramatized often in diametrically opposed ways, in *Henry VIII* and *The Schism in England.* Basic facts on the lives of the historical dramatis personae can also be gleaned from such palatable sources as Harold Barkley's *Likenesses in Line: An Anthology of Tudor and Stuart Engraved Portraits,* which provides bibliographic notes on the personages represented (e.g., Mary I; Philip II; Elizabeth I; Mary, Queen of Scots; James I; Shakespeare); and Peter Saccio's *Shakespeare's English Kings,* which, in juxtaposing the historical Henry VIII and those of his court with their fictional counterparts, enhances understanding not only of Shakespeare's text but also of Calderón's.

Drawing on information gleaned from the Morris text, students engage in self-conscious dialogue with the past as if they were journalists covering contemporary events in the history of two nations. Topics include the reign of Henry VIII (the ascendancy of Cardinal Wolsey and the Henrician Reformation); the rise of the Catholic monarchs, and Spain under Charles of Habsburg and Philip II (the Counter-Reformation, the reign of Mary Tudor, the proposed Spanish marriage, the division between the triumphant Spain of the first two Habsburgs and the disillusioned Spain of their successors, marked by the defeat of the Armada in 1588); and state, church, and society under Elizabeth I (the government of the realm, the religious settlement, the church and Puritanism). The return of history in literature through the influential if controversial movement new historicism, with its disruption of totalizing constructions of the past, provides a useful framework for probing fundamentally different dramatic appropriations of earlier events, by Shakespeare in *Henry VIII* and Calderón in *The Schism in England.*

Because students have already grappled with the slipperiness of historical investigation, they are more receptive to the enigmatic universe of *Henry VIII,* captured in its original, ambiguous title, *All Is True* (1613). It is "dominated by 'deceptive appearances' and the 'relativity of truth,' in which, in Pirandellian fashion, 'all is true' means precisely that *any* interpretation of the past may be true if one thinks it so, and no point of view is allowed to contain or control all others" (Rudnytsky 46). The students' task as readers is to comprehend the play's perspectivism in the depiction of character but, more important, in the conflicting versions of events leading to the great matter of the king's divorce. Ultimately, the idea is to see how Shakespeare, writing under James I, could both sustain and subvert the Elizabethan Protestant succession and the Tudor myth by confounding Henry's motives for abandoning his Spanish Queen Katherine. Was he moved more by the providential Protestant notion of a religious scruple regarding the lawfulness of his marriage to his brother's widow (Lev. 20.21); or, from a censorious Catholic standpoint, was the separation provoked by Henry's carnal desire for Anne Boleyn? (Shakespeare follows Cavendish's chronicle in insinuating that Henry's lust preceded the rumor of his divorce by having him meet Anne not in 1527 but around 1521; he disregards Holinshed, who is unambiguous in presenting the problem of conscience as a determining factor. Nevertheless, in Henry's apology for leaving Katherine, his conscience proves indistinguishable from his concupiscence: "Would it not grieve an able man to leave / So sweet a bedfellow? But conscience, conscience! / O 'tis a tender place, and I must leave her" [2.2.141–43]. Noteworthy, too, from a comparative perspective is the way that Shakespeare hints at the costs of the English Reformation, in his sympathetic portrayal of Katherine, who, in her dying moment, declares that Henry's "princely commendations" are "like a pardon after execution" [4.2.119, 121]).

Historical debate notwithstanding, Shakespeare can be read and taught "in ways that bring the dimensions of past constraint and modern viewpoint—the moment of production and the moment of reception—into dynamic reciprocity" (Ryan 15). Contemporary performance practices are crucial in this regard. In Greg Doran's 1996 staging of *Henry VIII* with the Royal Shakespeare Company, the ironic original title was emblazoned on the back wall of the Swan Theatre, thereby imprinting on the minds of spectators how the idea of truth is bent to suit individual purposes. That the play is accessible to modern audiences is also apparent, however anecdotally, from the response of the Prince of Wales, as recounted by the actor playing the part of Henry VIII in the Doran production: "It makes you realize how little things have changed. When one is born into a certain position you have people advising you all the time, whispering in your ear. It's only when you get to my age that you begin to work out who's telling you the truth" (Jesson 130–31). The perceived pertinence of Shakespeare to today's political sphere can foster a similar mind-set with respect to Calderón.

If Shakespeare composed an English history or chronicle play in which faithfulness to recorded history guides the structural pattern (notwithstanding some distortion of chronology and factual detail deployed, no doubt, to subvert the Protestant view of the schism), Calderón wrote not a history play but a conventional *comedia*. He offers a markedly Spanish perspective on a particular moment of English history, using as his source Pedro de Rivadeneira's chronicle *Historia ecclesiástica del scisma del reyno de Inglaterra* (1588). Students should be made aware that the play was written in late 1626 or early 1627, when England and Spain were once again at war. Consequently, attitudes were not especially conducive to the creation and performance of *comedias* complimentary to English history, as had perhaps been the case in 1623, during the so-called Spanish alliance. Not surprisingly, Calderón wrote from the perspective of an orthodox, nationalistic Catholic of the Counter Reformation; he had Anne Boleyn beheaded before Elizabeth I was ever conceived. In the final scene, the leaders of the English nation accept Mary as their future sovereign after she has sworn— albeit with a qualification about restoring Catholicism expressed in an aside—to obey the laws of the kingdom. It is as though "the danger of religious schism in England had been averted" (Loftis 214). María Cristina Quintero's analysis of those events in terms of the construction of gender is noteworthy—in particular, her point that "the misogyny and paranoia surrounding the question of women in power, especially for Spaniards, would have found justification in the formidable figure of Elizabeth" (262).

Read against *Henry VIII*, Calderon's *Schism in England* is a poignant reminder of the ways that nations appropriate history to (re)produce suitable ideological narratives. In George Mariscal's reading, for example, Shakespeare's Henry is presented in a variety of roles—administrator, husband, judge, lover, friend—but his improvisational shifting of subject position is thought to suggest the relative fluidity of Elizabethan social structures, whereas Calderón's Henry, despite his irrational comportment, is essentially a static character incapable of playing roles other than the one allotted to him by God (196). It is along the lines of fundamental social relations that other pairs of characters can be compared and contrasted.

By way of synthesis, sample topics for term papers featuring an interdisciplinary and comparative format are provided below. Students draft their essays after discussing and critiquing articles espousing a variety of critical or performance-oriented approaches to the two versions of Henry VIII (including my "Reader-Response" essay), and they are asked to address—by way of endorsement or refutation—a minimum of two external references in the construction of their arguments. The following assignments have worked well:

> *The sense of an ending.* "[W]hat's past is prologue" (*Tempest* 2.1.253) *Henry VIII* ends with the christening of the princess Elizabeth by the (Reformer) archbishop Cranmer, who prophesies that she will be a blessing to her kingdom and be followed by another ruler who will be equally admired (5.5.20). *The Schism in England* closes as though the schism had been averted, with public recognition of Mary as Henry's successor and without reference to Elizabeth. Why these different senses of an ending? How are they justified textually and historically? What "chosen truth" do they unveil (*Henry VIII*, Prologue, line 18). What truths do they obscure? What does it mean to say that "Shakespeare can no more justly be blamed for writing with an English bias than can Calderón for a Spanish—and Catholic—one" (Loftis 216)? Is one playwright more even-handed in his treatment of history than the other? If so, how?

> *Alter egos*   Henry VIII, Queen Katherine, Cardinal Wolsey, and Anne Boleyn all have so-called alter egos in *Henry VIII* and *The Schism in England*. Create an encounter between a pair of intertexual counterparts in which you compare and contrast them (e.g., Wolsey meets Wolsey) vis-à-vis their sociopolitical and religious contexts. To what extent are the infor-

mation and ideas you have about a character distorted or undermined in
the dramatic text as a result of power relations, changing material circumstances, internal growth and change, unconfirmed reports, private agendas, uninviting alternatives? What poetic images predominate in characters' self-descriptions and in the ways the personages are seen by others?
How have they been treated in performance (see articles by actors in the
case of Shakespeare), or how would you imagine them to be treated in performance (in the case of Calderón)?

Having grappled with what Louis Montrose dubs "the textuality of history"
("Professing" 20), and more particularly with the notion that elements of the literary text are inextricably linked to social relations at large, students are generally less awestruck by such outmoded concepts as honor and honorable revenge,
on which many Golden Age plays turn. *Comedia* performed in translation and in
foreign venues, in fact, can serve as a yardstick to measure student responses to
the plays because modern productions often identify major stumbling blocks for
today's theatergoers. Charles Spencer, for example, in his review of Rufus Norris's production of *Peribáñez* at the Young Vic Theater in 2003, makes a helpful
connection between "the apparently outdated concept of honour" and events in
today's world: "During the West's present battles against terrorism and rogue
states, these are surely knotty issues that resonate afresh. Could Lope's time have
come at last?" For Michael Billington, the play's interest goes beyond "the standard themes of honour, jealousy and class" as filtered through Lope's brand of
psychological subtlety. Positing a link with Angelo's query in *Measure for Measure*—"The tempter, or the tempted, who sins most?" (2.2.163)—Billington asserts that part of the greatness of Lope's play "lies in how it shows the technically
blameless Casilda driving the Commander mad and her husband to paroxysms
of jealousy" (28).

Indeed, in *Measure for Measure*, students are obliged to make sense of con-
cepts as alien to postmodern sensibilities as the tenets of the Spanish honor code.
How does one interpret, for example, Isabella's proclamation, "More than our
brother is our chastity" (2.4.185), or Duke Vincentio's assertion that Angelo is
Mariana's husband "on a pre-contract" (4.1.70)? Before attempting translations
of such anachronistic ideas vis-à-vis Shakespeare and Calderón, students read
Elizabeth Marie Pope's essay "The Renaissance Background of *Measure for
Measure*" and selections from Marcelin Defourneaux's *Daily Life in Spain in
the Golden Age*. Having perused such background material, they are better
equipped to contextualize the core of a Calderonian honor play and to attempt a
quasi-historicized exploration of the issues. This framework, too, enables them
to interrogate negative and untutored spectator reactions to *comedia* in performance, like Paul Taylor's offhand critique of the 1995 RSC production of *The
Painter of Dishonour*: "What this masochistic culture needed was a good dose
of Falstaff."

In answer to that sort of unproductive commentary, I assign my performance analysis "Historicizing *Painter of Dishonour* on the 'Foreign' Stage." Under-pinned by Dollimore's "radical" revision of tragedy, a materialist perspective that assumes human values to be informed by tangible conditions in a social and cul-tural process, the essay purports to circumvent encounters with the play in which the reaction is consternation rather than provocation, incredulity rather than outrage. How in fact do latter-day reading or spectating publics come to grips with *The Painter*'s "chilling" (Taylor) message in the last scene, which can be for-mulated as follows: Why does the play end tragically with undeserving deaths and contrived reprieve, yet fit structurally within the cadre of comedy? The sen-sitive reader or spectator who is steeped in the material reality of early modern honor is likely to have the richer understanding. These elements of discontinu-ity or rupture, which frustrate efforts to interpret the play in terms of a single generic code, may turn out to be less troublesome for students if they are viewed intertextually, along with the problematic ending of *Measure for Measure*, as a way of effecting a confrontation with the contradictory nature of society itself. Howard's essay on the difficulties of closure in Shakespearean comedy provides valuable insights on that score. Both *Measure* and *Painter*, instead of complying with the demands of formal generic harmony—the convention that would coun-tenance the attempt at resolution—conclude with irreconcilable events that challenge, if not undermine, the prospect of closure and restoration (Fischer, "Historicizing" 216).

The course's interdisciplinary and comparative approach to complex, rich plays like *Life Is a Dream* and *The Tempest* can best be schematized here by ref-erence to the final paper project, "Characters in Search of Each Other and of the Critics: Intertextual Encounters." I assign my comparative essay "'This Thing of Darkness I / Acknowledge Mine': Segismundo, Prospero, and *Shadow*" as a point of departure for this undertaking, which is divided into two separate but in-terrelated parts. First, students write an interactive or reactive autobiography of a character in *The Tempest*, who must be selected so as to be able to enter into dialogue with a counterpart from *Life Is a Dream* (e.g., Prospero and Segis-mundo; Prospero and Basilio; Caliban and Segismundo; Miranda and Rosaura; Trinculo or Stephano and Clarion; Ariel or Caliban and Segismundo; Courtiers and Astolfo or Estrella). In the second phase of the assignment, the character chosen from *The Tempest* engages dramatically with his or her alter ego, so to speak, or adversary from *Life Is a Dream*. Students may present a staged reading of the refashioned mini-play or of the resulting extradramatic scenes or acts.

Once themes common to the two plays have been identified, the pairing of characters falls readily into place. For example, both plays treat the issues of force and freedom; power or vengeance and forgiveness; passion (love, lust, rape = power) and honor (duty and ethical behavior); self-realization, wholeness and pride versus bestiality as instinct (nurture vs. nature); relations between father and offspring, between ruler and people; illusion and reality (all the world is a stage vs. life is a dream). Both the initial autobiography and the subsequent interactive dialogue are structured in accordance with leading questions used by actors imbued with the Konstantin Stanislavsky method: Who am I? Where am I? What are the circumstances? What is my relationship to total events, other characters, and to things? What do I want? Why do I want it? How will I get it? What must I overcome? The only guideline imposed is that Segismundo's stance with respect to the imprisonment of the rebel soldier must be addressed. From their intertextual explorations, students realize that the two plays can be said to end on a note of "precarious optimism" (Kott, *Shakespeare* 268) or, put another way, "The stage is a new purgatory in which everything is repeated but nothing is purified. . . . A play ends in oblivion. As does life. 'Our revels now are ended.' . . . What remains is a bare stage on which the same tragedy/comedy is replayed again and again" (Kott, *Bottom* 102).

Implicit in the culminating bipartite project on *The Tempest* and *Life Is a Dream* are several goals applicable to the entire course, insofar as students are obliged to *reflect* on the dilemmas posed by the characters and, more broadly, by the plays themselves in the historical context of production and in the contemporary (modern) moment of re-creation and contemplation; *make connections* among the themes seen in the context of their respective social worlds; *interact* with the characters and their critics; and *synthesize and integrate* their thoughts and insights by playing omniscient dramatist and engaging the characters intertextually in dialogue. If end-of-term evaluations are a useful barometer for measuring the subject matter of a course, it would seem that students who have experienced Reinventing Texts in a New (Historical) Context: Spanish *Comedia* and Shakespeare have ceased to think of *comedia* as a mere artifact, and Calderón (and Shakespeare) as autarkic prodigies, and have begun to explore the ways in which a seventeenth-century text relates both to its, and to their, culture.

Comedia and Comédie

Leah Middlebrook

In a public letter defending Pierre Corneille's *Le Cid* (1636) against attacks lev-eled at it by Georges de Scudéry—one of the play's many critics—an unnamed author wrote:

> Monsieur, C'est trop faire le bon François que de vouloir perdre le Cid, par ce qu'il est espagnol, il faut estre plux genereux . . . le traittant en prison-nier de guerre, souffrez que nous luy donnions nos cabinets pour prison: Il s'est assés rendu considerable pour nous obliger à le traitter favorable-ment, puis qu'il a eu l'honneur de plaire au Roy et aux grands Esprits du Royaume. (Gasté 152)

> Sir, One plays too much the good Frenchman in dismissing the Cid be-cause it is Spanish, one must be more generous . . . [instead of] treating it as a prisoner of war, allow us to offer our chambers as a prison: It has re-turned such results as to oblige us to treat it favorably, since it has had the honor of pleasing the King, and the great Souls of the Kingdom.[1]

He—or she—was right. French playwrights loved a good Spanish plot, and so did the French court. Despite the nearly constant state of war between the two countries and despite significant differences in audience and in rules for com-position, the principal French dramatic composers looked to the *comedia* for inspiration. If Corneille's reworking of Guillén de Castro's *Las mocedades del Cid* (published in 1618) is the most controversial example, there are more from which to draw. Pierre and Thomas Corneille, Molière: each turned to Spanish sources in fashioning some of their most popular works. If one is seeking a rea-son to teach a comparative course on *comedia* and *comédie*, the quest may end with the simple consideration of how indebted the French court theaters were to the Spanish *corrales*.

Yet there are other advantages of a comparative approach. Reading Spanish and French works in dialogue opens the way toward a broader examination of the similarities and differences in the political and ideological climates of two para-digmatic, and closely linked, societies. Spanish and French theater developed hand in hand with the early modern state; moreover, some of the principal re-orientations that lead us to designate the seventeenth century as incipiently "modern"—the breakdown of the feudal order and the emergence of a middle class, the rise of urbanism and of the "individual," the rise of absolutism and the elaboration of institutions and cultural forms disseminating its ideology—also changed the relation between a play and its audience. At the heart of much of Spanish and French seventeenth-century theater is a revived notion of Aristotelian catharsis. It is assumed that members of the audience will identify with main characters and interpret subtle, or not so subtle, messages about ways to think and be, taking in the lessons presented on the stage as directives for their own self-fashioning. Thus in the courses I teach on *comedia* and the *comédie* students compare versions of plots and of characters common to Spanish and French works, not only to gauge the distinct traits of the literary and dramatic conventions employed by Spanish and French playwrights, but also to understand the strategies by which writers inscribed specific matrices of values and repressions that brought into being model subjects of newly modern states.

Following is a description of my strategy for teaching seven plays: *Las mocedades del Cid, Primera Parte,* by Guillén de Castro; *Le Cid* and *Cinna* by Pierre Corneille; *Fuenteovejuna,* by Lope de Vega; *El alcalde de Zalamea,* by Calderón de la Barca; and *Le misanthrope* and *Le bourgeois gentilhomme,* by Molière. The readings represent the first two units of a three-part course, in which my chief aim is to encourage students to approach seventeenth-century plots analytically, as a means of recognizing when and how political and social imperatives of the state (the subjection of the nobility, the enfranchisement of the landed peasantry) are fused to psychological ones (separation from parents, first love, survival in the aftermath of rape), with the result that a social act (transformation into a good subject) is internalized as personal necessity. The last part of the course can be taken in a number of different directions. At the end of this essay, I suggest additional texts whose pairing has proven fruitful as a way of completing the term

Background and Context

Before we begin particular readings, we discuss important historical and cultural specifics. Liliane Picciola's *Corneille et la dramaturgie espagnole* has been useful in my own preparation. The following are good sources for supplementary student reading: *A New History of French Literature* (ed. Hollier); N. D. Shergold's *A History of the Spanish Stage;* and two books by William D. Howarth: *French Theatre in the Neoclassical Era, 1550–1789,* a compilation of original documents and reproductions of engravings and illustrations, and *Molière: The Playwright and His Audience,* for discussions of the Italian origins of both Spanish and French theater, the contact between Spanish and French theater troupes (also discussed by Finn, ch. 1), and French cultural phenomena such as *honnêteté* and the salons.

Comparative study should be situated in the context of important differences. The Spanish plays that drew the greatest interest from French playwrights and audiences presented, in their original form, multiple plots and a range of characters from low to high—the elements of the "new" comedy championed by Lope. In addition, many *comedia* plots inscribe the emergence of a type of Spanish subject—the modern warrior, the judicious peasant—as he or she comes into being in the political and social climate of a Castilian hegemony. In contrast, the rigors of French absolutism forced substantial changes in structure as works were adapted for the stage. For example, the Academie Française, which wielded significant power over what was published and shown, required adherence to neo-Aristotelian rules of unity of time, place, and action. Hence French playwrights pared down the diffuse focus of the Spanish plots, to create a fixed vanishing point—historically, the king, who at times occupied a privileged place on the stage (Howarth, *Molière,* ch. 2); diegetically, the absolute justice of a king allied with heaven. French playwrights also foregrounded the internal, psychological dramas of central characters, again in part because of the rigors of the cultural guidance administered by the Academie (see Greenberg; Murray; Rey). Fidelity to sources was sacrificed in the interest of achieving a narrowly construed, moralistic *vraisemblance,* or verisimilitude of individual motivation. Ironically, in the case of *Le Cid,* the original play was sheared of much of its historical accuracy. Corneille reduces the number of key figures in the royal household significantly, displacing the historical tensions between Sancho and Urraca onto the conventional structure of a love triangle. In *Cinna,* the extended soliloquies on the nature of kingship and just absolutist rule represent the modern, monarchic state as an intellectual phenomenon, as much as a military or historical one.

Whether or not the mystique of kingship was cultivated as assiduously in Spain as it was in France (and there has been debate on the question), French playwrights were more circumspect regarding the representation of kings, kingship, and, in Corneille's tragicomedy at least, patriarchs, than were Guillén de Castro, Lope, Tirso, and Calderón (Molière's satires lampoon bourgeois patriarchs because they misunderstand the responsibilities of the father in the paternal state, mistaking tyranny for legitimate authority). The nature of the distinction can be brought home by contrasting the early scenes of *Mocedades* with their counterparts in *Le Cid.* In the Spanish play, the fight between Don Diego and the Count takes place in the royal chambers, in front of the king, who must consider whether this affects his honor (act 1, lines 174–305). Corneille sets his version of the duel in a forecourt of the palace, thus shielding the king from the taint of dishonor; in fact, Don Fernand does not even appear onstage until well after the conflict has occurred, in act 2, scene 6. One might also contrast Diego's repeated mentions of his humiliation in act 1 of *Mocedades* with the single brief, if moving, speech he is assigned in *Le Cid* (1.4).

Finally, there is the question of audience. While both Molière and Lope claimed that they were writing for the general public, they clearly had different ideas about how general this public was. The *comedia* was, in Lope's famous phrasing, directed to the paying *vulgo* (*Arte nuevo* [Espasa ed.] 47–48), but the Corneilles and Molière wrote for the salons and the court. (Pierre Corneille's extensive writings on theater are difficult for undergraduates, but they are summarized well by Gutwirth.)

Unit 1: *The Subjection of the Nobility:* Le Cid; Las mocedades del Cid, primera parte; Cinna

Moving into the plays proper, I open with an examination of the eclipse of the feudal nobility, a narrative that follows a consistent formula: a young hero and heroine move from identification with a feudal order, associated with the world of the parents and governed by an exacting code of honor or vengeance, to voluntary subjection to the monarchic state. As the king asserts his power over his new subjects, mediated, legal ties—adoption, marriage, Rodrigo's renaming as El Cid—substitute for blood ties. Concomitantly, honor (*honra, honor, honneur*) is replaced by justice, and by publicly conferred glory (neoclassical French maintains a stronger distinction between *honneur* and *gloire* than Spanish plays do between *honra* and *honor*). I also call attention to the subtext of gender that accompanies these sociopolitical shifts, tracking how the central values of the feudal order—family, honor—are recast from heroic to "womanish" as the plots progress. In all three plays, the female protagonists (Ximena, Chimène, Emilie) mount the fiercest resistance to cultural change, while their final acquiescence brings dramatic closure. Although the women's acquiescence can be read as symptomatic of the patriarchal nature of absolutist ideology, I caution students that the historical agency of women in seventeenth-century politics was greater than they might assume. In France, this period was the era of the *précieuses*, and of two powerful regencies whose effect on theater have not yet, to my knowledge, been fully explored: Marie de Médicis, 1610–17, and the Spanish Anne of Austria, 1643–51. In addition, these plays' recalcitrant women are accompanied by a stock character who emerges during this time— the reasonable wife who gives counsel.

I begin our readings of the plays out of order. Pierre Corneille's *Le Cid* (1636) is an imitation of the first part of Guillén de Castro's *Las mocedades del Cid* (published 1618), but it is easier to read because of its tighter structure and focus. Like many Spanish plays, Guillén de Castro's maintains strong connections to the ballad tradition (evident in the scene of the encounter with St. Lazarus in act 3, for example) and to Spanish history, and the action is wide-ranging. In contrast, *Le Cid* develops as a clearly defined plot and subplot: the political drama of Rodrigue and Chimène's subjection to the monarchic order is punctuated by the travails of Sancho and Urraca, the unhappy, and unrequited, lovers of the drama's principal pair.

To encourage close reading, I ask my classes to prepare written answers to four questions for each play: Who acts in accordance with the wishes of the Count and

Don Diego? Who acts in accordance with the king? Does anyone change sides over the course of the play? If so, what emotional reasons does the play offer for the shift? In class, I work with their answers through a table written on the board:

Count/Diego	[transition]	King
Feudal		Absolutist
Honor		*Justice*

Columns 1 and 3 are self-explanatory. In the middle column, "transition," the emotional circumstances conditioning the characters' trajectories can be listed.

Once these circumstances are established, a number of interpretations become possible: the duel between Don Diego and the Count that sets the central action of the play in motion emerges as a metaphor for the political struggle over who is authorized to wield violence, the nobility or the king. Selections from Norbert Elias's *Power and Civility* on "courtierization" (258–70), on late-feudal self-restraint (229–47), and the rise of the state monopoly on violence (104–17) may be helpful. Taught in conjunction with key scenes in both *Le Cid* and *Mocedades* (the duel, speeches by Rodrigue and Chimène in which they pit duty against desire, for example: *Cid* 1.6 / *Mocedades* 1.518–85; *Cid* 3.905–32 / *Mocedades* 2.1155–185), Elias provides social background for understanding the honor code as the structuring principle of a nobleman's (and a noblewoman's) identity that restrains the violence characteristic of the warrior-nobility (thus, under the recently strengthened monarchy, fighting in the palace incurs dishonor). Student attention can then be drawn to the symbolic significance of the defeat of honor by justice: historically that the king and the state gained a monopoly on violence affects the fate of honor in these dramas. As warriors are eliminated from the social order in favor of courtiers, honor is increasingly elided with vengeance, a quality that is contrasted with the modern heroism of the Cid, in scenes in which Diego laments his humiliation and loss of virility in act 1 of both versions. Nevertheless, honor is associated with the shrill tirades of women who are losing credibility. Working in groups, students can track how, in the French plays in particular, honor and vengeance are linked with excesses of emotional suffering, with exploitation by parents, with tyranny . . . and with Chimène. Elvire speaks directly of Chimène's pursuit of "loi . . . tyrannique" (3.830) ("tyrannical law"), but in both versions of the story, Chimène's calls for "justice" are motivated by the blood debt owed to her family by Rodrigo (see, e.g., *Mocedades* 2.1036; *Le Cid* 2.689–90), and not by the objective consideration of the common good that the term ostensibly guarantees. At best, Chimène fails to understand true justice; at worst, she willfully manipulates language. In either case, she is cast in the wrong.

When we turn to Corneille's later tragicomedy *Cinna* (1641), a play similarly concerned with the domination of a treacherous nobility by a just and absolute king, the misogynist bent of French absolutism—and Corneille's embrace of it—is more evident: because the murder of the heroine Emilie's family takes place before the play begins, the ability of the audience to identify with the morality of her cries for revenge and justice is weakened. In a play rife with speeches comparing the disasters of the previous social order with the peace assured by the new, Emilie is firmly associated with a corrupt, discredited past.

Unit 2: *The Enfranchisement of a Middle Class:* Fuenteovejuna, El alcalde de Zalamea, Le bourgeois gentilhomme, Le misanthrope

In the second unit we move from dramas of the subjection of the nobility to ones that explore a relatively new cultural phenomenon: the social enfranchisement of the moneyed, nonnoble subject. Again, cultural and political context is provided. Here I emphasize the continuing breakdown of the feudal order; the ongoing wars between Spain and France; uprisings against the king's favorites, Lerma and Olivares, in Spain; in France, the revolt of the nobility commonly known as the Fronde. It was both fiscally and politically expedient during the seventeenth century for the crown to strengthen its links to the wealthy peasantry (Maravall, *Teatro* [1990 ed.], ch. 3; Castillo and Egginton). At the same time, the expansion of court culture and the demographic shift that resulted from the removal of members of the nobility from their estates to court had ambivalent consequences. As the architects of the political system had planned, the monarchic-seigneurial compact was reinforced, but urbanization was a factor in the so-called crisis of the baroque era (Maravall, chs. 1–5). Moreover, in both Spain and France, the social mobility facilitated by the expanded political role granted to subjects beyond the traditional nobility led to tension and even violence: for example, the prominence of *letrados*, or men of letters, in the court of Philip III (in France, the *noblesse de la robe*, or nobility of the robe, the group roundly lampooned by Molière) was a significant factor in the revolt against Lerma.

These social shifts occupied a significant space in the cultural imagination of both countries; onstage, however, they were played out in distinct ways. Noël Salomon, among others, has argued that the fashion for pastoral settings in the *comedia* reflects the complexity of the ideological climate in seventeenth-century Spain. People went to plays about the countryside because, having adapted themselves to the city and its sophisticated ways, they were "nostalgic" for a village life that existed primarily in the imagination (153–55). The plots that took place in these rural settings set forth an absolutist vision emphasizing the bonds of loyalty and justice that tied each subject, individually, to the king. Thus both Lope's *Fuenteovejuna* and Calderón's *El alcalde de Zalamea* present the king and state institutions, such as the law court, as purveyors of justice in a countryside ravaged by the petty tyrannies of the nobility and their soldiers. The ideology of the people's monarch was also operative in Paris, but French theatrical plots treating the enhanced social position of wealthy, nonnoble subjects are far more ambivalent. In discussing this contrast with students, I again call their attention to audience, often assigning side readings from Molière's *La critique de l'école des femmes* (scs. 5 and 6) and Lope's *Arte nuevo,* to bring the distinction home.

Turning to the plays, I reemphasize honor as the principle around which social identity is constituted, but this time I point out the different valences that accrue to honor when it ceases to be an exclusive attribute of the traditional nobility. My discussion questions are these: Who invokes honor as a principle of identity? When does such invocation begin? Is honor ever challenged as a social code by justice? What kinds of emotional narratives accompany that challenge? Students come to distinguish a less rigid, but nonetheless important, narrative formula at work in both *Fuenteovejuna* and *El alcalde de Zalamea.* After a preliminary set of reflections on the organic nature of self in a hierarchical society, the peasants Frondoso, Crespo, and to some extent Esteban recognize that the qualities by which they identify themselves—virtue, piety, integrity—also confer honor. Therefore, the characters who achieve it are newly "legible" within the monarchy, and they begin to participate in the rituals and institutions of the state: the townspeople of Fuenteovejuna take part in the trial, and Crespo becomes mayor of Zalamea. These protagonists have become viable, acting subjects; however, having crossed the threshold, they subject themselves to the king.

The opening scenes of act 3 of *El alcalde de Zalamea* provide a provocative elaboration of the paradigm. Isabel narrates her violation to her father and calls on him to kill her as a point of honor (3.275–80). Crespo's refusal to act in accordance with his daughter's version of the honor code (one she sets out in her opening soliloquy, 3.33–65) reproduces the gender dichotomy already discussed with reference to the nobility plays. Again, the burden of the old order is displaced onto the play's central female character. (This is also the case to some extent with Laurencia, in *Fuenteovejuna.* Consider her famous scene in act 3: "¡Vive Dios, que he de trazar / que solas mujeres cobren / la honra de estos tiranos" [lines 1774–776] ["My God, that I must show / how women alone recoup / our honor from those tyrants"].) Crespo's refusal, however, also indicates his modernity: he is aware that a worldview in which honor is remedied by an unjust vengeance is no longer viable. This personal act of self-restraint is immediately rewarded in the public sphere when a scribe arrives to announce Crespo's election to mayor (3.309–27).

The subtext is clear: Crespo maintains his honor by controlling his impulse to action, an impulse that is redirected after intervention by the state. Consequently, as mayor, Crespo continues to pursue a remedy to his honor, but he does so under the aegis of justice, not vengeance: "Cuando vengarme imagina, / me hace dueño de mi honor / la vara de la justicia" (3.328–30) ("When I imagine avenging myself, / the staff of justice / makes me master of my own honor"). Students can be guided to think of this chain of events and of subsequent developments in the subplot of Crespo's justice—such as the interviews with the Captain (3.405–550) and the king (3.850–947)—in terms of the state monopoly on violence. As in the nobility plays, the story of Crespo sends the message that personal agency must be sacrificed to absolutist control, to avoid the ravages brought about by rogue noblemen and officers. However, both *El alcalde de Zalamea* and *Fuenteovejuna* hold forth the promise that if this symbolic submission is made, the state will license its subjects to commit just acts of violence. In other words, the *comedia* continues to invest in honor as a personal code. If its meaning is shifted, from traditional birthright of the nobility to the "patrimonio del alma" (*Zalamea* 1.875) ("patrimony of the soul") of any honest man or woman, it nevertheless remains important as a principle of identity—perhaps, as David Castillo and William Egginton have argued—because the ideology of honor proved such a successful political tool in the interpellation of the Spanish peasantry.

Plays directed toward the emergent middle class thus insist that action, and particularly violence, is the prerogative of the king in the pacified absolutist state. Interestingly, the social and subjective costs of absolutism are brought into relief in a profoundly different work, Molière's *Le misanthrope*. Though, on first glance, it is a strange text to pair with the agrarian-peasant dramas of Lope and Calderón, the preoccupation subtending this witty, urban play is precisely the place of honor under absolutism. Alceste's compulsive refusal to participate in the social practice of *honnêteté*—or the social code of artful dissembling, comparable to Gracián's *prudencia,* and as central to French court culture as honor was to feudal Spain (Howarth on the *honnêtes gens* is useful for students; see *French Theatre* 57–63)—exposes the corrosive effects of trading on one's honor in the name of the social order. As Alceste rages through the play in search of a truly "honest"—as opposed to *honnête*—man or woman, I joke with my students that he has a "Spanish problem." That is, he is Pedro Crespo dropped into the outlying salons of French polite society, and bent on seeking an integrity that is properly the attribute of the agrarian peasant (Alceste's social rank is left somewhat ambiguous in the play; however, as this reading may suggest, it seems most likely that he is a member of the traditional "nobility of the sword," as opposed to the parvenu "nobility of the robe"). This view is strengthened by Alceste's final decision to retire to the country, as well as by the important information that he is being pursued by the Marshals of France (2.6). These royal officers were assigned by Richelieu the specific function of settling disputes having to do with honor, in the wake of state edicts outlawing the practice of dueling. Their presence on the margins of the society portrayed in *Le misanthrope* troubles the fiction that the modern state has secured absolute authority, and gestures to the fragility of the Sun King's pacified realm.

The degree of Molière's investment in this point of view is debatable. *Le misanthrope* is often viewed as a problem play within his oeuvre; that it was written in the aftermath the *Tartuffe* controversy explains, in part, his disillusionment with the court and with political favors. By following *Le misanthrope* with the satirical *Le bourgeois gentilhomme,* we observe a more conventional, if highly caricatured, view of modern, seventeenth-century Paris and of the social tensions arising from the coexistence of the traditional nobility and the newly powerful bourgeoisie.

Tracking the production of culturally viable subjects, the course can be rounded out with additional groupings: Thomas Corneille's *Le menteur* and Juan Ruiz de Alarcón's *La verdad sospechosa* offer a useful point of transition between questions of *honnêteté* and of hypocrisy; Tirso de Molina's *El burlador de sevilla* and Molière's *Dom Juan* also deal with hypocrisy, and with the dangers posed by the individual to the absolutist social order; Lope's *La dama boba,* and Molière's *L'école des femmes* and *L'école des maris* facilitate a deepened consideration of gender, since all three turn on the interpellation of the urban girl, and on the men who seek to usurp this function from an absolutist chance, or heaven. Taken as a group, these works might provide posthumous solace to Pierre Corneille's champion: when the *comedia* crossed the Pyrenees and entered Paris, its reception was evidently not that of the prisoner of war but of an honored guest.

NOTE

[1] All translations from the French and Spanish are mine.

Don Juan in Three Acts: Seduction across Time and Space

James Mandrell

Don Juan—also known as the *burlador de Sevilla,* or trickster of Seville—is the comparative topic par excellence. He first appears as a literary character in the seventeenth-century Spanish *comedia El burlador de Sevilla y convidado de piedra (The Trickster of Seville, or the Stone Guest)* and then travels throughout Spain and Europe as the protagonist of dramas, operas, poetry, and works of fiction. Eventually Don Juan becomes a psychological type, a concept, and a modern myth (see Feal; Rousset; Weinstein). Indeed, the protean nature of the *burlador* lends itself to Don Juan's reincarnation across time, space, and traditions.

Don Juan can lead us down a number of paths in the classroom. My rendering of his story begins with *El burlador de Sevilla,* a first act that could also incorporate any of the many versions that follow, including Molière's *Dom Juan* (1665), Lorenzo da Ponte's libretto for Mozart's *Don Giovanni* (1787), Byron's *Don Juan* (1819–24), and Alexandre Dumas's *Don Juan de Marana, ou la chute d'un ange (Don Juan de Marana; or, The Fall of an Angel)* (1836), to name some of the most obvious. The second act of my account considers Søren Kierkegaard's philosophical exploration of Don Juan, in *Either/Or* (1846), as well as psychological and psychoanalytic speculations, such as those of Gregorio Marañón, José Ortega y Gasset, and, perhaps most notable, Otto Rank. In the third and final act of this version of Don Juan, examining Derek Walcott's *The Joker of Seville* (1978) and Carlos Morton's *Johnny Tenorio* (1983) allows us to consider the figure in the light of Western culture and its effects on former colonies, and thereby to return to another reading of *El burlador de Sevilla.*

Act 1

The traditional Don Juan story as found in *El burlador de Sevilla* comprises two distinct aspects that were first brought together in one literary text by Tirso de Molina: the history of a dissolute nobleman, on the one hand, and the so-called double invitation, on the other.[1] Don Juan is a libertine who uses and abuses women, and also men, with impunity. Although the *burlador's* sexual liaisons with women are far better known than are his troubled relations with men, in both cases Don Juan proves to be a man without honor who compromises the honor of others. The double invitation occurs when, after committing a long line of personal and social affronts, Don Juan meets the funerary statue of one of his deceased victims, Don Gonzalo de Ulloa, the father of Doña Ana. The *burlador* mockingly invites the statue to dine in his home, only to be surprised when the statue arrives at the appointed time and place and responds with an invitation of his own, for Don Juan to dine in the Ulloa chapel. At the conclusion of the second meal, Tirso's Don Gonzalo, the comendador, acting as an agent of God, drags the *burlador* down to hell.

Don Juan's offenses against the honor of both women and men are the most obvious elements of the plot, but there is much more to Tirso's story of the *burlador.* The opening moments of *El burlador de Sevilla* give the lie to the types of concerns that will be taken up in other versions of Don Juan's story. The Duquesa Isabela leads a man she believes to be the Duque Octavio out of her bedchamber, only to realize, first, that the carefully structured exchange of her honor for a promise of marriage will not be fulfilled, and, second, that the man who made the false promise was in fact someone pretending to be her lover. "Duquesa, de nuevo os juro / de cumplir el dulce sí" (lines 3–4) ("Duchess, I once again swear to you to fulfill my sweet promise"), the man says; subsequently he reveals, in response to the duchess's questioning, that he is a "man without a name"—which is to say, not the duke.

The initial conversation presents the linguistic dimensions of Don Juan's modus operandi, which Shoshana Felman has brilliantly studied in relation to Molière's *Dom Juan.* Indeed, Felman's "meditation on promising" (11) brings into focus the similarities between the *burlador*'s seduction of women *and* men, achieved in both cases through the empty promises that pervade the *comedia.* The seductions of the Duquesa Isabela, the fisherwoman Tisbea, Doña Ana de Ulloa, and the peasant Aminta demonstrate the ways in which Don Juan uses his linguistic facility, especially his knack for making promises, to gain access to women and then to dishonor them. He is, in essence, a skilled actor who flaunts social conventions. But his verbal gifts extend, as well, to his dealings with men and the male preserves of state and honor, including the king of Naples, his uncle Don Pedro Tenorio, a group of fisherman, his friend the marqués de la Mota, and Doña Ana's father, Don Gonzalo. In a failed attempt to use words to plead his case, Don Juan tells Don Gonzalo's statue, "A tu hija no ofendí, / que vio mis engaños antes" (2851–52) ("I did not offend your daughter; she saw through my deceit"), to which the statue responds, "No importa, que ya pusiste / tu intento" (2853–54) ("It makes no difference; your intent was clear"). Seduction as practiced by Don Juan is not problematic simply or even principally because of its carnal implications but because of the way it unravels the social fabric. Again, words are the source of the unraveling. If the sacrament of marriage—which is nothing more nor less than an agreement effected by means of the spoken word (Mandrell 50–86)—was one of the fundamental contracts on which Spanish society rested, *El burlador de Sevilla* is not simply about the making and breaking of promises. It is also about the social chaos that false words create.

The linguistic thread runs through many of the literary works featuring Don Juan that follow Tirso's *El burlador de Sevilla* and Molière's *Dom Juan.* Not only is the strand a significant aspect of Spanish dramas about the *burlador,* such as José Zorrilla's *Don Juan Tenorio* (1844) and Miguel de Unamuno's *El hermano*

Juan (*Brother Juan*) (1939). It is also integral to texts from other traditions. Lord Byron's *Don Juan* is nothing if not a glorious display of linguistic facility—now of the author himself—with clear social and cultural implications. As Jerome J. McGann has observed: "*Don Juan* is intended first, to correct the degenerate literary practices of the day. . . . [It was] an attempt to restore poetry to its proper place and functions" (65, 78). So critical is the function of speech in George Bernard Shaw's *Man and Superman*—an extended portion of its third act is often performed independently, under the title "Don Juan in Hell"—that the play concludes with John Tanner, or Jack, Shaw's version of Don Juan, uttering, "Talking!" (209). Jack has progressed, through marriage, from authorship of "The Revolutionist's Handbook and Pocket Companion" to entry into the world of social discourse, as exemplified by his surprised concluding comment. And any consideration of the importance of Don Juan's linguistic skill should at least mention Mozart's *Don Giovanni*, which serves as testimony to the seductive beauty of the *burlador*'s language, now figured as music.

El *burlador de Sevilla* could easily be taken up in conjunction with other Golden Age *comedias* in an exploration of language and social action or of the dynamics of speech and writing—for example, Lope de Vega's *La dama boba* (1613), Andrés de Claramonte's *La estrella de Sevilla* (*The Star of Seville*) (c. 1630), and Ruiz de Alarcón's *La verdad sospechosa* (*The Suspect Truth*) (c. 1619). Tirso's play could also serve as the cornerstone of a study of Don Juan in the Spanish tradition, in dramas like Zorrilla's *Don Juan Tenorio*, Adelardo López de Ayala's *El nuevo don Juan* (1863), and Unamuno's *El hermano Juan*, as well as novels in which Don Juan figures explicitly—Azorín's *Don Juan* (1922), Ramón Pérez de Ayala's *Tigre Juan y el curandero de su honra* (*Tiger Juan and the Charlatan of His Honor*) (1926), and Gonzalo Torrente Ballester's *Don Juan* (1963)—and implicitly—Clarín's *La regenta* (*The Judge's Wife*) (1884–85) and Jacinto Octavio Picón's *Dulce y sabrosa* (*Sweet and Savory*) (1891).

Act 2

The phenomenon of seduction, which is key to Tirso's *El burlador de Sevilla*, leads beyond literary traditions to philosophical and psychological considerations of Don Juan. Whereas the *burlador* is originally seen as a destructive force deserving of condemnation, Zorrilla's Romantic, romanticized version of the *burlador*, in *Don Juan Tenorio*, introduces another possible denouement. Rather than descend into Hell, Don Juan ascends to heaven with Doña Inés, the woman who has saved him. At this point in the evolution of the story, Don Juan is perceived not as destructive but as an individual capable of a true desire to repent. This distinction at work in the presentation of Don Juan is also found in some of the philosophical discussions of the *burlador*, which will eventually lead to fullblown psychological studies of the literary character as a personality type.

Nowhere is this ambivalence more evident than in Kierkegaard's *Either/Or,* a pseudonymous collection of essays published in two volumes whose title signals an ambivalent approach to the topic. A vast and vastly complex work in its own right, it contains various essays pertinent to Don Juan. "The Seducer's Diary"—which relates, by means of a journal, letters, and recollections, the aesthetic seduction of Cordelia by Johannes—is a speculation on seduction, more a text *of* or *about* Don Juan than a commentary *on* him. "The Immediate Erotic Stages or the Musical Erotic," an extended reflection on Mozart's *Don Giovanni,* essentially begins and ends by making the point that the opera is one among a few "immortal" works and that it "ought to rank highest among all classic works" (135). "Silhouettes" examines sorrow in terms of the female characters Marie Beaumarchais, in Goethe's *Clavigo*; Donna Elvira, from *Don Giovanni*; and Margarete, from Goethe's *Faust*—although the reader quickly realizes that the women are not as interesting as the men who seduce them, something "due," in Kierkegaard's words, "not so much to the difference in the two feminine natures as to the essential difference between a Don Juan and Faust" (205). The essay thus shifts the focus from Don Juan's interactions with women to a discussion of men, as if women, no matter their importance to the *burlador* and his story, cannot be seen as agents of desire in and of themselves. Unlike Faust, Don Juan is no longer a singular character repeating through various texts but a type, as is clear from Kierkegaard's reference to "the essential difference between *a* Don Juan and Faust" (my italics).

The apparent ambivalence at work in *Either/Or* has less to do with Don Juan per se than with the workings of Kierkegaard's intricate text, in which Don Juan becomes an incarnation of life itself that rests in some ideal presentation of power. The ground traversed from Tirso to Kierkegaard, then, presents the alpha and omega of interpretations of Don Juan. For some, the *burlador* is a threat to social order; for others, he is an embodiment of the attractions of male power.

By seeing him as a type, Kierkegaard anticipates psychological considerations of Don Juan, such as Armand Hayem's 1886 study *Le Don Juanisme.* Even earlier than Hayem, López de Ayala identified an individual as a "new Don Juan" in his play of the same title. *El nuevo don Juan* offers not just a reworked version of the *burlador* but a critique of Zorrilla's Romantic view in *Don Juan Tenorio.* As López de Ayala's play draws to a close, Elena admonishes Paulina, who had hoped to reform and marry Juan de Alvarado, "Nada esperes de un Don Juan" (act 3, line 264) ("Do not hope for anything from a Don Juan").

López de Ayala's negative view of Don Juan as both a character and a type is shared by the medical researcher and clinician Marañón, whose interest in human sexuality and social development led him to devote several essays to the questions posed by the *burlador.* The most interesting of the essays are "Notas para la biología de don Juan" ("Notes for the Biology of Don Juan"), written in 1924, and "Gloria y miseria del conde de Villamediana" ("The Glory and Misery of the Count of Villamediana"), written in 1939 and 1940. Irrespective of the particular issue at hand, Marañón's conclusions all derive from the observation that the *burlador* is not just a literary character and a myth but a man of flesh and bone; so insistent is Marañón on this point that he provides Don Juan with a clinical history. Moreover, Don Juan serves as a kind of misguided masculine ideal that tricks men into both seducing women and abandoning the more pressing work of society. The man who devotes himself to seducing women, according to Marañón, is but "un varón a medias" ("half a man") ("Notas," *Obras completas* 4: 75, 80).

The philosopher and cultural critic Ortega y Gasset's commentary on the *burlador* furnishes a bitter and at times explicit correction to Marañón's views. In essays like "El tema de nuestro tiempo" ("The Topic of Our Time"), from 1923, and "Para una psicología del hombre interesante: Conocimiento del hombre" ("Toward a Psychology of the Interesting Man: Knowledge of Man"), from 1925, Ortega finds in Don Juan a spontaneity and vitality that hold forth the possibility of a new culture, one founded on "la plenitud vital" ("the vital plenitude") of the *burlador,* who is now an "hombre interesante" as well as a "figura equívoca que nuestro tiempo va afinando" ("equivocal figure that our age continues to refine") ("El tema," *Obras completas* 3: 178).

Marañón and Ortega move the discussion of Don Juan far from the types of theological considerations found in Tirso's *burlador* and even later in Zorrilla's Romantic revision. They locate the importance of the figure in, on the one hand, a biological reality that suggests actual individuals, and, on the other, a vital principle that pertains to social morals. The writers' reimaginings of the character ultimately result in a shift corresponding to the ways in which the twentieth century would frame explorations of culture and society in relation to the individual. The "equivocal figure" evoked by Ortega, who somewhat resembles Kierkegaard's object of study, offers no easy answers to those who would interpret him.

The modern appeal of Don Juan is apparent in Otto Rank's *The Don Juan Legend.* As does Kierkegaard in *Either/Or,* Rank regards Mozart's opera as a superlative work and certainly the most important one to deal with Don Juan. But Rank is primarily interested in using Don Giovanni to exemplify aspects of the Oedipus complex as well as Freud's theories of primitive social violence as found in *Totem and Taboo* and *Group Psychology and the Analysis of the Ego.* Rank remarks toward the end of his book-length essay that the first person to write of Don Juan articulates the inevitable, frightening nature of death—that is, "the psychological meaning of the vengeance of death." In other words, the *burlador's* spectacular demise performs for us the manner in which death overcomes and avenges all. But Don Juan is a protean figure, in Rank's words, "both eternal, and yet, as we have seen, capable of metamorphosis" (*Don Juan* 105–06).

Act 3

In 1973, Derek Walcott was asked by Britain's Royal Shakespeare Company to adapt Tirso's *El burlador de Sevilla*. Although unable to read the Spanish original, Walcott agreed and wrote *The Joker of Seville,* a drama in two acts, accompanied by music composed in the Caribbean style by Galt MacDermot (best known for the music in *Hair* [1979]) and songs, including stick-fight chants, supplied by Walcott. The result is a work in which a legend has found a new means of expression: as Walcott puts it, "legends find new vessels" (4). The Trinidadian poet follows the broad outlines of Tirso's story of the *burlador* (see Macdonald; Thieme). But he gives his play a local, metatheatrical twist by setting the action in the context of an All Souls' Eve celebration in Trinidad, during which the inhabitants of the village of San Juan resurrect "our champion, / the greatest stickman: Don Juan!" (8). By designating him as a "stickman," Walcott further entwines his version of Don Juan in Trinidadian culture. The stick dance, or *calinda,* was popular with male slaves throughout the West Indies. In its most benign form, it was a ritualized performance associated with carnival; it was also implicated in violent clashes with authorities in Trinidad and banned in the nineteenth century. (See Hill's discussion of carnival in Trinidad, esp. pp. 25–26.) After the All Souls' Eve celebration, the action shifts to Naples and to a recognizable recapitulation of both aspects of the traditional story of the *burlador:* the seductions and the double invitation.

Nevertheless, it is unclear whether or not Walcott's Juan is condemned, as is Tirso's *burlador.* The first act of *The Joker of Seville* bears as an epigraph a quotation from Ezra Pound's *Pisan Cantos:* "With a painted paradise at the end of it . . ." (7). At the end of this act and after Juan has killed Gonzalo, the chorus of Caribbean characters added by Walcott sings several times the refrain, "O Lord, let resurrection come / from this stickfight!" (86), recalling that this Juan himself has been resurrected. The second act, which is also introduced by a quotation from the *Pisan Cantos,* "Without a painted paradise at the end of it . . ." (87), ends not with Juan's ambiguous condemnation but with the ambivalence characteristic of modern versions of Don Juan's story. The King of Castile figures Don Juan's immortality as legendary when he comments, "May his [Juan's] death be, down all the ages, / told by the holy marriage bell," while Rafael, the village elder, intones, "Every man's life is a candle / that burns too fast, but, with your leave, / we lit his ritual death and ritual / resurrection on All Souls' Eve." But it is the Ace of Death, appearing alongside the Queen of Hearts and the Jack, who is most direct about this aspect of Walcott's adaptation when he sings, "*Now, whether Juan gone down to Hell / or up to Heaven, I cannot tell / . . . / but the truest joke he could play / is to come back to us one day, / because if there's resurrection, Death is the Joker: / sans humanité!*" (150). The end of *The Joker of Seville* therefore leaves us to ponder what Rank would identify as "the psychological meaning of the vengeance of death" as the Queen of Hearts closes the play with the refrain "*every heart has the right to its freedom*" (151). For Walcott, it seems that freedom, and not death or even the significance of desire, is the point of Don Juan's story.

Walcott's notion of freedom includes individual liberty as well as a broader sociopolitical freedom from oppression to be enjoyed by all individuals. In this way, he advances, in Errol Hill's words, a "politically liberal" view even as he offers a critique of the colonial impulses at work in Don Juan's story. Hill writes:

> [Walcott's] Don Juan has contempt for the peasants who create an imitation of ruling high culture. Walcott wants free disorder, not just a reversal of power relations. Don Juan liberates others from the social order by his violation of it, but he destroys those who do not use their freedom. (324)

This broadly sociopolitical understanding of freedom is implicated in a negative fashion in *El burlador de Sevilla*. The absence of individual liberty is most obvious in the way that the Rey de Castilla, or King of Castile, makes and remakes marriages, without regard for the preferences of the individuals, as a means of promoting social stability. Perhaps even more significant is the king himself, Alfonso XI (1311–50), a historical figure known for the vigor with which he reasserted authority over a restless Castilian nobility and for being only somewhat less aggressive than the son who succeeded him on the throne, Pedro I "el Cruel" (1334–69), also known as Peter the Just. Reflecting back from Walcott's play, we can read Don Juan's downfall at the hands of the comendador in Tirso's drama as a commentary on the extent to which individual action can fall victim to social stability. Central to a political reading is the degree to which the geography of *El burlador de Sevilla* establishes an imperial map. While not under Spanish control during the period of the play's action, Naples, having fallen to the Aragonese in the fifteenth century, belonged to Spain's vast empire when Tirso wrote the work. Seville would have resonated with Tirso's audiences both as a formerly Spanish-Muslim city, "reconquered" by Castile in the thirteenth century, and as one of the major ports for transatlantic trade in the early modern period; finally, Portugal, although independent in the fourteenth century, was under Spanish control at the time of the play's composition. Through these references, then, *El burlador de Sevilla* invites a reading that takes into account Spain's eventual hegemony over a vast empire.

This interpretation can be seen at work at numerous points in *The Joker of Seville*. For example, the act of rewriting a foundational text of one of the early colonizers of Trinidad—Spain—for a subsequent colonial authority, England, is itself worthy of remark, especially when the question of liberty is so pressing. Even more curious is that Walcott's adaptation of *El burlador de Sevilla* was commissioned by the Royal Shakespeare Company, an institution nominally charged with safeguarding and disseminating that most English of authors. Walcott's interest in cultural hegemony and colonialization is particularly evident in the revision of the so-called *loa* of Lisbon and in Don Juan's seduction of Tisbea. In the *loa* of Lisbon, Don Gonzalo, who serves as Alfonso's ambassador to Portugal, extols the virtues of the capital, defining it not as the greatest city in Portugal but as the "mayor ciudad de España" ("the greatest city in Spain") (1.717) (see ter

Horst, "*Loa*")—thus marking it as part of the Spanish empire. The lengthy passage in the original (1.722–858) is significantly different in Walcott's revision. At only thirty-three lines, it is now a much more circumspect and critical view of the place named for Ulysses, Ulissibona, or Lisbon. Picking up on the Homeric aspects of Tirso's *comedia* and deploying them throughout his play, Walcott has his Gonzalo assert, "Traveling from Lisbon, sir, I've come / into this wisdom. I have seen / that our greatest treasures are at home [in Seville]" (28). More acutely, when Juan and Catalinon are shipwrecked on the coast where they will meet Tisbea, the servant sings a painful lament punctuated by the chorus from the slaves on the boat that carried them. He compares their shipwreck with the "accident" of Columbus's encounter with the New World and then notes:

> I am the one slave to survive
> this shipwreck with my master.
> But I'm not sure, now I'm alive,
> which is the worse disaster.
> For this new world, its promised feasts,
> is nothing but the old one,
> as long as men are beasts, and beasts
> still bear their master's burden.

The chorus of slaves comments:

> Hey, hey, hey!
> Is the U.S.A.
> Once we get dere,
> we gonna be O.K!   (33–34)

Even Juan remarks, "Old World, New World. They're all one" (48).

What is notable about Walcott's adaptation is the ease with which he has plucked the story of Don Juan from a European context and resituated it in the creolized culture of the Caribbean. A similar strategy is at work in Carlos Morton's *Johnny Tenorio*, a one-act play set in the Chicano milieu of "Big Berta's Bar on the west side of San Antonio, Texas" (28). The action of the play itself is bracketed by a *corrido*, a traditional Mexican folk song epic and narrative. In this case, the song is Víctor Cordero's well-known "Corrido de Juan Charrasqueado," or "scar-faced Juan," the first part of which is sung by Berta herself as the play opens, and then, at the end, by a chorus of skeletons. The plot is a familiar one, involving a competition between Johnny and Louie to see who can seduce more women. One man goes to New York, the other to Mexico City; the work thus points to the two poles of Chicano culture, one in English, the other in Spanish.

However, Morton's *Johnny Tenorio* resists the pull of either of the colonizing cultures or languages by its insistence on a multilingual dialogue that races through Spanish, English, and Chicano slang. The result is a revision of the *burlador* that foregrounds the traditional tale, emphasizing the insidious nature of a patriarchal society, even as it admits to the many attractions of the character. Berta's summary judgment makes the case both for the *burlador* that Tirso condemns and for the Don Juan that Zorrilla saves. She asserts, on the one hand, "Here is Johnny Tenorio, el don Juan, a thorn in the soul of la raza since time immemorial. Ha traicionado a mujeres, asesinado a hombres y causado gran dolor. Por eso decimos . . . que muera!" ("He has betrayed women, assassinated men and caused great pain. That's why we say . . . let him die!") On the other hand, she recognizes that "he stood alone, defied all the rules, and fought the best he knew how. His heart pounds fiercely inside all of us—the men who desire to be like him, the women who lust after him. He is our lover, brother, father, and son. Por eso decimos—¡que viva!" ("That's why we say—let him live!") (51–52). We see here the mixing of Spanish and English—if not the use of Spanglish—as well as an acceptance of the bad and the good of the character. As does Walcott, Morton gives Don Juan a new context, but the original *burlador* is still present and accounted for.

If the passage of some 375 years has done little to diminish the *burlador*'s appeal and his centrality to diverse texts, traditions, and interpretations, the movement of the Don Juan through time and space reveals his ongoing pertinence to Western, if not world, culture (see Yokota-Murakami). As he assumes myriad forms and meanings, Don Juan invites approaches from varied perspectives and continuing discussions in multiple contexts. In this regard, Tirso's *El burlador de Sevilla* is as seductive as its hero, since the play's Don Juan continues to engage us in his unending reincarnations.

NOTE

[1] There has been extended controversy over the authorship, dating, and even the text of *El burlador de Sevilla*. For the purposes of my consideration, Tirso de Molina is assumed to be the author and the text is as found in Alfredo Rodríguez López-Vázquez's popular edition. Unless otherwise indicated, all translations are my own.

CROSS-CULTURAL APPROACHES

Lope de Vega and the Matter of America: Approaching the *Comedia* from a Transatlantic Perspective

José R. Cartagena-Calderón

A fundamental principle of the evolving field of transatlantic studies is that the "discovery," conquest, and colonization of the "New World" was not a one-way trip in which Europeans transformed the indigenous peoples they encountered without being transformed themselves. Instead, the encounter and its aftermath involved multiple round-trips that impacted forever the cultures on both sides of the Atlantic. A significant result of transatlantic approaches to early modern literature, culture, and history has been the study of New World resonances in Old World texts not customarily thought of as engaging the colonial experience. Another, perhaps more predictable, result is the attention critics are paying to Iberian texts (many of them noncanonical) that take the transoceanic ventures of the Spanish empire as their central preoccupation.

The Spanish theater of the sixteenth and seventeenth centuries is particularly suited for a transatlantic approach. Although only a handful of the thousands of plays written in early modern Spain take place in the New World, the matter of America is present even in dramatic works apparently concerned exclusively with metropolitan themes. We need only think, as Stephen Gilman reminded us, of "the considerable contribution of American expressions and references to Lope's immense poetic vocabulary as well as the inclusion of American types— 'mulattos,' 'indios,' and 'indianos'" (102). More than half a century ago Marcos Morínigo observed those references when he set out to write an article about the presence of America in the poetic imagination of Spain's preeminent playwright.

Morínigo's original article ended up becoming a book, *América en el teatro de Lope de Vega,* in which he identified plays that include episodes set in the New World or that make allusions to America. He also identified four plays by Lope specifically centered on Spain's transatlantic experience: *El Nuevo Mundo descubierto por Cristóbal Colón, Arauco domado, El Brasil restituido,* and the *auto sacramental La Araucana.*

The small number of existing New World plays (not more than fifteen, including the four by Lope) may seem like a blessing for teachers and students of a genre frequently described as a *mare magnum,* or bottomless sea. Interestingly enough, until recently what used to pose a challenge to teachers of the *comedia de Indias* was their noncanonical status and, consequently, the lack of readily accessible suitable editions for classroom use. The anthologies compiled by Francisco Ruiz Ramón (*América*) and Arturo Souto Alabarce of New World plays by major and minor writers in the early modern period have begun to remedy the problem. Additionally, Robert Shannon's bilingual edition of Lope's *El Nuevo Mundo descubierto por Cristóbal Colón* (2001), Ezra S. Engling's scholarly edition of Calderón de la Barca's *La aurora en Copacabana* (1994), Jesús Cañas Murillo's one-volume critical edition of Tirso de Molina's trilogy *Hazañas de los Pizarros* (1993), and Miguel Zugasti's three-volume critical edition of the same trilogy (1993) have made a much-needed contribution to the editing of the *comedia de Indias,* as well as to the reconfiguration of the theatrical canon.

My discussion on approaching the *comedia* from a transatlantic perspective will focus on *El Nuevo Mundo descubierto por Cristóbal Colón.* Most likely written between 1598 and 1603, it is the only extant early modern Spanish play that stages the "discovery" of the West Indies and the initial contact between Europeans and Amerindians. The other *comedias de Indias* center, by and large, on various aspects of the later conquest and colonization of the New World. Shannon's bilingual edition makes it possible to teach *El Nuevo Mundo* in different courses, on different levels, both in Spanish and in English translation. This particular New World play also has the advantage of reenacting Columbus's momentous voyage of 1492, a point of reference familiar to all students.

In the course Significant Other(s): Representing Alterity in the Early Modern Spanish Theater, I incorporate a reading of *El Nuevo Mundo* among a selection of Golden Age plays engaged in the representation of groups marked as other, against which an emerging national identity was constructed. In addition to Lope's play on the "discovery" of the Caribbean, the course examines *comedias* that center on the conquest of New World geographies, such as Mexico (Fernando de Zárate's *La conquista de México*), Peru (Tirso de Molina's *Amazonas en las Indias* [*Hazanas* 231–352] and Calderón's *La aurora en Copacabana*), Chile (Ricardo de Turia's *La bellígera española* and Lope's *Arauco domado*), and Brazil (Lope's *El Brasil restituido*). I also have students read Columbus's *Diario del primer viaje,* as well as excerpts from sixteenth-century chronicles of the Spanish experience in America, such as Francisco López de Gómara's *Historia general de las Indias y Vida de Hernán Cortés* (chs. 13–25) and the first part of Gonzalo Fernández de Oviedo's *Historia general y natural de las Indias* (bk. 2, chs. 4–6; bk. 3, chs. 5–6). Although Lope did not follow *al pie de la letra* Gómara's and Oviedo's chronicles, both texts served as the principal source for *El Nuevo Mundo descubierto por Cristóbal Colón*. Gómara's and Oviedo's accounts are a valuable tool when discussing how Lope rewrites the history of Spain's encounter with the New World. Students may explore, for instance, how Lope's characterization of Columbus as a saintly national hero differs from the chronicle sources; at the same time, the class can examine the ideological implications and contradictions of the playwright's portrait of the Admiral as an exemplary figure.

What should transpire in the students' engagement with the question of the other in a play like *El Nuevo Mundo* is an awareness of the complex processes at work in the imagining of early modern national and imperial identities vis-à-vis Spain's problems of coexistence, conflict, conversion, assimilation, and the expulsion of its non-Christian population. Thus it is important to point out that Moors and Amerindians share the stage in *El Nuevo Mundo* not at all accidentally, since the fall of Granada and Columbus's arrival in the West Indies both took place in 1492. That same year, the Jews were expelled from Spain. As students come to understand, Spain's internal and external others were central in the construction of the newly unified nation.

Lope justifies the conquest of the New World as an extension of the Reconquest of the Iberian Peninsula, just as López de Gómara had in his early chronicle: "[c]omenzaron las conquistas de indios acabada la de los moros, porque siempre guerreasen españoles contra infieles" (8) ("the conquest of the Indians commenced after that of the Moors was completed, so that Spaniards would ever fight the infidels"). When discussing historical events in class, such as the *Reconquista* and the *conquista* in the context of *El Nuevo Mundo,* or any other play, we must not forget Charles Gibson's reminder that the term *reconquista* is a neologism that finds its roots in the eighteenth century, far beyond the pre- and early modern period (*"Reconquista"* 21). We should also bear in mind that Spain's conflicts with Islam did not end in 1492 with the fall of Granada (Fuchs 7–8) but continued throughout the sixteenth and seventeenth centuries.

Key discussion questions regarding the representation of Moors and Amerindians in Lope's play are these: To what extent does the work establish for its metropolitan audience a firm sense of national Christian selfhood against a clearly defined cultural and religious other? Are there instances when distinctions between self and other collapse, pointing to the fragility of a collective self-image dictated by cultural exclusions? Such inquiries not only illuminate cultural contact and conflict on the early modern Spanish stage; they also help students come to terms with the still relevant fact that when dominant discourses seek to define marginal groups and register difference in them, they also, if inadvertently, define the hegemonic groups, individuals, and institutions that produced them. In other words, students are invited to reflect on structures of marginalization and exclusion that are operative in our increasingly diverse universities.

Another important issue is Lope's representation of the imperial and religious aspects of Columbus's venture. Lope revises history by fabricating a Columbus absolutely convinced of the existence of the Indies and driven by divine inspiration. After Ferdinand and Isabella achieve what Lope interprets to be their historical mission of erecting a Christian Spain with the fall of the Moorish kingdom of Granada, the next scene stages the Catholic monarchs' financing of Columbus's voyage. By having Columbus appeal to Ferdinand and Isabella mainly on religious terms, Lope suggests that the propagation of Christianity, more than the search for wealth, was the motivating force for exploration. King Ferdinand's response to Columbus highlights the idea that God himself wanted to repossess the New World and add it to the emerging Spanish empire after the Catholic monarchs won the long struggle against Spain's internal nonbelievers:

> Pues dádselo a Colón, y el cielo guíe
> sus altos pensamientos y deseos,
> porque a la fe se vuelvan los idólatras,
> y se ensanche de España el señorío.   (act 1, lines 973–76)

> Well, then, give Columbus what he needs, and may the heavens guide his noble thoughts and desires so that he may convert the idolaters to the faith and increase Spain's dominions.

For Lope, the Spanish rulers' support of Columbus is not motivated only by divine will but also by what Anthony Padgen has called Spain's depiction of itself as "the self-assured champion, guardian (and exporter) of Christian cultural values" (2). Indeed, Lope portrays Columbus as the "Christopherens," or Bearer of Christ, as Columbus liked to call himself and as he signed his name in his writings from 1501 on. To portray a Columbus more concerned with saving the souls of the Amerindians than with the search for gold, Lope has him arrive in the Caribbean accompanied by the missionary Fray Buyl, who, according to historical records, did not join the Admiral in the first voyage. In fact, the Admiral did not bring any clerics during his initial crossing. Lope, however, shows Columbus planting, with the help of Fray Buyl, a huge cross on the shores of the Caribbean island where he has made landfall. Columbus then fades away at the end of act 1; not until the end of act 3 does Lope return the Admiral to the stage, placing him in Barcelona before Ferdinand and Isabella, to whom he has brought a group of Amerindians to be baptized. The monarchs willingly accept the native Americans, announcing that Columbus's voyage has given the native inhabitants access to God and, to Spain, a New World to conquer. Columbus has carried the cross to the New World, and his mission to expand the Spanish empire beyond the borders of Christendom to the farthest pagan realms has been accomplished.

It is important to stress that Lope composed *El Nuevo Mundo* one century after Columbus's arrival in the Americas. It should be noted, as well, that the play was written roughly fifty years after the highly charged dispute over the rights of the Amerindians that culminated in the heated 1550 debate in Valladolid between the Spanish priest Fray Bartolomé de las Casas and Spain's leading humanist, Juan Ginés de Sepúlveda. To acquaint students with the polemic about Spain's presence in the Americas and the acceptable ways of exercising power over the Amerindians, I recommend Carlos Fuentes's history of Spain and the Spanish-speaking peoples *El espejo enterrado* (*The Buried Mirror*). The Discovery/BBC television series that inspired Fuentes's book is available in videos for classroom use. Students may also read Las Casas's *Brevísima relación de la destruición de las Indias* and scene 19 of Miguel de Carvajal and Luis Hurtado de Toledo's morality play *Las cortes de la muerte*, which stages some of the debates concerning the conquest of America and evokes some of Las Casas's ideas regarding the brutality of the conquistadores.

Familiarity with the issues raised by Las Casas's interrogation of Spain's actions and attitudes toward the Amerindians allows students to explore how Lope's New World play addresses the question of the legitimacy of the Spanish enterprise in America, as well as the truthfulness of Las Casas's account. Students may analyze, for instance, Lope's capacity to dramatize both sides of the debate, presenting a more complex view of the colonial experience in the New World. Is Lope merely a celebrant of and unreserved apologist for Spain's imperial expansion westward and the colonization process? Or is he ambivalent, constructing the conquistadores as lascivious, greedy sailors with an unquenchable thirst for the indigenous women's bodies and the island's gold? Does he thus suggest that the Amerindians had the right to rebel and defend themselves? Who are the truly idolatrous, the Amerindians who convert to Christianity at the end of the play or the Spanish sailors who die worshipping the American gold? Does Lope's depiction of the Spanish sailors' barbaric and unchristian behavior call into question the legitimization of the conquest and the colonial project as a missionary enterprise? These questions help students carry out a nuanced reading of Lope's *El Nuevo Mundo,* one that recognizes an official ideological stance but attends to substantial digressions from that position. We might thus see the play "as ideologically multiform or decentered" in its imagining of the encounter (Lauer, "Iberian" 38).

In my teaching of this play, I introduce other cultural variables, such as the interweaving of gender and colonialism, or what Louis Montrose has called the "gendering of the New World as feminine, and the sexualizing of its exploration, conquest, and settlement" ("Gender" 177). As one of the commonest colonialist tropes, the feminization and eroticization of the New World is present in Columbus's earliest writings as well as in numerous early modern visual materials. For instance, allegorical personifications of America as a female nude appeared throughout Western Europe in several drawings, engravings, and paintings, such as Jan van der Straet's famous drawing of Amerigo Vespucci's "discovery" of America, which was made widely available in print in the late sixteenth century by Theodor Galle's engraving. Montrose's (179–83) and Michel de Certau's (xxv–xxvi) analysis of the ideological implications of this well-known image are effective materials for teaching the importance of gender in the discourse of discovery in relation to Lope's New World play.

I point out that in *El Nuevo Mundo* the first native encountered by Columbus and his men is a woman who, describing the irresistible beauty of the European strangers, noticeably desires the conquistadores. Tellingly, Lope names the island where Columbus makes landfall La Deseada and not Guanahaní, as the natives called it, or San Salvador, as it was later named by the admiral. Students may also consider the scene in which Lope portrays the apparent lust of the New World females when one Spaniard makes an allusion to "the widely broadcast 'fact' [in the early modern period] that native women never liked to say no" (Brotherton 42). Lope presents a conquistador leaving the stage with an "india" in his arms, pleasantly amazed by the supposed "easiness" of the female and affirming that "por deshonra tienen éstas / el negar la voluntad" (3.2306–307) ("These women consider it dishonorable to deny the flesh"). That "india" brings to mind the allegorical personifications of America as a naked female native waiting to be conquered.

Lope presents Columbus's sailors as unable to resist their passions and the invitations of the willing native women who, like the newly found land, desire to be taken and conquered by the Spaniards. Even Tacuana, the female Amerindian protagonist who was abducted at the beginning of the play by the Indian chief Dulcanquellín, rejects her husband, Tapirazú, and her new Amerindian suitor to become the mistress of a conquistador. When considering Lope's characterization of Tacuana, many students hear the familiar ring of the story of Malinche, known by the Amerindians as Malintzín and as Doña Marina by the Spaniards. Granted to Hernán Cortés and his soldiers in one of the early continental encounters between Spaniards and Amerindians, Malinche became Cortés's interpreter and concubine, and the mother of his son. Over the centuries, Malinche has been perceived in Mexican national discourse as a symbol of treachery to her race and as a passive object of conquest. More recently, however, this complex, contradictory figure has been vindicated as a strategist, a translator or cultural bridge, the symbolic mother of the mestizo, and as a feminist symbol.

In viewing the Malinche story as a blueprint not only for the characterization of Tacuana but for the other female natives in Lope's play, who serve as intermediaries between the Spanish conquistadores and the Amerindian males (Carey–Webb 49–51), the class should highlight Tacuana's conscious alliance with the conquerors and her welcoming words to them. For instance, students may be asked to react to Tacuana's speech in which she invites the conquistadores to propagate Christianity "desde Haití a la Hermosa Chile" (3.2180) ("from Haiti to beautiful Chile") and then encourages them to bring their sons to the Indies so that the young men can marry "nuestras hijas, a donde, / mezclándose nuestra sangre, / seamos todos españoles" (2193–95) ("our daughters whereby, mixing with our blood, we may all be Spaniards"). In addition to exploring how Lope projects the Malinche story "backwards in time to the very earliest encounter of Spaniards and Native Americans" (Carey–Webb 51), students can probe how issues of *mestizaje* and national identity find their way into Lope's play. Did the mestizo offspring produced by the encounter change or challenge established ideas of what it meant to be a Spaniard? Who was Spanish and who was not? Later in the play the Spaniards who have sexual relations with the native women are killed by the native men. Does the ending reject the notion of the mixture of blood between Spaniards and Amerindians voiced by Tacuana?

These questions bring us back to the subject of Spain and its others with which I open my discussion of *El Nuevo Mundo* in the classroom and to a crucial idea that I endeavor to convey to my students: that for Lope, other dramatists, and their seventeenth-century audience, America did matter.

NOTE

Quotations of *El Nuevo Mundo descubierto por Cristóbal Colón* and English translations are from Robert M. Shannon's bilingual edition. For a verse translation, by Kenneth A. Stackhouse, see Vega Carpio, *Discovery*.

An Approach to Teaching Drama Written in Colonial Spanish America

Frederick Luciani

The corpus of colonial Spanish American theater is large, diverse, and rich in possibilities for undergraduate teaching, yet colonial drama is markedly under-represented in university curricula. A quick review of the course offerings in the Spanish programs of about thirty major American universities and colleges reveals not a single undergraduate course devoted solely to colonial Spanish American theater, and only a sprinkling of dramatic texts in more broadly based survey or thematic courses. The situation is perhaps not surprising: although academic attention to colonial Spanish American literature bourgeoned in the 1980s and 1990s, the field remains a relatively new one, and theater has received somewhat less scholarly treatment than other genres. There is, in effect, no set of canonical texts, and some of the most interesting, important examples of colonial theater cannot be found in easily accessible, well-edited modern editions.

But the lack of a well-established tradition of colonial Spanish American theater in the university curriculum is, in a sense, liberating. The field has grown simultaneously with the increasing emphasis on the interdisciplinary in the American academy, and with the trend toward cultural studies in departments of language and literature. Much scholarly work on colonial theater, of significance to the undergraduate classroom, reflects the move away from conventional forms of literary study. The teaching of the subject can be adapted to the diverse, fruit-fully idiosyncratic concerns of theme courses focusing on the colonial period, such as those I found in my review of Spanish and Latin American literature curricula: utopias, quest literature, "civilization versus barbarism," border crossings, self-fashioning in women writers, representations of cannibalism and piracy, and so on. Dramatic texts of the colonial period, if carefully chosen, can also have a central place in survey courses, whether the courses are limited to the co-lonial period or have a wider chronological range. Nor should colonial theater be overlooked when instructors are building a reading list embracing both peninsular Spanish and colonial texts, in accordance with the recent interest in transatlantic studies.

My course on colonial Spanish American literature, conducted in Spanish, has characteristics both of a survey and of a theme course. A primary goal is to give students a broad, representative sampling of the diverse forms of literature pro-duced in the colonies, from the first texts of the "discovery" through the end of the seventeenth century. The course focuses on a set of themes: the initial en-counter of Europeans and Amerindians as reflected in early texts and as refor-mulated in colonial-era texts to serve the diverse interests and agendas of later generations; the ongoing problematic of the representation of self and other in colonial texts; the emergence of creole and mestizo identities in the colonial period, as well as regional identities that prefigure the nationalist aspirations of the nineteenth century; the complicated processes of production and transmission of pre-Columbian texts that are necessarily colonial-era products and the concomicant deformation, manipulation, and reappropriation of cultural memory of the indigenous past; the early emergence of voices that challenged structures and institutions of power in the colonial world, along with the inevitable temporizing with those structures and institutions that the colonial situation demanded.

My audience for this advanced undergraduate course is itself diverse. Some of the students are Spanish majors or minors and have a grounding in early modern Hispanic culture and literary history, including that of Spain's Golden Age. These students have read, in Spanish, the belletristic genres: lyric and epic poetry, drama, the novel and short story, the essay. Other students are majors or minors in Latin American studies, and they usually have a good sense of the historical and cultural themes associated with the colonial period. A few of them have encountered in history classes (and in English) some of the texts and authors that I include in my course. Obviously, both groups of students bring strengths to the class. At the same time, there are elements of surprise or strangeness in our readings, for both groups of students. The Spanish majors are sometimes puzzled by genres they do not think of in connection with literature, such as letters and chronicles, or they may have instinctive misgivings about works produced anonymously, collectively, or by improvised writers—missionaries, conquistadores, and such. The Latin American studies students, for their part, tend to be less attuned to the aesthetic dimensions of our readings, as well as to the literary conventions within which an author's unique voice can be appreciated.

For this course, I choose theatrical texts that intersect with the thematic concerns I have listed here and that appeal to students' diverse strengths, while they productively challenge students' disciplinary assumptions and prejudices. The texts represent the two main geographical poles of colonial literary culture (Mexico and Peru), a range of authorial voices (indigenous, mestizo, creole, male, female), kinds of authorship (single author, anonymous, collective), and even languages (one of the plays is a translation into Spanish from the original Quechua). Peninsular Spanish theater provides a useful touchstone for these texts; the normative body of forms, tropes, and themes that it offers can help students recognize and explore the differences that characterize colonial theater. While often deferential to the prestige and influence of the drama of the metropolis, and undeniably imitative, colonial theater can also be self-consciously divergent—sometimes defiantly—from the peninsular tradition. Some examples contain indigenous, non-Western elements that stand in contrast to European dramatic forms. In either case, an important goal of the course is to encourage students to see that colonial theater, like colonial literature and cultural manifestations more broadly, is not merely derivative of, or lesser than, that of Spain.

Three of the theatrical texts in my syllabus take as their subject matter the first encounter of Spaniards and Amerindians and the conquest or conversion of the latter by the former. I have found that students often are predisposed to confront the conquest in stark moral terms—avaricious conquistadores, victimized Indians—and they may expect the texts either to ratify that moral posture (by offering a historically and ethically authentic view of the conquest) or to demonstrate a lack of awareness of it (the assumption being that our enlightened age is capable of recognizing what an earlier, benighted age could not). This is in fact a useful starting point for students' acquisition of a broader, more nuanced understanding of the passionate, contentious debate about the conquest that began in Spain and its colonies as early as the sixteenth century and evolved during the centuries to reflect diverse agendas and cultural identities.

An illustration of this idea can be seen in the first of our dramatic texts, the *Coloquio de los cuatros reyes de Tlaxcala* (Arrom and Rojas Garcidueñas). Before reading it, students will have learned that the Tlaxcaltecas, traditional enemies of the Mexicas, initially resisted the Spanish incursion on their territory as Cortés advanced toward Tenochtitlán; then, having been subdued by the Spaniards, joined forces with them and were instrumental in their eventual triumph. The *Coloquio,* of uncertain authorship, represents the legendary conversion to Christianity and baptism of the four Tlaxcalan kings in 1519. The play renders that story as a miraculous, providential event: the four kings, warned of the approach of the white foreigners by their god Hongol—who is none other than Lucifer—are inspired to abandon their idolatrous ways and convert to the new cult *before* their first meeting with Cortés. Their conversion is completed at the play's end, when, instructed in the rudiments of the faith by the friar who accompanies Cortés, they are baptized. The play makes no mention of armed resistance to the Spaniards by the Tlaxcalan nation.

The narrative is revisionist history, of course, and students immediately recognize it as such. The questions to explore with the students become, Who may have written this play, for what audience, and for what purpose? Working with a few scholarly studies of the play (Rojas Garcidueñas; W. A. Reynolds), I share with the students such meager knowledge of the play's provenance as is available: it was probably composed in Tlaxcala in the early seventeenth century— that is, about a hundred years after the events it portrays. I remind students that throughout the colonial period, the Tlaxcalans actively sought and were rewarded with special privileges by the Spanish crown in compensation for their role in the conquest. Here I am aided by a facsimile of the *Lienzo de Tlaxcala,* a mid-sixteenth-century pictorial work representing Tlaxcalan contributions to the conquest—and the legendary baptism of the four kings—a copy of which was sent to the king of Spain to promote Tlaxcalan interests; I view the facsimile with my students in my university's rare book collection.

The students themselves notice the lack of authenticity in the play's indigenous characters: before the kings encounter the Spaniards, their speech is peppered with references to Phoebus, Neptune, and Apelles, and there seems to be no language barrier between them and the Spaniards when they eventually meet. I drive home the point by revealing the probable source of the character Hongol, as discovered and explained by Winston A. Reynolds: the character is apparently derived from the fictional god Ongol in Lope de Vega's play *El Nuevo Mundo descubierto por Cristóbal Colón* (1614), and ultimately from the identically named character in Alonso de Ercilla's epic poem *La araucana* (1569), which deals with the conquest of the Araucanians of South America. Thus the *Coloquio de los cuatro reyes de Tlaxcala* is linked to the so-called *comedia de Indias* (see the article by Cartagena-Calderón in this volume), a genre practiced by Lope de Vega and Calderón de la Barca, among other peninsular playwrights. With its final emphasis on the Eucharist, the *Coloquio de los cuatro reyes de Tlaxcala* also can be seen as a variant of the *auto sacramental*—another genre that undergraduate students of Golden Age Spanish literature will have some familiarity with. In every sense, then, the play reflects Spanish and Catholic ideologies, literary traditions, and aesthetic sensibilities, while apparently promoting regional Tlaxcalan interests through revisionist historical apologetics.

The next play on my syllabus is the so-called *Tragedia del fin de Atahualpa*. This verse drama tells the story, from the indigenous perspective, of the prelude to the arrival of the Spanish in Inca realms, in the form of dreams and premonitions communicated to the Inca king Atahualpa; of the initial contacts between the Inca king and the conqueror Pizarro; of their eventual meeting, the murder of Atahualpa at Pizarro's hands, and Pizarro's death before "España"—the Spanish monarch—who is shocked and angered by the murder of the Inca. Despite this last scene, which seems to pull the play into the orbit of a Spanish worldview of authority and justice, the play seems fundamentally non-Western in outlook and in dramatic form. This point is evident in the powerful poetic imagery of a "world upside down" (Chang-Rodríguez 50–54) resulting from the slaying of the Inca and the overthrow of his kingdom, the interventions of a chorus of *ñustas* (princesses) to announce and comment on events, the use of elaborate formulas of address among the characters, and the constant repetition of verses and speeches. Significant, as well, is the play's insistence on the incomprehensibility to the natives of the Spanish language and forms of literate communication—most remarkable in the scenes in which Spaniards move their lips but no sound is heard, or in the set piece of the Incas' frustrated efforts to decipher the letter that Pizarro sends to Atahualpa. In the same vein, the play follows the historical tradition according to which Atahualpa's murder was precipitated by his impatient tossing aside of the Bible given to him by his captors, having failed to hear it say anything to him.

The *Tragedia del fin de Atahualpa* offers a valuable contrast to the accounts and judgments of the conquest we have read by the time we come to the play. But the inclusion of this work in a syllabus of colonial-era writings is not unproblematic. The *Tragedia* is known only through a copy of a lost nineteenth-century manuscript, although the work clearly is part of a centuries-long cycle of plays representing the death of the Incan emperor at the hands of Pizarro; early manifestations are described in sixteenth-century testimonies, and popular variants of the play are still performed in the Andean region. A number of prominent scholars, who first studied the play after its translation from Quechua and publication in 1957 by Jesús Lara, confidently dated it to the sixteenth century, and thus saw in it remnants of pre-Hispanic theatrical modes as well as a genuine expression of the so-called "vision of the vanquished." The play's seemingly non-Western form, and its poignant representation of the bewilderment and grief of the Incas on the murder of Atahualpa, would seem to confirm the play's attribution to the very early colonial era. Other scholars find evidence, in the text, of eighteenth-century revampings, connected with the resurgence, at that time, of indigenous insurrectionism in the Andean region. Recently, some scholars have expressed skepticism that the play is a colonial-era artifact at all. Pierre Duviols, for example, sees it as a fanciful nineteenth-century distillation of contemporary popular versions of the play, and, moreover, finds largely Spanish rather than indigenous theatrical origins in the Atahualpa cycle.

Instead of glossing over these controversies, I use them to discuss with the students the interesting challenges that such a layered text presents to the scholar, and even to the casual reader. The play's ideological and formal superimpositions and paradoxes are those of colonial culture itself—evident, for example, in the religious syncretism that evolved from the evangelization process, and in the professed allegiance to crown and church of leaders of armed rebellions against the colonial regime, such as José Gabriel Condorcanqui (Tupac Amaru II) in the late 1700s. Pertinent, as well, is the apparent conflation, throughout the long history of the "death of Atahualpa" theatrical cycle, of the executions of a series of leaders associated with the Inca dynasty—from Atahualpa and Tupac Amaru I in the sixteenth century, through Tupac Amaru II in the eighteenth (Chang-Rodríguez 43–49). For that matter, as Nathan Wachtel (35) has explained, representations of the Atahualpa story in recent popular theater have used scenic cues—such as dressing the conquistador characters in present-day military uniforms—to identify the Spanish oppressors with current repressive governments. Seen in this way, the *Tragedia del fin de Atahualpa* becomes less interesting as a colonial-era artifact representing a specific historical moment and more interesting as a text that encompasses distinct but parallel historical moments, and colonialism more broadly. The work graphically illustrates the problems of communication, of conflicting epistemologies, that occur when two cultures collide—a situation whose relevance today is thrown into sharper relief through the play's retrospective lens.

The third conquest play on my syllabus is the *loa* to *El divino Narciso*, by Sor Juana Inés de la Cruz (Mexico, 1648?-95), first published in 1690 (I use the Méndez Plancarte ed.). The play, an allegorical representation of the conquest and conversion of indigenous Mexicans, serves as prologue to an *auto sacramental* that uses the myth of Narcissus to allegorize Eucharistic doctrine. But the *loa* is significant as an autonomous short play. The characters are a noble indigenous couple, Occidente and América, and a Spanish couple, Celo (Zeal, dressed as a conquistador) and Religión (a Spanish lady). As the play opens, Occidente and América are singing and dancing a *tocotín* in honor of their God of Seeds. The entrance of Celo and Religión portrays the incursion by the Spanish and their overthrow of the Mexicans through the use of arms (carried out by Celo), followed by their efforts to convert the natives (realized by Religión). Religión serves to restrain Celo's violence; she advocates persuasion rather than force. She resorts to a syncretistic explanation of Christian doctrine by approximating the God of Seeds to the Christian God whom the natives, enlightened by a new truth, should now accept. The fact that the natives ceremonially consume their god— the rite alluded to was called *teocualo*, or "God is eaten" (Méndez Plancarte 503–04)—facilitates the explanation that Religión offers. To further convince Occidente and América, Religión invites them to witness the *auto sacramental* to follow, which will use the allegorical parallel of another pagan culture—that of ancient Greece—to illustrate the mysteries of the Eucharist.

The *loa* offers a useful recapitulation of themes developed throughout the course. While not actually meant for the religious instruction of native peoples (Sor Juana's *auto* was intended for performance in the Madrid court), the *loa* recalls the forms of missionary theater that, in the first decades following the conquest, sought equivalencies between native practices and Christian doctrine and capitalized on the benefits of visual spectacle (and native languages) to appeal to mass indigenous audiences. The tension between the methods of Celo and Religión, and the ascendancy of the latter over the former, suggests the sixteenth-century debates in Spain about the legitimacy and the methods of the conquest (which the students will have learned about through selected writings of Bartolomé de las Casas). Georgina Sabat-Rivers (283) helpfully observes that the characters Occidente and América defend their right to religious choice through the exercise of free will and reason; Sor Juana thus appears to validate the notion, supported by Las Casas and others, that the indigenous peoples possessed this fundamental right and capacity.

Unlike that of the *Coloquio* and, for that matter, *La tragedia del fin de Atahualpa*, the syncretism of Sor Juana's *loa* is not unwitting or naive. Rather, it brings to mind the deliberate efforts of erudite clerics of the colonial era to reconcile pre-Hispanic history, culture, and religion with those of the Christian West—to incorporate, in effect, indigenous history into what was understood as History itself. Such an attempt required, in Sor Juana as in other Creoles of her generation, a vigorous effort to recover and understand the legacy of Mexico's indigenous past. As Sabat-Rivers notes (272–73), the task involved a certain sentimental identification with and even mythicizing of that past, and can be related to a nascent sense of nationalism among the creole class.

Other elements of the *loa*, besides its erudition, bear the unique stamp of Sor Juana. By the time we read it, students have become familiar with the gender issues raised by Sor Juana's works. In her amorous and philosophical poetry, as in her theological and autobiographical prose, the Mexican nun promotes the idea that the female sex is capable of—in some instances is even the best custodian of—rationalism, learnedness, and moral wisdom. It seems no accident, then, that of the two Spanish characters, it is the lady, Religión, who carries the day, advocating the peaceful conversion of the natives through reason and persuasion. The male, Celo, in contrast, is characterized by his recourse to physical violence, with shadings of fanaticism and cruelty. Sor Juana revisits the conquest debates of an earlier century in a gendered framework. And, as so often occurs in her work, her subtle gender politics are self-referential. The *loa*, after all, introduces her *auto sacramental*, whose erudition, artistry, and mastery of theological allegory represent Sor Juana's bid to compete with the prestigious male practitioners of the form in the Spanish Peninsula, especially the acknowledged master, Calderón de la Barca.

I find that the three dramatic texts described here are not only broadly representative in terms of geography and authorial voice, in keeping with the survey structure of my course, but also illustrative of the course's thematic concerns. That they all deal with the conquest enables us to explore the diverse ways in which that cataclysmic event was viewed, by different interest groups and over time, during the colonial period. In these texts, Spanish majors and Latin American studies majors alike find formal and thematic properties that are both familiar and strange. All the students are coaxed away from a view of the conquest that is narrowly moralistic and acquire a better understanding of the layered quality of colonial Spanish American culture: the complicated fusions of thought and representation that the colonial situation produced and the intriguing assimilations and identifications that occurred across races, classes, and peoples.

Staging Captivity: Cervantes's Barbary Plays

María Antonia Garcés

Cervantes's plays *El trato de Argel* and *Los baños de Argel* reenact the author's traumatic experience as a slave of Algerian corsairs between 1575 and 1580, an indelible experience that inexorably recurs throughout his oeuvre (see my *Cervantes in Algiers*). On the borderline between autobiography and fiction, these plays function as poetic testimonies to the ordeals of human bondage. Cervantes, indeed, would be the first playwright in sixteenth-century Spain to stage the plight of Christian captives in Barbary, one of several innovations that make him a pioneer of the Spanish theater.

Since *El trato de Argel* and *Los baños de Argel* take place in Barbary, the name given by the early modern Europeans to the Maghreb—the North African region that now encompasses Morocco, Algeria, Tunisia, and Libya—I call these dramas the Barbary plays. They can be taught in a course on the Spanish theater of the Golden Age, in a cultural studies course on the early modern contacts between Spain and Islam in the Mediterranean, or in a survey of Cervantes's works. Always an exciting enterprise, teaching *El trato de Argel* and *Los baños de Argel* has acquired a particular relevance since the tragic events of 9/11 in the United States and the ensuing wars in Afghanistan and Iraq. The strife between Islam and Christianity for control of the Mediterranean that forms their backdrop can be discussed in the light of current conflicts between the two religions. These plays offer a multifaceted view of the Islamic world, for which Cervantes felt a conspicuous attraction throughout his life, even while they shed light on the complex interactions between Muslim and Christians in the early modern Mediterranean.

I introduce the history and geography of the region through a *PowerPoint* slide presentation of maps showing the geopolitical positions of the Hapsburg and Ottoman empires in the sixteenth century, including maps of Algiers and the Barbary Coast and early modern illustrations of Turks and Algerians, taken from European travel books. We review, as well, Spain's relations with North Africa after the fall of Granada in 1492, when the southern frontiers of Iberia were pushed to the Maghrebi coasts, where the Spaniards captured villages and constructed presidios, or fortresses.

Crucial for understanding Cervantes's Barbary plays is the examination of piracy and privateering in the early modern Mediterranean. An undeclared war practiced by Christians and Muslims alike, piracy was exacerbated by the presence of Morisco émigrés expelled by the *Reconquista,* who settled in the Maghreb in the sixteenth century (Braudel 2: 865–69). Joining the ranks of Muslim corsairs, they launched continuous attacks against Spain and its possessions. Their activities gained an enormous political significance under Barbarossa, the founder of the modern state of Algiers, who turned its capital into the apotheosis of privateering in the Mediterranean. Chapters from relevant studies of the sixteenth-century Maghreb, which stress its connections to Catholic Spain through war, commerce, and religious interactions (Garcés, *Cervantes*; García Arenal and de Bunes; Hess; Sola and de la Peña; Wolf), can help students appreciate the complex socioeconomic networks in the region during Cervantes's lifetime. As background reading for Cervantes's plays, we review accounts of the author's captivity, such as Jean Canavaggio, *Cervantes*; Garcés, "El cautiverio" and *Cervantes in Algiers*.

I begin the study of *El trato de Argel* (1581–83) by focusing on Cervantes's prologue to *Ocho comedias y ocho entremeses nunca representados* (*Obra completa*), an introduction that sheds light on the evolution of the Spanish theater before Lope, even while it emphasizes Cervantes's valuation of his dramatic production. Not only a pioneer of Spanish drama, Cervantes was one of its most informed critics, whose commentary on the theater of his time extends from its foundations to the attributes a good actor should have. The theater was, in fact, Cervantes's occupation in some periods of his career and a constant preoccupation throughout his life (A. Sánchez 15).

From the onset, *El trato* thrusts both the audience and the reader into Algiers, represented in the play's original title as if the city were a dungeon: *Comedia llamada* trato de Argel, *hecha por Miguel de Cervantes questuvo* [sic] *cautivo en él siete años* (A Play Entitled Life in Algiers, Composed by Miguel de Cervantes Who Was a Captive in This City for Seven Years).[1] The word *trato* means both "way of life" and "treatment", it also refers to a negotiation or commercial deal— in this case, the trade in human beings that constituted the central activity of Algiers in the sixteenth century. Cervantes called these transactions "*trato mísero intratable*" (miserable, untreatable *dealings*) and "*trato feo*" (ugly *dealings*) (1.15; 4.2535; emphasis added).[2] In effect, thousands of captives, rounded up in the assaults on Christian ships and on the coasts of Spain and Italy, were sold each year in the bustling slave trade of Algiers, the corsair capital of the Mediterranean. In his *Topografía, e historia general de Argel,* edited by Diego de Haedo (Valladolid, 1612), Antonio de Sosa claims that in the 1570s there were more than 25,000 Christian slaves in Algiers (Haedo, *Topografía* 1: 47).[3] Sosa was not only a close friend of Cervantes's in captivity but also his first biographer—see Sosa's account of Cervantes's second escape attempt, in his *Diálogo de los mártires de Argel* (178–81), and his ethnographic study of sixteenth-century Algiers (Haedo, *Topografía,* vol. 1), a marvelous complement to Cervantes's Barbary plays.

In the opening scene of *El trato,* the captive Aurelio appears alone and chained on the stage. If his solitary presence on the bare set underscores the bitter reality of captivity in Barbary, his initial soliloquy accentuates the incapacity of language to express catastrophic events. The captive ends by comparing the slaves' lives in Algiers with visions of purgatory and hell on earth: "¡Oh purgatorio en la vida, / infierno puesto en el mundo . . . !" (1.1–9) ("Oh Purgatory in life, / Hell placed in this world . . . !"). These images evoke the seventh circle of Dante's *Inferno,* focused on concentric rings of violence, torture, and death. All forms of violence contained in this medieval *Inferno* are represented in Cervantes's depiction of life in Algiers. The physical and spiritual afflictions adumbrated by Aurelio invoke the abysmal image of a hell, illustrated by a city surrounded by the desert and the sea, an inferno symbolized by the endless sufferings and punishments of the captives (Zimic, "Los tratos" 41–45). In his *Diálogo de la cautividad en Argel,* Sosa compares the city of Algiers to an inferno where one continuously "hears nothing but beatings, torments, and cries" from the tortures invented to kill Christians (Haedo 2: 125). For both Sosa and Cervantes, captivity represents a confrontation with death—that is, death experienced in advance by the captives. Death is also anticipated in the tortures inflicted on the Christian slaves, as well as in the escapes they staged, such as that of Per Álvarez, who reenacts Cervantes's first escape attempt, in January or February 1576 (Garcés, *Cervantes* 151–56).

Intertwining autobiography and history in uncanny ways, Cervantes's Barbary plays invite exploration from the perspective of trauma studies (see Caruth; Felman and Laub). The vertiginous, fragmented images of captivity that crisscross *El trato,* as well as the various doubles of the former slave Cervantes, signal the presence of trauma in the play (see Garcés, *Cervantes*). Indeed, acute trauma is distinguished by profound forms of splitting, so that separate selves seem to coexist in the subject (Lifton 175). In survivors of a catastrophic experience, splitting signals the impossibility of the subject to relive the event directly; creating doubles permits the subject to approach that which he or she cannot experience face to face. Doubling illuminates the relation between Aurelio and Saavedra, who stand for two parts of Cervantes in *El trato,* and sheds light on the other refracted couples of this drama.

El trato is organized through the representation of reversed and complementary couples who frequently mirror each other in a distorted way: each has an inverted double, embodied by another character (Zmantar 192). While Aurelio depicts the captive confined to a private home, Saavedra, his double and complement, belongs to the street. Per Álvarez, the fugitive who is miraculously saved in Cervantes's play, also has a double, another runaway slave who is caught and clubbed to death as the pasha watches and orders more beatings. This anonymous slave evokes the image of Cervantes, who failed in four breakout attempts from his prison, barely escaping death (Zmantar 192–93). Whereas the anonymous slave is punished to death, however, Cervantes's life was twice spared by Hasan Pasha, the bey (governor) of Algiers, when the Spanish captive appeared fettered and chained before him. The reiterative doubling revealed by *El trato* (between Cervantes and Per Álvarez, and between Per Álvarez and the anonymous slave, among others) testifies to trauma, in its construction of a fictional reality consisting of two antithetical tableaux with no connections between them. In addition, the fragmented scenes and discourses of *El trato* mimic the way in which trauma returns in shards to the memory of the survivor, reflecting the difficulty of reliving and reenacting the traumatic event (Garcés, *Cervantes* 170–73).

Through his spokesman Aurelio, Cervantes characterized *El trato* as a "trasunto de la vida de Argel" (3.2534–535) ("reflection of life in Algiers"). Containing detailed descriptions of life in Algiers in the 1570s, this drama includes a number of historical personages, from renegade corsairs and Algerian leaders to notable Spanish and Portuguese captives. The precision with which Cervantes portrays the multicultural milieu of the city—its corsair raids; its slave market with its auctions of human beings; its renegades with eclectic identities; its Christian captives with their torments, love affairs, apostasies, and ransoms—stages a prodigious image of life in Barbary never before seen in Europe. The number of renegades who appear in Cervantes's works, the roles he gives them, and the sympathy with which he usually portrays them reveal both his enlightened curiosity and a real compassion for their plight.

In regard to apostasy, Cervantes shows in *El trato* and other works that the temptation to convert to Islam was a constant for the captives. Multiple Christian slaves, in effect, ended up converting to Islam to free themselves from their chains. Sosa claims that more than half the inhabitants of Algiers in the 1570s were renegades, born and brought up in the Christian faith, who had apostatized by their own free will (Haedo 1: 52). An illuminating dialogue in *El trato*, between the autobiographical character named Saavedra and a Spanish captive named Pedro, illustrates these dangers. Pedro, who has decided to apostatize, adopting the name Mamí, explains that he will become a Muslim, albeit only in appearance, to gain his liberty. He hopes to run away during a privateering expedition to a Christian land (4.2142–155). With deep-felt sympathy and compassion, Saavedra persuades the doubting Pedro not to renounce his Christian faith (4.2159–161). The parallels to Cervantes's experiences with renegades are remarkable, as revealed by the testimonies of other captives (Garcés, *Cervantes* 57–59).

The moral dangers of captivity in Algiers are dramatized in another scene, from act 3, in which the Moorish Zahara, enamored of her slave Aurelio, torments him with her enticements. Two allegorical figures, representing Aurelio's internal strife—Necesidad (Need) and Ocasión (Occasion)—stage a debate with Aurelio, who wavers between his desire for sensuous Zahara and his love for virginal Silvia, another Spanish slave. The climax of the play occurs when Aurelio practically surrenders to Zahara's seduction (4.1764–765). As Bartolomé Bennassar and Lucile Bennassar have demonstrated in their study of fifteen hundred renegades tried by the Spanish and Portuguese Inquisitions, apostatizing meant not only obtaining freedom and prosperity as a renegade in Barbary but also gaining access to the sensual pleasures offered by the societies of the Maghreb

(474). Aurelio's final triumph over his inner torments underlines the victory of Christian fortitude over the temptations of Islam, even as it underscores the multiple attractions and the perils of a long enslavement in Barbary.

As a collective tragedy in the style of *Numancia*, *El trato* represents the drama of a group connected by a common destiny: captivity in Algiers (Meregalli 403). That the author's traumatic experience is rewritten and reenacted by the thirty-eight characters who embody the ordeal of human bondage transforms this drama into a polyphonic testimony of captivity. Their common catastrophic experience turns *El trato* into a tragedy in the present, post-Holocaust sense (Garcés, *Cervantes* 170–73).

In contrast, *Los baños de Argel* represents a refined elaboration of the experience of captivity. The work was probably composed between 1609 and 1610, when Cervantes was already renowned as the author of *Don Quijote*. As traumatic images of the writer's captivity continue to intrude in his fictions down the years, they unfold into fantastic representations that open the window of creation. *Los baños de Argel* bears witness to the creative reworking of these unforgettable events thirty years after Cervantes's liberation.

In *La gran comedia de los cautivos de Argel* (1599), Lope de Vega had imitated Cervantes's *El trato*, reproducing much of its plot, especially the crisscrossing infatuations of the Moorish and Christian couples. At the same time, Lope introduced innovations, such as the reduction of long monologues, more freedom in the change of locations within the play, and the inclusion of a gracioso (jester). These innovations, in turn, passed to *Los baños*, which Cervantes probably wrote with the explicit intention of refuting and emulating his rival (Fothergill-Payne, "Los tratos" 180–81). Despite the novelties borrowed from Lope's play, the main plots of *Los baños* follow Cervantes's own works, as Antonio Rey Hazas has claimed (44). *Los baños* is a synthesis of *El trato*, with a secondary plot taken from *La historia del cautivo*, interpolated in *Don Quijote* 1, a story that we compare in class with *Los baños* because it rehearses some of the same motifs.

Paying attention to the historical underpinnings of both the play and the narrative, we focus on the alleged Christianity of the historical personage who inspired Cervantes's Zoraida, in *La historia del cautivo*, and her counterpart Zahara, in *Los baños*. In regard to this Algerian woman, whom Cervantes surely met, I inform students that her Christian grandmother was still alive in Algiers in 1580 (Garcés, *Cervantes* 208–11). We also focus on the female slaves in Algiers and other Maghrebi centers, many of whom practiced their Christian religion in secret, just as the pampered wives of certain rich men in Algiers regularly prayed to "Christ our Lord and to his blessed Mother" and "had many masses said" (Haedo 1: 165). This leads us to explore the role of women in Algerian society, as portrayed in *La historia del cautivo* and in Cervantes's Barbary plays, where the Moorish woman often speaks for the author. Likewise, as Cervantes intimates in his fiction, some Muslim women in Algiers and other North African cities committed adultery with Christian men, despite the harsh punishments contemplated by Islamic law (see Bennassar and Bennassar 384, 472, 477; and Garcés, *Cervantes* 168–70).

In *Los baños,* Cervantes deploys special theatrical effects intended to move and surprise the spectator, including violent actions that provoke terror in the audience. The play opens with a nocturnal *rebato* (assault) perpetrated by Algerian corsairs on a coastal village in Spain. Infused with epic grandeur, this pathetic scene stresses the confusion and desperation of the women, children, and old people who are torn from their country. The melodramatic effects of the scene are highlighted by a contrast between "high" and "low" stage settings: the town walls, where a captain and a soldier appear, describing the corsair's attack below; and a rock that Don Fernando climbs while delivering a monologue that laments the abduction of his fiancée, Costança. The high ramparts in this play are contrasted with the sea (the "low"), which appears to swallow both the corsairs and Don Fernando, who throws himself from the cliffs in desperation. I ask students to read the stage directions, paying particular attention to where the action takes place, including the changes in stage settings. Reminding students that this is a performance, I ask, for instance: How is the theatrical space constructed? What does the architecture tell us about a scene? These questions seem pertinent in view of the abrupt shifts of scene, such as the sharp drop from the city walls in Spain to the *baño* in Algiers, a scene that opens with the chief guardian calling the captives to hard labor in the city. The radical change of scenario accentuates the visual contrast between high and low stage settings, evoking both the fall of Don Fernando into the sea and the fall into captivity, in images that provide a symbolic commentary on the horrors of slavery in Barbary.

The presence of city walls and cliffs in *Los baños,* as well as of clear stage directions, reveals Cervantes's vivid interest in theatrical settings and effects. Accordingly, the portrayal of life in the Algerian *baños* becomes more and more spectacular in this play, as disclosed by the stage directions: "Sale un cautivo cristiano, que viene huyendo del Guardián, que viene tras él dándoles palos" (*Baños,* act 1, p. 35) ("A Christian captive comes out running away from the guard, who comes after him beating him"). The scene portrays the beatings inflicted on a weak and bloodstained slave, discovered in hiding by a guard. The captive is mortally ill, which elicits a wry comment from another slave: "Y cuando muerto le ven, / Dicen: '¡Gualá, que el mezquino / Estaba malo, sin duda!'" (1.297–302) ("And when they see him dead, / They say: 'By Allah! The poor man / was, in effect, sick!'"). The apotheosis of visual effects occurs with the martyrdom of Francisquito, who dies onstage as a result of the tortures inflicted by his master: "Córrese una cortina, descúbrese Francisquito, atado a una columna, en la forma que pueda mover a más piedad" (3.254) ("A curtain opens, showing Francisquito tied to a pillar, in the way that can inspire more pity"). The accumulation of sensational effects in *Los baños* appears, then, as an integral part of the play, designed to astonish and move the spectators.

Cervantes's emphasis on the theatrical in *Los baños* extends to the depiction of exotic Algerian customs, such as the lavish wedding celebrated between Hajji Murad's daughter Zahara and Sultan 'Abd al-Malik of Morocco. Historically, the daughter first married the aspirant to the Moroccan throne 'Abd al-Malik in 1570, remaining in Algiers while he returned to Marrakech in 1575. After the sultan's death in the Battle of Alcazarquivir in 1578, his widow married none other than Hasan Pasha, who became Cervantes's master in 1579. In *Los baños*, Cervantes alters these historical facts, separating the future sultan from his bride on the day of the wedding, as Zahara refuses her suitor. The ceremony is nevertheless celebrated with great fanfare, but the veiled woman carried on shoulders in the nuptial cortege is not Hajji Murad's daughter but a friend of hers, the married Halima. If the lavish staging of this wedding allows Cervantes to portray the marriage customs of Algiers in a spectacular way, his alteration of history permits the development of the plot, including the love affair between Zahara and the Christian captive Lope, with whom she finally escapes.

The fantastic wedding celebrated in *Los baños* enables students to focus on the staging of life in Algiers. The play can be read, indeed, as an ethnographic work that re-creates Algerian customs in the 1570s. Concomitantly, I ask students to list and be ready to discuss such images and aspects of Algerian life as the market scene where slaves are sold to the highest bidders, homosexuality, punishments applied to the captives, the status of renegades, and love between men and women from different religions. I also request students to compare scenes that depict Algerian customs with pertinent passages from Sosa's *Topografía* (Haedo, vol. 1) or from Sosa's *Diálogo de los mártires de Argel*.

The extraordinary scene of the theater within the theater in *Los baños* underscores the relevance of a dramatic recourse that reappears in other plays by Cervantes, such as *La entretenida* and *Pedro de Urdemalas*, as well as in his best-known interlude, *El retablo de las maravillas*. Revealing Cervantes's interest in mirror games, the most spectacular scene of *Los baños*, in act 3, represents the staging, in the *baños* of Algiers, of a pastoral play by Lope de Rueda, interpreted by some benevolent actors (captives) for an audience also made up of Spanish captives. The common condition of spectators and actors—all experiencing the drama of captivity—unifies the two actions of the play within the play. To stress the melodramatic effects of these mirror games, I ask some students to act out this scene, enhanced by the interruptions and buffooneries of the sacristan, which elicit the violent reactions of Cauralí, a corsair captain of Algiers. The pitiful comedy played by captives is finally halted by the tragic news of the death of various captives, killed by janissaries who mistakenly believed that a Christian fleet had arrived in Algiers.

The innovative scenarios and experimental nature of *Los baños de Argel*, among other of his plays, place Cervantes next to Bertolt Brecht, Eugène Ionesco, and Fernando Arrabal in our day, as Bruce Wardropper has observed ("Comedias" 158). The extraordinary success of *Los baños de Argel* and other *comedias de cautivos* by Cervantes, recently staged in Spain (see Monleón) and other countries, demonstrates that Cervantes's theater is *"un théâtre à naître"* (a theater not yet born), as Jean Canavaggio proclaimed in his *Cervantès dramaturge* (448–50)—that is, a theater ready for new readings and interpretations.

NOTES

[1] The play is mentioned as both *El trato de Argel* and *Los tratos de Argel*. The extant manuscript in Madrid's Biblioteca Nacional is entitled *Comedia llamada* trato de Argel *hecha por Miguel de Cervantes.* . . . See Canavaggio, "À propos."

[2] All translations from the Spanish are mine. Parenthetical references for quotations from plays refer to act and line numbers.

[3] Sosa's monumental work, which includes five books, was edited and published by Diego de Haedo; it appears in the works-cited listing under the name of its editor, Haedo, as *Topografía*. One of Sosa's works, *Diálogo de los mártires de Argel*, appears in the works-cited listing under its author's name, Antonio de Sosa.

Teaching Race and the Performances of Whiteness in *El valiente negro en Flandes*, by Andrés de Claramonte

John Beusterien

ANTÓN. Pues ¿quién damo comirá a Antón?
JUAN. Yo.
ANTÓN. Comiendo Antón, el paje olvidamo, y a Juan por sior tendremo. Damo y llevamo alabarda.
JUAN. ¿Prometes lealtad?
ANTÓN. Prometo.
[Juan le pasa a Antón la alabarda.]
JUAN. Pues toma, y sígueme.
ANTÓN. Vamo.
JUAN. Más espacio y más severo.
ANTÓN. Aspacio y severo andamo.
JUAN. Antonillo, ¿qué parezco?
ANTÓN. Rey mago, y yo sun lacayo.
JUAN. ¿Antón?
ANTÓN. ¿Sioro?
JUAN. Respeto; que soy sargento de Flandes.
ANTÓN. Turu lu mundo sabremo.
JUAN. ¿Antón?
ANTÓN. ¿Sioro?
JUAN. Camina.
ANTÓN. Parecen cosas de negros. (59–60)

ANTÓN. Who's going to provide Antón his food now?
JUAN. I am.
ANTÓN With Antón's belly full, he can forget the page and accept Juan as his master. Give me the halberd; I'll carry it.
JUAN. Do you promise to be loyal?
ANTÓN. I do.
[Juan hands him the halberd.]
JUAN. Take it and follow me.
ANTÓN. Let's go.
JUAN. Slow down and chin up.
ANTÓN. I'm going slow and my chin's up.
JUAN. My little Antón, what do I look like?
ANTÓN. Like one of the three Magi, and I his servant.
JUAN. Antón?
ANTÓN. Master?

JUAN. Show some respect; I am an army sergeant in Flanders.
ANTÓN. Everyone knows that.
JUAN. Antón?
ANTÓN. Master?
JUAN. March.
ANTÓN. It's all just a black thing.[1]

I teach Andrés de Claramonte's play *El valiente negro en Flandes* to make a postcolonial intervention into *comedia* studies, shedding light on this genre in the context of the history of race and imperialism. I include Andrés de Claramonte's play in an advanced undergraduate seminar, The Invention of Race, devoting approximately four hours of teaching time to it. This class, designed for Spanish majors, examines race in the Hispanic and Anglo-American world. Aside from offering credit toward a major in Spanish, the course meets an ethnicity studies core curriculum requirement for graduation. A modern edition of *El negro valiente en Flandes* (ed. Rodríguez López-Vázquez) has made the work more easily available for the undergraduate classroom. Although Claramonte is less popular in college and university classrooms than Calderón, Lope, Tirso, and Sor Juana, many of his plays were extremely well liked in their time. The first known edition of *El valiente negro en Flandes* is from 1638 (although the play was written in approximately 1620); along with a sequel written by Manuel Vicente Guerrero, it can be found in seventeenth- and eighteenth-century editions of plays from Madrid, Valencia, Seville, and Barcelona (Rodríguez López-Vázquez 213). By the mid-seventeenth century, the black protagonist of the play, Juan, was sufficiently well known that he made an appearance in a comic skit performed as part of the birthday festivities for King Philip IV's daughter Margarita (Restori 141–54). He is referred to in the skit by his popular nicknames *el valiente* and *el perro de Alba*.

Performance

I begin my teaching of this play by having students perform the selection I've provided here, in front of the classroom. After reading the passage out loud, many, even those whose Spanish is rusty, point out words that are not quite right. While they may not all immediately understand the words *sun* (the nasalized possessive—an *n* added to *su*) or *sioro* (a common word that black characters use for *señor*), most hear (and, in the case of native and advanced speakers, may even notice as a phonetic tendency in their own speech) that the final *s* has been dropped from the forms *vamo, andamo,* and *sabremo*. Having recognized that Antón's spoken Spanish differs from the standard and knowing that he is a black character, the class raises questions about language and race: Why does the secondary character Antón speak in a different way from the standard spoken by

Juan and the other characters in the play? If Antón is black and speaks a form of black Spanish, why does his companion Juan, the black protagonist, speak like the white characters in the play? These questions can trigger a class discussion about students' experiences with language and race, ranging from hip-hop music to rap to Ebonics and even to the revived film genre blaxploitation.

Critical Interventions

After the live performance, the class considers the play as well as the question of race alongside two articles from *comedia* criticism and one article that examines early modern English drama from a postcolonial perspective. The students will have read these three articles—Arnold G. Reichenberger's "The Uniqueness of the *Comedia*," Melveena McKendrick's "Honour/Vengeance in the *Comedia:* A Case of Mimetic Transference," and Ania Loomba's "'Delicious Traffick': Racial and Religious Difference on Early Modern Stages"—and have prepared answers to the following questions before class: What is unique about the *comedia* for Reichenberger? If Reichenberger describes the ending of the *comedia* as depicting "restored order," from whose point of view is order restored? What political or social institutions are implicated in that order? For McKendrick, what are the important issues posed by the *comedia*? To what degree are historical events significant for McKendrick's analysis? In what dramatic cases does she describe honor and vengeance? How do those characters seeking honor compare with those who are seeking honor and vengeance in *El valiente negro en Flandes*? What specific aspects of imperial culture does Loomba consider important in her analysis of early modern drama? What national stage tradition is the focus of her analysis? Why? In discussing Loomba's article, the students list examples from *El valiente negro en Flandes* that correspond to her category "religious difference."

In relation to Reichenberger's notion of "restored order," I point out that here it is a black-white marriage that restores the order, and we discuss the marriage from a transatlantic perspective. If we consider Spain in the context of its American territories, then the question of representing color in the *comedia*—the nature of the representation of race that originates in the cultural production from the metropole—is especially significant. The population of Africans and those of African descent in Spanish America nearly doubled that of whites, as early as in the sixteenth century (Martínez 195). Further, *comedias* that represent black protagonists such as *El valiente negro en Flandes* were not performed just on the national stages in Madrid but in the *corrales* of the viceroy capitals such as Mexico City—Enrique de Olavarría y Ferrari comments that it was one of the most popular plays there in the second half of the eighteenth century (28).

With the third question on the McKendrick article, my intention is to amplify and complicate the notion of honor in the *comedia*. A trademark *comedia* notion itself, honor has connotations primarily of social status, class relations, purity of blood, and a woman's social place. In this play (as in others, such as *El negro del cuerpo blanco, y el esclavo de su honra,* by Francisco de Leiva Ramírez de Arellano, from the mid-seventeenth century, in which the protagonist disguises himself by appearing on stage in blackface, to avenge and symbolically personify his tainted honor) the performance and visualization of skin color is also connected to the seventeenth-century concept of honor and status. Placing the concept again in a transatlantic perspective, I explain that in Spanish America, the aristocratic title *Don* would soon be associated with one's whiteness, in a context in which social status and lighter skin could literally be bought. Thus, for example, one eighteenth-century royal edict decreed that a *Don* could be purchased by *blancos de orilla* (lesser whites) for 1,400 *reales* and that free blacks could move up to the rank of *pardo* (another term for mulatto) for 700 *reales,* or to *quinterón* (one-fifth African blood) for 1,100 *reales* (Maingot 227). My interest in presenting such information is not meant to elide Spain's historical realities. The *comedia* reflects social status based more on religious orthodoxy and nobility than on race and skin color. Nonetheless, skin color contributed to the way in which Spanish society visualized and articulated hierarchies of difference in the seventeenth century, a fact largely occluded from *comedia* criticism.

I include the Loomba article as an example of a postcolonial approach to early modern English drama. The questions are designed to ascertain to what degree such an approach can be applied to Spanish drama, which Loomba does not include in her early modern stages. In examining the play from the Spanish colonial point of view, I suggest to students that the Spanish experience in the Americas also informs the character of Juan, even though the work is set in Flanders and Spain. Africans played a significant role in the development of the Spanish empire by aiding the campaigns of the early conquistadores, including Pedrarias Dávila in Panama, Pedro de Alvarado in Guatamala, and Hernán Cortés in Mexico. Most important, Juan Valiente, the hero in the conquest of Chile and the most famous sixteenth-century black of the early frontier (Kamen, *Empire* 139), seems to have served as an important historical source for the fictional protagonist of *El valiente negro.*

Symptomatic Analysis

In small groups, students discuss the following two scenes from the *comedia:*

Scene A

JUAN: Llamarse un negro Juan de Alba
hoy, de la misma manera
que es llamarse Juan Blanco
mas juro de hacer eterna vuestra Alba
en estos países;

que he de ser contra estas fieras
gentes, lebrel generoso
que los ladre y que los muerda. (48)

To call a black man Juan de Alba
from today on means the same thing
as calling him Juan White.
I swear that I will make
your name Alba eternal
in these lands.
I will set myself against
these fierce peoples like a generous rabbit-dog
that barks and bites them.

Scene A is important because it emblematizes the primary plot of the play, which has to do with the character Juan, who joins the Spanish army to fight the Flemish (the inhabitants of Flanders, which today corresponds to the Flemish part of Belgium) and single-handedly conquers them. In discussing Scene A, I encourage students to describe the characteristics of whiteness as performance. Juan creates for himself a paradoxical situation: although he is the black protagonist and hero, he aspires to be an exemplary model of whiteness. Juan experiences a fundamental anxiety with respect to the category of whiteness: he calls himself Juan Blanco, but the rest of the characters see him as the "black." In fact, he sets the terms of whiteness in a way that increases that anxiety. By proposing to make "Alba eternal," he makes whiteness an ahistoricized concept, without origin.

After discussing the implications of Juan as Alba's, or the "white's," dog, I provide students with a gloss of the secondary title of the play, "El perro de Alba." The alternative title indicates that people connected the play with a poem from the period—the ballad, or *romance*, of the same name; the poem had circulated orally and in chapbooks for nearly a century before the writing of the play (Gillet). Andrés de Claramonte introduces a direct anti-Semitic reference in the play, beyond the connotations of the alternative title, when Juan is fighting against the Flemish and shouts, "El perro de Alba soy; vengan judíos" (61) ("I am the dog from Alba; bring on the Jews"). Different versions of this *romance* existed, but it always contained the same plot, about a dog that could sniff out Jews. The versatility of the category of whiteness exists both in the play and in the *romance*, present and invisible in the name Alba. In the poem, *Alba* principally refers not to the duke or "dawn" but to the town of that name. Whiteness thereby is a secondary, concealed meaning, inscribed both in and onto Spanish geography as well as onto the body of the nation's military leader. *El valiente negro en Flandes* incorporates the anti-Jewish discourse from the poem and includes it within the meaning of whiteness, at the same time that it erases that notion behind the meaning of the proper name.

Scene B

Doña Leonor.	Tomad mi mano.
Juan.	Es muy tierna y muy blanca, y tiznaráse . . .
Juan.	Détente . . . Yo a los hombres desde lejos los abrazo.
Doña Leonor.	Eso es ser piedra. (51, 57)

Doña Leonor.	Take my hand.
Juan.	It's very tender and very white, and it will be stained . . .
Juan.	Stay back . . . I only hug men from a distance.
Doña Leonor.	You have a heart of stone.

Scene B is important because it deals with the secondary plot of the play, in which Leonor dresses as a man to avenge herself of Agustín, who has loved her and left her: he has stolen her honor. In a comic interlude, dressed as a page (the one whom Antón abandons for Juan), Leonor forgets her quest to find Agustín and begins to woo Juan. The purpose of the discussion of the scene is to let students describe how Juan associates the category of whiteness with compulsory heterosexuality. Juan is repulsed by the possibility of a relationship with Leonor, whom he sees as a man, and he suggests, following some Inquisition trials of the time, that she should be burned. A reading of Juan's desires in this scene, such as his desire to see "him" burned, underlines how this scene maps out a normative position with respect to masculinity and race. The original performance of the scene, though, can reveal a materiality to the words that question those norms. The reference to staining her white hand, in the verb *tiznarse,* evokes the soot, or *tizne,* that the actor playing Juan may have used for his makeup.[2] This moment of humor—the evocation of the artificiality of his color, through a reference to the fact that he may literally stain—disturbs the language of essentialism associated with Juan's blackness and by extension Leonor's whiteness.

Repeat Performance

To conclude my teaching of the play, we perform the scene in the epigraph once again. As we act it out in class, this time I may give a student a ruler, a stick, a rolled-up piece of paper, or any other prop that can serve as the halberd, and ask the student playing Juan to pass the weapon, at the cue, to Antón, the other black character and gracioso of the play. This action might be interpreted as one in which Juan makes Antón his servant, charged with carrying his weapon. Antón, however, carrying the hero's long spear-like weapon (halberds are about two meters long), suddenly finds himself with a certain strength and authority. One student performs these lines just as the audience—the class—listens to them. Speaking for Antón, the student uses a nonstandard form of Spanish, one that does not follow the white imperial syntax of Juan (and countless white male protagonists in other *comedias*). Rather than read the scene and the entire play as one that mocks or suppresses Antón's voice (Fra Molinero), a teacher can showcase this voice, precisely because it belongs to a minor character. Such direction can provide the opportunity to discuss how Antón's voice reflects an ideolect, a marginal way of speaking, in Spain, on the west coast of Africa, and in many parts of the Americas in the sixteenth and seventeenth centuries (Beusterien; Granda). Included as a part of the postcolonial intervention that I intend with this pedagogy, then, is my effort to show how theater can give a voice, a new halberd with each acting out of this scene, to the powerless.

The *comedia* may be understood as a symptomatic site that maps out normative spectator positions regarding not only whiteness but also gender, as well as monarchy and social class. Nonetheless, with the restaging of scenes such as this one in class, the combination of its present enactment and the contexts of its past performance, I teach the *comedia* as a disruptive body, the material manifestation of a silent academic reading, a site where the class as the performers and spectators resignify the norms of a constraining social script. In a play that represents norms of whiteness, there also exists a potential performance waiting to happen, in which the experience of the play subverts those norms. Antón gains a degree of dominance in his possession of the weapon—a possible metonym for the Greek scepter as well as the phallus, classical and psychoanalytic emblems of the power of speech.

Further, Antón, by saying that Juan looks "like one of the three Magi," refers to Juan as a theatrical character who would resonate with an audience all too familiar with the representation of Baltasar, the black king of the Magi, one of the oldest and most widespread characters in the history of popular Spanish drama (scholars typically cite the twelfth-century *Auto de los reyes magos* as the earliest surviving Spanish play). Through his overtly metatheatrical reference, he makes blackness artificial in that it constitutes a part of performativity. Even as I provide students with the past historical-theatrical context of Antón's remark, present student experiences with gender and racial performances surface in class. In one session a Jamaican student related her experience in a study-abroad program in a town in Burgos during January, in which she was asked to play the role of Baltasar for the Epiphany celebration.

Acting out this initial scene can trigger, again, a series of questions about the way in which it should be performed in class. What physically happens onstage with the reference to Juan's remark about "más espacio"? Is Juan asking Antón to slow down and give him space? Has Antón, then, been making fun of Juan's white mentality that men should keep their distance? When Juan demands more respect from Antón, can we assume that Antón is making faces or somehow mocking Juan onstage? Although we cannot know how the director or the actors interpreted this scene in any one of its many productions across the Spanish empire, the class re-creation of this ephemeral stage moment is pedagogically vital—not just because it can be interpreted as a moment in which Antón mocks Juan and, by implication, the white normativity associated with his character but also because it gives students an opportunity to recognize whiteness as performance rather than as immutable essence. This pedagogy connects with the trajectory of race and whiteness we will debate in future class discussions, including contemporary manifestations of white privilege (Wiegman) and its connections with anti-Semitism (Mills 74) and normative heterosexuality (R. Dyer; Stokes).

NOTES

[1] All translations from the Spanish are mine.

[2] Callaghan has studied blackfacing in early modern English theater, but no such study exists for Spanish theater of the same period. Blackfacing may not have existed in some productions, since black actors may have taken on black roles (Ruano de la Haza and Allen 310; V. Williamsen, *Minor Dramatists* 42). Nevertheless, direct references from plays— *Virtudes vencen señales,* by Luis Vélez de Guevara (86) and *El negro del cuerpo blanco,* by Leiva Ramírez (12)—and from written accounts by theatergoers (Shergold, *History* 47) clearly show that blackfacing was commonplace.

Teaching the *Comedia* to Nonmajors: Golden Age Drama in a Cultural Studies Context

Cory A. Reed

This class is about culture. It shouldn't be about literature.
—Middle Eastern studies major

We studied a lot of literature. I found myself wondering
how this would be beneficial. Literature should be studied
only as background for understanding how the people
actually lived.
—Geography major

Teaching nonmajors can be a daunting task. As *comedia* specialists, we share certain assumptions about the study of language, literature, and drama, as well as the expectation that our students have an appreciation of literature and at least a nominal interest in learning about it. Enter the nonmajor, and all assumptions are out the window. Nothing seems to violate an instructor's horizon of teaching expectations faster than a student who questions the value of the very subject we profess to teach. Nonmajors sometimes have little experience in the study of language and literature and may even question the value of exploring literature at all. Instead of being familiar with the critical apparatus of literary analysis, they may be locked into the scholarly paradigms of other disciplines—from the perspective of which literature appears soft or divorced from the real issues they are accustomed to studying. Increasingly, these students bring a cultural studies perspective, as issues of race, class, gender, ethnicity, and identity formation become prominent in the liberal arts curriculum.

The advent of cultural studies as a field of rising interest and influence on American campuses presents challenges, as well as opportunities, for faculty members who teach what has become known as the literature of dead white males. Despite our field's broadening focus to include female dramatists and critical approaches that reflect new theoretical sensibilities, undergraduates persist in viewing old literature as a relic of the past, irrelevant to a university culture afflicted by a kind of presentism that considers any period predating its own generation as ancient history. How do you explain the 1600s to students for whom the twentieth century exists largely in history books? Making old literature meaningful to a modern audience is always difficult, but the recent scholarly interest in cultural studies, the primacy of political readings of literary texts, and the shift in Hispanism from Spain to all things Latin American has, more than ever, cast Golden Age literature not only in the distant past but also as the cultural product of a decadent, oppressive society that students would rather scorn than examine.

In cultural studies and other area studies programs, undergraduates sometimes possess a predetermined antagonistic stance toward the study of Spain in general, and early modern Spain in particular, which they see as an evil empire bent on military conquest and ethnic cleansing. Recent scholarship has done much to correct misperceptions of the past that had favored an unbalanced, Eurocentric view of the Spanish-Amerindian encounter, but student attitudes have now rebounded far in the opposite direction. It has become fashionable to dis Spain. A few years ago, I happened to overhear a student describing my course to a friend. "It's about Spain," she said. "Why do they make us study Spain, anyway?" As our departments have responded to changes in the field, the culture of Spanish America is increasingly seen as sexy, while Spain and its literary production have been cast not so much the ugly stepsister as the wicked stepmother.

Nevertheless, student perspectives and biases about literature and historical periods can enrich our readings of the *comedia* even as we seek to disprove the myths, preconceptions, and prejudices students carry with them. The key to finding relevance for nonmajors is to relate the *comedia* to what they do understand and appreciate. Students in cultural studies are interested in cultural conflicts, discourses of power, religious violence, and social constructions of self and other. Many of these concepts inform the corpus of Golden Age plays that are regularly taught in our field. By drawing attention to these topics in our study of the *comedia,* we can address the meaty issues that appeal to our students, and maybe even reverse the bias against Spain at the same time, restoring part of the transatlantic balance that has been lost. These approaches to the *comedia* have received critical attention in current research; the trick is to foreground them, consistently and creatively, in the undergraduate classroom as well.

I direct an interdisciplinary cultural studies program that traces the historical roots of southwestern culture into Mexico, Spain, and North Africa. I also teach a seminar in the program that introduces art history, music, literature, and drama, among other topics, into the discussion. Because the students are seldom literature majors, they are scarcely prepared for rigorous literary analysis. Some do not even like literature and question why it should play a part in a cultural studies program (as evidenced by the surveys quoted at the beginning of this essay). Many of the students do not speak Spanish, so the literary readings are offered in translation (those who can, read in the original). Yet the students' biases against Spain and literature are really ones of unfamiliarity, not overt hostility. Our job is to dispel the myth that literature doesn't matter and to promote the idea that the dramatic literature of Spain, in particular, can enrich their understanding of the issues they enjoy studying.

Our semester begins with a comprehensive study of *convivencia* in medieval Iberia as a way of introducing topics familiar to cultural studies majors. Students with backgrounds in other disciplines, having studied Spain only as a monolithic presence that sought to destroy the diversity of the indigenous population of the Americas, are often surprised to discover Spain's multicultural roots. They learn that Spain, too, was part of a cultural mix fraught with tensions and violence, which helps explain the country's preoccupation with blood purity and racial and ethnic classifications in the New World, codified in the *casta* system of New Spain, for example. Throughout the semester, I introduce literary, cultural, and theoretical readings that illustrate moments of multicultural interaction in Spain and colonial Mexico. Nondramatic readings include excerpts from Edward Said's *Culture and Imperialism*; lyric poetry from the *jarchas* and the Hebrew poets to the *romances fronterizos*; *Castaways*, by Alvar Núñez Cabeza de Vaca; selections from Olivia Remie Constable's excellent reader *Medieval Iberia* (including Columbus's letter and historical and philosophical treatises by Christian, Muslim, and Jewish authors); the first few chapters of Octavio Paz's *Sor Juana; or, The Traps of Faith*; and readings on honor and syncretism in the New World. I also include two *comedias* and an *entremés*. The references in these texts to *limpieza de sangre;* the Mediterranean codes of honor and shame; the *encomienda* system (in both Spain and the colonies), and the Catholic kings' project of unifying and ordering Spanish society all lay the framework for a lively discussion of Lope de Vega's *Fuenteovejuna* (ed. Flores). The conspicuous absence of *convivencia* in the River Duero's prophecy in Cervantes's *Numancia* (ed. Bentley) raises issues of lineage and ethnic purity in the context of developing a creation myth for the Spanish empire. Cervantes's *entremés El retablo de las maravillas* serves as a comic counterpoint to the serious exposition of personal and national honor in the two *comedias,* by exposing the preoccupation with blood purity as illusion and by providing valuable evidence of Spain's concern and dissatisfaction with its racial and ethnic prejudices.

Our approach to the *comedia* is not exclusively political or devoid of aesthetic discussion. On the contrary, in the light of students' heightened interest in all things political, I take the opportunity to link politics and aesthetics by presenting two camps of literary criticism for them to investigate during the semester: the moral and political views of the Platonic mode of criticism, and the aesthetic critique of the Aristotelian branch. The distinction between those who condemn art for its potential for moral corruption and those who define literary value in aesthetic terms is particularly meaningful to cultural studies students, who see similar debates playing out today among politicians and filmmakers and who are prone to moral criticism themselves as a first response to reading literature. They quickly appreciate the differences between these critical approaches as we study *Numancia* and *Fuenteovejuna* in the light of neo-Aristotelian literary-critical debates, Lope's *Arte nuevo de hacer comedias,* and the pragmatic, financial concerns of the theatrical industry of the time. Rather than fight students' misconceptions about literature and their tendency to diminish its importance, I encourage them to bring materials and approaches from their other classes to broaden our discussion and arrive at an interdisciplinary synthesis. Indeed, I periodically assign brief essays that require students to apply theories from their other classes as tools for textual analysis in ours.

A useful prism through which to view *Numancia,* for example, is the discourse of civilization and barbarism, already familiar to many students of Latin America with a cultural studies background. The play's juxtaposition of the fierce but initially undisciplined Roman forces, who represent institutional values in the relentless pursuit of fame and conquest, and the valorous Numantinos, who depict self-sacrifice, human values, and personal virtue, throws the traditional contrast between supposedly civilized Rome and the barbarous tribes on its side. Escipión's obsession culminates in his bribing the only remaining Numantino youth with promises of favors and riches if he will allow the general a military victory through conquest of a single individual. For the Romans, military conquest is a process that, once undertaken, must be carried to its conclusion and can be satisfied only by the subjugation of other human beings and their incorporation into the social order of the metropolis. In contrast, the Numantinos, largely through the love interest between Marandro and Lira and their friendship with Leonicio, represent virtue and integrity. Where the Romans are given to the vice of lechery, the Numantinos offer true love. The Romans want military victory at all costs, while the Numantinos propose humane resolutions to the conflict in the form of truce and singular battle as alternatives to mass destruction. The inversion of the traditional roles of civilization and barbarism naturally leads the students to sympathize with the indigenous Celtiberians and to accuse the Romans of imperial oppression.

Just before studying *Numancia,* the students read selections from *The Devastation of the Indies,* by Bartolomé de las Casas; the two works prompt interesting parallels between the Roman imperial conquest of an indigenous population and the Spanish conquest of the Americas. To balance the discussion, they also read Charles Gibson's introduction to *The Black Legend.* Some students interpret Cervantes's play as an allegory of the Spanish empire's military and political designs that acknowledges the controversy surrounding the treatment of the Indians and portrays the indigenous protagonists with sympathy and respect. At the very least, the students come to an understanding that the colonial project was a matter of intense debate in Golden Age Spain and that a substantial portion of the public was concerned about the ethical, humane treatment of the indigenous populations of America. The class also learns how Spain's military rivals used evidence of Spanish atrocities to project perversity and immorality onto the Spanish character, the basis of the so-called *leyenda negra,* itself a northern European bias against Mediterranean culture, with ethnic, racial, and religious overtones.

These issues raise questions of identity formation, definitions of self versus the other, and the relation among political power, religion, and violence, with which the cultural studies students can readily identify. We then discuss *Numancia* in terms of its establishment of a creation myth for imperial Spain, a myth that evokes a kind of innate nobility and integrity in the Spanish national character predating the Roman invasion and that survives intact into the early modern period, ultimately belying the *leyenda negra.* Here the allegorical figures come into play, particularly the River Duero's prophecy in act 1 and Fama's speech at the play's conclusion. The Duero's prophecy, which predicts (retroactively, for Cervantes's audience) the rise and fall of Spanish power throughout history, failing to mention the nearly eight centuries of Islamic presence, raises eyebrows among students who have just studied the *convivencia* period in detail. They note the omission and comment on Spanish racial and ethnic prejudices. Then they pursue a more sophisticated understanding of the omission: that it establishes an indelible historical link between the Visigoths and the people of Cervantes's time, echoing his society's preoccupation with blood purity and lineage. Fama's speech at the end of the play completes Duero's prophecy by connecting the sacrificial fall of Numancia to the future (Spain's imperial present, for Cervantes). Nobility, honor, and self-sacrifice are shown as indigenous to Spain, preceding Roman times, but coalescing during the Romanization of Iberia, and surviving oppression, violence, and repeated invasion to culminate in an empire destined to unite the world through Catholicism. The tragedy of collective suicide is thus cast in heroic terms that approach manifest destiny. Simultaneously, the play warns its audience of the danger of meeting the same fate as Rome, and raises the question of how the nobility and heroism of the Spanish character are reflected in the controversial actions of the nation's imperial project.

While discussing the rise of the Spanish empire, we consider Ibn Khaldun's notion of *asabiyah,* or "group feeling," which the Arab historian proposes in his *Muqaddimah* as the glue that holds societies together and allows them to define themselves and others. Arising from Iberian *convivencia,* the concept serves as a theoretical bridge between the imperial creation myth of *Numancia* and the dynamics of empire building represented in the political background of Lope's *Fuenteovejuna.* We study *Fuenteovejuna* as an analysis of authority in early modern Spain, in the context of the birth of imperial politics and the Catholic monarchs' consolidation of power, but also as a drama composed during the time of Spain's military and colonial hegemony. We discuss the Order of Calatrava and the other military orders of the Reconquest, the *encomienda* system in both Spain and colonial America, the tensions between the monarchs and the nobility as the rulers sought to centralize political power, and the play's overall movement from a broken social hierarchy to the restoration of order through collective civic action and the imposition of royal authority. In this light, the comendador is presented as the root of violence, political abuse, and oppression, responsible for undermining the established order by manipulating his superior, Rodrigo Téllez Girón; by attacking forces loyal to Ferdinand and Isabella (the legitimate power recognized by Lope's play); and by abusing the villagers of Fuenteovejuna. (Blue's article, "The Politics of Lope's *Fuenteovejuna,*" is useful in preparation for this class, as is Kagan's study "The Spain of Ferdinand and Isabella.") The play's pervasive theme of honor attracts attention, and we discuss the elusive term with reference to Américo Castro (*Edad conflictiva*), who postulates the caste-based origins of Spanish *honor* and *honra* in the *convivencia* period, and the Mediterranean values of honor and shame (see also Peristiany's *Honour and Shame*). The students appreciate the traditional distinctions between honor derived from birthright and social position (represented by the comendador) and honor that reflects virtue through good works and actions (manifest in the villagers of Fuenteovejuna). They conclude that Lope favored the form of virtuous honor in dramatizing sympathetic villagers confronted by an abusive, authoritarian overlord. As we delve deeper into the subject of the play, however, the students become aware of the inherent contradictions in the honor code. The comendador represents not only the hierarchical, vertical honor but also the loss of honor through actions, regardless of social position. The villagers, who gain our sympathy with their desire to live honorably under the comendador, become problematic when they reveal their ethnic prejudices by raising a blood purity complaint against him. We discuss the Golden Age rural prejudices against the urban nobility and its reputation for immorality and tainted blood. We then extend our commentary on the social conception of honor in Spain to include the exportation of Mediterranean honor codes to the New World, along with the *encomienda* system. This exploration helps the students understand, from a different perspective, the Spanish preoccupation with racial and ethnic classification in colonial New Spain, as represented by the delineation of multiple *castas* in the complex *mestizaje* of European, African, and indigenous blood lines. We also consider how the establishment of the *casta* and *encomienda* systems results in the awarding of habits and honorific titles to Spaniards and criollos in colonial Mexico, as a way of separating "purebloods" from the ethnic mix of the *castas*, thus perpetuating Spanish hegemony abroad (see Johnson and Lipsett-Rivera). Through these discussions of race, ethnicity, power, and oppression, bridging the periods of the Catholic monarchs and Lope's seventeenth century, the students see *Fuenteovejuna* as a window on the Golden Age not divorced from the paradigms they've examined previously but inexorably linked to them; the connection adds a level of complexity to the transatlantic study of imperial Spain and colonialism.

The final dramatic work in our course is Cervantes's *El retablo de las maravillas*. The farcical *entremés*, with its carnivalesque humor, serves not only as a welcome moment of comic relief in our program of study but as a concise, burlesque critique of the very institutions of honor and blood purity we have studied throughout the semester. We read the play aloud in parts so that the class can appreciate Cervantes's humor (I use my unpublished translation). As we progress through our dramatic reading, we stop periodically to consider the play's witty criticism of honor, legitimacy, and blood purity, and the way the work comments on the theatrical enterprise of the Golden Age, cast in terms of Lope's *comedia nueva*. The tricksters, Chanfalla and Chirinos, masquerade as *autores de comedias*, who plan to deceive the leadership class of the village with an honor play, revealed to the reader (or theatrical audience) as illusion, as there are no actors, characters, props, or scenery. The farcical treatment of the honor code unmasks the villagers' hypocritical obsession with blood purity as they dramatize themselves through their self-conscious actions, motivated by ethnic and racial prejudice. In this short, funny play, the students find further evidence that Spanish society was engaged in a dialogue about its problematic social beliefs and political behavior in its imperial moment. After we've read *Fuenteovejuna,* we raise the question as to whether this *entremés* could function in its traditionally subordinate position between the acts of a *comedia,* especially if the *comedia* was an honor play. Could the audience return to the second act of *Fuenteovejuna* and still take seriously its thematic presentation of honor after having seen it exposed as a sham in the *entremés*? While structural and pragmatic concerns in this intricate *entremés* might have been responsible for Cervantes's inability to find a producer, the students also conclude that the subject matter, with its biting critique of Spanish prejudice, may have been too subversive to be performed as a Golden Age theatrical representation without interfering with the reception of the *comedia.*

If the course is successful, by the end of the semester the students have gained an understanding of the complexity of early modern Spain through literary and cultural readings, including Golden Age dramas. What to do with the student who continues to resist literary exploration or wants to subordinate it to other fields? Compromise is the key, not active attempts at conversion. While it is nearly impossible to please every student in such a class, the ultimate goal is to demonstrate that literature can be a tool for learning about other cultures and "how the people actually lived" (as the student may demand) without diminishing its intrinsic value as art. If nothing else, the course achieves an important objective if the students begin to question their assumptions about Spain and literature and to think critically about the themes of the course that dovetail with their major fields of study. They recognize the dangers in judging the past by the morality of the twenty-first century. They can appreciate the positive literary contributions of early modern Spain while acknowledging the negative aspects of cultural conflicts and imperial politics, rather than condemn an entire nation on the basis of its checkered history. By these standards, the culture of Golden Age Spain, as examined through its literary and dramatic production, evinces a critical, multicultural complexity that challenges the reductionist tendency to dismiss the nation as a monolithic entity morally unworthy of study.

Trials: Teaching the Spanish Baroque *Comedia* in the Twenty-First Century

A. Robert Lauer

A problem one often encounters when teaching older, foreign literature is its alleged lack of relevance. The situation is compounded when a scholar of the specialized literature tries to show its worldview as different (archaeologized) from one's own. In vain one tries to explain concepts like honor or the king as fossilized worldviews that at one time might have been pertinent to a certain culture in a particular period, or so one thinks. Hence one remains linked, perhaps even chained, to the familiar Reichenberger concept of the "uniqueness" of the *comedia,* which continues thus to render as other Spain's most important literary period into an imaginary bank of meaninglessness or *curiositas,* in spite of Eric Bentley's defense of its universality. The usual teaching model, consisting of an instructor, or furnisher of knowledge (see the Latin root of *instruere*), who imparts wisdom to students, the recipients of such august lore—what Kenneth A. Bruffee calls the "foundational" approach to knowledge (222–23)—is perhaps as fossilized and ineffective a method of instruction (see Pease 6) as the (imaginary) Platonic formula—or obsolete banking model—on which it is based.

There are, of course, other approaches to knowledge besides the foundational (or accumulative)—depending, of course, on the kind of learning one wishes to postulate. The first approach is traditional and teacher-centered. It also presupposes a passive learning strategy on the part of the student. Herein the teacher is a seer or prophet, a messianic cultural worker with a mission of freedom (see hooks 2–3), a model citizen, a role model, and a master teacher;

and the student, following the medieval pattern on which the approach is based, is a vassal-vessel, an apprentice, a subject, a receptacle. There is always an implied formality and imaginary boundary between teacher and learner, at times made visible by physically elevating the professorial space above that of the learner. The teacher dresses professionally. Learners and teachers address each other by title. The teacher gives lectures, usually from notes, which are delivered slowly for students to write down the information imparted therein. The idea of making copies of the teacher's notes is unthinkable, for the teaching style at work here is based on orality and power. The delivery lasts ninety percent of the time allotted per class session, with ten percent left for students to ask questions. Some friendly or approachable instructors tell their students to interrupt at any time during the lecture to ask questions, but this directive is merely a form of rhetorical courtesy, as any student who would ask more than one or two questions in a row would soon realize. The teacher is in total control of this learning experience. The students, in true medieval fashion, learn to be subservient, sheepish vassals. They do not offer opinions or points of view that differ radically from the teacher's. To do so would be improper and imprudent. It is of course polite to ask a question. That is proof that the lesson has been delivered and accepted by the learner. A polite question (one the teacher can answer with a knowing smile and without perspiring profusely) is tantamount to a clap at the end of a theatrical performance. After all, the teacher has performed for a class (one teacher fondly recalls that a student referred to his class as "The Litvak Show" [Litvak 19]). The actual verbal impact of this kind of aqueductory form of teaching is less than ten percent (Pease [6] reminds one that in any oral message, one apprehends 7% of its verbal component, 38% of its vocal force, and 55% of its physical or nonverbal impetus). However, learners internalize important citizen functions this way (silence, timing, appropriate mimicking, humility, attentive listening, and proper decorum) that become survival tools in the real, professional, and hierarchical world (in academies, colleges, schools, the business world, any political arena, and any civic, military, or religious organization). This environment does not stimulate intellectual growth. Knowledge is transmitted orally, in imitation of preliterate cultures, and is then possessed and transmitted to others by means of secondary orality. A model of this kind of genetic cultural exchange is seen in G. W. F. Hegel's *Philosophy of Fine Art,* put together posthumously by his students.

As a reaction to this highly autocratic and aristocratic teaching style, the highly democratic student-centered classroom of free active learning came to be. Teachers here claim to be just one more learner. They dress informally and bring pertinent gadgets to class to visualize something effectively. They are full of jokes and anecdotes (anecdotal evidence, of course, is what a lot of cultural studies people do, as Berlant asseverates [109]). They shake students' hands before or after class (in the heyday of the Dartmouth method, of course, hugs and kisses were not uncommon) and call students not only by their first names but, if preferred, even by their nicknames (Muffy, Big Dude). Students are treated like children (although this would be flatly denied by all parties involved) who are provided with a safe environment (a playground, as it were) where they can express themselves without fear. Everything they say has value and is important, even if dead wrong. There is a lot of talk about feelings. Any attempt by the instructor to raise the level of discourse to a higher register might disrupt the comfort stasis already created by this humane teacher. Little work is done. Few challenges are met. High grades are received (and if they are not, students will feel betrayed). Students have a good—gemütlich—learning (at times called life) experience. In the future they might recall this teacher with fondness and give an endowment to the university. At times, of course, there is a backlash effect, as demonstrated in the testimony of the feminist pedagogue Jane Gallop (*Feminist Accused*).

The excesses of the student-centered approach produced the critical thinking method, which creates an idea-centered classroom. Both teacher and students have a problem or an issue that needs to be resolved. Many points of view are brought in, to arrive at an adequate solution to a problem. The classroom, in effect, becomes an operating table, a laboratory, a war room. Participants must feel very secure in their opinions and be ready to defend them or give them up for better ones. There is a great deal of psychological intensity in this approach, for the solution is arrived at only at a critical node that requires that a point of view become dominant. To ease the blow of easily crushed egos, the teacher declares that the group is arriving at a consensus. This is a highly intellectual approach where new (nonfoundational) knowledge (see Bruffee 222–23) is created and old (foundational) knowledge is challenged and declared either invalid or, at best, temporarily viable. Sweat prevails in this milieu. Some of the problems of this last approach are resolved in the technology-centered method. Here the student works in a room with a notebook. Class attendance is optional, and teachers neither expect students to be there nor are surprised if, while they indulge in a *PowerPoint* presentation, a student is doing e-mail or surfing through the Playboy Channel. The idea of the class as a social event is gone. Discussing an idea critically is also gone, unless it is done in a computerized chat room in the privacy of one's home. Knowledge is easily accessible, depending only on the technological memory and speed of a laptop. Instant communication is possible, with sounds, colors, graphics, pictures, and alphanumeric texts. This is probably the fastest method of learning and teaching there is now. Knowledge, however, is transmitted uncritically, although more sophisticated Web pages might solve this problem.

Each of the methods listed here has advantages and disadvantages. As a supplement, I would like to propose a complete, eclectic, and functional methodology. In this fifth teaching and learning approach, the teacher retains some of the authority of the autocratic, foundational, or traditional teacher-centered approach, as well as some of the props of the democratic, or student-centered, strategy. Herein, the instructor should lecture for a limited time, twenty minutes at most, to satisfy the reasonable and expected needs of a student clientele that in effect has paid for qualitative and quantitative information. Moreover, to satisfy the exigencies of a community of learners who must engage in nonfoundational approaches to knowledge to gain proficiency in their development of cognitive skills, which includes the creation of critical thought, the instructor must allow ample opportunities for student engagements. In effect, the teacher should form sundry heteroglossic units consisting of an even number (2, 4, 6) of groups of, ideally, five students each (Bruffee 32), scientifically designed to avoid homogeneity of any kind: by gender, race, age, previous knowledge, competence, and, if appropriate, even class. The groups should be formed at the end of the second week of class to allow the instructor enough time to notice seating patterns, competence levels, personal inclinations or gravitations, and the like. The groups should also be permanent for the duration of the semester, to allow each group to establish an identity, a functional approach to problem solving, and a unique negotiating style for the members of what in effect becomes a long-term (10–14 weeks) learning community. Moreover, functional groups should have individualized and open-ended topics, tasks, problems, experiments, or hypotheses to consider, discuss, or solve by the end of an assigned period of time (10–15 minutes). During a group work activity, the teacher becomes a silent observer or supervisor who notices the activities of each group but does not intervene in their job or function, even if asked ("I would prefer that you try to discuss and resolve that issue collaboratively with your group members"). There should be four to five group activities throughout the semester. More than that would be counterproductive as far as learning foundational material is concerned; less than that would not be enough to create a dynamic sense of community among the students. Each group should also have a roving secretary, representative, or synthesizer, who will put together (usually in writing) the ideas of the group and give a public report to the rest of the class afterward. The other students have the right to interject additional material at the end of each report, or even express minority views excluded in the majority report. In this fashion all views are heard, weighed, and considered, even if not adopted by the group in general. As a final addendum, the teacher may ask for a class vote afterward, based on the persuasiveness and information presented by any one of the groups. This approach requires that the teacher be willing to lose some control or power, which, in effect, turns to well-organized communities that will be willing to function on their own precisely because they have been scientifically formed by the teacher. When the groups are fully functional, they are allowed to choose a name by consensus (Los relámpagos, Las golondrinas, Los lauercitos, etc.). This eclectic method incorporates the authority of the first approach discussed, the democracy of the second, and, once the groups are formed, the aristocracy of the third. An effective, contemporary class must also provide the technology of the fourth (films, disks, pictures, slides, e-mail, Web pages, laser pointers, photostats, *PowerPoint* presentations, transparencies, etc.) and be on the cutting edge of research. This complete approach (the eclectic functional method) also uses all possible cognitive skills (attentive listening, close textual reading, extended oral discourse in the target language, and several examples of writing samples, ranging from a five-minute report [consisting of discrete sentences and strings of sentences] to a research paper [composed of extended paragraph-style discourse]); all are recommended by ACTFL (American Council on the Teaching of Foreign Languages; see the ACTFL Proficiency Guidelines in Buck).

A variant of this collaborative method that I have used when teaching the *comedia* at the graduate and undergraduate levels is the trial of ambiguous characters in baroque works like Lope Félix de Vega Carpio's *Fuenteovejuna,* Tirso de Molina's *El burlador de Sevilla,* and Pedro Calderón de la Barca's *La vida es sueño* (although I have used group trials for other works, like Cervantes's *Don Quijote,* the anonymous *Lazarillo de Tormes,* Fernando de Rojas's *La Celestina,* José Zorrilla's *Don Juan Tenorio,* and Benito Pérez Galdós's *Doña Perfecta*). In fall 2002, in a University of Oklahoma Spanish capstone class, my students and I tried Segismundo, the ambiguous prince of *La vida es sueño,* as part of a final examination. We did so in the following fashion: first we read, analyzed, and discussed the play; then we saw and compared it with the 1968 Radio y Televisión Española's superb filmed version (with Julio Núñez as Segismundo); then we read sundry critical articles on the play (Carter; de Armas, *Prince*; Lauer, "Leal"; A. A. Parker, "Tower"; Ruiz Ramón, "Uranos"). Afterward, the class was divided into five clusters (there were thirteen undergraduate students and one graduate auditor)· two clusters of plaintiffs played by seven students faced two clusters of defendants played by six students. The fifth cluster consisted of five observers (the graduate auditor and four graduate student volunteers) facing the podium on the opposite side of the room (see fig. below).

Podium		
Plaintiffs Clotaldo (2) Rosaura (2)	**Empty space** (buffer zone)	**Defendants** Segismundo (2) Estrella (1)
Plaintiffs Astolfo (1) Basilio (1) Soldado (1)		**Defendants** Clarín (2) Soldado (1)
Observers (ambassadors of the Holy Roman Empire)		

It had been determined in advance that the end of the play raised doubts about the capacity of Prince Segismundo to reign. Forgiving his enemies (Clotaldo, Basilio, Astolfo) was seen either as an act of magnanimity or as a Machiavellian ploy to retain power. Marrying Rosaura to Astolfo was perceived as either cruel or sad; moreover, Segismundo's sudden interest in Estrella was judged merely as a self-serving political act. Punishing the so-called rebel loyal soldier at the end was appraised as a show of force, quite unnecessary under the circumstances. Concern about being ruled by a tyrant motivated some of the notable members of the *rokosz,* or Polish aristocratic parliament, to appeal to the Holy Roman Empire. Subsequently the empire called an imperial diet and sent five ambassadors who would observe the vanquished elements of the realm (Basilio, Astolfo, Clotaldo, Rosaura, and a soldier) accuse the triumphant group (Segismundo, Estrella, the ghost of the dead Clarín, and a soldier) of tyranny (*absque titulo* [by usurpation] and *in regimine* [in administration]) and of dividing the realm in factions (as indeed happens in the play). The nobles were concerned that a weak Poland would not be able to withstand an attack from its national enemies to the east, the Orthodox Muscovites; the Lutheran Swedes to the west (the House of Vasa frequently intervened in Polish affairs); assorted German principalities of dubious faith to the north; and, in the south, the conquering infidels, the Ottoman Turks, who in the seventeenth century practically bordered on Poland. Royal coats of arms of the Houses of Russia, Sweden, and the Ottomans had been posted throughout the room to visualize the terror of an invasion that would endanger the territorial integrity of Poland. The plaintiffs considered their options. One of them would be to depose Segismundo (Basilio was seen as an inept *rex inutilis* [useless king]) and keep Estrella as their queen. Ideally, she would then marry an Austrian or a Catholic German and create an alliance with a powerful coreligionist. But other options were possible, like having Estrella marry Astolfo (as was Basilio's plan) and, hence, avoid more bloodshed between two national enemies. It was perhaps even likely that if Astolfo was to be given the Polish crown, all hostilities between the two kingdoms would disappear, although at the cost of Polish independence. Some traditional forces would perhaps like to retain Basilio for a while longer (with the proviso that the ruler keep his *dignitas* but lose his *potestas*). Other pragmatic elements would not mind having an interregnum under Habsburg tutelage until a more capable ruler was found among the Poles. After all, early modern Poland had a "noble republic" (1572–1795), where power resided mainly in the aristocracy; the monarchy therein was elective. It goes without saying that the House of Austria was interested in intervening in Polish affairs for fear that if Poland disappeared from the map (as indeed happened historically), there would no longer be a stalwart buffer zone to protect the Holy Roman Empire against invading Russians, Swedes, and Ottomans. For that reason the Austrians sent observers (goodwill ambassadors) who in effect would hear out all sides and make a determination that would best serve the interests of Poland and, of course, the empire and its way of life.

The day of the trial (20 Dec. 2002), the impersonating students showed up in costumes and sat in their designated places. The hearing was to last ninety minutes. The instructor, now the secretary of His Imperial Majesty the Emperor, explained the reason for the tribunal and went over the appropriate protocol. All members had to stand behind the podium with the Polish eagle, address the ambassadors politely ("Eminentes señores embajadores"), make themselves known ("Yo, Clotaldo"), and voice their opinions and requests without fear of interruption (this practice allowed all students to narrate and hypothesize, using extended discourse in the target language). The plaintiffs had thirty minutes to bring up all the charges against Segismundo and to make a recommendation to the ambassadors. They could use notes and whatever rhetorical tactics (including *actio*) or props they desired, provided they did not depart from the spirit of the transcript (the Calderonian text itself). Afterward, the defendants had thirty minutes to counter the charges and explain why Segismundo should reign. Subsequently, the plaintiffs and, later, the defendants had fifteen minutes each to counter additional arguments raised during the first sixty minutes (this thirty-minute period is always the most dynamic and competitive part of the trial). After ninety minutes, a recess was deemed necessary to psychologically disembody the students from their roles. Later, they were to act as jurors and, based on the evidence they had just heard, cast a written ballot for or against Segismundo. The instructor-secretary invited the ambassadors to exit the room so that the jurors could determine their choice freely. The secretary then informed the ambassadors that the vote of the jurors in the *rokosz* could only be advisory, for they had appealed to a higher authority to resolve their conflicts. Hence, any ambassador could veto the Polish vote if it proved detrimental to the interests of the Holy Roman Empire. Nevertheless, all efforts would be made to accommodate the wishes of the Poles to the interests of Austria.

On 20 December 2002, one was ninety days away from the coalition conflict in Iraq. Perhaps the impending war had an impact on the way the trial and the final vote ensued. Although the plaintiffs had begun their attack in a vehement and vociferous fashion and the defendants were not entirely convincing in demonstrating their right to reign, Clarín, the final defendant to speak, was very persuasive in showing that the only traitor in the realm was the former king, Basilio. From that moment on, the plaintiffs caved in one by one. Basilio admitted his guilt. Clotaldo remained stupefied. Astolfo declared that he would give up all claims to the Polish throne, since he would never reign secure. Rosaura mentioned that Segismundo deserved another opportunity to reign. Estrella offered to help Segismundo in his administration. The rebel soldier, in an unexpected turn, declared that he would gladly die, if necessary, to keep Segismundo enthroned and Poland united. Segismundo asked for patience and help as he dealt with the needs of the realm. The ambassadors grabbed this opportunity immediately to ask the Poles if they would vote to have imperial military and technical advisers for a number of years, until Segismundo could reign on his own. Ten of twelve students voted yes. When the imperial secretary placed a crown on Segismundo's head, the students-jurors probably realized that they were now under imperial influence.

In brief, the trial brought out multiple perspectives that the teacher might not even have imagined. In the process, old institutions (an imperial diet, a parliamentary *rokosz*) and political concepts (*rex inutilis, tyrannus absque titulo, tyrannus in regimine*) became timely and relevant; in a sense, they foreshadowed current and ongoing conflicts. At first, the students were shy and hesitant to open their mouths and express opinions. However, by the end of class, they actually would not let the trial end, for every student had something at stake to defend or support: his or her dramatic identity as well as the honor or integrity of each other's respective groups. Trial time had to be limited to ninety minutes, for the forensic sections of the trial (especially the confirmation and the refutation parts) required extensive oral discourse of a persuasive nature (which ACTFL considers a high or advanced level of proficiency), very attentive listening, and instant feedback in a highly dynamic and healthily competitive fashion. In the end, the trial provided one with the ultimate satisfaction of knowing that one's view was heard well by all, even if it did not ultimately prevail. The trial also enabled teacher and student to use all prevailing pedagogical methodologies in an eclectic way, thus giving the participants a sense of completion and, hence, maximizing the learning and teaching experience in a realistic, playful, and effective manner.

And is this not, in effect, what life too—not just language, literature, and culture—is about? Trials have to do with communication, hypothesis, learning and knowing the facts, persuasion, "otherification," ongoing "conversations" (Bruffee 113; Heidegger 760) between the I and the Thou, the here and the now, the then and the there; performance (Litvak 22), connections, translations, simulations (see Baudrillard 152); bridge building, interpretative communities, empire formation; life, capstone, or senior experience; the dramatization of life, "la vida es sueño," and, in the plainly and simply stated asseveration of Jane Gallop, im-personation ("Im-Personation" 17).

Life is a trial; and all of us, *comediantes*, are merely *farsantes*, as Everett W. Hesse, the founding editor of the *Bulletin of the Comediantes,* once jovially said. The stakes, nevertheless, are high indeed, for they have to do with continuity, pedagogy, reacculturation (Bruffee 225–26), and paradigm formation (Kuhn 383). Old knowledge and facts are pertinent today because they were pertinent then. It's all a matter of how that knowledge is translated and made new again. The surface structure changes, but not the deep structure. Our task, both as teachers and as learners, is first to understand that which has not changed and then to enable others to go back to it to bring it into consciousness again. We are cultural exorcists fighting even our demons of misunderstanding. And in this sensitive task, our students and we are there to help each other make the necessary connections, with toys and ThinkPads if necessary, to return to the real after a mighty battle between the imaginary forces of chaos and semiotic disorder and the soothing symbolic forces of order and intelligibility. Let us not worry. The connections will be made. It is not a matter of *what* but of *how* one impersonates. Hence, may one's performance in this trying *gran teatro del mundo* be a good one. And may one never forget, as Everett never did, also to have fun and enjoy the *comedia* (and life) with gusto.

Mentoring Environments and Golden Age Theater Production

Dale J. Pratt and Valerie Hegstrom

We believe that the best way to teach theater is through performance. If supplemented with a set of carefully designed (but not rigid) mentoring experiences, including a substantial writing component, exposure to current critical discourse in the field, and service to the greater community, the performance of a Golden Age play can become a transformative event in the lives of the students and the department. We have had two wonderful semesters mentoring groups of twenty-four and twenty-six students in producing *La dama duende* and the *loa* to *El divino Orfeo*, and then *Don Gil de las calzas verdes* and *El retablo de las maravillas*, as part of our course Spanish Theater Production. Two very generous university grants designed to foster increased interaction between faculty members, graduate students, and undergraduates through mentoring supported our efforts.[1] While most literature professors cannot count on such lavish support for their classes, we believe that even in the smallest classes and programs, teachers can implement many of the methods we tried in our Golden Age theater group.

Collaboration between the students and the professor(s) forms the foundation of mentored learning. Although teachers often feel that they can cover more of the material they have spent long years studying if they stand in front of the class and lecture, students and teachers need to uncover ideas and truths for learning to actually take place. Mentoring clearly helps students discover truth and create knowledge in ways unmatched by the efforts of a single professor, however scholarly and dedicated.[2] From our personal experience as professors and as former students, we realize that sometimes student collaboration can lead to sloppy research and writing and uneven workloads. We both can recall carrying the burden for a group when it became clear our own grades were in jeopardy. Mentoring goes beyond the student group format by including the professor in the collaboration, and provides the additional check of "I don't want to let Professor X down." Also, the students who in traditional collaborative learning tend to bear much of the workload for the group can serve as mentors in areas where their particular talents help the most.

Our Spanish 439R-639R teaches as much about a new way to learn as about the *comedia*. Mentored theater production draws from other performance-oriented classes[3] and requires the professor to relinquish authority and delegate to the student mentors responsibility for dispensing knowledge. Pratt's syllabus for the course on *La dama duende* had a calendar with only nine entries, including four days for the read-through and auditions for the play; the remainder of the syllabus, which for a typical class would be filled with readings, homework assignments, exam dates, and grading criteria, he left blank. After he organized mentoring groups (each consisting of one graduate student and four or five undergraduates), the students took responsibility for the rest of the semester. In her version of the course, Hegstrom never lectured on the *comedia;* she gave only two vocabulary quizzes and led a discussion once the whole semester, leaving class meetings for student mentors to plan. The advantages to the professor of relinquishing traditional roles include not having to direct the production or attend every rehearsal and being able to count on several other pairs of eyes to read the drafts of the papers, thus freeing up energy and time to devote to individual and small-group needs.

From the students' point of view, the mentoring experience can become the most difficult and rewarding educational opportunity of their college careers. They cannot passively take notes in class, read assigned texts, and grudgingly complete papers and exams. Instead, students become responsible not only for their roles in one or two plays but also for gathering information, through library research and interactions with theater professionals and *comedia* scholars, that will have a direct impact on the production of the play. They have to research and write with the urgent, specific purposes of learning how to do what they need to do, and to explain it to their audiences. As a result of our collaboration with our students, they learned about Golden Age stagecraft and what it takes to produce a play, attended the Chamizal International Siglo de Oro Theater Festival and the Association for Hispanic Classical Theater (AHCT) conference, participated in outreach to elementary and secondary school students, learned to write with a purpose and published extensive program notes, and performed four Golden Age plays for very enthusiastic audiences.

This course started with a student director and a few flyers announcing the production of *La dama duende,* and Pratt deferred to the director's choices in casting both that play and the *loa.* Several students who did not receive major roles dropped the course immediately, but the others quickly became involved in the read-through of the play and the other behind-the-scenes work of the production. The decision to produce the *loa,* with its large cast of characters with brief parts, gave everyone a chance to be onstage without memorizing hundreds of lines. The director and the principals of *La dama duende* met with the professor during evenings for two weeks to go over the roles and to cut lines. Pratt found that the students did not have a good ear for the poetry and often wanted to cut lines in ways that would destroy the patterns and sometimes the meaning. He also had to fight to preserve the sonnets in a love scene between Don Juan and Doña Beatriz, which the students found boring (in the finished production this scene turned out beautifully, to great applause). Because the students in *La dama duende* struggled with the language and the length of the play as they learned their parts in one semester, we decided to cast *Don Gil* and *El retablo de las maravillas* several months in advance, thus giving the actors a full semester to memorize their lines before our first class meeting. When we cast both plays, the group included some of our veterans from *La dama duende* and several others who had seen the play and wanted to get involved in the next one. Within a couple of weeks, we met with both casts to do a complete read-through of the plays. This experience helped them to understand the plays line by line before beginning to memorize their parts. The students also got to know each other and to enjoy both plays.

Beyond the challenge of turning Spanish majors and other Spanish-speaking students into actors, a mentored theater production can force students to learn the theatrical context of *comedia* performance, to learn Golden Age stagecraft. Our conception of the *Dama duende* staging as a presentation in a *corral de comedias* required the students to do research on the *corrales,* their construction, their conventions, and the specifications of the *alacena,* or secret door, which would allow the *duende* and her maid to appear and disappear. The group read articles on the subject and built a model of the stage they designed, complete with secret door and discovery space. The students chose an outdoor patio on the west side of the university's library as the *corral.* After careful planning, the construction began a few days before the first show. The next year, the student director suggested we perform *Don Gil* as if staged by a traveling company. This exciting goal required the construction of a *carro,* or large wagon, that could convert into a stage. We enlisted a graduate student who had experience building houses and roofing to design the wagon and mentor other students in its construction. To help all the students understand the concept, we held a workshop in the fall before our class started. The director showed them slides of drawings of *corrales* and other stages used in medieval and Renaissance Spain and elsewhere in Europe, as well as a virtual tour of the Corral del Príncipe. Our set designer displayed his cardboard model of our future *carro.* A few weeks later, the professor made her only teaching presentation before the group. The students prepared by reading Cervantes's prologue to his *Entremeses,* the *Maese Pedro* and *Las cortes de la muerte* episodes from the *Quijote,* Lope's *Arte nuevo* and the "Prólogo dialogístico" to the *parte 16* of his *Comedias,* and excerpts from Tirso's *Cigarrales de Toledo.* They also read a children's picture book, Tomie de Paola's *The Clown of God.* In her presentation, with the help of the director and student production manager, Hegstrom brought in images of medieval and early Renaissance *carros,* as well as a few modern stagings of mystery play cycles. She also showed video clips depicting traveling theater troupes, street theater, and puppet shows: for example, *The Seventh Seal, Hamlet* (Mel Gibson), *The Hunchback of Notre Dame* (Disney), and *Rosencrantz and Guildenstern Are Dead.* The class discussed how these materials might affect our production of *Don Gil* and *El retablo de las maravillas.* The students brainstormed about their roles as actors and production committee members, as well as what the group as a whole might need to accomplish to make our production a reality.

The production committees constitute a key aspect in the mentoring experience. For our productions, group assignments included sets and props, house and atmosphere, acting and characters, costuming, publicity and Web site, educational outreach, music and dance, writing and editing, and project history. One of our most passionate, organized students from *La dama duende* suggested we appoint a production manager to oversee the work of all the other student committees; she of course received the job. We recruited some of our best graduate students to lead the committees, with the charge that they mentor the undergraduates on their committees as they worked on specific tasks. Two undergraduates, however, directed *La dama duende* and *El retablo de las maravillas* and proved themselves superb mentors. The student mentors received instructions about how to mentor their groups from the professor in frequent production meetings. There we also learned about which students made huge contributions, and even more often about which students avoided their work.[4] Students revealed their personalities: some mentors felt content to leave work undone, some did most or all the work themselves, others found different ways to inspire the students to do their fair share.

As part of the mentoring project, most of the members of the class traveled to El Paso, Texas, to attend the annual Chamizal festival and the accompanying AHCT conference.[5] Each night the students saw a Golden Age play and participated in roundtable discussions with the directors and actors, sometimes asking the majority of the questions. They identified with the performers, thinking of themselves as novice actors rather than just spectators. They asked about working together as a group, seeking advice to help with our project. Because we stayed at the same motel as the acting companies, our students could continue their conversations in the parking lot and restaurant and be further mentored by acting groups from Colombia and Spain.[6] These priceless moments allowed our students to appreciate Golden Age theater from the perspective of professional actors who really care about the *comedia*.

We required our students to attend at least a session each day of the AHCT conference, to explore the *comedia* with experts in the field. They learned how scholars make presentations and interact, and met many of the people whose articles and books they had read while preparing the program notes and study guide. Our student director also presented a paper on our experience with *La dama duende*. The AHCT conference enhances the academic component of the course.

Before the second trip, we coordinated with Virginia Ness, the National Park Service organizer of the Chamizal festival, to have our students visit area schools as part of the NPS educational outreach program. We visited six elementary and high schools, with audiences ranging from 50 to 350 students. Our students explained why Spanish Golden Age playwrights and their works matter, performed a few scenes, and then invited some of the schoolchildren onstage to behave like *damas* and *galanes* in scenes of their own. The outreach helped our students practice their lines, teach what they had learned, and see how Golden Age theater can appeal to diverse audiences. The heritage speakers, in particular, lit up when our students told them how many hundreds more plays Lope wrote than

Shakespeare; this response helped our students recognize the value of their performance. Our group was able to reach nearly one thousand students in El Paso.

Later in Provo, Utah, our education committee wrote letters and made phone calls to two dozen local high school and immersion program teachers. They sent out biographies of our authors and plot summaries of our plays, along with a short study guide. We made presentations to several Provo High School classes. We also invited a group of homeschool families on campus to see our educational presentation. In the end, three high schools and several homeschool groups attended our matinee performances.

An important part of Pratt's vision of our mentoring project gave the students the opportunity to write with a specific purpose and a specific audience in mind: they would publish extensive programs or play guides to teach the audience about Golden Age theater. The students conducted research and wrote short essays that had value for real readers. They read each others' papers and discussed numerous scholarly articles about *La dama duende* chosen by Pratt and the mentors. During the first week of the *Don Gil* class, our writing mentor made assignments to the undergraduates to research a specific topic related to their roles in the plays or their job as a committee member. For example, the principal actors researched and thought through their characters and wrote articles about their situations and motivations. Thus Angela from *La dama duende* wrote about the status of women in the Golden Age, while Doña Juana from *Don Gil* wrote about cross-dressing women. Other papers dealt with topics germane to our productions, such as the purpose of the *loa* or the *entremés,* night scenes in a *corral* theater, honor in the *comedia,* traveling theater companies, and the medieval or Renaissance marketplace. The student mentor later invited the university librarian in charge of Spanish acquisitions to teach the students how to research the *comedia,* and a graduate writing instructor to help them develop and organize their arguments. Several of them learned about interlibrary loans for the first time. Student mentors helped with finding library resources and read and edited multiple drafts of papers, the final versions of which were due before students boarded the plane for El Paso. Our editors worked late nights to make the copy camera-ready and to meet deadlines with the press.[7] When the boxes of books arrived a day or two before each play opened, the students reacted with pride and enthusiasm; they could see the purpose of their writing.

When audience members entered our *corral* to see *La dama duende* in April 2002, they received a program, "tomatoes" (beanbags created by the students), and a comic book version of *La dama duende* in English. "Armed" guards escorted them to their seats, men up front, women in the back of the theater in the *cazuela.* Spanish noblemen and women (paintings) stared down at them from the *aposentos* (library windows). The show began with the *loa,* which, surprisingly, delighted all with its alphabet characters, who displayed their individual traits (*H* for *la honra,* for example, cheered each time *Dama duende* characters mentioned *honor*) and performed a dance choreographed by one of the students. The *Dama duende* actors entered through the audience, directed all their asides and soliloquies to the spectators, complained and otherwise responded when rowdy audience members threw beanbags, and sometimes stopped to visit with someone they recognized in the audience. These interactions engaged the spectators in ways impossible in fourth-wall theater. *La dama duende* played to standing-room-only audiences and received "solid gold" reviews from the Salt Lake *Tribune.*

On opening day in April 2003, *El retablo de las maravillas* was a jewel, but the cast members of *Don Gil* still did not understand the play and they disliked one another. The second and third days' performances snowed out, and the cast did one read-through of the play. Then magic happened. Friday evening the audience arrived in the marketplace to find the decorations, preshows, and food booth arranged for by the house committee. Costumed class members handed out printed information about market activities and a *Don Gil* comic book in English, hawked programs, passed out "tomatoes" and small bags of money (washers with Carlos V stickers on them), performed period Spanish violin pieces and songs, and begged for money. Spanish and Portuguese professors volunteered to dress as inquisitors and distribute prohibited-book lists. The audience mingled, munched on chorizo and churros, waited, and wondered. There was no sign of any stage or theater. Suddenly at show time, the actors arrived, pulling and riding in our *carro* and dragging carts full of folding chairs. Our students sang, played instruments, passed out chairs, and within ten minutes they had opened the *carro,* unloaded the props, raised the curtain, and secured the sides of the wagon horizontally to increase the area of the stage. One of the more experienced students (who played the father in *Don Gil* and the gobernador in *El retablo*) also took on the role of the *autor de comedias.* He called for the audience's attention, explained the rules of proper beanbag throwing, and introduced the show. Miraculously, the two down days created enough anxiety and anticipation in the students that the show came together, they got its meaning, and they began to enjoy themselves onstage. The audience responded; they threw beanbags and sometimes even coins; they bought programs and more food; they smiled as our guards and inquisitors handcuffed them, put them in the stocks, or forced them to wear a *sambenito;* and they participated in the play whenever our actors asked them to and sometimes on their own.

Following each performance, our director led roundtable discussions for groups of two dozen or more interested audience members. Sometimes the spectators had lots of questions and comments about the *cazuela,* the beanbags and coins, the paintings of the nobility, our goals and plans. Sometimes the director prodded them with questions of our own: Did they speak Spanish? If not, could they enjoy the play anyway? How did they respond to Golden Age stagecraft and conventions? What did they think about the *loa* or the *entremés* preceding or interrupting the major play? Had they heard of any Spanish Golden Age playwrights or any of their works? Had they ever seen one performed before? At *Don Gil,* we had many repeat customers, so they could affirm that they had experience with the *comedia.* They had seen *La dama duende* and had come back for more.

At BYU, we have between 350 and 500 Spanish and Portuguese majors during any given semester; thousands of BYU students speak Spanish. Thus we have a large potential audience for our plays among the members of our campus community. We teach nine sections of Introduction to Hispanic Literature and three or four sections of Survey of Spanish Literature every semester. We encourage our colleagues teaching the introductory class to include our one-act play among course readings. All of the survey courses include the shorter work and the full-length *comedia,* sometimes taught by our theater production students. Several sections of these classes require attendance at the plays and a written review assignment. In this way, the production of the plays benefits many more Spanish students than those participating in the theater class. Because our plays engage the audience and we provide program and comic book help for them, we attract many non-Spanish speakers. Most of our graduate teaching assistants award their 100- and 200-level students extra credit points for attending. Additionally, we have reached out to native Spanish speakers in Utah Valley by distributing posters and flyers in restaurants and *mercados.*[8]

We recorded both years' performances and created DVDs including the plays and a photo scrapbook of our service and production travails, to provide inspiration for future groups and serve as treasured records of these wonderful experiences.[9]

NOTES

[1] Brigham Young University's Office of Research and Creative Activities specifically designs its Mentoring Environments grants to encourage regular and close interaction between students and faculty members as they carry out research and creative activities. The principles of mentoring at BYU include these: "Students should have access to faculty (and/or mentoring teams) for sufficient time to allow development of personal and professional relationships. Students should be involved in programs and processes wherein scholarship and/or central academic activities in its several forms constitute the core of their experiences. Students should be given the opportunity for growth in skills and increase in responsibility in the project or experience. Mentored experiences should be pertinent to future situations of the students involved and ideally would assist the students in attaining the 'next level' of their chosen disciplines" (*Brigham Young* 3).

[2] Barbara Gross Davis cites numerous studies that indicate that "regardless of the subject matter, students working in small groups tend to learn more of what is taught and retain it longer than when the same content is presented in other instructional formats. Students who work in collaborative groups also appear more satisfied with their classes" (147).

[3] Other titles in the MLA's Options for Teaching and Approaches to Teaching World Literature series offer useful performance-based articles, such as James F. Gaines's

"From Classroom to Stage and Back: Using Molière in Performance," Lois Potter's "Teaching Shakespeare: The Participatory Approach," and Cynthia Lewis's "Performing Shakespeare: The Outward Bound of the English Department."

[4] The greatest challenge of a mentoring project is the Little Red Hen syndrome—who will stay up until 3 (or 6) A.M. to finish the costumes? Who will spend nine hours putting the stage together, or set up the Web site, or call the schools to schedule the outreach work? The answers to these questions can come only from dedicated individuals. The ideal outcomes include regular, careful work throughout the semester, so that in the week before the show opens there will be no marathon sewing sessions or stage-building problems. At one dire moment a few weeks into the *Don Gil* class, Hegstrom gave what has come to be known among the students as "The Lecture"—a dressing-down of students not taking their opportunities seriously. Pratt's group met in BYU's engineering building, and at one point when the drafts of the papers for the program did not look so good, Pratt mentioned to the students that all around them in the building their peers construct high-tech machinery to do real work in the real world. He told them that as seniors in a university major, they should produce a substantial document of very high quality. With a few exceptions, these students rose to the task. This outcome can result when students understand that the class is not a play in Spanish, but rather a multifaceted learning and service experience.

[5] The BYU Mentoring grants funded these trips. We recognize that the cost of such an excursion will likely prove prohibitive but suggest that teachers encourage individuals or small groups of students to attend Chamizal when possible.

[6] Before our second trip, we gave one of our graduate student mentors the title cruise director, and put him in charge of lodging, food, and other trip arrangements. The responsibilities gave our student more headaches but relieved Hegstrom from some of the burden Pratt previously had carried.

[7] Our grants subvented the publication of the programs, but both years' ticket sales easily covered those costs.

[8] Since writing this essay, we have taken Angela de Azevedo's *El muerto disimulado* and Lope's *El caballero de Olmedo* and *Las cortes de la muerte* on the road to visit university and community audiences in Utah, Idaho, Arizona, New Mexico, Texas, and Ciudad Juárez, Mexico.

[9] We would like to thank several students who have been involved in these productions from the beginning and without whom the projects might have failed. Director, prop maker, stage builder, and visionary Jason Yancey, assistant director Wesley Pack, editors David Richter and Collin McKinney, and costume seamstress, stage designer, and production manager Melissa Mills (the Little Red Hen).

The Digital *Comedia:* Teaching Golden Age Theater with New and Emerging Technologies

Diane E. Sieber

I have often heard instructors lament the need to convince their students that Golden Age drama is relevant to students' lives and concerns, but given the visual sophistication of a generation raised on video games and the Internet, few topics can be made more engaging than the most visual of literary genres, the theater. New media technologies can provide an immediate, compelling, and memorable student experience with Golden Age drama. Multimedia teaching brings to the classroom intertexts that are particularly suited to new-historicist, anthropological, and cultural studies approaches to dramatic works.

In 1993, D. E. Kinnaman identified the danger of adopting new teaching technologies:

> There is no doubt that technology will change the classroom. But that doesn't mean that technology will improve education. Unless we take a fresh look at the strategies we use for teaching and learning, we are likely to spend a lot of time, energy, and money to create a new way to deliver the same old school experience.

I have taught Golden Age theater since 1993, employing technologies that range from e-mail to interactive Web sites, Flash animations, and three-dimensional modeling. In the process, I have noted real improvements in student research and learning and more sophisticated classroom discussions and written work. I have also enjoyed the enthusiasm with which my students embrace both the mass media of the Internet and film and the early modern *cultura de masas* that was the Golden Age theater.

Student Use of Information Technology

The students have provided me with some cultural context of their own. I received my first e-mail from a student in 1993. The event was so transformative that I distributed the first of my surveys of student technological proficiency. These surveys have been issued on the first day of each Spanish literature class for fifteen consecutive semesters, from fall 1993 through spring 2003. I have evolved with my students, adopting more advanced pedagogical approaches as students have become more proficient in media technologies.

In 1993, only 29% of my students used their e-mail accounts with any frequency. By spring 2004, 100% sent or checked their e-mail daily. In 1993, 68% of my students were using a word processing program to produce written work for class. Four years later they all used such programs for class assignments. Virtual office hours and digital paper submissions were among my earliest accommodations to technological progress. Virtual office hours, supplemental to physical office hours, are the set times when I answer student e-mails.

In 1995, 60% of my students were already using the World Wide Web to conduct research for their classes. By fall 2000, 100% were using the Web daily for academic research; only 20% reported that they performed any research in the university libraries. That number has since dropped to 4%. For 96% of my students, then, the Web has become the exclusive information-gathering medium for research projects. I developed my course Web sites as a defensive instructional tool that pointed students to reliable sources of information and suggested how to distinguish the credible sites from the incredible, the more dispassionate sites from the agenda-driven.

My students' use of computers and the Internet has changed substantially since I began using these technologies, as has their assumption that technology would be integrated into the learning experience. On the first day of class in 2003, 85% of my students indicated that they expected to have access to a class Web site; 65% expected me to use the Internet, *PowerPoint*, or digital video in the classroom. Their increased expectation of up-to-the-minute communication, their growing facility with reading text and data online, and their almost universal preparation of written work on a scrolling screen signal a student culture that differs significantly from the culture of my undergraduate experience.

Student Information Literacy

Students who use information technology (IT) are not necessarily IT literate. To be information technology literate, one "must be able to recognize when information is needed and have the ability to locate, evaluate, and use effectively the needed information. . . . Information literate people are those who have learned how to learn" (Green and Gilbert 8). The 96% of students who conduct research for my class exclusively on the Web have already learned to read printed texts critically, but many have yet to deal with the implications of the networked information age for research: they must sift through vast amounts of unsorted and unrefereed information, and they have little academic training to do so.

My theater and survey courses now begin with a one-week introduction to effective information searching, critical reading, and citation of digital sources. Students discover basic search techniques, such as how to find and use a Spanish-language search engine, how to conduct Boolean and advanced searches, and strategies for narrowing down search results. They engage in a number of evaluative exercises that I have mounted to the course Web site, such as comparisons of reliable and unreliable sites. Excellent resources for university-level instruction in digital information literacy have been developed by the Association of College and Research Libraries. Both literacy standards and intructors' toolkits can be found on the American Library Association Web site. Scholars such as Cheryl Gould and Diana Laurillard address the urgent need to teach research methods in newer digital media.

As a group, my theater students produce guidelines for analyzing the reliability of a Web site. They also need a reminder that digital sources, like print sources, must be credited in research papers. The students are learning to read new media using techniques that they had taken for granted in a society of refereed publications. They are learning to read in the networked information age.

Web-Based Technologies

Several aspects of technologizing my teaching approach have helped me strengthen the fabric of my courses. Once I moved beyond the initial adoption phase, during which I grafted new technology onto an existing course by posting text to a static Web site, I found that using new media caused me to rethink the content and delivery of my courses. In his study of the transition to teaching with technology, Stephen Ehrmann cautions instructors to shift to new types of course materials, "creating new types of assignments, and inventing new ways of assessing student learning" (29). Each semester I redesign my courses by refining my messages and expectations, visualizing the course materials anew, and engaging in storyboarding, the process of creating the physical layout and information flow of a Web site.

Web-based technologies have proved to have the greatest impact on my theater courses. The Web provides an excellent supplement to classroom contact. The class Web site has become a portal for students of Spanish theater and history. Eschewing printed anthologies, I am able to assemble and disseminate my own. A hypertext (clickable) syllabus links to primary and secondary readings and to contextual information pertinent to each day's class. Excellent virtual tours of museums, regions, and historic sites are available, and the major Spanish archives and libraries are digitizing their collections for the Web.

There are excellent Web resources for teachers of Golden Age drama. The Association for Hispanic Classical Theater site features multiformat digital texts of both canonical and less-accessible works (over 250 as of summer 2003). A video collection, a library of teaching and research tools, and an association virtual community complement this extraordinary resource. Matthew Stroud's database of characters and plots in Tirso's *comedias* is also heavily used by students; the *Corral del Príncipe* virtual site of José María Ruano de la Haza, the *Biblioteca Virtual Miguel de Cervantes, Parnaseo,* and *Teatro de los Siglos de Oro* sites provide text, supplemental materials, and indispensable links. *Cibertextos* offers interactive digital texts with glossaries and other materials (all site addresses appear by title in the Works Cited section of this volume). New resources appear online weekly and offer fresh insights into approaches to Spanish Golden Age drama worldwide.

The creative flexibility of the Web has allowed me to craft immediacy rooms, which introduce students to particularly difficult or complex material. The immediacy room is a password-protected Web page that condenses a wide range of cultural artifacts pertinent to a particular topic into a localized multimedia experience. For example, when we discuss the term *baroque* in class, I no longer begin with a lecture and slide show. Students arrive for class having visited the baroque room, where they play music (Alessandro Scarlatti and Domenico Scarlatti) while they read selected sonnets and excerpts from *La vida es sueño,* examine a gallery of paintings (by Velázquez, Valdés Leal, Caravaggio, Rubens), sculpture and architecture (by Bernini, Borromini), and emblems (Covarrubias Orozco, Saavedra Fajardo), and read firsthand accounts of seventeenth-century social and political events. By the time we get to class, students already have an experience of the many ways in which we might think of the baroque. Virtual rooms have become indispensable for communicating concepts like courtly love, *desengaño,* the *mujer varonil,* good kingship, the labyrinth and the minotaur, the wild man, the *cultura de masas;* and the historical and cultural contexts of the Reformation and the Counter Reformation, the New World, the Turkish threat, the Moriscos, and so on. In fact, it is now possible to render almost any temporally and geographically distant event or concept more immediate, more memorable, and more compelling by presenting a collection of related cultural artifacts for student examination. The immediacy rooms further serve the course by spotlighting themes and concepts that inform multiple plays during the semester. The *mujer varonil* page, which includes quotations from several plays and prose works; depictions of emblems, painting, and sculpture; and excerpts from treatises on the duties of women, refers students to *La vida es sueño, El perro del hortelano, El nuevo rey Gallinato,* and other works examined during the semester. Students often bring up these Web pages as we read a play, comparing the cultural artifacts with each character and suggesting ways in which a character confirms or confounds student expectations. One of my immediacy rooms provides images of Moriscos from the Royal Chapel in Granada and Weiditz sketches, facsimiles of the decrees of diaspora (1571) and expulsion (1609), commentaries by proponents and opponents of expulsion, *aljamiado* texts, satirical ballads, maps of population concentration and expulsion routes, and Morisco letters of appeal (1609–14). This collection of artifacts informs plays like Calderón's *Amar despues de la muerte,* which both employs and subverts negative imagery of the Morisco in Spanish Golden Age culture. Because of copyright and fair use limitations on Web publication of these artifacts, immediacy rooms must remain behind password protection on a course site. These materials are accessible only to the specific theater class and are available for educational use only during the semester. Students are provided with a user identification and password to access these resources. To see a public example of an immediacy room, visit my resource Web site: http://spot.colorado.edu/~sieberd/technology.

Streaming video, which at current bandwidths rarely can be used in increments of more than twenty minutes, delivers video of performances directly to students from a course Web site. Scenes from visually complex plays can be viewed in advance by students and again during the class period for more detailed scene-by-scene commentary. My students have used study questions in combination with key segments of the Compañía Nacional de Teatro Clásico's Madrid performances of *La dama duende* and *El médico de su honra* (unfortunately, videotapes of these productions are not available for public use). Without exception, students who have seen the final moments of *El médico de su honra* perceive the flaws in King Don Pedro (*el Cruel*) and ask if Calderón implicitly condemns wife-murderer Don Gutierre. I have never had this experience with students who read the play without visual cues or detailed historical explanations. Historical context is still discussed in the class, but our reading no longer relies exclusively on my lectures about don Pedro and dynastic conflict.

Macromedia Flash is a digital tool that provides excellent compression rates for Web-delivered animations. Flash animations can be used to demonstrate many theatrical concepts in a dynamic or interactive way. One excellent use of Flash is for visualization of the discovery space or inner stage in the Golden Age theater. A simple animation of the stage can be altered to show the variety of *apariencias* used at key moments in dramas: changes of location, thematic revelation, scenes of violence, or emblematic incidents. Students can explore the discovery spaces as they relate, for example, to Segismundo's tower, don Manuel's room in *La dama duende,* the horrific results of the bloodletting in *El médico de su honra,* or the heads of the *Infantes de Lara* in Lope's *El bastardo Mudarra.*

The Web site also allows student learning to become self-guided. I had hoped to move away from the history and arts lectures that the original course seemed to require. I began to design the Web site so that every learner could wander down unexpected paths and make discoveries. Judith Boettcher and G. Philip Cartwright noticed by 1997 that new technologies were ideal for initiating the decentering process (62). The research, arts, history, and world literature pages on the Web site connect to subordinate pages dedicated to related information, topics, and Internet resources that students can explore freely. In-class discussion brings student discoveries to light. Two students who were particularly disengaged during the first weeks of my course began to speak up enthusiastically after their first visits to the Web site. They brought up topics not covered directly in the syllabus: urban delinquency and the picaresque novel. As a result, we all learned about two aspects of Spain that we would not have discussed as thoroughly otherwise, and two students who began the course with little interest became the most active learners of the group.

A course Web site presents opportunities for peer-to-peer learning. Students post three-page descriptions of their oral presentations to a password-protected section of the Web site one week before they present to the class. Each posted summary has three assigned respondents, who provide feedback on grammar, accuracy, and argument, and who recommend further research before the big day. Students likewise post final-paper proposals to the password-protected Web site for critique. We have achieved a much higher level of discourse as a result. The written and oral work by my students has improved, projects are more carefully researched, and my office hours are dedicated to discussion of thought rather than fact questions.

A vexing problem in senior seminars has been how to convince students to go to the reserve desk at the library, check out and read critical articles on reserve. Many campus libraries are currently switching to digital reserves, which allow instructors to submit digitized course readings in PDF file format. Students can access these password-protected readings on the library server from the course Web site at any hour and from most locations. Because these literary works are linked to the plays and cultural artifacts on our course site, students are more likely to seek information or explanations from the critical readings as they explore a Golden Age *comedia.* Secondary readings are no longer an afterthought because they are available when and where students need them.

A number of scholars have developed hypertext editions of Golden Age plays. Harry Vélez Quiñones points out that such editions "enable instructors to tailor textual annotations to the linguistic level of competence of their students . . . and make it easier to integrate relevant cultural material." Among the scholars pioneering the field are Vern Williamsen, Eduardo Urbina, Alix Ingber, Vélez Quiñones, Matthew Stroud and others (see the essay by Stroud in this book). Such hypertext-enhanced editions can be published to a course Web site or password-protected digital reserve, or distributed to students on CD-ROM. Those of us who frequently incorporate noncanonical works into our course design find it difficult—at times impossible—to locate and order a modern edition. For my undergraduate survey course, I created a hypertext-enriched edition of

Andrés de Claramonte's *El valiente negro en Flandes.* I had assigned this play several times, always photocopied from a reader-unfriendly nineteenth-century edition. Students found it difficult to read on their own, and often came to class with many more questions about the plot than comments about the play's meaning. By creating an HTML-based version of the text, I could provide basic clarifications of syntax and meaning with examples drawn from the *Tesoro de la lengua castellana o española* (Covarrubias) and the *Diccionario de autoridades.* My approach to this play is spatial, but most students do not know the map of the Mediterranean world, nor do they intuit the poetic significance of geographical spaces within the play, such as Mérida, Flanders, Madrid, and Guinea. I inserted a collection of maps, some interactive, at key moments of geographical transition. Students were able to see the physical patterns of space representation in the play, and they first suspected and then investigated the potential spatial arguments in the text. One student presentation, on the no-man's-land that divides the Spanish and Flemish forces in act 1, argued that only in such a space could the *valiente negro* don a mask and become a Spanish hero. The student's use of maps had led him to an independent discovery of liminal spaces. Other supplements to the Claramonte text include Alciato's emblem 59, "Impossibile," information on slavery and race in the Spanish empire, and associated theoretical and critical articles on digital reserve. The resulting (hyper)text of the play reaches more students than did the paper version: the poorly prepared students are able to find the extra information they need before class, so they can participate more confidently in discussions, and the more advanced students can explore their interests beyond what we cover during the average class meeting.

Instructors who have Internet access in their classrooms can use such editions and other Web site materials to enhance discussion. Multimedia artifacts and examples for class can now be accessed without recourse to multiple machineries during class time. We used to negotiate a slide projector, a video machine, a music player, and an overhead projector during a fifty-minute class. Now materials can be preloaded and seamlessly delivered as needed in the classroom.

Three-Dimensional Modeling and Future Technologies

Three-dimensional modeling is another technology application that creates teaching and learning opportunities. Form Z, a three-dimensional visualization tool used by architects, engineers, industrial designers, and animators, is one of several programs that allow instructors to model complex architectural and dramatic settings. Through a combination of its basic wire frame modeling tools and rendered surfaces, I am developing a three-dimensional model of the *corral del príncipe,* based on the sketches and physical model in John J. Allen's widely used *The Reconstruction of a Spanish Golden Age Playhouse.* Using the program's animation capabilities, I provide students with the experience of a casual walk through the theater and across the stage at several different times of the day. Discussions of staging, of lighting effects, and of spectators' interactions with each other and with the play have become immediate and experiential to the students, who have not studied in Spain, visited the theater at Almagro, or experienced a modern staging of the plays that we examine in the course. Armed with the *corral* model, students discover the visual impact of the rare candle mentioned in a play and the intricacies of the *alacena* mechanism in *La dama duende*; they gain a clearer appreciation of the uses of vertical space in *La vida es sueño* and *El burlador de Sevilla*. Future modeling projects might include the *carros* for an *auto sacramental*. The *auto* is particularly difficult for students to visualize without three-dimensional models.

Likewise, a three-dimensional model of the spaces connected by the *alacena* in Calderón's *La dama duende* helps us examine the approaches to staging and spatial relations in critical articles by María Martino Crocetti; J. M. Ruano de la Haza, "Staging"; J. E. Varey, *Símbolos*; N. D. Shergold, *Ses acteurs*. Students debate with surprising vigor the extent to which scholars can determine staging details from dramatic *acotaciones*, the plausibility of the staging schemes we can arrange in our 3D model of the *corral*, and the dramatic efficacy of a variety of stagings for both Golden Age and modern audiences. The modeling resolves for me the long-standing question of how to give students a clear sense of the complex spatial games in Calderón's dramatic works.

More sophisticated animation tools, such as Director combined with an AI (artificial intelligence) Toolkit, are becoming accessible for the amateur. Our ability to create credible human figures, place them in a three-dimensional space, and walk them through an interactive gaming environment promises new ways of communicating the significance of theatrical proxemics and power relations among dramatic characters. Many technology theorists claim that we are now experiencing only the beginning of a networked age, and that true virtual reality and artificial intelligence will alter everything we know about teaching and learning. The acceleration of technological discovery and the convergence of technology devices—cell phones that are personal digital assistants and music players, PDAs that connect wirelessly to computer networks—will certainly change how we access and deliver information about the past.

For further information on acquiring and implementing technology skills for the classroom and for examples of Web sites that utilize these technologies, visit the resource Web site (spot.colorado.edu/~sieberd/technology). I am indebted to the Carnegie Academy for the Scholarship of Teaching and Learning for financial support and academic guidance as I examine effective teaching with new technologies.

The Closest Reading: Creating Annotated Online Editions

Matthew D. Stroud

Teaching old literature of any kind to undergraduates is a challenge. The language is difficult, the themes often lack resonance for today's students, and the cultural references are abstruse. When one adds to the mix that the works are in an archaic version of Spanish, not the native language of most students in the United States, and that the plays are written in florid, baroque poetry, the task of helping students to appreciate the Spanish *comedia* for its literary value is made considerably more demanding. A great many students simply do not understand what is going on with the plots and characters when they read a play. One sign of their lack of engagement with the text is the fact that rarely do undergraduates make marginal notes in their editions. It appears they read the texts blankly, waiting for the professor or someone else to tell them what they were supposed to think about them. In class, the students rarely ask questions on their own and do not usually give anything but the most rudimentary answers to questions regarding the basic themes, much less more esoteric topics such as baroque prosody. Faced with fifty minutes of silence, the professor breaks down and lectures, giving the students the information that he or she thinks they need. The overall experience of a class run in this fashion is abysmal for both the students and the professor. The problem is not that students are uninterested in the topics of the *comedia*. Once they understand what the plays are about—sex, honor, intrigue—students are forthcoming with their opinions and insights.

One strategy to help students comprehend the texts is to bring reader and text together much more intensively than usual, through the creation of annotated editions of the dramas. Rarely at the undergraduate level does one even discuss the critical editions they are reading: the variants, the modernizations, sometimes the latter-day additions of lengthy stage directions. As a result, to have students develop critical editions means they must deal with texts and textual issues much more directly. It also requires an enormous amount of preparation on the part of the professor, who must have in mind what the entire project will look like at the end (texts, notes, plot summaries, author biographies, critical studies, and the like); and, ultimately, the professor, as general editor, is responsible for bringing together all the student contributions to form a useful whole. When I had students prepare critical editions, they were excited about the project from the start. Perhaps they were happy that our meetings were not just going to be another lecture course, or perhaps they did not yet realize exactly how much work would be involved. More than anything, though, this kind of project gives students the feeling that they are an integral part of the course and, therefore, they have a significant stake in the outcome—in this case, a deeper understanding of six important *comedias*.

One of the first decisions to be made is how many plays one can handle in a semester; work goes much more slowly when dealing with text at this level of close reading. For one course on the Spanish *comedia,* the class was to focus on only six plays at a pace of roughly one three-act play every two weeks. Even that rate is quite rushed, but at some point one must keep in mind that these are undergraduates and a semester spent on only one *comedia* might not best serve their long-term educational goals. The next decision involved specifying the particular plays to study. To add a bit of interest, the six *comedias* included three by men (Lope's *El castigo sin venganza,* Tirso's *El burlador de Sevilla,* and Calderón's *La vida es sueño*) and three by women (Caro's *Valor, agravio y mujer,* Zayas's *La traición en la amistad,* and Sor Juana's *Los empeños de una casa*). These choices were somewhat arbitrary but did reflect a desire to include standard masterpieces and less-studied plays. The three plays by men were readily available in a number of scholarly editions, including online editions. The plays by women were, tellingly, less available in current annotated editions but at least all of them had been printed.

Another early decision was the final format—that is, what the result of the class effort would look like, and we chose to publish the editions online for three primary reasons. First, online publication gave the students the greatest stake in the outcome: knowing that anyone could access the plays and see their work, they tended to be more critical of themselves and one another in order to create a product they could be proud of. Second, online publication was much more feasible, and not just in terms of access to the Internet; publishing otherwise would have involved considerable expense. Third, Web-based pages allowed for the insertion of hypertextual material that would have been difficult to incorporate in a linear publication. More specifically, there was a desire to help readers of these editions by including plot summaries available at the click of a mouse. Since the works were now going to be electronic editions, it was important to establish from the beginning the ultimate look of the plays on the computer screen. Glosses were to appear on the screen with the text itself, to allow us to print out the text and annotations on the same page. Line numbers and versification were also considered essential, as was the more general notion that the text should resemble its counterpart in a regular printed edition—that is, with indentations and other familiar features.

Had this been a graduate course in paleography, we would have started with seventeenth-century editions or even manuscripts, which would have meant dealing effectively with even fewer texts during the semester. For the purposes of the undergraduate course, however, it was enough to start with modern editions. Because five of the plays were already in the database of the Association for Hispanic Classical Theater (AHCT), we did not have to type in the complete text of those plays. The decision to include line numbers, though, meant that the AHCT database editions needed to be completely reformatted. Much of the conversion was accomplished using macros created in Microsoft Word, but some of the conversion simply involved a great deal of retyping. In some ways, the play by Zayas, which was not available online, was easier because it involved no conversion. Based on the version in Manuel Serrano y Sanz, with some changes, the play had to be typed in manually, but I created the tables as I typed, thus omitting the middle step.

An additional problem of conversion dealt with page layout, especially indentations and the spacing between the text and the line numbers. At the time, Web page standards offered few options, none of which was perfect. We could just insert spaces, but all the text would have appeared in courier font, and the goal was for the Web pages to look more like printed than typed pages. The solution came through the use of the color option: I declared the background white and inserted white periods to move the text to its appropriate place. (Unfortunately, some printers do not recognize the white-on-white periods as spaces to be left blank; instead, they print a row of black periods. An alternative would be to create a small white spacing graphic and use it to insert a spacer.) As a general rule, I preferred to limit myself to earlier Web page standards, so that almost any browser could view the texts properly, not just those with the latest technology. Another major advancement is the growing popularity of *Adobe Acrobat* (PDF) files. Anyone with a relatively recent browser can download the *Acrobat* files at no cost. The advantage of using *Acrobat* is that one can format pages in Word or another high-end word-processing program with no limit on special effects (indentations, font, kerning, even graphics). As a result, pages look the same to all viewers both on screen and printed. The disadvantages are minimal: the necessity of using the *Acrobat Reader* and the fact that the files viewed with *Acrobat* are not editable if downloaded the same way that HTML files are. So impressive are *Acrobat* files that the AHCT collection includes PDF as one of its standard formats for dramatic texts.

The preparation of the texts of the six plays, including the input process for the Zayas work, required approximately one hundred hours, spent over the summer before the course, and that figure does not include the creation of title pages, buttons, and other features of the finished product, much less the work done later by the students. Essentially the plays were to be presented along with a brief biography of the writer and a brief introduction to the work itself; then the text pages would include notes to words and expressions students found difficult and a synopsis of the action, together with an analysis of the versification. There were fourteen assignments for each play, or eighty-four in all, and seventeen students; each student had four assignments, leaving sixteen for me to do. (As it turns out, I had to do even more, because one student simply didn't hand in his work.) Finally, at the end of the semester, students were required to submit a study, also in electronic form, of some aspect of a play or plays we had read.

One final consideration was to balance the time students devoted to *comedia* texts with that they spent on Web page creation. I had originally thought about having the students do their own Web page creation, but I abandoned that idea early on because consistency of style was important and because we simply could not rely on students to have Web-creation skills in a Spanish literature course. Despite what we are told, even today students are not universally computer literate to the same degree. Some did not understand the difference between a Mac and a Power Mac (an important difference at the time, since we were using PC-based formats), and many had no idea how to add accents to their work. Therefore, part of the course involved teaching about computers as well as about the *comedia*. The key here is to evaluate the computer literacy of the class and then decide where to draw the line so that the technology aspect does not overwhelm the study of literature.

As for the *comedias* themselves, I realized immediately that the students understood little on reading the texts the first time (and for undergraduates, the first time is usually the last time). Perhaps it was because they were dealing with raw text, without notes (still to be created), but we spent an inordinate amount of time in class just going over what happens. This experience makes me wonder just how much students in more traditional *comedia* classes have grasped the texts; maybe their usual lack of participation is largely a function of their lack of understanding. At any rate, by dealing with the text on a minute level, the students discovered a number of truths about the plays.

The first thing they noted was that the plays are very difficult. The plots are astonishingly complicated, and the language is poetic and archaic at the same time. Perhaps because of poor training in the essentials of poetry in any language, students had great trouble identifying the different verse forms. Students used to modern literature are not prepared for intrigues built on intrigues or the use of certain names over and over (Juan, Leonor, and Pedro, for example). They also noted the difficulty of the vocabulary and grammar. About a third of the class were native speakers (from Mexico, Guatemala, and Colombia), but they seemed to have almost as hard a time with the texts as the native speakers of English did. The students' first impulse was to gloss everything, from every appearance of archaisms such as *agora* and *oílde* to every mention of *Cupido*. Some of the words they glossed left me wondering about their basic ability in Spanish: *aurora, furor, desespera, presagio, magnánimo, desdichada,* and almost every form of the verb *errar* (*erremos, erró, yerro*). If they had trouble with these words, one can only imagine their helplessness when confronted with lyrical passages. Not only did they seem to be at sea when dealing directly with poetry; I sensed a lack of commitment based on what I perceive to be their narrative approach to all literature. If a passage did not advance the plot, they tended to discount it; if it was difficult as well, they just gave up. Again, this approach forced the students to confront their worst fears—that is, baroque poetry—head on; they were simply not allowed to pass over difficult passages lightly and then move on to the next scene.

On their own, the students came up with topics of interest in *comedia* criticism: metatheater (without my having mentioned it, the students noted how the intrigues could be seen as theater within theater and remarked on the generally unreal aspect of the action of the plays); gender studies (they questioned what defines one's sex if a woman can become a man, at least as far as other characters are concerned, just by a change of clothing); theater semiotics (since there are no meaningful stage directions, they learned to read signs in the text: articles of clothing, adjective endings, and the like); themes, such as desire and honor, that motivate the characters; and historical and cultural studies (they asked a surprising number of questions regarding "the way it was" in seventeenth-century Spain, in an attempt to put the action of the plays into context).

Most interesting to me was the reaction to plays written by men versus those written by women. The students' first insight was that the works by women were much harder to read than those by men. It is tricky to generalize from such a small sample, but apparently the works by women are significantly more challenging, in terms of grammar, vocabulary, and plot structure, and they assume considerable erudition on the part of the spectator (or reader). Sor Juana's *Los empeños de una casa* had the most complicated plot to keep up with (not surprising, considering the three couples, the mistaken identities, and the like); students found Zayas's poetry difficult (not in a Calderonian sense, with words like *hipogrifo*, but in a more organic way; there are six sonnets in the play in which the action stops and all the focus is poetic).

The difference in mythological, historical, and other cultural references proved to be one of the more surprising discoveries by the students. The first act of Caro's *Valor, agravio y mujer* presented the densest web of references, many of which had to be explained to us (me included) by experts such as María José Delgado and Vern Williamsen, via e-mail. Both Caro and Zayas made considerably greater use of such references than the other playwrights did. *Valor, agravio y mujer* had 38 references and *La traición en la amistad* had 41 (Lope had 29, Tirso 19, Calderón 28, and Sor Juana 16). Moreover, the references used by all the women seemed more erudite and arcane, at least to us. While Lope referred to Circe (line 2138) and Troy (1472, 1670) and Tirso mentioned Ulysses (816) and Medea (2205), Caro dazzled her audience with references to Mavorte (72), Aneo Galión (250–51), Marcelo (292), Camila (504), and Sor Juana taxed our general knowledge by referring to Clicie (826) and Garatuza (2395).

Quite unexpectedly, this project ended up being an experiment I had long wanted to do: I gave an essentially naive audience *comedia* texts by men and women with no notes and, therefore, no hints about what students were supposed to find. They found that these texts by men and women differed not only at the level of subject matter (friendship versus honor) but also at the level of the text itself. Why the women's plays were much more difficult than the men's is anyone's guess. It could be that the audience for the plays was different, more educated. It could be that in general the women's plays were written later than the men's, when the baroque was marked more profoundly by excess. It could be something psychological in the relation of women to signification and language. It could also be a function of the particular references chosen by women: not just the familiar masculine images (Marte, Paris, Adonis, and others) but also less familiar feminine images (Camila, Clicie, and Salmacis). In addition, there are definitely more references to Spanish literature and history in the plays by women: Góngora, Calderón, Magallanes, and Doña Urraca all appear as cultural references. There was no time to investigate this phenomenon during the course, but the students came up with their plausible if impressionistic hypothesis: maybe the women felt they had more to prove, so they threw all their erudition and poetic virtuosity into their work. Whatever the reason, this kind of insight could not have taken place in an undergraduate course without the intimate textual work required by the creation of these online editions.

What did the students think of their project? Without exception, the course evaluations revealed that having their work appear on the Internet was motivating, although several students found it "scary" to have their assignments accessible by anyone in the world. Fortunately, the more frequent descriptions included "stimulating," "a good idea," "exciting," "fun," "important," the reasons given being that computers and the Internet are the wave of the future and that, as one student put it, the results made students feel as though they had accomplished something (I dread to ponder what this says about their other courses). As for the actual assignments (notes, synopses, etc.), while a couple of students thought they were boring (they would have rather expressed their opinions about the plays, for example), almost all praised the effort as an excellent way to get to know the *comedia* up close. The incorporation of technology into literature courses is daunting, but, at least in this class, the rewards made the effort worthwhile. Moreover, and more important, students left the course not just having read those particular six *comedias* but truly understanding and appreciating them.

GLOSSARY OF KEY TERMS

aposento upper-level box-seat sections of the theaters occupied by wealthy patrons

autor (de comedias) theater company owner and director as well as actor; hence, the "author" of performances

auto sacramental one-act allegorical religious drama (see, e.g., the essay by Martin)

baile dance; see also *entremés*

barba literally, "beard"; the role of an older man, or the actor who portrayed it; companies typically included one or two "barba" actors

carro cart or wagon that could convert into a stage, used especially for *autos sacramentales*

cazuela literally, "stew pot"; gallery in the back of the theater reserved for women attending a play

cofradía charitable confraternity; performances in public theaters were sponsored by *cofradías* to generate income for hospitals and other charities they supported

comedia typically a three-act poetic drama, combining comic and tragic elements and including both noble and lower-born characters; a generic term applied to comic, tragicomic, and tragic dramas alike; sometimes referred to as the *comedia nueva,* to indicate the form as defined by Lope de Vega

comedia de capa y espada literally, a cape-and-sword play (see, e.g, the essay by García Santo-Tomás); a comedy of love and its obstacles involving members of the lower nobility and set in the author's time period

conceptismo a witty poetic style, marked by conceits (*conceptos*) or surprising metaphors, ingenious comparisons, puns, and paradoxes, among other poetic devices (see, e.g., the essay by Gaylord)

corral originally, a courtyard that served as the site for early performances of *comedias;* term later used for theaters

corral de comedias commercial open-air public playhouse that succeeded the earlier *corrales* and served as the principal venue of *comedia* performances from about 1580 onward; the two enduring *corrales* in Madrid were the Corral de la Cruz and the Corral del Príncipe

dama lady; the leading and supporting female roles in the play, assigned to actresses designated in the company's cast lists as *primera, segunda,* and *tercera dama*

décima a stanza of ten lines, rhyming *abbaaccddc* (see, e.g., the essay by Gaylord)

desengaño disillusion, the state of being free of worldly illusions; a major theme in Counter Reformation Spanish philosophy and in early modern Spanish drama (see, e.g., the essay by Delgado)

entremés originally, a dramatic interlude presented between the acts of a court banquet; a short farce or burlesque entertainment presented between the acts of *comedias* and with *autos sacramentales;* related types of interludes are the *mojiganga* (farce), the *jácara* (ruffian ballad), the *baile* (dance), and *baile entremesado* (dramatized dance) (see, e.g., the essay by Martin)

galán literally, gallant or handsome; also used to designate a suitor; the leading men in theater companies were referred to as *primero, segundo,* or *tercer galán*

gracioso comic plebian character, typically the servant of a noble protagonist; a standard presence in virtually all *comedias* (e.g., Clarín in *La vida es sueño*)

honor and **honra** both defined in English as "honor" but sometimes having distinct meanings in early modern Spain; *honor* pertains to private or internal virtue, moral integrity, dignity, nobility of mind; *honra* pertains to public or social esteem, respect, reputation, good name; both are key themes in early modern Spanish drama (see, e.g., the essays by McKendrick and Barahona)

jácara ruffian ballad; see *entremés* and the essay by Martin

jornada act of a play; a term derived from a day's journey or the length of a day's work, to be followed by rest

lacayo lackey; the servant and foil of the noble *galán,* equivalent to the *gracioso* role

leyenda negra literally, "black legend"; a term coined in the early twentieth century, pertaining to early modern and modern European representations of Spain as greedy, cruel, and tyrannical, especially relating to atrocities of the conquest and colonization of the New World (see, e.g., the essay by Reed)

limpieza de sangre purity of blood, i.e., the absence of Jewish, Moorish, or, in some instances, plebian ancestry; stressed by Spanish nobility as a barrier separating them from the lower classes, and by commoners asserting their worth against nobility suspected of ancestral intermarriage with wealthy Jews or Jewish converts (see, e.g., the essay by McKendrick)

loa prologue of a play in the form of a monologue or a skit

mestizaje term indicating the ethnic or cultural mixing of European and indigenous peoples in the New World (see, e.g., the essays by Cartagena-Calderón and Reed)

mojiganga farce; see *entremés* and the essay by Martin

mosquesteros literally, musket-bearing soldiers; male spectators occupying standing space at the rear of the *patio,* famous for disrupting performances that displeased or bored them

paso comic episode, sometimes used interchangeably with *entremés*

patio the ground-level, uncovered standing space for male spectators paying the minimum entry fee to the *corral;* those paying an additional fee could rent a seat at the front of the patio

quintilla a stanza of five lines, rhyming in different patterns, such as *ababa* or *abbab* (see, e.g., the essay by Gaylord)

redondilla a stanza of four lines, rhyming *abba* (see, e.g., the essay by Gaylord)

romance a ballad sequence of unspecified length, with even-numbered lines rhyming in assonance; often narrative in nature (see, e.g., the essay by Gaylord)

Siglo de Oro literally, "Age of Gold"; sometimes used to describe Spain of the sixteenth and seventeenth centuries

tertulia gallery reserved for clerics attending a play

tramoya stage machine used for special effects

vestuario dressing room; the women's dressing room at the rear of the stage doubled as a discovery space for special effects

villancico poetic composition or song, with a refrain, descended from or in imitation of the traditional songs sung by *villanos;* the meter and rhyme are variable

villano commoner; lowborn inhabitant of a village or town

vulgo the masses or crowd; used to designate a popular as opposed to elite audience

NOTES ON CONTRIBUTORS

Renato Barahona is professor of history at the University of Illinois, Chicago. His research and teaching center on the social history of Spain and early modern Europe. His publications include *Sex Crimes, Honour and the Law in Early Modern Spain: Vizcaya, 1528–1735*; and *Vizcaya on the Eve of Carlism: Politics and Society, 1800–1833*. His current research focuses on how victims' narratives were shaped by the legal establishment.

Laura R. Bass is assistant professor at Tulane University. She teaches courses on early modern Spanish and colonial Latin American literature, art, and culture and has won awards for her work in the classroom. She has published articles on literature from the fifteenth through the seventeenth centuries. Her book manuscript "The Drama of the Portrait: Theater and Visual Culture in Early Modern Spain" is currently under review.

John Beusterien is associate professor at Texas Tech University. He has published articles on the question of race, anti-Semitism, and the *comedia*. His book *An Eye on Race: Perspectives from Theater in Imperial Spain* is forthcoming. He is a contributing author to *Culturas de España*, a textbook on Spanish cultures.

Bruce R. Burningham is assistant professor at Illinois State University, where he teaches courses on medieval and early modern Spanish literature, Hispanic drama, and performance theory. He is the author of *Radical Theatricality: Jongleuresque Performance on the Early Spanish Stage* (forthcoming). His most recent book project, "Tinted Mirrors: Baroque Reflections on Contemporary Culture," examines the intersection of the Spanish baroque and contemporary Anglo-American culture.

José R. Cartagena-Calderón is visiting assistant professor at Stanford University. He has published articles on the construction of masculinity in early modern Spanish literature. He has completed a book, "Masculinidades en obras: Los avatares de la hombría en la España imperial," on the intersections of empire, ethnicity, sexuality, and masculinity in early modern Hispanic literature.

Frederick A. de Armas is Andrew W. Mellon Professor in Humanities and chair of the Department of Romance Languages and Literatures at the University of Chicago. His publications focus on the literature of the Spanish Golden Age, often from a comparative perspective. His books include *A Star-Crossed Golden Age: Myth and the Spanish Comedia*; *Cervantes, Raphael, and the Classics*; and *Writing for the Eyes in the Spanish Golden Age*.

Manuel Delgado is professor of Spanish at Bucknell University. He has authored *Tiranía y derecho de resistencia en el teatro de Guillén de Castro* and many essays on Golden Age and twentieth-century literature. He has edited *The Calderonian Stage: Body and Soul*; Calderón's *La devoción de la cruz*; and, with Alice Poust, *Lorca, Buñuel, Dalí: Art and Theory*. He is currently editing Calderón's *Amar después de la muerte*.

Susan L. Fischer is professor of Spanish and comparative literature at Bucknell University. She is the editor of, and contributor to, two volumes of essays: *Comedias del Siglo de*

Oro and *Shakespeare and Self-Conscious Art: A Tribute to John W. Kronik.* Her recent publications include "'Some Are Born Great' and 'Have Greatness Thrust upon Them': Staging Lope's *El perro del hortelano* on the Boards of the Bard"; "Staging Lope de Vega's *Peribañez:* The Problem of an Ending"; and "'De l'ironie avant tout': Andreï Serban's (In)human (Re)invention of *The Merchant of Venice* at La Comédie-Française."

Edward H. Friedman is professor of Spanish and comparative literature at Vanderbilt University. His research centers on early modern Spanish literature and contemporary narrative and drama. His publications include *The Unifying Concept: Approaches to Cervantes' Comedias*; *The Antiheroine's Voice: Narrative Discourse and Transformations of the Picaresque*; *Wit's End: An Adaptation of Lope de Vega's* La dama boba; and *El cuento: Arte y análisis.* He is editor of the *Bulletin of the Comediantes.*

María Antonia Garcés is associate professor of Spanish at Cornell University. In 2003, she was awarded the MLA's James Russell Lowell Prize for her book *Cervantes in Algiers: A Captive's Tale,* which she has translated and revised for publication in Spain. She has published articles on Cervantes, Montaigne, and Inca Garcilaso de la Vega. Forthcoming works include a critical edition of Antonio de Sosa's *Topografiá e historia general de Argel,* edited by Diego de Haedo.

Carmen García de la Rasilla is assistant professor of Spanish at the University of New Hampshire. She has published articles on comparative literature and a book on contemporary Spanish history. She has just finished a book manuscript on Salvador Dalí's autobiography *The Secret Life.*

Enrique García Santo-Tomás is associate professor of Spanish at the University of Michigan, Ann Arbor. He is author of the award-winning books *La creación del Fénix: Recepción crítica y formación canónica del teatro de Lope de Vega* and *Espacio urbano y creación literaria en el Madrid de Felipe IV.* He is editor of *El teatro del Siglo de Oro ante los espacios de la crítica* and editions of Tirso and Lope. He has just completed a book on Salas Barbadillo.

Mary Malcolm Gaylord is Sosland Family Professor of Romance Languages and Literatures at Harvard University. She is the author of *The Historical Prose of Fernando de Herrera* and editor of *Frames for Reading: Cervantes Studies in Honor of Peter N. Dunn* and of *Fray Luis de Leon and San Juan de la Cruz: An International Symposium.* Her writings on Golden Age literature include essays on the plays of Fernando de Rojas, Cervantes, Lope de Vega, Ruiz de Alarcón, and Calderón.

Margaret R. Greer is chair and professor of Spanish in the Department of Romance Studies, Duke University. Her publications include *María de Zayas Tells Baroque Tales of Love and the Cruelty of Men*; *The Play of Power: Mythological Court Dramas of Pedro Calderón de la Barca*; and two editions of Calderón plays. She is working on books on early modern Spanish tragedy and on hunting in Spanish and colonial literature, art, and law.

Valerie Hegstrom is associate professor of Spanish and comparative literature at Brigham Young University. Her publications include an edition of Zayas's *La traición en la amistad / Friendship Betrayed* (trans. Catherine Larson); *Engendering the Early Modern Stage: Women Playwrights in the Spanish Empire* (coedited with Amy Williamsen); and articles on Zayas, Tirso, and Golden Age women playwrights. She is working on editions of the plays of Sor Maria do Ceo and Joanna Theodora de Souza.

A. Robert Lauer is professor of Spanish and film at the University of Oklahoma. He is the author of four books, including *Tyrannicide and Drama,* and sixty essays, mostly on the Spanish Golden Age. He is general editor of *Ibérica,* treasurer of AITENSO, board member of the *Bulletin of the Comediantes,* and member of the MLA Sixteenth- and Seventeenth-Century Spanish Drama Division.

Frederick Luciani is professor of Spanish at Colgate University. He is the general editor of *Colonial Latin American Review* and author of *Literary Self-Fashioning in Sor Juana Inés de la Cruz.* His current project is a critical edition of a 1756 *festejo* from the convent of San Jerónimo in Mexico City.

James Mandrell is associate professor of Spanish, comparative literature, women's studies, and film studies at Brandeis University. He is the author of *Don Juan and the Point of Honor: Seduction, Patriarchal Society, and Literary Tradition,* as well as articles on Hispanic and comparative topics. He is currently at work on a comparative study of Canadian, United States, and Mexican film.

Vincent Martin is assistant professor of Spanish at the University of Delaware. He has published editions of two of Calderón's plays for student use; an edited volume, *Clarines de pluma: Homenaje a Antonio Regalado*; and two monographs: *El concepto de "representación" en los autos sacramentales de Calderón* and *Calderón (1600–1681).* With Electa Arenal, he is currently preparing a critical edition of Sor Juana's *Neptuno alegórico.*

Melveena McKendrick is professor of Spanish Golden Age literature, culture, and society and pro-vice-chancellor for education at the University of Cambridge and a Fellow of the British Academy. She is author of *Woman and Society in the Spanish Drama of the Golden Age; Theatre in Spain 1490–1700; Playing the King: Lope de Vega and the Limits of Conformity*; and *Identities in Crisis: Essays on Honour, Gender and Women in the Comedia.*

Leah Middlebrook is assistant professor of Romance languages and comparative literature at the University of Oregon. She has published articles on Spanish and French Petrarchism and on women and court politics in sixteenth-century France. She is currently completing a book manuscript on Spanish poets and early modernity, "Imperial Lyric."

Dale J. Pratt is associate professor of Spanish and comparative literature at Brigham Young University. He has published on the *auto sacramental,* metatheater in José Triana, and the nexus between literature and science in Spain. He is currently working on a book that analyzes uses of the term *human,* including chapters on Galdós and germs, Iberian cave people, degeneracy, artificial intelligences, cyborgs and virtual realities. He is a board member of the AHCT.

Cory A. Reed is associate professor in the Department of Spanish and Portuguese at the University of Texas, Austin. He is the author of *The Novelist as Playwright: Cervantes and the* Entremés Nuevo and has published articles on Cervantes's drama, the *Novelas ejemplares, Don Quijote,* and Calderón. He is an award-winning teacher and a faculty director of the interdisciplinary Tracking Cultures Program in the College of Liberal Arts. He is currently completing a book on scientific and technological imagery in *Don Quixote*.

Diane E. Sieber is associate professor, Herbst Program for Humanities in Engineering, and codirector of the ATLAS Institute at the University of Colorado, Boulder. She has published *Historiography and Marginal Identity in Sixteenth-Century Spain* and articles on colonial New Mexico, Spanish historiography, *Don Quijote,* the *moriscos,* and Golden Age theater. A Carnegie Teaching Scholar, she is currently researching effective teaching with new and emerging technologies and writing a book on the monster in Golden Age Theater.

Teresa S. Soufas is professor of Spanish at Tulane University. Her publications include *Melancholy and the Secular Mind in Spanish Golden Age Literature*; *Dramas of Distinction: Plays by Golden Age Spanish Women*; *Women's Acts: Plays by Women*; and articles on the culture of early modern Spain, particularly women authors and gender issues. She is currently working on a project about Queen Isabel I of Spain.

Matthew D. Stroud is professor of Spanish, director of the Self-Instructional Language Program in Arabic, and recipient of an outstanding teacher award at Trinity University, San Antonio. His publications include *Fatal Union: A Pluralistic Approach to the Spanish Wife-Murder* Comedias; *The Play in the Mirror: Lacanian Perspectives on Spanish Baroque Theater*; and an edition of Calderón's *Celos aun del aire matan*. He has recently completed a monograph on queer approaches to early modern Spanish drama.

SURVEY PARTICIPANTS

Following are the names and affiliations of the other scholars and teachers who took time from their busy schedules to respond to the questionnaire on approaches to teaching early modern Spanish drama. These responses and the information provided were invaluable to the editors of the volume.

John J. Allen, *University of Kentucky*
Belén Atienza, *Clark University*
Luis F. Avilés, *University of California, Irvine*
Ed Aylward, *University of South Carolina*
Amy R. Barber, *Grove City College*
Bernard P. E. Bentley, *The University, St. Andrews, Scotland*
Catalina Buezo Canalejo, *Universidad Europea de Madrid*
José R. Cartagena-Calderón, *Stanford University*
Catherine Connor, *University of Vermont*
Frederick A. de Armas, *University of Chicago*
Nancy D'Antuono, *Saint Mary's College, Notre Dame, Indiana*
Denise DiPuccio, *University of North Carolina, Wilmington*
Victor Dixon, *Trinity College, University of Dublin*
Peter N. Dunn, *Wesleyan University*
Enrique Fernández, *University of Manitoba*
Edward H. Friedman, *Vanderbilt University*
Susan L. Fischer, *Bucknell University*
Enrique García Santo-Tomás, *University of Michigan*
Christopher D. Gascón, *SUNY Cortland*
Chad M. Gasta, *Iowa State University*
Cleveland Johnson, *Spelman College*
Carol Bingham Kirby, *State University College at Buffalo*
Hilary W. Landwehr, *Northern Kentucky University*
A. Robert Lauer, *University of Oklahoma*
Julia R. Lieberman, *Saint Louis University*
Ann L. Mackenzie, *University of Glasgow*
Michael McGaha, *Pomona College*
Melveena McKendrick, *Cambridge University*
Patricia W. Manning, *The University of Kansas*
Vincent Martin, *University of Delaware*
Ignacio Navarrete, *University of California, Berkeley*
Bradley J. Nelson, *Concordia University, Montreal*
Lisa J. Nowak, *Albion College*
Mary Parker, Independent scholar, New York City
Vicente Pérez de León, *Oberlin College*
Dale J. Pratt, *Brigham Young University*
Carmen Rasilla, *University of New Hampshire*

Cory A. Reed, *University of Texas at Austin*
Joseph V. Ricapito, *Louisiana State University*
Theresa Ann Sears, *University of North Carolina, Greensboro*
Diane E. Sieber, *University of Colorado at Boulder*
Ana María Snell, *Johns Hopkins University*
Matthew D. Stroud, *Trinity University*
Eric W. Vogt, *Seattle Pacific University*
Sharon Voros, *US Naval Academy*
Barbara Weissberger, *University of Minnesota, Minneapolis*

WORKS CITED

Abel, Lionel. *Metatheatre: A New View of Dramatic Form.* New York: Hill, 1963.

Abre los ojos [*Open Your Eyes*]. Dir. Alejandro Amenábar. Artisan Entertainment, 1997.

Adams, Hazard, and Leroy Searle, eds. *Critical Theory since 1965.* Tallahassee, Florida State UP, 1990.

Alarcón, Juan Ruiz de. *Obras completas.* Ed. Alva V. Ebersole. 2 vols. Valencia: Albatros Hispanófila, 1990.

———. *The Truth Can't Be Trusted.* Trans. Dakin Matthews. New Orleans: UP of the South, 1998; North Hollywood: Andak Theatrical Services, 2000.

———. *La verdad sospechosa.* Ed. Alva M. Ebersole. Madrid: Cátedra, 1980.

———. *La verdad sospechosa.* Ed. Gloria B. Clark. Newark: Cervantes & Co., 2002.

———. *La verdad sospechosa.* Ed. José Montero Reguera. Madrid: Castalia, 1999.

Albrecht, Jane. *The Playgoing Public of Madrid in the Time of Tirso de Molina.* New Orleans: UP of the South, 2001.

Alín, José María, and María Begoña Barrio Alonso. *El cancionero teatral de Lope de Vega.* London: Tamesis, 1997.

Allen, John J. *The Reconstruction of a Spanish Golden Age Playhouse: El Corral del Príncipe (1583–1744).* Gainesville: UP of Florida, 1983.

Alonso, Dámaso. "La correlación en la estructura del teatro calderoniano." *Seis calas en la expresión literaria española.* By Alonso and Carlos Bousoño. Madrid: Gredos, 1951. 109–75.

Alvar Ezquerra, Alfredo. *El nacimiento de una capital europea: Madrid entre 1561 y 1606.* Madrid: Turner, 1989.

Anthony (El Saffar), Ruth. "Violante: The Place of Rejection." De Armas, *Prince* 165–82.

Aparicio Maydeu, Javier, ed. *Estudios sobre Calderón.* 2 vols. Madrid: Istmo, 2000.

Arellano, Ignacio. *Historia del teatro español del siglo XVII.* Madrid: Cátedra, 1995.

Arellano, Ignacio, et al., eds. *Comedias burlescas del Siglo de Oro.* Austral 463. Madrid: Espasa, 1999.

Argente del Castillo Ocaña, Carmen. "De la realidad a la ficción: El vestido en la escena." *Las mujeres en la sociedad española del Siglo de Oro: Ficción teatral y realidad histórica. Actas del II coloquio del Aula-Biblioteca Mira Amescua.* Ed. Juan Antonio Martínez Berbel and Roberto Castillo Pérez. Granada: U de Granada, 1998. 161–84.

Aristotle. *Aristotle's Poetics.* Ed. and trans. James Hutton. New York: Norton, 1982.

———. *The Poetics of Aristotle.* Trans. and commentary by Stephen Halliwell. Chapel Hill: U of North Carolina P, 1987.

Arrom, José Juan, and José Rojas Garcidueñas, eds. *Coloquio de los cuatro reyes de Tlaxcala. Tres piezas teatrales del Virreinato.* México: Instituto de Investigaciones Estéticas, U.N.A.M., 1976.

Ars theatrica. Ed. José L. Canet, Evangelina Rodríguez, and Josep Lluís Serra. Parnaseo, U de València. 10 Sept. 2004 <http://parnaseo.uv.es/ars.htm>.

Asensio, Eugenio. *Itinerario del entremés desde Lope de Rueda a Quiñones de Benavente, con cinco entremeses inéditos de Francisco de Quevedo.* Madrid: Gredos, 1965.

Asociación Internacional de Teatro Español y Novohispano de los Siglos de Oro (AITENSO). Ed. A. Robert Lauer. 10 Sept. 2004 <http://faculty-staff.ou.edu/L/A-Robert.R.Lauer-1/AITENSO.html>.

Association for Hispanic Classical Theater. Ed. Matthew Stroud. 10 Sept. 2004 <http://www.comedias.org>. <http://www.trinity.edu/org/comedia/index.html>.

Austin, J. L. *How to Do Things with Words.* Cambridge: Harvard UP, 1962.

Azar, Inés. "Self, Responsibility, Discourse: An Introduction to Speech Act Theory." Rivers, *Things* 1–13.

Bakhtin, Mikhail. *Rabelais and His World.* Trans. Hélène Iswolsky. Bloomington: Indiana UP, 1984.

Bakker, Jan. "Versificación y estructura de la comedia de Lope." *Diálogos hispánicos de Amsterdam* 2 (1981): 93–101.

Bandrés Oto, Maribel. *La moda en la pintura: Velázquez. Usos y costumbres del siglo XVII.* Pamplona: EUNSA, 2002.

Barahona, Renato. *Sex Crimes, Honour and the Law in Early Modern Spain: Vizcaya, 1528–1735.* Toronto: U of Toronto P, 2003.

Barbera, Raymond R. "An Instance of Medieval Iconography in *Fuenteovejuna.*" *Romance Notes* 10 (1968): 160–62.

Barkley, Harold. *Likenesses in Line: An Anthology of Tudor and Stuart Engraved Portraits.* London: Her Majesty's Stationery Office, 1982.

Barton, John. *Playing Shakespeare.* London: Methuen in assn. with Channel 4 Television, 1984.

Baudrillard, Jean. "On Seduction." *Selected Writings.* Ed. Mark Poster. Trans. Jacques Mourrain. Stanford: Stanford UP, 1988. 149–65.

Bazán Díaz, Iñaki. *Delincuencia y criminalidad en el País Vasco en la transición de la edad media a la moderna.* Servicio de Publicaciones del Gobierno Vasco: Gasteiz-Vitoria, 1995.

Bennassar, Bartolomé. *La España del Siglo de Oro.* Barcelona: Crítica, 1983.

———. "Honor and Violence." *The Spanish Character: Attitudes and Mentalities from the Sixteenth to the Nineteenth Century.* Trans. Benjamin Keen. Berkeley: U of California P, 1979. 213–36.

———. *Valladolid au Siècle d'Or.* Paris: Mouton, 1967.

Bennassar, Bartolomé, and Lucile Bennassar. *Los cristianos de Alá: La fascinante aventura de los renegados.* Trans. José Luis Aristu. Madrid: Nerea, 1989.

Bentley, Eric, ed. *Spanish Plays.* Vol. 3 of *The Classic Theatre.* Garden City: Doubleday, 1959. Rpt. in part as Life Is a Dream *and Other Spanish Classics.* New York: Applause, 1990.

————. "The Universality of the *Comedia.*" *Hispanic Review* 38 (1970): 147–62.

Bergman, Hannah E., ed. *Ramillete de entremeses y bailes nuevamente recogidos de los antiguos poetas de España, siglo XVII.* Madrid: Castalia, 1970.

Bergmann, Emilie L. "Reading and Writing in the *Comedia.*" *The Golden Age Comedia: Text, Theory, and Performance.* Ganelin and Mancing 276–92.

Berlant, Lauren. "Collegiality, Crisis, and Cultural Studies." *Profession 1998.* New York: MLA, 1998. 105–16.

Bernat Vistarini, Antonio, and John T. Cull. *Emblemas españoles ilustrados.* Madrid: Akal, 1999.

Bernis, Carmen. "La moda en la España de Felipe II a través del retrato de Corte." *Alonso Sánchez Coello y el retrato en la corte de Felipe II.* Madrid: Museo del Prado, 1990. 66–111.

————. *El traje y los tipos sociales en* El Quijote. Madrid: Viso, 2001.

————. "Los trajes." Castillejo 123–86.

Beusterien, John. "Talking Black in Spanish: An Unfinished Black Spanish Glossary." *Bulletin of the Comediantes* 51 (1999): 83–104.

Biblioteca Virtual Miguel de Cervantes. <http://cervantesvirtual.com>.

Billington, Michael. Rev. of *"Peribáñez." Guardian* (London) 9 May 2003: 28+.

Blessing, Jennifer. Introduction. *Rrose Is a Rrose Is a Rrose: Gender Performance in Photography.* Ed. Blessing. New York: Guggenheim Foundation, 1997. 6–17.

Bloom, Harold. *The Western Canon: The Books and School of the Ages.* New York: Harcourt, 1994.

Blue, William R. "The Politics of Lope's *Fuenteovejuna.*" *Hispanic Review* 59 (1991): 295–315.

————. *Spanish Comedies and Historical Contexts in the 1620s.* University Park: Pennsylvania State UP, 1996.

Boettcher, Judith, and G. Philip Cartwright. "Technology: Designing and Supporting Courses on the Web." *Change* 29.5 (1997): 10, 62–63.

Bonete, Enrique. *Éticas en esbozo: De política, felicidad y muerte.* Bilbao: Desclée de Brouwer, 2003.

Bowman, Sylvia, et al., eds. *Studies in Honor of Gerald E. Wade.* Madrid: J. Porrúa, [1979].

Braudel, Fernad. *The Mediterranean and the Mediterranean World in the Age of Philip II.* Trans. Siân Reynolds. 2 vols. New York: Harper, 1972.

Braunmuller, A. R., and J. C. Bulman. *Essays in Honor of Eugene M. Waith.* Newark: U of Delaware P, 1986.

Braveheart. Dir. Mel Gibson. Paramount, 1995.

Brigham Young University's Mentoring Environments Grants Application. "Principles of Mentoring at BYU." Provo: Brigham Young U, 2002.

Brockett, Oscar G., and Franklin J. Hildy. *History of the Theatre.* 9th ed. Boston: Allyn, 2003.

Brook, Peter. *The Empty Space.* New York: Atheneum, 1968.

Brotherton, John. *"El Nuevo Mundo descubierto por Cristóbal Colón:* Convention and Ideology." *Bulletin of the Comediantes* 46 (1994): 33–47.

Brown, Joan L., and Crista Johnson. "Required Reading: The Canon in Spanish and Spanish American Literature." *Hispania* 81 (1998): 1–17.

Brown, Jonathan. *The Golden Age of Painting in Spain.* New Haven: Yale UP, 1991.

———. *Painting in Spain: 1500–1700.* New Haven: Yale UP, 1998.

Brown, Jonathan, and J. H. Elliott. *A Palace for a King: The Buen Retiro and the Court of Philip IV.* Rev. and expanded ed. New Haven: Yale UP, 2003.

Bruerton, Courtney. "La versificación dramática española en el período 1587–1610." *Nueva Revista de Filología Hispánica* 10 (1956): 337–64.

Bruffee, Kenneth A. *Collaborative Learning: Higher Education, Interdependence, and the Authority of Knowledge.* Baltimore: Johns Hopkins UP, 1995.

Buck, Kathryn, ed. *The ACTFL Oral Proficiency Interview Tester Training Manual.* Yonkers: ACTFL, 1989.

Buezo, Catalina. *El Carnaval y otras procesiones burlescas del viejo Madrid.* Madrid: Avapiés, 1992.

———. *La mojiganga dramática: De la fiesta al teatro.* Madrid: Caja Madrid; Kassel: Reichenberger, 1993.

———. *Prácticas festivas en el teatro breve del siglo XVII.* Kassel: Reichenberger, 2004.

———, ed. *Teatro breve de los Siglos de Oro: Antología.* Madrid: Castalia Didáctica, 1992.

Burningham, Bruce R. "Barbarians at the Gates: The Invasive Discourse of Medieval Performance in Lope's *Arte nuevo." Theatre Journal* 50 (1998): 289–302.

Butler, Judith. *Gender Trouble: Feminism and the Subversion of Identity.* New York: Routledge, 1990.

Caballero Fernández-Rufete, Carmelo. "La música en el teatro clásico." Huerta Calvo, *Historia* 1: 677–715.

Calderón de la Barca, Pedro. *El alcalde de Zalamea.* Ed. José María Díez Borque. Madrid: Castalia, 1976.

———. *El alcalde de Zalamea.* Ed. José María Ruano de la Haza. Madrid: Espasa, 1988.

———. *El alcalde de Zalamea.* Ed. José Enríquez Martínez. Madrid: Biblioteca Didáctica Anaya, 1992.

———. *El alcalde de Zalamea.* Ed. José Montero Reguera. Madrid: Castalia Didáctica, 1996.

———. *La aurora en Copacabana.* Ed. Ezra S. Engling. London: Tamesis, 1994.

———. *Las carnestolendas.* Calderón de la Barca, *Entremeses* 139–55.

———. *Celos aun del aire matan.* Ed. and trans. Matthew D. Stroud. San Antonio: Trinity UP, 1981.

———. *La cisma de Inglaterra.* Ed. Francisco Ruiz Ramón. Madrid: Castalia, 1981.

———. *Colección de autos sacramentales completos de Calderón.* 49 vols. to date. Pamplona: U de Navarra; Kassel: Reichenberger, 1992– .

———. *La dama duende.* Ed. A. J. Valbuena Briones. Madrid: Cátedra, 1994.

————. *La devoción de la cruz*. Ed. Manuel Delgado. Madrid: Cátedra, 2000.

————. *Eight Dramas of Calderón*. 1853. Ed. and trans. Edward FitzGerald. Foreword by Margaret R. Greer. Urbana: U of Illinois P, 2000.

————. *Entremeses, jácaras y mojigangas*. Ed. Evangelina Rodríguez and Antonio Tordera. Madrid: Castalia, 1982.

————. *La fiera, el rayo y la piedra*. Ed. Aurora Egido. Madrid: Cátedra, 1989.

————. *El gran teatro del mundo*. Ed. Eugenio Frutos Cortés. Madrid: Cátedra, 1983.

————. *El gran teatro del mundo. El gran mercado del mundo*. Ed. Eugenio Frutos Cortés. 8th ed. Madrid: Cátedra, 1985.

————. *El gran teatro del mundo*. Ed. John J. Allen y Domingo Ynduráin. Barcelona: Crítica, 1997.

————. *The Great Stage of the World: An Allegorical* Auto Sacramental. Trans. George W. Brandt. Manchester: Manchester UP, 1976.

————. *Guárdate de la agua mansa / Beware of Still Waters*. Ed. and trans. David M. Gitlitz. San Antonio: Trinity UP, 1984.

————. *La hija del aire: Tragedia en dos partes*. Ed. Francisco Ruiz Ramón. Madrid: Cátedra, 1987.

————. *Love Is No Laughing Matter / No hay burlas con el amor.* Ed. and trans. Don Cruickshank and Seán Page. Warminster, Eng.: Aris, 1986.

————. *El mágico prodigioso*. Ed. Ángel Valbuena Prat. Madrid: Espasa, 1970.

————. *El mágico prodigioso*. Ed. Bruce W. Wardropper. Madrid: Cátedra, 1985.

————. *El mágico prodigioso*. Ed. Michael J. McGrath. Newark: Cervantes & Co., 2003.

————. *El mayor monstruo del mundo*. Ed. José M. Ruano de la Haza. Madrid: Espasa, 1989.

————. *The Mayor of Zalamea. Eight Dramas of Calderón*. Trans. Edward Fitzgerald. Urbana: U of Illinois P, 2000. 221–62.

————. *El médico de su honra*. Ed. Don William Cruickshank. Madrid: Castalia, 1981.

————. *No hay instante sin milagro*. Ed. Ignacio Arellano, Ildefonso Adeva, and Rafael Zafra. Pamplona: U de Navarra; Kassel: Reichenberger, 1995.

————. *The Painter of His Dishonour / El pintor de su deshonra*. Ed. and trans. A. K. G. Paterson. Warminister, Eng.: Aris, 1991.

————. *The Phantom Lady*. Ed. and trans. Donald Beecher and James Nelson Novoa. Ottawa: Dovehouse, 2002.

————. *El príncipe constante*. Ed. Alberto Porqueras Mayo. Madrid: Espasa, 1975.

————. *El príncipe constante*. Ed. Fernando Cantalapiedra y Alfredo Rodríguez López-Vázquez. Madrid: Cátedra, 1996.

————. *The Schism in England / La cisma de Inglaterra*. Ed. and trans. Kenneth Muir and Ann L. MacKenzie. Warminster, Eng.: Aris, 1990.

————. *El sitio de Bredá. Dramas*. Ed. A. Valbuena Briones. Madrid: Aguilar, 1987. 103–39. Vol. 2 of *Obras completas*.

————. *Three Plays*. Ed. and trans. Adrian Mitchell and John Barton. Bath: Absolute Classics, 1990.

——. *La vida es sueño.* Ed. Ana Suárez Miramón. Madrid: Biblioteca Didáctica Anaya, 1985.

——. *La vida es sueño.* Ed. Ciriaco Morón. Madrid: Cátedra, 2001.

——. *La vida es sueño.* Ed. J. M. García Martín. Madrid: Castalia Didáctica, 1992.

——. *La vida es sueño.* Ed. Javier Azpeitia. Madrid: McGraw, 1997.

——. *La vida es sueño.* Ed. José M. Ruano de la Haza. Madrid: Castalia, 2000.

——. *La vida es sueño [y] El alcalde de Zalamea.* Ed. Augusto Cortina. Madrid: Espasa, 1955.

——. *La vida es sueño.* Ed. Vincent Martin. Newark: Cervantes & Co., 2003.

——. *La vida es sueño.* Trinity U. 12 May 2003. <http://www.trinity.edu/mstroud/comedia/vidsue.html>.

Calderón de la Barca y la España del Barroco. Madrid: Sociedad Estatal España Nuevo Milenio, 2000.

Callaghan, Dympna. *Shakespeare without Women: Representing Gender and Race on the Renaissance Stage.* London: Routledge, 2000.

Calvo Poyato, José. *Así vivían en el Siglo de Oro.* Madrid: Anaya, 2000.

Canavaggio, Jean. "À propos de deux 'Comedias' de Cervantès: Quelques remarques sur un manuscrit récemment retrouvé." *Bulletin hispanique* 68 (1966): 5–29.

——. *Cervantes.* Trans. J. R. Jones. New York: Norton, 1990.

——. *Cervantès dramaturge: Un théâtre à naître.* Paris: PUF, 1977.

Carey-Webb, Allen. *Making Subject(s): Literature and the Emergence of National Identity.* New York: Garland, 1998.

Carmona, Ramón. *Cómo se comenta un texto fílmico.* Madrid: Cátedra, 1996.

Caro Baroja, Julio. *El Carnaval: Análisis histórico-cultural.* 2nd ed. Madrid: Taurus, 1979.

——. *Las formas complejas de la vida religiosa. Religión, sociedad y carácter en la España de los siglos XVI y XVII.* Corrected ed. Barcelona: Galaxia Gutenberg; Valencia: Círculo de Lectores, 1995.

——. "Honor y vergüenza." *Revista de dialectología y tradiciones populares* 20.4 (1964): 410–60. English trans. in Peristiany 79–138.

Caro Mallén de Soto, Ana. *Valor, agravio y mujer.* Ed. Lola Luna. Madrid: Castalia, 1993.

——. *Valor, agravio y mujer.* 26 June 2002. Assn. for Hispanic Classical Theater. 12 May 2003. <http://www.trinity.edu/org/comedia/caro/valagr.html>.

——. *Valor, agravio y mujer.* 12 May 2003. Trinity U. <http://www.trinity.edu/mstroud/comedia/valagr.html>.

Carr, Raymond, ed. *Spain: A History.* New York: Oxford UP, 2000.

Carrasco Ferrer, Marta. "Charles V in Rome: The Triumph of a New Scipio." *Carolus. Museo de Santa Cruz, Toledo.* Madrid: Sociedad Estatal para la Conmemoración de los Centenarios de Felipe II y Carlos V, 2000. 81–101.

Carreño, Antonio. "Del romancero nuevo a la comedia nueva de Lope de Vega: Constantes e interpolaciones." *Hispanic Review* 50 (1982): 33–52.

Carrión, María M. "The Queen's Too Bawdies: *El burlador de Sevilla* and the Teasing of Historicity." Fradenburg and Freccero 45–69.

Cartagena-Calderón, José. *Entre telones masculinos: Teatro, literatura y construcción de masculinidades en la España aurisecular.* Diss. Harvard U, 2000.

Carter, Robin. "Liberty, Comedy, and Irony in *La vida es sueño.*" *Forum for Modern Language Studies* 32 (1996): 354–71.

Caruth, Cathy. *Trauma: Explorations in Memory.* Baltimore: Johns Hopkins UP, 1995.

———, ed. *Unclaimed Experience: Trauma, Narrative, and History.* Baltimore: Johns Hopkins UP, 1996.

Carvajal, Miguel de, and Luis Hurtado de Toledo. *Las cortes de la muerte.* Scene 19. Ruiz Ramón, *América* 259–68.

Casa, Frank P., Luciano García Lorenzo, and Germán Vega García-Luengos, eds. *Diccionario de la comedia del Siglo de Oro.* Madrid: Castalia, 2002.

Casalduero, Joaquín. *Estudios sobre el teatro español.* Madrid: Gredos, 1962.

———. *The Devastation of the Indies: A Brief Account.* Trans. Herma Briffault. Baltimore: Johns Hopkins UP, 1992.

Cascardi, Anthony J. *Ideologies of History in the Spanish Golden Age.* University Park: Pennsylvania State UP, 1997.

Casey, James. *Early Modern Spain: A Social History.* London: Routledge, 1999.

Castillejo, David, ed. *El corral de comedias: Escenarios, sociedad, actores.* Madrid: Teatro Español / Ayuntamiento de Madrid, 1984.

Castillo, David, and Egginton, William. "All the King's Subjects: Honor in Early Modernity." *Romance Language Annual* 6 (1994): 422–27.

Castro, Américo. *De la edad conflictiva: Crisis de la cultura española en el siglo XVII.* 4th ed. Madrid: Taurus, 1976.

Castro, Guillén de. *Las mocedades del Cid. Primera parte.* Ed. Victor Said Armesto. Madrid: Espasa, 1952. 1–136.

———. *Las mocedades del Cid.* Ed. Luciano García Lorenzo. Madrid: Cátedra, 1984.

———. *Las mocedades del Cid.* Ed. Stefano Arata. Barcelona: Crítica, 1996.

———. *Las mocedades del Cid.* Ed. James Crapotta and Marcia L. Welles. Newark: Cervantes & Co., 2002.

———. *Obras completas.* Ed. Joan Oleza. 5 vols. Madrid: Biblioteca Castro, 1997.

———. *The Youthful Deeds of the Cid.* Trans. Robert R. La Du, Luis Soto-Ruiz, and Giles A. Daeger. New York. Exposition, 1969.

Catherein, V. "Ethics." *The Catholic Encyclopedia.* 2002. 15 May 2003. <http://www.newadvent.org/cathen//05556a.htm>.

Certau, Michel de. *The Writing of History.* Trans. Tom Conley. New York: Columbia UP, 1988.

Cervantes, Miguel de. *Los baños de Argel.* Ed. Florencio Sevilla Arroyo and Antonio Rey Hazas. Madrid: Alianza, 1998. Vol. 14 of *Obras completas.*

———. *El cerco de Numancia.* Ed. Robert Marrast. 4th ed. Madrid: Cátedra, 1999.

————. Don Quixote: *The Ormsby Translation Revised, Backgrounds and Sources, Criticism.* Ed. Joseph R. Jones and Kenneth Douglas. Norton Critical Ed. New York: Norton, 1981.

————. *Eight Interludes.* Ed. and trans. Dawn L. Smith. London: Everyman, 1996.

————. *Entremeses.* Ed. Miguel Herrero García. Madrid: Espasa, 1966.

————. *Entremeses.* Ed. Eugenio Asensio. Madrid: Castalia, 1971.

————. *Entremeses.* Ed. Nicholas Spadaccini. Madrid: Cátedra, 1982.

————. *The Great Pretender.* Trans. Philip Osment. London: Oberon, 2004.

————. *El ingenioso hidalgo don Quijote de la Mancha.* Ed. Luis Andrés Murillo. 2 vols. Madrid: Castalia, 1978.

————. *La Numancia.* Ed. Robert Marrast. Madrid: Cátedra, 1984.

————. *La Numancia.* Ed. Alfredo Hermenegildo. Madrid: Castalia, 1994.

————. *Obras completas de Miguel de Cervantes.* Ed. Florencio Sevilla Arroyo and Antonio Rey Hazas. 18 vols. Madrid: Alianza, 1998.

————. *Ocho comedias y ocho entremeses nunca representados.* Ed. Florencio Sevilla Arrollo and Antonio Rey Hazas. Madrid: Alianza, 1998. Vol. 17 of *Obras completas.*

————. The Siege of Numantia, Life Is a Dream, *and Other Spanish Classics.* Trans. Roy Campbell. Ed. Eric Bentley. New York: Harper, 1985. 97–160.

————. *El trato de Argel.* Ed. Florencio Sevilla Arroyo and Antonio Rey Hazas. Madrid: Alianza, 1996. Vol. 2 of *Obras completas.*

Cervantes, Miguel de, and Federico García Lorca. *Dos retablos y un retablillo.* Ed. Ana Herrero Riopérez. Madrid: Castalia Prima, 2000.

Chaffee-Sorace, Diane. "Animal Imagery in Lope de Vega's *Fuenteovejuna." Bulletin of the Comediantes* 42 (1990): 199–214.

Chang-Rodríguez, Raquel. *Hidden Messages: Representation and Resistance in Andean Colonial Drama.* Lewisburg: Bucknell UP, 1999.

Chauchadis, Claude. *Honneur, morale et société dans l'Espagne de Philippe II.* Paris: CNRS, 1984.

Chittenden, Jean S. *The Characters and Plots of Tirso's* Comedias. Don Gil de las Calzas Verdes. <www.trinity.edu/mstroud/tirso/DGilCV.html>.

Cibertextos. Miguel Garci-Gómez. <http://aaswebsv.aas.duke.edu/cibertextos/index.html>.

Civil, Pierre. "Corps, vêtement et société: Le costume aristocratique espagnol dans la deuxième moitié du XVIe siècle." *Le corps dans la société espagnole des XVIe et XVIIe siècles.* Ed. Agustín Redondo. Paris: Sorbonne, 1990. 307–19.

Claramonte, Andrés de. *La estrella de Sevilla.* Ed. Alfredo Rodríguez López-Vázquez. Madrid: Cátedra, 1991.

————. *El valiente negro en Flandes.* Ed. Alfredo Rodríguez López-Vázquez. Alcalá: U de Alcalá, 1997.

Cohen, Walter. *Drama of a Nation: Public Theater in Renaissance England and Spain.* Ithaca: Cornell U, 1985.

Cohn, Ruby. "Dramatic Poetry." *The New Princeton Encyclopedia of Poetry and Poetics.* Ed. Alex Preminger and T. V. F. Brogan. Princeton: Princeton UP, 1993. 304–11.

Cole, Toby, and Helen Krich Chinoy, eds. *Actors on Acting*. New York: Crown: 1949.

Collard, Andrée. *Nueva poesía: Conceptismo, culteranismo en la poesía española*. Madrid: Castalia, 1967.

Columbus, Christopher. *The Journal of the First Voyage / Diario del primer viaje*. Ed. B. W. Ife. Warminster, Eng.: Aris, 1990.

Comedia in Translation. Ed. Susan Paun de García. <http://www.denison.edu/collaborations/comedia/translations>.

Compañía Nacional de Teatro Clásico. 10 Sept. 2004. <http://teatroclasico.mcu.es>.

Constable, Olivia Remie, ed. *Medieval Iberia: Readings from Christian, Muslim, and Jewish Sources*. Philadelphia: U of Pennsylvania P, 1997.

Córdoba de la Llave, Ricardo. *El instinto diabólico: Agresiones sexuales en la Castilla medieval*. Córdoba: U de Córdoba, 1994.

Corneille, Pierre. *Le Cid. Œuvres complètes*. Ed. André Stegmann. Paris: Seuil. 1963. 215–41.

———. *The Cid*. Ed. John Cairncross. New York: Penguin, 1975. 23–109.

———. *Le Cid*. Trans. Vincent J. Cheng. Newark: U of Delaware P, 1987.

———. *Cinna. Œuvres complètes*. Ed. André Stegmann. Paris: Seuil. 1963. 268–88.

———. *Cinna*. Ed. John Cairncross. New York: Penguin, 1975. 113 92.

Corral del Príncipe. <http://aix1.uottowa.ca/%7Ejmruano/corral.html>.

Coso Marín, Miguel Ángel, Mercedes Higuera Sánchez-Pardo, and Juan Sanz Ballesteros. *El Teatro Cervantes de Alcalá de Henares, 1602–1866: Estudio y documentos*. London: Tamesis, 1989.

Cotarelo y Mori, Emilio. *Bibliografía de las controversias sobre la licitud del teatro en España*. Madrid: Est. de la Revista de Archivos, Bibliotecas y Museos, 1904. Facsimile ed. Ed. José Luis Suárez García. Granada: U de Granada, 1997.

———. *Ensayo sobre la vida y obras de D. Pedro Calderón de la Barca*. Madrid: Tipografía de la Revista de Archivos, Bibliotecas y Museos, 1924. Facsimile ed. Ed. Ignacio Arellano and Juan Manuel Escudero. Pamplona: U de Navarra; Madrid: Iberoamericana; Frankfurt: Vervuert, 2001.

Covarrubias Orozco, Sebastián de. *Emblemas morales*. Ed. Carmen Bravo-Villasante. Madrid: Fundación Universitaria Española, 1978.

———. *Tesoro de la lengua castellana o española*. Ed. Felipe Maldonado. Rev. Manuel Camarero. Madrid: Castalia, 1994.

Cox, Harvey. *The Feast of Fools: A Theological Essay on Festivity and Fantasy*. Cambridge: Harvard UP, 1969.

Crocetti, María Martino. "*La dama duende*: Spatial and Hymeneal Dialectics." Stoll and Smith 51–66.

Cruikshank, Don William. *Calderón de la Barca: El médico de su honra*. London: Grant, 2003.

Cummins, John G., ed. *The Spanish Traditional Lyric*. Oxford: Pergamon, 1977.

Dandelet, Thomas James. *Spanish Rome, 1500–1700*. New Haven: Yale UP, 2001.

Darst, David H. "Lope's Strategy for Tragedy in *El caballero de Olmedo*." *Crítica hispánica* 6.1 (1984): 11–17.

Davis, Barbara Gross. *Tools for Teaching*. San Francisco: Jossey-Bass, 1993.

de Armas, Frederick A. "The Allure of the Oriental Other: Titian's *Rossa Sultana* and Lope de Vega's *La Santa Liga*." Friedman and Larson 191–208.

———. *Cervantes, Raphael, and the Classics*. Cambridge: Cambridge UP, 1998.

———, ed. *The Prince in the Tower: Perceptions of* La vida es sueño. Lewisburg: Bucknell UP, 1993.

———, ed. *Writing for the Eyes in the Spanish Golden Age*. Lewisburg: Bucknell UP, 2004.

Defourneaux, Marcelin. *Daily Life in Spain in the Golden Age*. Stanford: Stanford UP, 1979.

Delano, Lucille K. *A Critical Index of Sonnets in the Plays of Lope de Vega*. Toronto: U of Toronto P, 1935.

Deleito y Piñuela, José. *También se divierte el pueblo*. Madrid: Alianza, 1988.

Delgado, Manuel. "La melancolía amorosa de Cipriano en *El mágico prodigioso*." *Bulletin of Spanish Studies* 8 (2004): 37–48.

———. "Sindéresis, ley natural y sentido moral en *La vida es sueño*." *Ayer y hoy de Calderón*. Ed. José María Ruano de la Haza and Jesús Pérez Magallón. Madrid: Castalia, 2002. 107–23.

Delgado, María José, and Alain Saint-Saëns, eds. *Lesbianism and Homosexuality in Early Modern Spain: Literature and Theater in Context*. New Orleans: UP of the South, 2000.

Della Porta, Giovanni Battista. *Ars Reminscendi: Agiunta l'arte di ricordare tradotta da Dorandino Falcone da Gioia*. Ed. Raffaele Sirri. Napoli: Scientifische Italiane, 1996.

dePaola, Tomie. *The Clown of God*. New York: Harcourt, 1978.

Diccionario de autoridades . . . 1726–39. 6 vols. Madrid: Gredos, 1990. 3 vols. Facsimile ed. <http://www.rae.es>.

Díez Borque, José María. "El auto sacramental calderoniano y su público: Funciones del texto cantado." *Calderón and the Baroque Tradition*. Ed. Kurt Levy, Jésus Ara, and Gettin Hughes. Waterloo: Wilfred Laurier UP, 1985. 49–67.

———, ed. *Una fiesta sacramental barroca*. Madrid: Taurus, 1984.

———. *Los géneros dramáticos en el siglo XVI: El teatro hasta Lope de Vega*. Madrid: Taurus, 1987.

———. "Relaciones de teatro y fiesta en el barroco español." *Teatro y fiesta en el Barroco: España e Iberoamérica*. Ed. Díez Borque. Barcelona: Serbal, 1986.

———. *Sociedad y teatro en la España de Lope de Vega*. Barcelona: Bosch, 1978.

———. *Sociología de la comedia española del siglo XVII*. Madrid: Cátedra, 1975.

———, ed. *Teatro y fiesta del Siglo de Oro en tierras europeas de los Austrias*. Madrid: Sociedad Estatal para la Acción Cultural Exterior, 2003.

Díez de Revenga, Francisco Javier. *Teatro de Lope de Vega y lírica tradicional*. Murcia: U de Murcia, 1983.

Dixon, Victor. "The Uses of Polymetry: An Approach to Editing the *Comedia* as Verse

Drama." *Editing the Comedia.* Ed. Frank P. Casa and Michael D. McGaha. Ann Arbor: U of Michigan P, 1985. 104–25.

Dolan, Frances E. *Whores of Babylon: Catholicism, Gender, and Seventeenth-Century Print Culture.* Ithaca: Cornell UP, 1999.

Dollimore, Jonathan. *Radical Tragedy: Religion, Ideology and Power in the Drama of Shakespeare and His Contemporaries.* 2nd ed. London: Harvester Wheatsheaf, 1989.

———. "Shakespeare, Cultural Materialism, and the New Historicism." *Political Shakespeare: New Essays in Cultural Materialism.* Ed. Dollimore and Alan Sinfield. Manchester: Manchester UP, 1985. 2–18. Rpt. in Wilson and Dutton 45–56.

Domínguez Ortíz, Antonio. *The Golden Age of Spain, 1516–1659.* Trans. James Casey. New York: Basic, 1971.

Don Juan de Marco. Dir. Jeremy Leven. With Marlon Brando, Johnny Depp, and Faye Dunaway. 1995. DVD. New Line Home Entertainment, 2004.

Donnell, Sidney. *Feminizing the Enemy: Imperial Spain, Transvestite Drama, and the Crisis of Masculinity.* Lewisburg: Bucknell UP, 2003.

Dopico Black, Georgina. "Mencía Perfected: Strategies of Containment in Calderón's *El médico de su honra.*" Friedman, Manzari, and Miller 59–72.

———. *Perfect Wives, Other Women.* Durham: Duke UP, 2001.

Dunn, Peter. "Honour and the Christian Background in Calderón." *Bulletin of Hispanic Studies* 37 (1960): 75–105.

———. "Some Uses of Sonnets in the Plays of Lope de Vega." *Bulletin of Hispanic Studies* 24 (1957): 213–22.

Durán, Manuel, and Roberto González Echeverría, eds. *Calderón y la crítica: Historia y antología.* 2 vols. Madrid: Gredos, 1976.

Duviols, Pierre. "Las representaciones andinas de *La muerte de Atahuallpa:* Sus orígenes culturales y sus fuentes." *La formación de la cultura virreinal.* Ed. Karl Kohut and Sonia V. Rose. Vol. 1. Madrid: Iberoamericana, 2000. 213–47.

Dyer, Abigail. "Heresy and Dishonor: Sexual Crimes before the Courts of Early Modern Spain." Diss. Columbia U, 2000.

Dyer, Richard. *White: Essays on Race and Culture.* London: Routledge, 1997.

Egginton, William. *How the World Became a Stage: Presence, Theatricality, and the Question of Modernity.* Albany: SU of New York P, 2003.

———. "Psychoanalysis and the *Comedia:* Skepticism and the Paternal Function in *La vida es sueño.*" *Bulletin of the Comediantes* 52 (2000): 97–122.

Ehrmann, Stephen C. "What Does Research Tell Us about Technology and Higher Learning?" *Change* 27.2 (1995): 24–41.

Elam, Kier. "Language in the Theater." *Substance* 18-19 (1977): 139–61.

Elias, Norbert. *The Court Society.* Trans. Edmund Jephcott. London: Blackwell, 1983.

———. *Power and Civility.* New York, Pantheon, 1982. Vol. 2 of *The Civilizing Process.*

Elliott, J. H. *Imperial Spain, 1469–1716.* 1963. London: Penguin, 1970. Trans. as *La España imperial, 1469–1716.* Trans. J. Marfany. 5th ed. Barcelona: Vives, 1986.

————. *Spain and Its World, 1500–1700.* New Haven: Yale UP, 1989.

Encyclopedia of the Renaissance. Ed. Paul Grendler. 6 vols. New York: Scribner, 1999.

Esquerdo, Vicenta. "Indumentaria con la que los cómicos representaban en el siglo XVII." *Boletín de la Real Academia Española* 58 (1978): 447–544.

Evans, Peter W. "The Roots of Desire in *El burlador de Sevilla." Forum for Modern Language Studies* 22 (1986): 232–47.

Feal, Carlos. *En nombre de don Juan (Estructura de un mito literario).* Amsterdam: Benjamins, 1984.

Felman, Shoshana. *The Literary Speech Act: Don Juan with J. L. Austin; or, Seduction in Two Languages.* Trans. Catherine Porter. Ithaca: Cornell UP, 1983.

Felman, Shoshana, and Dori Laub. *Testimony: Crises of Witnessing in Literature, Psychoanalysis, and History.* New York: Routledge, 1992.

Fernández de Oviedo, Gonzalo. *Historia general y natural de las Indias.* Ed. Juan Pérez de Tuleda Bueso. Biblioteca de Autores Españoles 117. Madrid: Atlas, 1959.

Ferrater Mora, José. *La filosofía, en el mundo de hoy.* Madrid: Revista de Occidente, 1967. Vol. 2 of *Obras selectas.*

Ferrell, William K. *Literature and Film as Modern Mythology.* London: Praeger, 2000.

Festival Internacional de Teatro Clásico de Almagro. 10 Sept. 2004. <http://www.festivaldealmagro.com>.

Finn, Thomas P. *Molière's Spanish Connection: Seventeenth-Century Spanish Theatrical Influence on Imaginary Identity in Molière.* New York: Lang, 2001.

Fischer, Susan L. "Historicizing *Painter of Dishonour* on the 'Foreign' Stage: A Radical Interrogation of Tragedy." Mackenzie 183–216.

————. "Reader-Response Criticism and the *Comedia:* Creation of Meaning in Calderón's *La cisma de Ingalaterra." Bulletin of the Comediantes* 31 (1979): 109–25. Rpt. in Everett W. Hesse and Catherine Larson, eds. *Approaches to Teaching Spanish Golden Age Drama.* York: Spanish Literature, 1989. 92–111.

————. "'This Thing of Darkness I / Acknowledge Mine': Segismundo, Prospero, and *Shadow." De* Armas, *Prince* 147–64.

Fish, Stanley. "How to Do Things with Austin and Searle: Speech Act Theory and Literary Criticism." *MLN* 91 (1976): 983–1025.

————. *Is There a Text in This Class? The Authority of Interpretive Communities.* Cambridge: Harvard UP, 1980.

Fothergill-Payne, Louise. *La alegoría en los autos y farsas anteriores a Calderón.* London: Tamesis, 1977.

————. "*Los tratos de Argel, Los cautivos de Argel* y *Los baños de Argel:* Tres 'trasuntos' de un 'asunto.'" *El mundo del teatro español en el Siglo de Oro: Ensayos dedicados a John E. Varey.* Ed. José María Ruano de la Haza. Ottawa: Dovehouse, 1989. 177–96.

Fothergill-Payne, Louise, and Peter Fothergill-Payne, eds. *Parallel Lives: Spanish and English National Drama, 1580–1680.* Lewisburg: Bucknell UP, 1991.

Fox, Dian. "History, Tragedy, and the Ballad Tradition in *El caballero de Olmedo*." Ganelin and Mancing 9–23.

Fox, Dian, Harry Sieber, and Robert ter Horst, eds. *Studies in Honor of Bruce W. Wardropper*. Newark: Juan de la Cuesta, 1989.

Fradenburg, Louise, and Carla Freccero, eds. *Premodern Sexualities*. New York: Routledge, 1996.

Fra Molinero, Baltasar. *La imagen de los negros en el teatro del Siglo de Oro*. Mexico: Siglo Veintiuno, 1995.

Frenk Alatorre, Margit, ed. *Lirica española de tipo popular: Edad Media y Renacimiento*. Madrid: Cátedra, 1977.

Friedman, Edward H. "Theater Semiotics and Lope de Vega's *El caballero de Olmedo*." *El arte nuevo de estudiar comedias: Literary Theory and Spanish Golden Age Drama*. Ed. Barbara Simerka. Lewisburg: Bucknell UP, 1996. 66–85.

Friedman, Edward H., and Catherine Larson, eds. *Brave New Words: Studies in Spanish Golden Age Literature*. New Orleans: UP of the South, 1996.

Friedman, Edward H., H. J. Manzari, and Donald D. Miller, eds. *A Society on Stage: Essays on Golden Age Drama*. New Orleans: UP of the South, 1998.

Fuchs, Barbara. *Mimesis and Empire: The New World, Islam, and European Identities*. Cambridge: Cambridge UP, 2001.

Fuenteovejuna. Prod. Radio y Televisión Española (RTVE). 1980. Videocassette. Films for the Humanities and Sciences. <http://www.films.com>.

Fuentes, Carlos. *El espejo enterrado*. Madrid: Taurus, 1992.

Fuss, Diana. *Essentially Speaking: Feminism, Nature, and Difference*. New York: Routledge, 1989.

Gadamer, Hans Georg. *Truth and Method*. Trans. and rev. Joel Weinsheimer and Donald G. Marshall. 2nd rev. ed. New York: Crossroad, 1989.

Gaines, James F. "From Classroom to Stage and Back: Using Molière in Performance." *Approaches to Teaching Molière's* Tartuffe *and Other Plays*. Ed. James F. Gaines and Michael S. Koppisch. New York: MLA, 1995. 145–51.

Gallop, Jane. *Feminist Accused of Sexual Harassment*. Durham: Duke UP, 1997.

———. "Im-Personation: A Reading in the Guise of an Introduction." Gallop, *Pedagogy* 1–18.

———, ed. *Pedagogy: The Question of Impersonation*. Bloomington: Indiana UP, 1995.

Ganelin, Charles, and Howard Mancing, eds. *The Golden Age* Comedia: *Text, Theory, and Performance*. West Lafayette: Purdue UP, 1994.

Garber, Marjorie. *Vested Interests: Cross-Dressing and Cultural Anxiety*. New York: Harper Perennial, 1993.

Garcés, María Antonia. "El cautiverio: Meollo de la obra cervantina." *El Quijote en Colombia ayer y siempre*. Spec. issue of *Senderos* 9.33 (1998): 1322–335.

———. *Cervantes in Algiers: A Captive's Tale*. Nashville: Vanderbilt UP, 2002.

García Arenal, Mercedes, and Miguel Ángel de Bunes. *Los españoles en el Norte de Africa: Siglos XV–XVIII*. Madrid: MAPFRE, 1992.

García de Enterría, María Concepción. "Función de la 'letra para cantar' en las comedias de Lope de Vega: Comedia engendrada por una canción." *Boletín de la Biblioteca Menéndez Pelayo* 41 (1965): 3–62.

García García, Bernardo J. "Los hatos de actores y compañías." Reyes Peña 165–90.

García Lorca, Federico. *Blood Wedding.* Trans. Gwynne Edwards. London: Methuen, 1997.

———. *Bodas de sangre.* Ed. Allen Josephs and Juan Caballero. Madrid: Cátedra, 1998.

García Lorenzo, Luciano, ed. *El teatro menor en España a partir del siglo XVI: Actas del coloquio celebrado en Madrid, 20–22 de mayo de 1982.* Anejos de la Revista *Segismundo* 5. Madrid: CSIC, 1983.

García Santo-Tomás, Enrique, ed. *El teatro del Siglo de Oro ante los espacios de la crítica: Encuentros y revisiones.* Madrid: Iberoamericana, 2002.

Gasté, Armand. *La querelle du Cid: Pièces et pamphlets publiés d'après les originaux.* Geneva: Slatkine, 1970.

Gaylord Randel, Mary. "The Grammar of Femininity in the Traditional Spanish Lyric." *Revista / Review Interamericana* 12 (1984): 115–24.

Geckle, George L., ed. *Twentieth-Century Interpretations of* Measure for Measure. Englewood Cliffs: Prentice, 1970.

Geertz, Clifford. "Centers, Kings, and Charisma: Reflections on the Symbolics of Power." *Rites of Power: Symbolism, Ritual, and Politics since the Middle Ages.* Ed. Sean Wilentz. Philadelphia: U of Pennsylvania P, 1985. 13–38.

Gerli, Michael. "The Hunt of Love: The Literalization of a Metaphor in *Fuenteovejuna.*" *Neophilologus* 63 (1979): 54–58.

Gibson, Charles. Introduction. *The Black Legend: Anti-Spanish Attitudes in the Old World and the New.* Ed. Gibson. New York: Knopf, 1971. 3–27.

———. "*Reconquista* and *Conquista.*" *Homage to Irving A. Leonard: Essays on Hispanic Art, History, and Literature.* Ed. Raquel Chang-Rodríguez and Donald A. Yates. New York: Mensaje, 1977. 19–28.

Gillet, Joseph E. "The *Coplas del perro de Alba.*" *Modern Philology* 23 (1925–26): 417–44.

Gilman, Stephen A. "Lope de Vega and the 'Indias en su ingenio.'" *Spanische Literatur im Goldenen Zeitalter.* Ed. Horst Baader and Erich Loos. Frankfurt: Klostermann, 1973. 102–16.

———. "On *Romancero* as a Poetic Language." *Homenaje a Casalduero: Crítica y poesía.* Ed. Rizel Pincus Sigele and Gonzalo Sobejano. Madrid: Gredos, 1972. 151–60.

Gilmore, David D., ed. *Honor and Shame and the Unity of the Mediterranean.* Amer. Anthropological Assn. Spec. Pub. 22. Washington: AAA, 1987.

Godzich, Wlad, and Nicholas Spadaccini, eds. *Literature among Discourses: The Spanish Golden Age.* Minneapolis: U of Minnesota P, 1986.

Gómez, María Asunción. *Del escenario a la pantalla: La adaptación cinematográfica del teatro español.* Chapel Hill: U of North Carolina, Dept. of Romance Langs., 2000.

Góngora, Luis de. *Las firmezas de Isabela.* Ed. Robert James. Madrid: Castalia, 1984.

———. *Teatro completo.* Ed. Laura Dolfi. Madrid: Cátedra, 1993.

González de Salas, Jusepe Antonio. *Nueva idea de la tragedia antigua.* 1633. Ed. Luis Sánchez Laílla. 2 vols. Kassel: Reichenberger, 2003.

González García, Serafín. "El tema de la nobleza en *El vergonzoso en palacio.*" *Mira de Amescua en el candelero: Actas del congreso internacional sobre Mira de Amescua y el teatro español del siglo XVII.* Ed. Agustín de la Granja and Juan A. Martínez Berbel. Granada: U de Granada, 1996. 239–49.

González Maestro, Jesús. "Hacia una tragedia moderna: La poética de lo trágico en la *Numancia.*" *La escena imaginaria: Poética del teatro de Miguel de Cervantes.* Madrid: Iberoamericana, 2000: 155–98.

Gould, Cheryl. *Searching Smart on the World Wide Web.* Berkeley: Library Solutions, 1998.

Granda, Germán de. "Sobre el origen del 'habla de negro' en la literatura peninsular del Siglo de Oro." *Prohemio* 2 (1971): 97–109.

Green, Kenneth C., and Stephen W. Gilbert. "Great Expectations: Content, Communications, Productivity, and the Role of Information Technology in Higher Education." *Change* 27.2 (1995): 8–18.

Green, Robert A. "Instinct of Nature: Natural Law, Synderesis, and the Moral Sense." *Journal of the History of Ideas* 58.2 (1997): 173–98.

Greenberg, Mitchell. "Towards French Classical Tragedy." Hollier 273–78.

Greer, Margaret Rich. "Embodying the Faith: The *Auto* Program of 1670." *The Theater of Calderón: Body and Soul.* Ed. Manuel Delgado. Lewisburg: Bucknell UP, 1997. 133–53.

———. *The Play of Power: Mythological Court Dramas of Pedro Calderón de la Barca.* Princeton: Princeton UP, 1991.

———. "The (Self)Representation of Control in *La dama duende.*" Ganelin and Mancing 87–196.

———. "A Tale of Three Cities: The Place of the Theatre in Early Modern Madrid, Paris and London." *Bulletin of Hispanic Studies* 77 (2000): 391–419.

Gregory, Derek. *Geographical Imaginations.* Oxford: Blackwell, 1994.

Grupo Investigación Siglo de Oro (GRISO). U de Navarra. 10 Sept. 2004. <http://griso.cti.unav.es/docs/inicio/principal.html>.

Gutwirth, Marcel. "Autocritical Dramaturgy." Hollier 309–14.

Haedo, Diego de, ed. *Topografía e historia general de Argel.* By Antonio de Sosa. Ed. Ignacio Bauer y Landauer. 3 vols. Madrid: Sociedad de Bibliófilos Españoles, 1927–29.

Hale, J. R. *Artists and Warfare in the Renaissance.* New Haven: Yale UP, 1990.

Halkoree, Premraj. *Calderón de la Barca: El alcalde de Zalamea.* London: Grant, 1972.

Hall, J. B. *Lope de Vega: Fuenteovejuna.* London: Grant, 1985.

Hardison, O. B. *Christian Rite and Christian Drama in the Middle Ages: Essays in the Origin and Early History of Modern Drama.* Baltimore: Johns Hopkins UP, 1965.

Harris, Max. "Carnival in Galicia." *Drama Review* 44.3 (2000): 154–70.

Hart, Thomas R. *Gil Vicente: Casandra and* Don Duardos. London: Grant, 1994.

Hartt, Frederick. *History of Renaissance Art*. Rev. David G. Wilkins. 4th ed. New York: Abrams, 1994.

Harvey, David. *The Condition of Postmodernity: An Enquiry into the Origins of Social Change*. Baltimore: Johns Hopkins UP, 1989.

———. *Consciousness and the Urban Experience: Studies in the History and Theory of Capitalist Urbanization*. Baltimore: Johns Hopkins UP, 1985.

Harvey, John. *Men in Black*. Chicago: U of Chicago P, 1995.

Hayem, Armand. *Le Don Juanisme*. Paris: Alphonse Lemerre, 1886.

Heers, Jacques. *Carnavales y fiestas de locos*. Trans. Xavier Riu y Camps. Barcelona: Península, 1988.

Hegstrom, Valerie, ed. *La traición en la amistad / Friendship Betrayed*. By María de Zayas. Trans. Catherine Larson. Lewisburg: Bucknell UP, 1999.

Hegstrom, Valerie, and Amy R. Williamsen, eds. *Engendering the Early Modern Stage: Women Playwrights in the Spanish Empire*. New Orleans: UP of the South, 1999.

Heidegger, Martin. "Hölderlin and the Essence of Poetry." Adams and Searle 758-65.

Heise, Ursula K. "Transvestism and Stage Controversy in Spain and England, 1580–1680." *Theater Journal* 44 (1992): 357–74.

Henry V. By William Shakespeare. Screenplay by Alan Dent and Laurence Olivier. Dir. Olivier. Perf. Olivier. 1944. Rank, 1999.

Henry V. By William Shakespeare. Screenplay by Kenneth Branagh. Dir. Branagh. Perf. Derek Jacobi, Branagh. 1989. MGM Home Entertainment, 2000.

Hermenegildo, Alfredo. *El teatro del siglo XVI*. Madrid: Júcar, 1994.

Herrero, Javier. "The New Monarchy: A Structural Reintepretation of *Fuenteovejuna*." *Revista hispánica moderna* 36 (1970–71): 173–85.

Hess, Andrew C. *The Forgotten Frontier: A History of the Sixteenth-Century Ibero-African Frontier*. Chicago: U of Chicago P, 1978.

Hesse, Everett W. "Calderón's Concept of the Perfect Prince in *La vida es sueño*." Wardropper, *Critical Essays* 14–33.

Hilborn, Harry Warren. *A Chronology of the Plays of D. Pedro Calderón de la Barca*. Toronto: U of Toronto P, 1938.

Hill, Errol. *The Trinidad Carnival: Mandate for a National Theatre*. Austin: U of Texas P, 1972.

Hollier, Dennis, ed. *A New History of French Literature*. Cambridge: Harvard UP, 1989.

Honig, Edwin. *Calderón and the Seizures of Honor*. Cambridge: Harvard UP, 1972.

hooks, bell. *Teaching to Transgress: Education as the Practice of Freedom*. New York: Routledge, 1994.

Hooper, John. *The New Spaniards*. Harmondsworth: Penguin, 1995.

Horapollo. *The Hieroglyphs of Horapollo*. Trans. George Boas. Fwd. Anthony T. Grafton. Princeton: Princeton UP, 1993.

Hornblower, Simon, and Antony Spawforth, eds. *The Oxford Companion to Classical Civilization*. Oxford: Oxford UP, 1998.

Howard, Jean E. "The Difficulties of Closure: An Approach to the Problematic in Shakespearean Comedy." Braunmuller and Bulman 113–28.

———. "The New Historicism in Renaissance Studies." Wilson and Dutton 13–43.

Howarth, William D., ed. *French Theatre in the Neoclassical Era, 1550–1789*. Cambridge: Cambridge UP, 1997.

———. *Molière: The Playwright and His Audience*. Cambridge: Cambridge UP, 1982.

Huerta Calvo, Javier, dir. *Historia del teatro español*. Vol. 1: *De la Edad Media a los Siglos de Oro*. Abraham Madroñal Durán and Héctor Urzáiz Tortajada, coords. Vol. 2: *Del siglo XVIII a la época actual*. Fernando Doménech Rico and Emilio Peral Vega, coords. Madrid: Gredos, 2003.

———, ed. *Teatro breve de los siglos XVI y XVII: Entremeses, loas, bailes, jácaras y mojigangas*. Madrid: Taurus, 1985.

———. *El teatro breve en la Edad de Oro*. Madrid: Laberinto, 2001.

Huerta Calvo, Javier, and Hector Urzáiz Tortajada, eds. *Diccionario de personajes de Calderón*. Madrid: Pliegos, 2002.

Huizinga, Johan. *Homo Ludens: A Study of the Play Element in Culture*. 1938. Boston: Beacon, 1966.

Huston, Hollis. *The Actor's Instrument: Body, Theory, Stage*. Ann Arbor: U of Michigan P, 1992.

Ibn Khaldun. *The Muqaddimah: An Introduction to History*. Trans. Franz Rosenthal. Ed. N. J. Dawood. Abr. ed. Princeton: Princeton UP, 1989.

Jesson, Paul. "Henry VIII." Smallwood 114–31.

Johnson, Lyman L., and Sonya Lipsett-Rivera, eds. *The Faces of Honor: Sex, Shame, and Violence in Colonial Latin America*. Albuquerque: U of New Mexico P, 1998.

Jones, Ann Rosalind. "Writing the Body: Toward an Understanding of *l'Écriture Féminine*." *The New Feminist Criticism: Essays on Women, Literature and Theory*. Ed. Elaine Showalter. New York: Pantheon, 1985. 361–77.

Jones, C. A. "Spanish Honour as Historical Phenomenon, Convention and Artistic Motive." *Hispanic Review* 33 (1965): 32–39.

Jones, R. O. *Studies in Spanish Literature of the Golden Age: Presented to E. M. Wilson*. London: Tamesis, 1973.

Jordan, Constance. *Renaissance Feminism: Literary Texts and Political Models*. Ithaca: Cornell UP, 1990.

Jorgens, Jack J. *Shakespeare on Film*. Bloomington: Indiana UP, 1977.

Juana Inés de la Cruz, Sor. *Los empeños de una casa*. Ed. Celsa Carmen García Valdés. Barcelona: PPU, 1989.

———. *Los empeños de una casa*. Trinity U. 12 May 2003. <http://www.trinity.edu/org/comedia/textlist.html>.

———. *House of Desires*. Trans. Catherine Boyle. London: Oberon, 2004.

——. *The House of Trials: A Translation of* Los empeños de una casa. Ed. and trans. David Pasto. New York: Lang, 1997.

——. *Obras completas.* Ed. Francisco Monterde. Mexico: Porrúa, 1989.

——. *Pawns of a House / Los empeños de una casa.* Ed. and trans. Susana Hernández-Araico and Michael D. McGaha. Tempe: Bilingual Review, 2006.

Juárez, Encarnación. "El discurso sartorial y el conflicto amoroso social en *El caballero de Olmedo.*" *Bulletin of the Comediantes* 53 (2001): 247–66.

Kagan, Richard L. "The Spain of Ferdinand and Isabella." *Circa 1492: Art in the Age of Exploration.* Ed. Jay A. Levenson. Washington: Natl. Gallery; New Haven: Yale UP, 1991. 55–61.

Kamen, Henry. *Empire: How Spain Became a World Power, 1492–1763.* New York: Harper, 2003.

——. *Spain, 1469–1714: A Society of Conflict.* London: Longman, 1983. Trans. as *Una sociedad conflictiva: España, 1469–1714.* Madrid: Alianza, 1984.

Kienzle, Beverly Mayne, and Teresa Méndez-Faith, eds. *Panoramas literarios España.* Boston: Houghton, 1998.

Kierkegaard, Søren. *Either/Or.* 1846. Trans. Howard V. Hong and Edna H. Hong. 2 vols. Princeton: Princeton UP, 1987.

King, Willard F. "Cervantes's *Numancia* and Imperial Spain." *MLN* 94 (1979): 200–21.

Kinnaman, Daniel E. "Technology and Situated Cognition." *Technology and Learning* 14.1 (1993): 86.

Kirschner, Teresa. *El protagonista colectivo en* Fuenteovejuna. Salamanca: U de Salamanca, 1979.

Klibansky, Raymond, Erwin Panofsky, and Fritz Saxl. *Saturn and Melancholy: Studies in the History of Natural Philosophy, Religion, and Art.* New York: Basic, 1964.

Korolec, J. B. "Free Will and Free Choice." *The Cambridge History of Later Medieval Philosophy.* Ed. Norman Kretzmann, Anthony Kenny, and John Pinborg. Cambridge: Cambridge UP, 1982. 629–41.

Kott, Jan. *The Bottom Translation.* Trans. Daniela Miedzyrzecka. Evanston: Northwestern UP, 1987.

——. *Shakespeare Our Contemporary.* Trans. Boleslaw Taborski. London: Methuen, 1965.

Kraye, Jill A. "Moral Philosophy." *The Cambridge History of Renaissance Philosophy.* Ed. Q. Skinner and E. Kessler. Cambridge: Cambridge UP, 1988. 303–86.

Krieger, Murray. *Ekphrasis: The Illusion of the Natural Sign.* Baltimore: Johns Hopkins UP, 1992.

Kuhn, Thomas S. "Objectivity, Value Judgment, and Theory Choice." Adams and Searle 383–93.

Kurtz, Barbara. *The Play of Allegory in the* Autos Sacramentales *of Pedro Calderón de la Barca.* Washington: Catholic UP, 1991.

Laqueur, Thomas. *Making Sex: Body and Gender from the Greeks to Freud.* Cambridge: Harvard UP, 1990.

Lara, Jesús, ed. and trans. *Tragedia del fin de Atawallpa.* 1957. Buenos Aires: Sol, 1989.

Laroque, François. *The Age of Shakespeare.* Trans. Alexandra Campbell. London: Thames, 1993.

Larson, Donald. *The Honor Plays of Lope de Vega.* Cambridge: Harvard UP, 1977.

Larson, Paul E. "*Fuente Ovejuna:* History, Historiography, and Literary History." *Bulletin of the Comediantes* 53 (2001): 267–90.

Las Casas, Bartolomé de. *Brevísima relación de la destruición de las Indias.* Ed. André Saint-Lu. Madrid: Cátedra, 1996.

Lauer, A. Robert. "La función dramática de Clarín en *La vida es sueño* de Calderón: Prolegómenos para un estudio del 'gracioso' en la tragedia barroca calderoniana." *Calderón 1600–2000: Jornadas de investigación calderoniana.* Ed. Aurelio González. Mexico: Colegio de México, 2002. 151–67.

———. "The Iberian Encounter of America in the Spanish Theater of the Golden Age." *Pacific Coast Philology.* 28.1 (1993): 32–42.

———. "El leal traidor de *La vida es sueño* de Calderón." Mackenzie 133–44.

———."A New-Historical Reading of *Fuenteovejuna.*" Friedman and Larson 209–19.

———. "El rey Basilio y el discurso del poder." *Hacia Calderón: Décimo congreso anglogermano, Passau, 1993.* Ed. Hans Flasche. Stuttgart: Steiner, 1994. 253–65.

Laurillard, Diana. *Rethinking University Teaching: A Conversational Framework for the Effective Use of Learning Technologies.* London: Routledge, 2002.

Lefebvre, Henri. *The Production of Space.* Oxford: Blackwell, 1991.

Leiva Ramírez de Arellano, Francisco de. *El negro del cuerpo blanco, y el esclavo de su honra: Comedias antiguas de varios ingenios.* New Haven: Research Pubs. 1972. *Spanish Drama of the Golden Age.* Reel 77. Part 1 of 1.

Lévinas, Emmanuel. *Alterity and Transcendence.* New York: Columbia UP, 1999.

———. *Totality and Infinity: An Essay on Eternity.* Pittsburgh: Duquesne UP, 1969.

Lewis, Cynthia. "Performing Shakespeare: The Outward Bound of the English Department." Riggio 295–306.

Lewis-Smith, Paul. *Calderón de la Barca:* La vida es sueño. London: Grant, 1998.

———. "Cervantes' *Numancia* as Tragedy and as Tragicomedy." *Bulletin of Hispanic Studies* 64 (1987): 15–26.

Lifton, Robert Jay. *The Broken Connection: On Death and the Continuity of Life.* New York: Basic, 1983.

Litvak, Joseph. "Discipline, Spectacle, and Melancholia in and around the Gay Studies Classroom." Gallop, *Pedagogy* 19–27.

Loftis, John. "*Henry VIII* and Calderón's *La cisma de Inglaterra.*" *Comparative Literature* 34 (1992): 208–22.

Loomba, Ania. "'Delicious Traffick': Racial and Religious Difference on Early Modern Stages." *Shakespeare and Race.* Ed. Catherine M. S. Alexander and Stanley Wells. Cambridge: Cambridge UP, 2000. 203–24.

———. *Gender, Race, Renaissance Drama.* Manchester: Manchester UP, 1989.

Lope de Vega Carpio. See Vega Carpio, Félix Lope de.

López de Ayala, Adelardo. *Obras completas*. Ed. José María Castro y Calvo. 3 vols. BAE 182. Madrid: Atlas 1965.

López de Gómara, Francisco. *Historia general de las Indias y Vida de Hernán Cortés*. Ed. Jorge Curria Lacroix. Caracas: Ayacucho, 1979.

López Torrijos, Rosa. *La mitología en la pintura española del Siglo de Oro*. Madrid: Cátedra, 1985.

———. *Mythology and History in the Great Paintings of the Prado*. London: Scala, 1989.

Lord, Albert B. *The Singer of Tales*. Cambridge: Harvard UP, 1960.

Lottin, D. Odon. *Psychologie et morale aux XIIe et XIIIe siècles*. Vol. 2. Louvain: Abbaye du Mont César, 1948.

Lozano, Jesús, dir. *Entroido en Laza*. Film. Madrid: Europ Documenta and New York Univ. in Spain, 1989.

Lynch, John. *The Hispanic World in Crisis and Change: 1598–1700*. Cambridge: Blackwell, 1992.

———. *Spain, 1516–1598: From Nation State to World Empire*. Cambridge: Blackwell, 1992.

MacCurdy, Raymond R., ed. *Spanish Drama of the Golden Age: Twelve Plays*. New York: Appleton, 1971.

Macdonald, D. L. "Derek Walcott's Don Juans." *Connotations* 4.1–2 (1994–95): 98–118.

Mackenzie, Ann L., ed. *Calderón 1600–1681: Quartercentenary Studies in Memory of John E. Varey*. Spec. issue of *Bulletin of Hispanic Studies* 77 [Glasgow] (2000).

Madrigal, José A., ed. *New Historicism and the* Comedia: *Poetics, Politics, and Praxis*. Lincoln: Soc. of Spanish and Spanish-Amer. Studies, 1997.

Madroñal Durán, Abraham. "Quiñones de Benavente y el teatro breve." Huerta Calvo, *Historia* 1: 1025–68.

Maingot, Anthony P. "Race, Color, and Class in the Caribbean." *Americas: New Interpretive Essays*. Ed. Alfred Stepan. New York: Oxford UP, 1992. 220–47.

Maiorino, Giancarlo. *Leonardo da Vinci: The Daedalian Mythmaker*. University Park: Pennsylvania State UP, 1992.

Maire Bobes, Jesús, ed. *Teatro breve de la Edad Media y del Siglo de Oro*. Madrid: Akal, 2003.

Mallory, Nina Ayala. *El Greco to Murillo: Spanish Painting in the Golden Age, 1556–1700*. New York: Harper, 1990.

Mandrell, James. *Don Juan and the Point of Honor: Seduction, Patriarchal Society, and Literary Tradition*. University Park: Penn State UP, 1992.

Mangan, Michael. *A Preface to Shakespeare's Tragedies*. London: Longman, 1991.

Marañón, Gregorio. *Obras completas*. Ed. Alfredo Juderías. 10 vols. Madrid: Espasa, 1966–77.

Maravall, José Antonio. *La cultura del Barroco: Análisis de una estructura histórica*. Barcelona: Ariel, 1980. *The Culture of the Baroque: Analysis of a Historical Structure*. Trans. Terry Cochran. Minneapolis: U of Minnesota P, 1986.

————. "La función del honor en la sociedad tradicional." *Ideologies and Literature* 2.7 (1978): 9–27.

————. *Poder, honor y élites en el siglo XVII.* Madrid: Siglo XXI, 1989.

————. *Teatro y literatura en la sociedad barroca.* 1972. Barcelona: Crítica, 1990.

Marín, Diego. "On the Dramatic Function of Versification in Lope de Vega." *Theatre Annual* 19 (1962): 27–42.

————. *Uso y función de la versificación dramática en Lope de Vega.* Valencia: Hispanófila, 1968.

Mariscal, George. "Calderón and Shakespeare: The Subject of Henry VIII." *Bulletin of the Comediantes* 39 (1987): 189–213.

Maroto Camino, Mercedes. "María de Zayas and Ana Caro: The Space of Woman's Solidarity in the Spanish Golden Age." *Hispanic Review* 67 (1999): 1–16.

Martel, José, and Hymen Alpern, eds. *Diez comedias del Siglo de Oro.* 1939. Long Grove: Waveland, 1985.

Martin, Vincent. *El concepto de 'representación' en los autos sacramentales de Calderón.* Pamplona: U de Navarra; Kassel: Reichenberger, 2002.

————. "The Play of Illusion in Cervantes's Interludes." *Bulletin of the Comediantes* 56 (2004): 367–85.

Martínez, José Luis. *Pasajeros de Indias.* Madrid: Alianza, 1983.

Martínez Gómez, Luis. "Síntesis de historia de la filosofía española." App. *Historia de la filosofía.* By Johannes Hirscheberger. 2nd ed. Barcelona: Herder, 1977. 600–10.

The Matrix. Dir. Andy Wachowski and Larry Wachowski. Warner, 1999.

McGann, Jerome J. *Don Juan in Context.* Chicago: U of Chicago P, 1976.

McKendrick, Melveena, ed. *Golden-Age Studies in Honour of A. A. Parker.* Spec. issue of *Bulletin of Hispanic Studies* 64 [Liverpool] (1984).

————. "Honour/Vengeance in the *Comedia*: A Case of Mimetic Transference." *Modern Language Review* 79 (1984): 313–35.

————. *Identities in Crisis: Essays on Honour, Gender and Women in the Comedia.* Kassel: Reichenberger, 2002.

————. *Playing the King: Lope de Vega and the Limits of Conformity.* London: Tamesis, 2000.

————. *Theatre in Spain, 1490–1700.* Cambridge: Cambridge UP, 1989. Trans. as *El teatro en España, 1490–1700.* Trans. José Antonio Desmonts. 2nd ed. Palma de Mallorca: Olañeta, 2003.

————. *Woman and Society in the Spanish Drama of the Golden Age: A Study of the Mujer Varonil.* London: Cambridge UP, 1974.

McKim-Smith, Gridley. "Why Spaniards Wore Black." MLA Annual Convention. Washington Hilton Hotel, Washington. 29 Dec. 2000.

Méndez Plancarte, Alfonso, ed. *Autos y loas.* México: Fondo de Cultura Económica, 1955. Vol. 3 of *Obras completas of Sor Juana Inés de la Cruz.*

Meregalli, Franco. "De *Los tratos de Argel* a *Los baños de Argel.*" *Homenaje a*

Casalduero. Ed. Rizel Pincus and Gonzalo Sobejano. Madrid: Gredos, 1972. 395–409.

Miguel, Amando de. *Los españoles: Sociología de la vida cotidiana.* Madrid: Temas de Hoy, 1990.

Mills, Charles W. *Blackness Visible: Essays on Philosophy and Race.* Ithaca: Cornell UP, 1998.

Mira de Amescua, Antonio. *The Devil's Slave.* Ed. and trans. Michael D. McGaha and José M. Ruano de la Haza. Ottawa: Dovehouse, 1989.

Moir, Duncan W. "Lope de Vega's *Fuenteovejuna* and the *Emblemas Morales* of Sebastián de Covarrubias Orozco (with a Few Remarks on *El villano en su rincón*)." *Homenaje a William L. Fichter.* Ed. A. David Kossoff and José Amor y Vázquez. Madrid: Castalia, 1971. 537–46.

Molière. *Le bourgeois gentilhomme.* Molière, *Théâtre complet* 2: 433–518.

———. *The Bourgeois Gentleman.* Tartuffe *and* The Bourgeois Gentleman / Le Tartuffe *et* Le bourgeois gentilhomme: *A Dual Language Book.* Trans. Stanley Appelbaum. Mineola: Dover, 1998. 175–395.

———. *La critique de l'école des femmes.* Molière, *Théâtre complet* 1: 477–512.

———. *Le misanthrope.* Molière, *Théâtre Complet* 1: 816–77.

———. *The Misanthrope.* The Misanthrope *and Other Plays.* Ed. and trans. John Wood and David Coward. London: Penguin, 2000. 95–146.

———. *Théâtre Complet.* Ed. Robert Jouanny. 2 vols. Paris: Garnier, 1962.

Monleón, José, ed. Los baños de Argel *de Miguel de Cervantes: Un trabajo teatral de Francisco Nieva, música de Tomás Marco.* Madrid: Centro Dramático Nacional, 1980.

Montrose, Louis. "Professing the Renaissance: The Poetics and Politics of Culture." *The New Historicism.* Ed. H. Aram Veeser. New York: Routledge, 1989. 15–36.

———. "The Work of Gender in the Discourse of Discovery." *New World Encounters.* Ed. Stephen Greenblatt. Berkeley: U of California P, 1993. 177–217.

Moreto, Agustín de. *El desdén con el desdén [y] Las galeras de la honra [y] Los oficios.* Ed. Francisco Rico. Madrid: Castalia, 1978.

———. *El lindo don Diego.* Ed. Frank P. Casa and Berislav Primorac. Madrid: Cátedra, 1977.

———. *Loas, entremeses y bailes de Agustín Moreto.* Ed. María Luisa Lobato. 2 vols. Kassel: Reichenberger, 2003.

Morínigo, Marcos A. *América en el teatro de Lope de Vega.* Buenos Aires: Revista de Filología Hispánica, 1946.

Morley, S. Griswold. "Studies in Spanish Dramatic Versification of the *Siglo de Oro:* Alarcón and Moreto." *Publications in Modern Philology* 7 (1918): 131–73.

Morley, S. Griswold, and Courtney Bruerton. *The Chronology of Lope de Vega's Comedias.* New York: MLA, 1940.

———. *Cronología de las comedias de Lope de Vega.* Madrid: Gredos, 1968.

Morris, T. A. *Europe and England in the Sixteenth Century.* London: Routledge, 1998.

Morton, Carlos. *Johnny Tenorio.* 1983. Johnny Tenorio *and Other Plays.* Houston: Arte Publico, 1992. 25–52.

Mujica, Barbara. *Texto y vida: Introducción a la literatura española.* Hoboken: Wiley, 1992.

———, ed. *Women Writers of Early Modern Spain: Sophia's Daughters.* New Haven: Yale UP, 2004.

Murray, Timothy. "The Academie Française." Hollier 267–73.

Nalle, Sara. "Literacy and Culture in Early Modern Castille." *Past and Present* 125 (1989): 65–96.

Narbona Vizcaíno, Rafael. *Pueblo, poder y sexo: Valencia medieval (1306–1420).* Valencia: Diputació de València, 1992.

Navarro Tomás, Tomás. *Métrica española.* Barcelona: Labor, 1983.

Nelson, Bradley J. "The Marriage of Art and Honor: Anamorphosis and Control in Calderón's *La dama duende.*" *Bulletin of the Comediantes* 54 (2002): 407–41.

Núñez Cabeza de Vaca, Alvar. *Castaways: The Narrative of Alvar Núñez Cabeza de Vaca.* Ed. Enrique Pupo-Walker. Trans. Frances M. López-Morillas. Berkeley: U of California P, 1993.

Oakley, R. J. *Tirso de Molina:* El condenado por desconfiado. London: Grant, 1994.

Oehrlein, Josef. *El actor en el teatro español del Siglo de Oro.* Madrid: Castalia, 1993.

Offen, Karen. "Defining Feminism: A Comparative Approach." *Signs: Journal of Women in Culture and Society* 14 (1988): 119–57.

Olavarría y Ferrari, Enrique de. *Reseña histórica del teatro en México, 1538–1911.* Vol. 1. Mexico: Porrúa, 1961.

Ong, Walter J. *Orality and Literacy: The Technologizing of the Word.* London: Methuen, 1982.

Oriel, Charles. "Text and Textile in *El caballero de Olmedo.*" *Indiana Journal of Hispanic Literatures* 2.2 (1994): 131–56.

Ortega y Gasset, José. *Obras completas.* 12 vols. Madrid: Alianza–Revista de Occidente, 1946–83.

Padgen, Anthony. *Spanish Imperialism and the Political Imagination.* New Haven: Yale UP, 1990.

Parker, Alexander A. *The Allegorical Drama of Calderón: An Introduction to the* Autos Sacramentales. Oxford: Dolphin, 1943.

———. "The Approach to the Spanish Drama of the Golden Age." *Tulane Drama Review* 4 (1959): 42–59.

———. *La imaginación y el arte de Calderón: Ensayos sobre sus comedias.* Madrid: Cátedra, 1991.

———. "Segismundo's Tower: A Calderonian Myth." *Bulletin of Hispanic Studies* 59 (1982): 247–56.

———. "The Spanish Drama of the Golden Age: A Method of Analysis and Interpretation." *The Great Playwrights: Twenty-Five Plays with Commentaries by Critics and Scholars.* 2 vols. Ed. Eric Bentley. New York: Doubleday, 1970. 1:

679–707. Trans. of "Aproximación al drama español del Siglo de Oro." Durán and Echevarría 1: 329–57.

Parker, Mary, ed. *Spanish Dramatists of the Golden Age: A Bio-Bibliographical Sourcebook*. Westport: Greenwood, 1998.

Parnaseo. Ed. José Luis Canet. U de València. <http://parnaseo.uv.es/>.

Paz, Octavio. *Sor Juana; or, The Traps of Faith*. Trans. Margaret Sayers Peden. Cambridge: Harvard UP, 1988.

Pease, Allan. *Signals*. New York: Bantam, 1984.

Pelorson, J. M. "Aspectos ideológicos." *La frustración de un imperio (1476–1714)*. Ed. Jean-Paul le Flem et al. Barcelona: Labor, 1982. 261–318. Vol. 5 of *Historia de España*. Ed. Manuel Tuñon de Lara.

Pérez Chico, David, and Martín López Corredoira. "Sobre el libre albedrío: Dos únicas opciones, dualismo o materialismo." *El Catoblepas* 2 (2002). 10 May 2004. <http://www.nodulo.org/ec/2002/n002p01.htm>.

Pérez Pastor, Cristóbal. *Nuevos datos acerca del histrionismo español en los siglos XVI y XVII (primera serie)*. Madrid: Revista Española, 1901.

———. "Nuevos datos acerca del histrionismo español en los siglos XVI y XVII (segunda serie)." *Bulletin Hispanique* 8 (1906): 71–78, 148–53, 363–73; 10 (1908): 243–58; 12 (1910): 303–16; 13 (1911): 47–60, 306–15; 14 (1913): 300–17, 408–32; 15 (1913): 300–05, 424–44; 16 (1914): 209–24, 458–87.

Peristiany, John G., ed. *Honour and Shame: The Values of Mediterranean Society*. Chicago: U of Chicago P, 1966.

El perro del hortelano. Dir. Pilar Miró. Columbia TriStar Films de España, 1996.

Perry, Mary Elizabeth. *Gender and Disorder in Early Modern Seville*. Princeton: Princeton UP, 1990.

Picciola, Liliane. *Corneille et la dramaturgie espagnole*. Tübingen: Biblio 17, 2002.

Pope, Elizabeth Marie. "The Renaissance Background of *Measure for Measure*." Geckle 50–72.

Potter, Lois. "Teaching Shakespeare: The Participatory Approach." Riggio 235–43.

Pound, Ezra. *The Pisan Cantos*. Ed. Richard Sieburth. New York: New Directions, 2003.

Querol, Miguel. *Cancionero musical de Lope de Vega*. Vol. 3. *Poesías cantadas en las comedias*. Madrid: CSIC, 1991.

Quiñones de Benavente, Luis. *Entremeses*. Ed. Christian Andrès. Madrid: Cátedra, 1991.

Quintero, María Cristina. "English Queens and the Body Politic in *La cisma de Inglaterra* and Rivadeneira's *Historia ecclesiástica del scisma del reyno de Inglaterra*." *MLN* 113 (1998): 259–82.

Racine, Jean. *Phèdre*. Trans. Margaret Rawlings. New York: Dutton, 1989.

Rank, Otto. *The Don Juan Legend*. Trans. David G. Winter. Princeton: Princeton UP, 1975.

———. *The Incest Theme in Literature and Legend: Fundamentals of a Psychology of*

Literary Creation. Trans. Gregory C. Richter. Baltimore: Johns Hopkins UP, 1992.

Rappaport, Roy A. "The Obvious Aspects of Ritual." *Ecology, Meaning, and Religion.* 2nd ed. Berkeley: North Atlantic, 1979. 173–221.

———. *Ritual and Religion in the Making of Humanity.* Cambridge: Cambridge UP, 1999.

Reade, Brian. *The Dominance of Spain, 1550–1650.* London: Harrap, 1951.

Reckert, Stephen. *Lyra Minima: Structure and Symbol in Iberian Traditional Verse.* London: King's College, 1970.

Regalado, Mariana. "*Entroido* in Laza, Spain: A Continuing Rural Carnival Tradition." *¡Carnaval!* Ed. Barbara Mauldin. Seattle: U of Washington P, 2004. 21–43.

Regueiro, José M. *Spanish Drama of the Golden Age: A Catalog of the* Comedia *Collection in the University of Pennsylvania Libraries.* New Haven: Research, 1971.

Reichenberger, Arnold G. "The Uniqueness of the *Comedia.*" *Hispanic Review* 27 (1959): 303-16.

Rennert, Hugo A. *The Life of Lope de Vega (1562–1635).* Glasgow: Gowans; Philadelphia: Campion, 1904. Freely trans. and emended by Américo Castro as *Vida de Lope de Vega (1562–1635).* Madrid: Impresor de los sucesores de Hernando, 1919.

Resina, Joan Ramon. "What Sort of Wedding? The Orders of Discourse in *El burlador de Sevilla.*" *MLQ* 57 (1996): 545–78.

Restori, Antonio. *Piezas de titulos de comedias: Saggi e documenti inediti o rari del teatro spagnuolo dei secoli XVII e XVIII.* Messina: Muglia, 1903.

Rey, Alain. "Linguistic Absolutism." Hollier 373–79.

Rey Hazas, Antonio. "Las comedias de cautivos de Cervantes." *Los imperios orientales en el teatro del Siglo de Oro: Actas de las XVI jornadas de teatro clásico, Almagro, Julio de 1993.* Ed. Felipe B. Pedraza Jiménez and Rafael González Cañal. Almagro: U Castilla–La Mancha y Festival de Almagro, 1994. 29–56.

El rey pasmado. Dir. Imanol Uribe. 1991. Based on *Crónica del rey pasmado,* by Gonzalo Torrente Ballester. <http://www.fnac.es>.

Reyes Peña, Mercedes de los, ed. *El vestuario en el teatro español del Siglo de Oro.* Cuadernos de Teatro Clásico 13–14. Madrid: Compañía Nacional de Teatro Clásico, 2000.

Reynolds, John J., and Szilvia E. Szmuk. *Spanish Golden Age Drama: An Annotated Bibliography of United States Doctoral Dissertations, 1899–1992, with a Supplement of Non–United States Dissertations.* New York: MLA, 1998.

Reynolds, Winston A. "El demonio y Lope de Vega en el manuscrito mexicano *Coloquio de la nueva conversión y bautismo de los cuatro últimos reyes de Tlaxcala en la Nueva España.*" *Cuadernos americanos* 163 (1969): 172–84.

Rhodes, Elizabeth. "Gender and the Monstrous in *El burlador de Sevilla.*" *MLN* 117 (2002): 267–85.

Ribbans, Geoffrey W. "The Meaning and Structure of Lope's *Fuenteovejuna*." *Bulletin of Hispanic Studies* 31 (1954): 150–70.

Riggio, Milla Cozart, ed. *Teaching Shakespeare through Performance.* New York: MLA, 1999.

Ringrose, David. *Madrid and the Spanish Economy, 1560–1850.* Berkeley: U of California P, 1983.

Rist, John M. "The Stoic Concept of Detachment." *The Stoics.* Ed. Rist. Berkeley: U of California P, 1978. 259–72.

Rivers, Elias L. "The *Comedia* as Discursive Action." Fox, Sieber, and ter Horst 249–56.

———, ed. *Poesía lírica del Siglo de Oro.* Madrid: Cátedra, 1979.

———, ed. *Renaissance and Baroque Poetry of Spain, with English Prose Translations.* Prospect Heights: Waveland, 1988.

———, ed. *Things Done with Words: Speech Acts in Spanish Drama.* Newark: Cuesta, 1986.

Robayo Alonso, Álvaro, ed. *Poesia de cansionero.* Madrid: Cátedra, 1995.

Robertson, Sandra. "Life Is Virtual Dream: Amenábar Reading Calderón." *Cine-Lit 2000: Essays on Hispanic Film and Fiction.* Ed. George Cabello-Castellet, Jaume Marti-Olivella, and Guy H. Wood. Corvalis: Oregon SU, 2000. 115–25.

Rodríguez, Evangelina, and Antonio Tordera. "Introducción biográfica y crítica." Calderón de la Barca. *Entremeses* 9–49.

Rodríguez Cuadros, Evangelina. *La técnica del actor español en el Barroco: Hipótesis y documentos.* Madrid: Castalia, 1998.

Rodríguez de la Flor, Fernando. *Barroco: Representación e ideología en el mundo hispánico (1580–1680).* Madrid: Cátedra, 2002.

Rodríguez López-Vázquez, Alfredo. *Lope, Tirso, Claramonte: La autoría de las comedias más famosas del Siglo de Oro.* Kassel: Reichenberger, 1999.

Rogers, Daniel. "Fearful Symmetry: The Ending of *El burlador de Sevilla*." *Bulletin of Hispanic Studies* 41 (1964): 141–59.

———. *Tirso de Molina:* El burlador de Sevilla. London: Grant, 1977.

Rogers, Edith Randam. *The Perilous Hunt: Symbols in Hispanic and European Balladry.* Lexington: UP of Kentucky, 1980.

Rojas Garcidueñas, José. Prólogo. Arrom and Rojas Garcidueñas 149–81.

Rojas Zorrilla, Francisco de. *Del rey abajo, ninguno.* Ed. Jean Testas. Madrid: Castalia, 1971.

———. *Entre bobos anda el juego.* Ed. María Grazia Profeti. Barcelona: Crítica, 1998.

El romancero viejo. Ed. Mercedes Díaz Roig. Madrid: Cátedra, 1980.

Roskill, Mark W. *Dolce's* Aretino *and Venetian Art Theory of the Cinquecento.* New York: New York UP, 1968.

Rousset, Jean. *Le mythe de Don Juan.* Paris: Colin, 1978.

Rowland, Ingrid D. "Pop Esoterica! Leonardo da Vinci at the Beach." *New Republic* 16 and 23 Aug. 2004: 21–26.

Royal Shakespeare Company. *Great Performances.* Videocassette. Guardian TV, 1995.

Ruano de la Haza, José María. *La puesta en escena en los teatros comerciales del Siglo de Oro.* Madrid: Castalia, 2000.

———. "The Staging of Calderón's *La vida es sueño* and *La dama duende.*" *Bulletin of Hispanic Studies* 64 (1987): 51–63.

Ruano de la Haza, José María, and John J. Allen. *Los teatros comerciales del siglo XVII y la escenificación de la comedia.* Madrid: Castalia, 1994.

Rudnytsky, Peter L. "Shakespeare and the Deconstruction of History." *Shakespeare Survey* 43 (1991): 43–47.

Rueda, Lope de. *The Interludes (Los pasos).* Ed. and trans. Randall W. Listerman. Ottawa: Dovehouse, 1988.

———. *Pasos completos.* Ed. Juan María Marín. Madrid: Espasa, 1990.

Ruiz, Teófilo. *Spanish Society, 1400–1600.* Harlow: Longman, 2001. Trans. as *Historia social de España, 1400–1600.* Barcelona: Crítica, 2002.

Ruiz Ramón, Francisco, ed. *América en el teatro clásico español: Estudio y textos.* Pamplona: U de Navarra, 1993.

———. *Historia del teatro español.* 2 vols. Madrid: Alianza, 1967–71.

———. "El 'mito de Uranos' en *La vida es sueño.*" *Teatro del Siglo de Oro: Homenaje a Alberto Navarro González.* Ed. Víctor García de la Concha. Kassel: Reichenberger, 1990. 547–62.

———. "Segismundo en palacio: Reflejos en el espejo." Tietz 227–39.

Ryan, Kiernan. *Shakespeare.* 3rd ed. New York: Palgrave, 2002.

Saavedra Fajardo, Diego de. *Idea de un príncipe político-cristiano: Obras de don Diego de Saavedra Fajardo.* 1640. BAE 25. Madrid: Atlas, 1947.

Sabat-Rivers, Georgina. "Apología de América y del mundo azteca en tres loas de Sor Juana." *Revista de estudios hispánicos* (Río Piedras) 19 (1992): 267–91.

Saccio, Peter. *Shakespeare's English Kings.* Oxford: Oxford UP, 1977.

Sage, Jack W. "Calderón y la música teatral." *Bulletin hispanique* 58 (1956): 275–300.

———. *Lope de Vega:* El caballero de Olmedo. London: Grant, 1974.

Said, Edward. *Culture and Imperialism.* New York: Knopf, 1993.

Salomon, Noël. *Recherches sur le thème paysan dans la "comedia" au temps de Lope de Vega.* Bordeaux: Institut d'Études et Ibéro-Americaines de l'U de Bordeaux, 1965. *Lo villano en el teatro del Siglo de Oro.* Trans. Beatriz Chenot. Madrid: Castalia, 1985.

Sánchez, Alberto. "Aproximación al teatro de Cervantes." *Cervantes y el teatro.* Cuadernos de Teatro Clásico 7. Madrid: Compañia Nacional de Teatro Clásico, 1992. 11–30.

Sánchez, María Ángeles. *Fiestas populares: España día a día.* Madrid: Maeva, 1998.

Sánchez Escribano, Federico, and Alberto Porqueras Mayo. *Preceptiva dramática española del Renacimiento y el Barroco.* 2nd ed. Madrid: Gredos, 1972.

Sánchez Jiménez, Antonio. "Cuellos, valonas y golillas: Leyes suntuarias y crítica política en *No hay mal que por bien no venga,* de Juan Ruiz de Alarcón." *Bulletin of the Comediantes* 54: 91–113.

Sánchez Noriega, José Luis. *De la literatura al cine.* Barcelona: Paidós, 2000.

Sánchez-Romeraldo, Antonio, and Fernando Ibarra. *Antología de autores españoles: Antiguos y modernos.* Vol 1. New York: Prentice, 1972.

Santamaría Gari, Mikel Gotzon. *Acción, persona, libertad: Max Scheller-Tomás de Aquino,* Pamplona: EUNSA, 2002.

Sanz Ayán, Carmen. "Fiestas, diversiones, juegos y espectáculos." *La vida cotidiana en la España de Velázquez.* Ed. José N. Alcalá-Zamora. Madrid: Temas de Hoy, 1994. 195–215, 376–78.

Sanz Ayán, Carmen, and Bernardo J. García García. *Teatros y comediantes en el Madrid de Felipe II.* Madrid: Editorial Complutense, 2000.

Schechner, Richard. *Essays on Performance Theory.* New York: Drama Book Specialists, 1977.

——, ed. *Performance Studies: An Introduction.* London: Routledge, 2002.

——. *Performance Theory.* New York: Routledge, 1988.

Schwartz, Lía. "Velázquez and Two Poets of the Baroque: Luis de Góngora and Francisco de Quevedo." *The Cambridge Companion to Velázquez.* Ed. Suzanne L. Stratton-Pruit. Cambridge: Cambridge UP, 2002. 130–48.

Searle, John R. *Speech Acts.* Cambridge: Cambridge UP, 1976.

Sempere, Antonio. *Alejandro Amenábar: Cine en las venas.* Madrid: Nuer, 2000.

Sempere y Guarinos, Juan. *Historia del lujo y de las leyes suntuarias de España.* Madrid: Real, 1788.

Serlio, Sebastiano. *Sebastiano Serlio on Architecture: Books I–V of* Tutte l'opere d'architettura et prospetivà. Ed. Vaughan Hart and Peter Hicks. New Haven: Yale UP, 1996.

Shakespeare, William. *The Riverside Shakespeare.* Ed. G. Blakemore Evans. Boston: Houghton, 1997.

Shaw, George Bernard. *Man and Superman: A Comedy and a Philosophy.* Ed. Dan H. Laurence. London: Penguin, 1957.

Sheppard, Philippa. "Fair Counterfeits: A Bibliography of Visual Aids for Renaissance Drama." *Approaches to Teaching English Renaissance Drama.* Ed. Karen Bramford and Alexander Leggatt. New York: MLA, 2002. 43–50.

Shergold, N. D. *A History of the Spanish Stage from Medieval Times until the End of the Seventeenth Century.* Oxford: Claredon, 1967.

——. "*La vida es sueño:* Ses acteurs, son théâtre et son publique." *Dramaturgie et société.* Ed. Jean Jacquot. Paris: CNRS, 1968. 93–103.

Silveira y Montes de Oca, Jorge A. "El romancero y el teatro nacional español: De Juan de la Cueva a Lope de Vega." *Lope de Vega y los orígenes del teatro español.* Ed. Manuel Criado de Val. Madrid: Edi-8, 1981. 73–81.

Simerka, Barbara, ed. *El arte nuevo de estudiar comedias: Literary Theory and Spanish Golden Age Drama.* Lewisburg: Bucknell UP, 1996.

Simerka, Barbara A., and Christopher B. Weimer, eds. *Echoes and Inscriptions: Comparative Approaches to Early Modern Spanish Literatures.* Lewisburg: Bucknell UP; London: Associated UP, 2000.

Sinfield, Alan. *Faultlines: Cultural Materialism and the Politics of Dissident Reading.* Oxford: Oxford UP, 1992.

Smallwood, Robert, ed. *Players of Shakespeare 4: Further Essays in Shakespearean Performance with the Royal Shakespeare Company.* Cambridge: Cambridge UP, 1998.

Smith, Dawn L. *"El vergonzoso en palacio:* A Play for Actors." *Tirso de Molina: His Originality Then and Now.* Ed. Henry W. Sullivan and Raúl Galoppe. Ottawa: Dovehouse, 1996. 80–101.

Smith, Paul Julian. "The Rhetoric of Inscription in the *Comedia." Writing in the Margin: Spanish Literature of the Golden Age.* Oxford: Clarendon, 1988.

Smith, Rhea Marsh. *Spain: A Modern History.* Ann Arbor: U of Michigan P, 1965.

Soja, Edward. *Postmodern Geographies: The Reassertion of Space in Critical Social Theory.* London: Verso, 1989.

Sola, Emilio, and José F. de la Peña. *Cervantes y la Berbería: Cervantes, mundo turco-berberisco y servicios secretos en la época de Felipe II.* Mexico: Fondo de Cutura Económica, 1995.

Sor Juana Inés de la Cruz. *See* Juana Inés de la Cruz

Sosa, Antonio de. *Diálogo de la cautividad de Argel.* Haedo, *Topografía* 2: 1–216.

———. *Diálogo de los mártires de Argel.* Ed. Emilio Sola and José M. Parreño. Madrid: Hiperión, 1990.

Soufas, C. Christopher, and Teresa Scott Soufas. *"La vida es sueño* and Post-modern Sensibilities: Towards a New Method of Analysis and Interpretation." Fox, Sieber, and ter Horst 291–303.

Soufas, Teresa Scott. *Dramas of Distinction: A Study of Plays by Golden Age Women.* Lexington: UP of Kentucky, 1997.

———. "María de Zayas's (Un)Conventional Play, *La traición en la amistad."* Ganelin and Mancing 148–64.

———, ed. *Women's Acts: Plays by Women Dramatists of Spain's Golden Age.* Lexington: UP of Kentucky, 1996.

Souto Alabarce, Arturo. *Teatro indiano de los Siglos de Oro.* Mexico: Trillas, 1988.

Spanish Drama of the Golden Age: Comedia *Collection.* 86 microfilm reels. New Haven: Research, 1972.

Spencer, Charles. Rev. of *"Peribáñez."* Prod. by Rufus Norris. *Daily Telegraph* [London] 10 May 2003: 22.

Stallybrass, Peter. "Patriarchal Territories: The Body Enclosed." *Rewriting the Renaissance: The Discourses of Sexual Difference in Early Modern Europe.* Ed. Maureen Quilligan, Margaret W. Ferguson, and Nancy J. Vickers. Chicago: U of Chicago P, 1986. 123–42.

Stein, Louise K. *Songs of Mortals, Dialogue of the Gods: Music and Theatre in Seventeenth-Century Spain.* Oxford: Clarendon; New York: Oxford UP, 1993.

Stoicism. *Internet Encyclopedia of Philosophy.* 2001. 10 May 2003 <http://www.utm.edu/research/iep/s/stoicism.htm>.

Stokes, Mason. *In the Color of Sex: Whiteness, Heterosexuality, and the Fiction of White Supremacy.* Durham: Duke UP, 2001.

Stoll, Anita K., and Dawn Smith, eds. *Gender, Identity, and Representation in Spain's Golden Age.* Lewisburg: Bucknell UP, 2000.

———. *The Perception of Women in Spanish Theater of the Golden Age.* Lewisburg: Bucknell UP, 1991.

Stroud, Matthew. "The Characters and Plots in Tirso's *Comedias.*" 10 May 2005. <http://www.trinity.edu/mstroud/tirso>.

———. "La comedia española del Siglo de Oro." Trinity U. 12 May 2003. <http://www.trinity.edu/mstroud/comedia/>.

———. *Fatal Union: A Pluralistic Approach to the Spanish Wife-Murder* Comedias. Lewisburg: Bucknell UP, 1990.

———. *The Play in the Mirror: Lacanian Perspectives on Spanish Baroque Theater.* Lewisburg: Bucknell UP, 1996.

Suárez-Galbán Guerra, Eugenio. *Antología del teatro del Siglo de Oro.* Madrid: Orígenes, 1989.

Sullivan, Henry W. "Jacques Lacan and the Golden Age Drama." Simerka 105–24.

Surtz, Ronald E. *The Birth of a Theater: Dramatic Convention in the Spanish Theater from Juan del Encina to Lope de Vega.* Princeton: Princeton UP; Madrid: Castalia, 1979.

———. "Daughter of Night, Daughter of Light: The Imagery of Finea's Transformation in *La dama boba.*" *Bulletin of the Comediantes* 33 (1981): 161–67.

Swislocki, Marsha. "Discurso romancístico y significación poética en la comedia lopesca." *Actas Irvine-92.* Ed. Juan Villegas Morales. Newark: Cuesta, 1994. 1: 187–95.

———. "El romance de *La adúltera* en algunas obras dramáticas de Lope de Vega: Pretextos, intertextos y contextos." *Bulletin of Hispanic Studies* 63 (1986): 213–23.

Talvacchia, Bette. *Taking Positions: On the Erotic in Renaissance Culture.* Princeton: Princeton UP, 1999.

Taylor, Paul. Rev. of *"The Painter of His Dishonour."* By Calderón de la Barca. Prod. Royal Shakespeare Co. *Independent Weekend* [London] 8 July 1995.

Teatro cómico popular. Ed. Beatriz Pérez Sánchez and Angel Muñoz Calvo. Madrid: Castalia Prima, 2001.

Teatro de los Siglos de Oro. U du Québec à Trois-Rivières. <http://www.uqtr.uquebec.ca/dlmo/TEATRO/teatro.html>.

Teatro español del Siglo de Oro (TESO). Electronic resource. Alexandria: Chadwick-Healy, 1997.

Teatro y fiesta del Siglo de Oro en tierras europeas de los Austrias. [Madrid]: Sociedad Estatal para la Acción Cultural de España, 2003.

ter Horst, Robert. "The *Loa* of Lisbon and the Mythical Substructure of *El burlador de Sevilla.*" *Bulletin of Hispanic Studies* 50 (1973): 147–65.

———. "The True Mind of Marriage: Ironies of the Intellect in Lope's *La dama boba.*" *Romanistisches Jahrbuch* 27 (1976): 347–63.

Thieme, John. *Derek Walcott*. Contemporary World Writers. Manchester: Manchester UP, 1999.

Tietz, Manfred, ed. *Texto e imagen en Calderón*. Stuttgart: Steiner, 1998.

Tillyard, E. M. W. *The Elizabethan World Picture*. New York: Vintage, 1943.

Tirso de Molina (Fray Gabriel Téllez). *Amazonas en las Indias*. Tirso de Molina, *Hazañas* 231–352.

——. *El amor médico*. Ed. Blanca Oteiza. Pamplona: GRISO, U de Navarra, 1997.

——. *The Bashful Man at Court*. Trans. John Browning and Fiorigio Minelli. *The Bashful Man at Court [y] Don Gil of the Breeches Green [y] The Doubter Damned*. Ottawa: Dovehouse, 1991. 89–199.

——. *El burlador de Sevilla*. Ed. Ignacio Arrellano. Madrid: Espasa, 1989.

——. *El burlador de Sevilla*. Ed. Mercedes Sánchez Sánchez. Madrid : Castalia Didáctica, 1997.

——. *El burlador de Sevilla y convidado de piedra*. Ed. Alfredo Rodríguez López-Vázquez. Madrid: Cátedra, 2002.

——. *El burlador de Sevilla*. Assn. for Hispanic Classical Theater. 12 May 2003. <http://www.trinity.edu/org/comedia/tirso/bursev.html>.

——. *El burlador de Sevilla*. Ed. R. John McCaw. Newark: Cervantes & Co., 2003.

——. *El condenado por desconfiado*. Ed. Ángel Ciriaco Morón Arroyo and Rolena Adorno. Madrid: Cátedra, 1989.

——. *El condenado por desconfiado*. Ed. Ángel Raimundo Fernández González. Madrid: Espasa, 1990.

——. *Damned for despair / El condonado por desconfiado*. Ed. and trans. Nicholas G. Round. Warminster, Eng.: Aris, 1986.

——. *Don Gil de las calzas verdes*. Ed. Alonso Zamora Vicente. Madrid: Castalia, 1990.

——. *Don Gil of the Green Breeches / Don Gil de las calzas verdes*. Ed. Gordon Minter. Warminster, Eng.: Aris, 1991.

——. *Hazañas de los Pizarro (tres comedias): Todo es dar en una cosa, Amazonas en las Indias, La lealtad contra la envidia*. Ed. Jesús Cañas Murillo. Mérida: Extremadura, 1993.

——. *Obras completas*. Publicaciones del Instituto de Estudios Tirsianos. 14 vols. to date. Pamplona: GRISO, U de Navarra, 1997– .

——. *Tamar's Revenge*. Trans. James Fenton and Simon Masterson. London: Oberon Books, 2004.

——. *Tamar's Revenge / La venganza de Tamar*. Ed and trans. John Lyon. Warminster, Eng.: Aris, 1988.

——. *The Trickster of Seville and the Stone Guest / El burlador de Sevilla y el convidado de piedra*. Ed. and trans. Gwynne Edwards. Warminster, Eng.: Aris, 1986.

——. *La Trilogía de los Pizarros*. Ed. Miguel Zugasti. Kassel: Reichenberger, 1993.

————. *Two Plays*. Ed. and trans. Laurence Boswell, Jonathan Thacker, and Deirde McKenna. Bath: Absolute Classics, 1992.

————. *El vergonzoso en palacio*. Ed. Francisco Ayala. Madrid: Castalia, 1971.

————. *El vergonzoso en palacio*. Ed. Ciriaco Morón Arroyo and Rolena Adorno. Madrid: Cátedra, 1974.

Tomlinson, Janis A. *From El Greco to Goya: Painting in Spain, 1561–1828*. New York: Abrams, 1997.

Torres Naharro, Bartolomé de. *Comedias:* Soldadesca, Tinelaria, Himenea. Ed. D. W. McPheeters. Madrid: Castalia, 1973.

Traub, Valerie. *Desire and Anxiety: Circulations of Sexuality in Shakespearean Drama*. New York: Routledge, 1992.

Trujillo, Tomás de. *Libro llamado reprobación des trajes, y abuso de juramentos*. Estella, Navarra: Anuers, 1563.

The Truman Show. Dir. Peter Weir. Paramount, 1998.

Tuan, Yi-Fu. *Space and Place: The Perspective of Experience*. London: Arnold, 1977.

Turia, Ricardo de. *La bellígera española*. Ruiz Ramón, *América* 141–205.

Turner, Victor. *From Ritual to Theatre: The Human Seriousness of Play*. New York: Performing Arts Journal, 1982.

Tyler, Richard W., and Sergio D. Elizondo. *The Characters, Plots, and Settings of Calderón's Comedias*. Lincoln: Soc. of Spanish and Spanish-American Studies, 1981.

Umpierre, Gustavo. *Songs in the Plays of Lope de Vega: A Study of Their Dramatic Function*. London: Tamesis, 1975.

Usunáriz, Jesús María. "El matrimonio y su reforma en el mundo hispánico durante el Siglo de Oro: Un ejemplo de disciplinamiento social." *Temas del Barroco hispánico. Actas del congreso internacional, Valparaíso, Chile, noviembre 2003*. Ed. Ignacio Arellano. Navarra, 2004. 291–312.

————. "'Volved ya las riendas, porque no os perdáis': La transformación de los comportamientos morales en la España del XVI." *El mundo social y cultural de La Celestina: Actas del congreso internacional, Universidad de Navarra, junio 2001*. Ed. Ignacio Arellano and Usunáriz. Madrid: Iberoamericana; Frankfurt am Main: Vervuert, 2003. 295–321.

Vanilla Sky. Dir. Cameron Crowe. Paramount, 2001.

Varey, John E. *Cosmovisión y escenografía: El teatro español en el Siglo de Oro*. Madrid: Castalia, 1987.

————. "*La dama duende* de Calderón: Símbolos y escenografía." *Actas del congreso internacional sobre Calderón y el teatro español del Siglo de Oro, Madrid, 1981*. Madrid: CSIC, 1983. 1: 165–83.

Veeser, H. Aram, ed. *The New Historicism*. New York: Routledge, 1989.

Vega Carpio, Félix Lope de. *El acero de Madrid*. Ed. Stefano Arata. Madrid: Castalia, 2000.

————. *El anzuelo de Fenisa / Fenisa's Hook,* or *Fenisa the Hooker*. Ed. and trans. David M. Gitlitz. San Antonio: Trinity UP, 1988.

————. *La Araucana. Obras de Lope de Vega*. Ed. Marcelino Menéndez Pelago. Vol. 7. Madrid: Atlas, 1963, 417–29.

———. *Arauco domado*. Ruiz Ramón, *América* 75–140.

———. *El arte nuevo de hacer comedias*. Madrid: Espasa, 1948.

———. *El arte nuevo de hacer comedias en este tiempo*. Ed. Juana de José Prades. Madrid: CSIC, 1971.

———. *The Best Boy in Spain / El mejor mozo de España*. Ed. and trans. David M. Gitlitz. Tempe: Bilingual Review, 1999.

———. *El Brasil restituido*. Ed. Gino de Solenni. New York: Instituto de las Españas en los Estados Unidos, 1929.

———. *El caballero de Olmedo*. Ed. Joseph Pérez. Madrid: Castalia, 1970.

———. *El caballero de Olmedo*. Ed. Francisco Rico. Madrid: Cátedra, 1981.

———. *El caballero de Olmedo*. Ed. Ignacio Sáez Jiménez. Madrid: Biblioteca Didáctica Anaya, 1985.

———. *El caballero de Olmedo*. Ed. Juan Maria Marín Martínez. Madrid: Castalia Didáctica, 1993.

———. *El caballero de Olmedo*. Eds. Ignacio Arellano and Juan Manuel Escudero. Madrid: Espasa, 1998.

———. *El caballero de Olmedo*. Ed. Edward H. Friedman. Newark: Cervantes & Co., 2004.

———. *El castigo sin venganza [y] El perro del Hortelano*. Ed. A. David Kossoff. Madrid: Castalia: 1970.

———. *El castigo sin venganza*. Ed. Antonio Carreño. Madrid: Cátedra, 1990.

———. *El castigo sin venganza*. Assn. for Hispanic Classical Theater. 12 May 2003. ‹http://www.trinity.edu/mstroud/comedia/casven.html›.

———. *El castigo sin venganza*. Trinity U. 12 May 2003. <http://www.trinity.edu/org/comedia/lope/castsv.html>.

———. *Comedia la famosa de los guanches de Tenerife y conquista de Canaria*. Ed. Eyda M. Merediz. Newark: Juan de la Cuesta, 2003.

———. *Comedias de Lope de Vega*. Multiple editors. 4 vols. to date. Barcelona: PROLOPE, U Autònoma de Barcelona. Lleida: Milenio, 1997– .

———. *Los comendadores de Córdoba*. BAE 215. Madrid: Atlas, 1868. Vol. 24 of *Obras de Lope de Vega*.

———. *La dama boba*. Ed. Diego Marín. Madrid: Cátedra, 1976.

———. *The Discovery of the New World. Translations of the American Plays of Lope de Vega: The Discovery of the New World, The Conquest of Araucania, Brazil Restored*. Ed. and trans. Kenneth A. Stackhouse. Lewiston: Mellen, 2003. 123–80.

———. *The Dog in the Manger.* Ed. and trans. Victor Dixon. Ottawa: Dovehouse, 1999.

———. *The Dog in the Manger.* Trans. David Johnson. London: Oberon, 2004.

———. *The Duchess of Amalfi's Steward.* Ed. and trans. Cynthia Rodriguez-Badendyck. Ottawa: Dovehouse, 1985.

———. *Five Plays.* Trans. Jill Booty. New York: Hill, 1961.

———. *Fuenteovejuna. Spanish Drama.* Trans. Angel Flores and Muriel Kittel. Ed. Flores. New York: Bantam, 1962. 33–80.

————. *Fuente Ovejuna.* Ed. Juan María Marín. Madrid: Cátedra, 1982.

————. *Fuente Ovejuna.* Ed. Francisco López Estrada y María Teresa López García-Bordoy. Madrid: Castalia Didáctica, 1987.

————. *Fuente Ovejuna.* Ed. and trans. Victor Dixon. Warminster, Eng.: Aris, 1989.

————. *Fuente Ovejuna.* Ed. Donald McGrady. Barcelona: Crítica, 1993.

————. *Fuente Ovejuna.* Ed. Juan José Amate Blanco. Madrid: Biblioteca Didáctica Anaya, 1995.

————. *Fuente Ovejuna.* Ed. Antonio Orejudo. Madrid: McGraw, 1996.

————. *Fuente Ovejuna.* Ed. Francisco López Estrada. Madrid: Castalia Didactica, 1997.

————. *Fuenteovejuna.* Ed. Matthew A. Wyszynski. Newark: Cervantes & Co., 2003.

————. *La gran comedia de los cautivos de Argel. Parte veintecinco perfeta y verdadera, de las comedias del Fenix de España Frey Lope Felix de Vega Carpio.* Folios 231–78. Zaragoza: Viuda de Pedro Verges, 1647.

————. The Great Pretenders, The Gentleman from Olmedo: *Two Plays.* Ed. and trans. David Johnston. Bath: Absolute Classics, 1992.

————. *Lady Nitwit / La dama boba.* Ed. and trans. William I. Oliver. Tempe: Bilingual, 1998.

————. *El mejor alcalde, el rey.* Madrid: Espasa, 1981.

————. *El mejor alcalde, el rey [y] Fuente Ovejuna.* 5th ed. Ed. Alonso Zamora Vicente. Madrid: Espasa, 1985.

————. *El mejor alcalde, el rey.* Ed. J. Mª. Marín Martínez. Madrid: Espasa, 1990.

————. *El mejor alcalde, el rey.* Ed. Frank P. Casa and Berislav Primorac. Madrid: Cátedra, 1993.

————. *The New Art of Writing Plays.* Trans. William T. Brewster. New York: Dramatic Museum of Columbia U. 1914.

————. *El Nuevo Mundo descubierto por Cristóbal Colón / The New World Discovered by Christopher Columbus: Una edición crítica y bilingüe / A Critical and Bilingual Edition.* Ed. Robert M. Shannon. New York: Lang, 2001.

————. *Obras escogidas.* Ed. Federico Carlos Sainz de Robles. 5th ed. 3 vols. Madrid: Aguilar, 1990.

————. *Obras.* BAE. Vols. 24–250. Madrid: Atlas, 1853–1972.

————. *Peribáñez and the comendador of Ocaña / Peribáñez y el comendador de Ocaña.* Ed. and trans. James Lloyd. Warminster, Eng.: Aris, 1990.

————. *Peribáñez y el comendador de Ocaña.* Ed. Alonso Zamora Vicente. Madrid: Espasa, 1987.

————. *Peribáñez y el comendador de Ocaña.* Ed. F. B. Pedraza. Madrid: Castalia Didáctica, 1989.

————. *Peribáñez y el comendador de Ocaña.* Ed. Juan María Marín. Madrid: Cátedra, 2002.

————. *Peribáñez y el comendador de Ocaña.* Ed. Donald McGrady. Barcelona: Crítica, 2002.

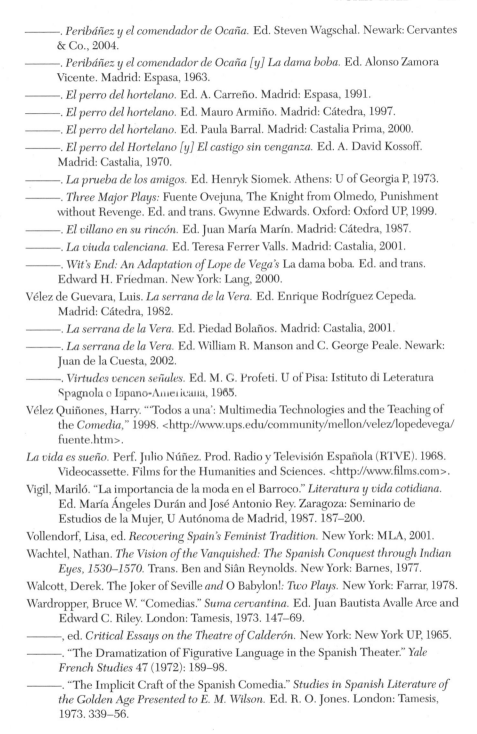

———. *Peribáñez y el comendador de Ocaña.* Ed. Steven Wagschal. Newark: Cervantes & Co., 2004.

———. *Peribáñez y el comendador de Ocaña [y] La dama boba.* Ed. Alonso Zamora Vicente. Madrid: Espasa, 1963.

———. *El perro del hortelano.* Ed. A. Carreño. Madrid: Espasa, 1991.

———. *El perro del hortelano.* Ed. Mauro Armiño. Madrid: Cátedra, 1997.

———. *El perro del hortelano.* Ed. Paula Barral. Madrid: Castalia Prima, 2000.

———. *El perro del Hortelano [y] El castigo sin venganza.* Ed. A. David Kossoff. Madrid: Castalia, 1970.

———. *La prueba de los amigos.* Ed. Henryk Siomek. Athens: U of Georgia P, 1973.

———. *Three Major Plays:* Fuente Ovejuna, The Knight from Olmedo, Punishment without Revenge. Ed. and trans. Gwynne Edwards. Oxford: Oxford UP, 1999.

———. *El villano en su rincón.* Ed. Juan María Marín. Madrid: Cátedra, 1987.

———. *La viuda valenciana.* Ed. Teresa Ferrer Valls. Madrid: Castalia, 2001.

———. *Wit's End: An Adaptation of Lope de Vega's* La dama boba. Ed. and trans. Edward H. Friedman. New York: Lang, 2000.

Vélez de Guevara, Luis. *La serrana de la Vera.* Ed. Enrique Rodríguez Cepeda. Madrid: Cátedra, 1982.

———. *La serrana de la Vera.* Ed. Piedad Bolaños. Madrid: Castalia, 2001.

———. *La serrana de la Vera.* Ed. William R. Manson and C. George Peale. Newark: Juan de la Cuesta, 2002.

———. *Virtudes vencen señales.* Ed. M. G. Profeti. U of Pisa: Istituto di Leteratura Spagnola o Ispano-Americana, 1965.

Vélez Quiñones, Harry. "'Todos a una': Multimedia Technologies and the Teaching of the *Comedia,*" 1998. <http://www.ups.edu/community/mellon/velez/lopedevega/fuente.htm>.

La vida es sueño. Perf. Julio Núñez. Prod. Radio y Televisión Española (RTVE). 1968. Videocassette. Films for the Humanities and Sciences. <http://www.films.com>.

Vigil, Mariló. "La importancia de la moda en el Barroco." *Literatura y vida cotidiana.* Ed. María Ángeles Durán and José Antonio Rey. Zaragoza: Seminario de Estudios de la Mujer, U Autónoma de Madrid, 1987. 187–200.

Vollendorf, Lisa, ed. *Recovering Spain's Feminist Tradition.* New York: MLA, 2001.

Wachtel, Nathan. *The Vision of the Vanquished: The Spanish Conquest through Indian Eyes, 1530–1570.* Trans. Ben and Siân Reynolds. New York: Barnes, 1977.

Walcott, Derek. The Joker of Seville *and* O Babylon!: Two Plays. New York: Farrar, 1978.

Wardropper, Bruce W. "Comedias." *Suma cervantina.* Ed. Juan Bautista Avalle Arce and Edward C. Riley. London: Tamesis, 1973. 147–69.

———, ed. *Critical Essays on the Theatre of Calderón.* New York: New York UP, 1965.

———. "The Dramatization of Figurative Language in the Spanish Theater." *Yale French Studies* 47 (1972): 189–98.

———. "The Implicit Craft of the Spanish Comedia." *Studies in Spanish Literature of the Golden Age Presented to E. M. Wilson.* Ed. R. O. Jones. London: Tamesis, 1973. 339–56.

————. *Introducción al teatro religioso del Siglo de Oro (la evolución del auto sacramental, 1500–1648)*. Madrid: Revista del Occidente, 1953.

————, comp. *Teatro español del Siglo de Oro: Masterpieces by Lope de Vega, Calderón, and Their Contemporaries*. New York: Scribner, 1970.

Weinberg, Bernard. *A History of Literary Criticism in the Italian Renaissance*. 2 vols. Chicago: U of Chicago P, 1961.

Weinstein, Leo. *The Metamorphoses of Don Juan*. Stanford: Stanford UP, 1959.

Welles, Marcia. *Persephone's Girdle: Narratives of Rape in Seventeenth-Century Spanish Literature*. Nashville: Vanderbilt UP, 2000.

West Side Story. Dir. Robert Wise and Jerome Rogers. United Artists, 1961.

Whitby, William. "Rosaura's Role in *La vida es sueño*." Wardropper, *Critical Essays* 101–13.

White, Hayden. "New Historicism: A Comment." Veeser 293–302.

————. *Tropics of Discourse*. Baltimore: Johns Hopkins UP, 1978.

Whittock, Trevor. *Metaphor and Film*. New York: Cambridge UP, 1990.

Wiegman, Robyn. "Whiteness Studies and the Paradox of Particularity." *Boundary* 2 (1999): 115–50.

Williamsen, Amy R. "Fatal Formulas: Mencía, Men, and Verbal Manipulation." *Indiana Journal of Hispanic Literatures* 2.2 (1994): 28–37.

Williamsen, Vern. *The Minor Dramatists of Seventeenth-Century Spain*. Boston: Twayne, 1982.

————. "Rhyme as a Form of Audible 'Sign' in Two Calderonian Plays." *Neophilologus* 68 (1984): 546–56.

————. "The Structural Function of Polymetry in the Spanish *Comedia*." *Perspectivas de la Comedia*. Ed. Alva V. Ebersole. Valencia: Estudios de Hispanófila, 1978. 33–47.

Wilson, Edward M. "The Four Elements in the Imagery of Calderón." *Modern Language Review* 31 (1936): 34–43.

Wilson, Edward M., and D. W. Moir. *The Golden Age: Drama, 1492–1700*. London: Benn; New York: Barnes, 1971. Trans. as *Siglo de oro: Teatro*. Barcelona: Ariel, 1974.

Wilson, Edward M., and Jack W. Sage. *Poesías líricas en las obras dramáticas de Calderón*. London: Tamesis, 1964.

Wilson, Margaret. *Spanish Drama of the Golden Age*. Oxford: Pergamon, 1969.

Wilson, Richard, and Richard Dutton, eds. *New Historicism and Renaissance Drama*. London: Longman, 1992.

Wolf, John B. *The Barbary Coast: Algiers under the Turks, 1500 to 1830*. New York: Norton, 1979.

Yarbro-Bejarano, Yvonne. *Feminism and the Honor Plays of Lope de Vega*. West Lafayette: Purdue UP, 1994.

Yates, Frances A. *The Art of Memory*. Chicago: U of Chicago P, 1966.

Yokota-Murakami, Takayuki. *Don Juan East/West: On the Problematics of Comparative Literature*. Albany: State U of New York P, 1998.

Zárate, Fernando de (Antonio Enríquez Gómez). *La conquista de México*. Ruiz Ramón, *América* 207–58.

Zayas, María de. *La traición en la amistad*. Trinity U. 12 May 2003. <http://www.trinity .edu/mstroud/comedia/traicion.html>.

———. *La traición en la amistad*. *Apuntes para una biblioteca de escritoras españolas*. Ed. Manuel Serrano y Sanz. Vol. 1. Madrid: Ribadeneyra, 1903. Rpt. BAE 268. 590–620.

———. *La traición en la amistad / Friendship Betrayed*. Ed. and trans. Valerie Hegstrom and Catherine Larson. Lewisburg: Bucknell UP, 1999.

Zimic, Stanislav. "Los tratos de Argel." *El teatro de Cervantes*. Madrid: Castalia, 1992. 37–56.

Zmantar, Françoise. "Saavedra et les captifs du *Trato de Argel* de Miguel de Cervantes." *L'autobiographie dans le monde hispanique. Actes du colloque international de la Baume-lès-Aix, 11–13 Mai, 1979*. Aix-en-Provence: U de Provence, 1980. 185–203.

INDEX OF PLAYS

INDEX OF PLAYWRIGHTS

INDEX OF NAMES

Modern Language Association of America

Approaches to Teaching World Literature

Joseph Gibaldi, series editor

Works of Louise Erdrich. Ed. Gregg Sarris, Connie A. Jacobs, and James R. Giles. 2004.

Dramas of Euripides. Ed. Robin Mitchell-Boyask. 2002.

Faulkner's The Sound and the Fury. Ed. Stephen Hahn and Arthur F. Kinney. 1996.

Flaubert's Madame Bovary. Ed. Laurence M. Porter and Eugene F. Gray. 1995.

García Márquez's One Hundred Years of Solitude. Ed. María Elena de Valdés and Mario J. Valdés. 1990.

Gilman's "The Yellow Wall-Paper" and Herland. Ed. Denise D. Knight and Cynthia J. Davis. 2003.

Goethe's Faust. Ed. Douglas J. McMillan. 1987.

Gothic Fiction: The British and American Traditions. Ed. Diane Long Hoeveler and Tamar Heller. 2003.

Hebrew Bible as Literature in Translation. Ed. Barry N. Olshen and Yael S. Feldman. 1989.

Homer's Iliad *and* Odyssey. Ed. Kostas Myrsiades. 1987.

Ibsen's A Doll House. Ed. Yvonne Shafer. 1985.

Henry James's Daisy Miller *and* The Turn of the Screw. Ed. Kimberly C. Reed and Peter G. Beidler. 2005.

Works of Samuel Johnson. Ed. David R. Anderson and Gwin J. Kolb. 1993.

Joyce's Ulysses. Ed. Kathleen McCormick and Erwin R. Steinberg. 1993.

Kafka's Short Fiction. Ed. Richard T. Gray. 1995.

Keats's Poetry. Ed. Walter H. Evert and Jack W. Rhodes. 1991.

Kingston's The Woman Warrior. Ed. Shirley Geok-lin Lim. 1991.

Lafayette's The Princess of Clèves. Ed. Faith E. Beasley and Katharine Ann Jensen. 1998.

Works of D. H. Lawrence. Ed. M. Elizabeth Sargent and Garry Watson. 2001.

Lessing's The Golden Notebook. Ed. Carey Kaplan and Ellen Cronan Rose. 1989.

Mann's Death in Venice *and Other Short Fiction*. Ed. Jeffrey B. Berlin. 1992.

Medieval English Drama. Ed. Richard K. Emmerson. 1990.

Melville's Moby-Dick. Ed. Martin Bickman. 1985.

Metaphysical Poets. Ed. Sidney Gottlieb. 1990.

Miller's Death of a Salesman. Ed. Matthew C. Roudané. 1995.

Milton's Paradise Lost. Ed. Galbraith M. Crump. 1986.

Molière's Tartuffe *and Other Plays*. Ed. James F. Gaines and Michael S. Koppisch. 1995.

Momaday's The Way to Rainy Mountain. Ed. Kenneth M. Roemer. 1988.

Montaigne's Essays. Ed. Patrick Henry. 1994.

Novels of Toni Morrison. Ed. Nellie Y. McKay and Kathryn Earle. 1997.

Murasaki Shikibu's The Tale of Genji. Ed. Edward Kamens. 1993.

Pope's Poetry. Ed. Wallace Jackson and R. Paul Yoder. 1993.

Proust's Fiction and Criticism. Ed. Elyane Dezon-Jones and Inge Crosman Wimmers. 2003.

Novels of Samuel Richardson. Ed. Lisa Zunshine and Jocelyn Harris. 2006.

Rousseau's Confessions *and* Reveries of the Solitary Walker. Ed. John C. O'Neal and Ourida Mostefai. 2003.

Shakespeare's Hamlet. Ed. Bernice W. Kliman. 2001.

Shakespeare's King Lear. Ed. Robert H. Ray. 1986.

Shakespeare's Othello. Ed. Peter Erickson and Maurice Hunt. 2005.

Shakespeare's Romeo and Juliet. Ed. Maurice Hunt. 2000.

Shakespeare's The Tempest *and Other Late Romances.* Ed. Maurice Hunt. 1992.

Shelley's Frankenstein. Ed. Stephen C. Behrendt. 1990.

Shelley's Poetry. Ed. Spencer Hall. 1990.

Sir Gawain and the Green Knight. Ed. Miriam Youngerman Miller and Jane Chance. 1986.

Spenser's Faerie Queene. Ed. David Lee Miller and Alexander Dunlop. 1994.

Stendhal's The Red and the Black. Ed. Dean de la Motte and Stirling Haig. 1999.

Sterne's Tristram Shandy. Ed. Melvyn New. 1989.

Stowe's Uncle Tom's Cabin. Ed. Elizabeth Ammons and Susan Belasco. 2000.

Swift's Gulliver's Travels. Ed. Edward J. Rielly. 1988.

Thoreau's Walden *and Other Works.* Ed. Richard J. Schneider. 1996.

Tolstoy's Anna Karenina. Ed. Liza Knapp and Amy Mandelker. 2003.

Vergil's Aeneid. Ed. William S. Anderson and Lorina N. Quartarone. 2002.

Voltaire's Candide. Ed. Renée Waldinger. 1987.

Whitman's Leaves of Grass. Ed. Donald D. Kummings. 1990.

Woolf's To the Lighthouse. Ed. Beth Rigel Daugherty and Mary Beth Pringle. 2001.

Wordsworth's Poetry. Ed. Spencer Hall, with Jonathan Ramsey. 1986.

Wright's Native Son. Ed. James A. Miller. 1997.